NOTHING BUT COURAGE

ALSO BY JAMES DONOVAN

Shoot for the Moon: The Space Race and the Extraordinary Voyage of Apollo 11

The Blood of Heroes: The 13-Day Struggle for the Alamo—and the Sacrifice That Forged a Nation

A Terrible Glory: Custer and the Little Bighorn—the Last Great Battle of the American West

Custer and the Little Bighorn: The Man, the Mystery, the Myth

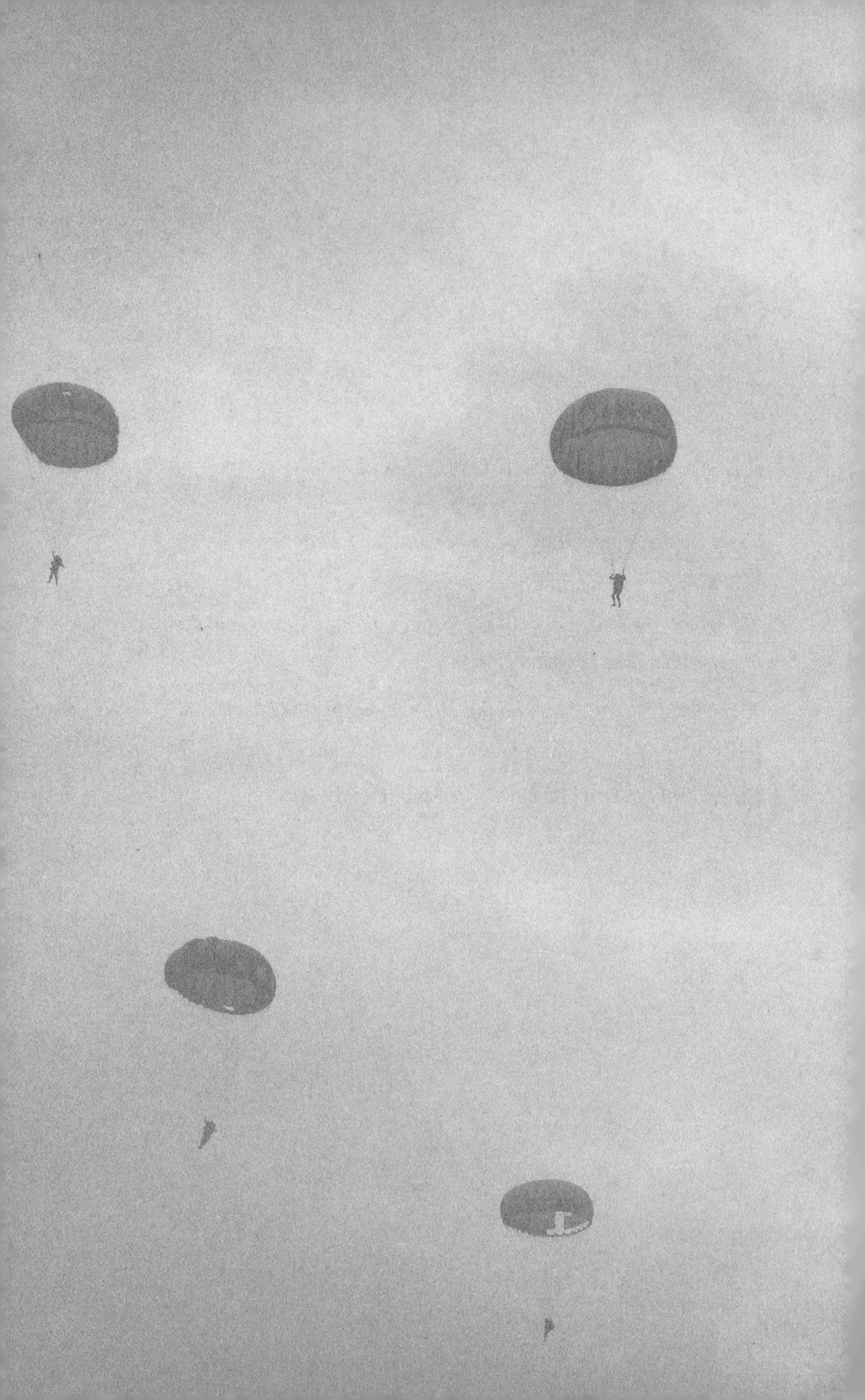

NOTHING BUT COURAGE

The 82nd Airborne's Daring D-Day Mission—and Their Heroic Charge Across the La Fière Bridge

JAMES DONOVAN

CALIBER

CALIBER
An imprint of Penguin Random House LLC
1745 Broadway, New York, NY 10019
penguinrandomhouse.com

Copyright © 2025 by James Donovan
Penguin Random House values and supports copyright. Copyright fuels creativity, encourages diverse voices, promotes free speech, and creates a vibrant culture. Thank you for buying an authorized edition of this book and for complying with copyright laws by not reproducing, scanning, or distributing any part of it in any form without permission. You are supporting writers and allowing Penguin Random House to continue to publish books for every reader. Please note that no part of this book may be used or reproduced in any manner for the purpose of training artificial intelligence technologies or systems.

DUTTON CALIBER and the D CALIBER colophon are registered trademarks of Penguin Random House LLC.

BOOK DESIGN BY LORIE PAGNOZZI

Map © 2025 by Jeffrey L. Ward
Title page and part opener photograph: Shutterstock

LIBRARY OF CONGRESS CATALOGING-IN-PUBLICATION DATA
has been applied for.

ISBN 9780593184875 (hardcover)
ISBN 9780593184899 (ebook)

Printed in the United States of America
1 3 5 7 9 10 8 6 4 2

The authorized representative in the EU for product safety and compliance is Penguin Random House Ireland, Morrison Chambers, 32 Nassau Street, Dublin D02 YH68, Ireland, https://eu-contact.penguin.ie.

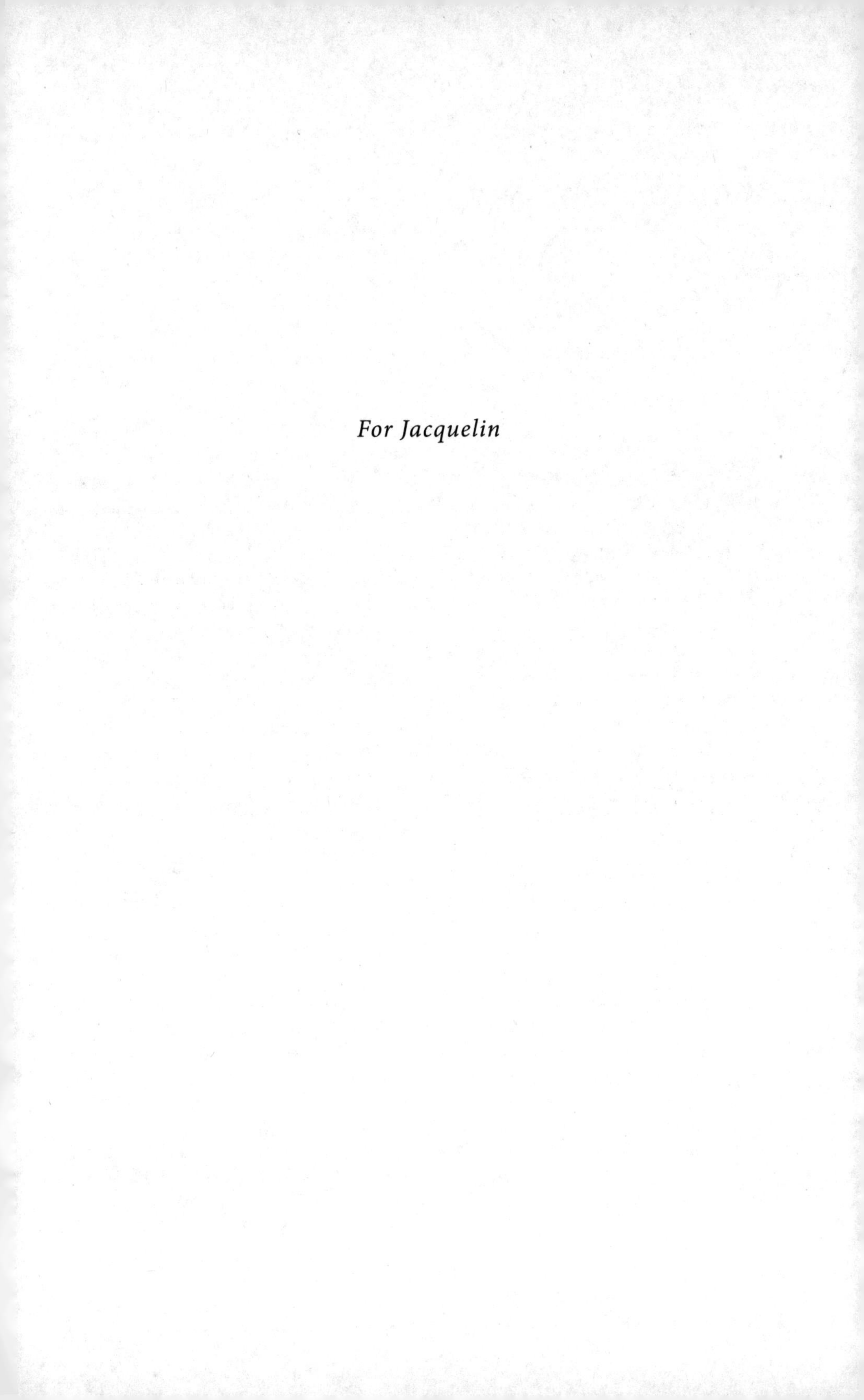

For Jacquelin

CONTENTS

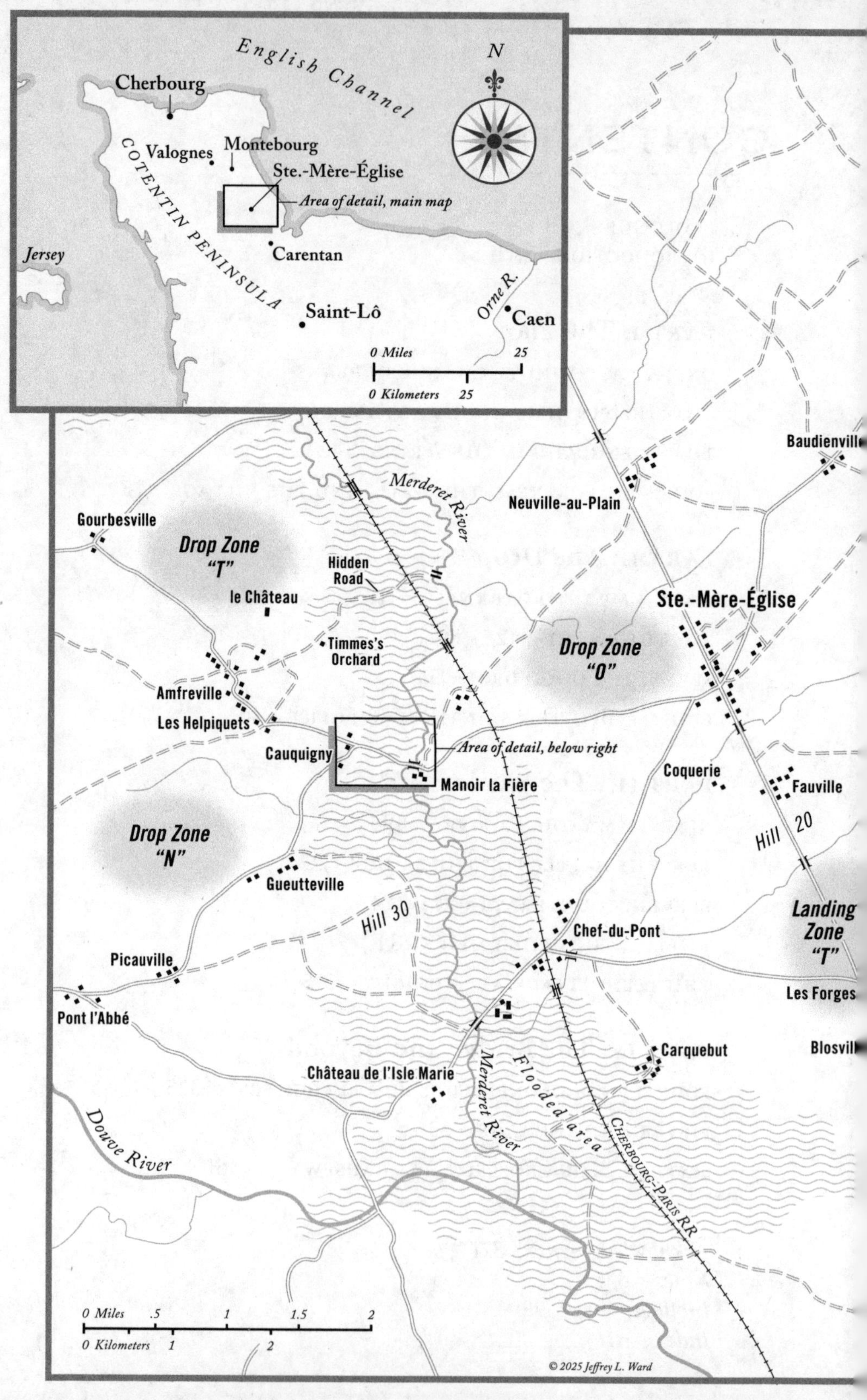
English Channel
N
Cherbourg
Valognes
Montebourg
Ste.-Mère-Église
Area of detail, main map
COTENTIN PENINSULA
Jersey
Carentan
Saint-Lô
Orne R.
Caen
0 Miles
25
0 Kilometers
25
Baudienville
Merderet River
Neuville-au-Plain
Gourbesville
Drop Zone "T"
Hidden Road
le Château
Ste.-Mère-Église
Timmes's Orchard
Drop Zone "O"
Amfreville
Les Helpiquets
Cauquigny
Area of detail, below right
Manoir la Fière
Coquerie
Fauville
Drop Zone "N"
Hill 20
Gueutteville
Hill 30
Landing Zone "T"
Chef-du-Pont
Picauville
Les Forges
Pont l'Abbé
Carquebut
Blosvil
Château de l'Isle Marie
Merderet River
Flooded area
Douve River
CHERBOURG–PARIS RR
0 Miles
.5
1
1.5
2
0 Kilometers
1
2
© 2025 Jeffrey L. Ward

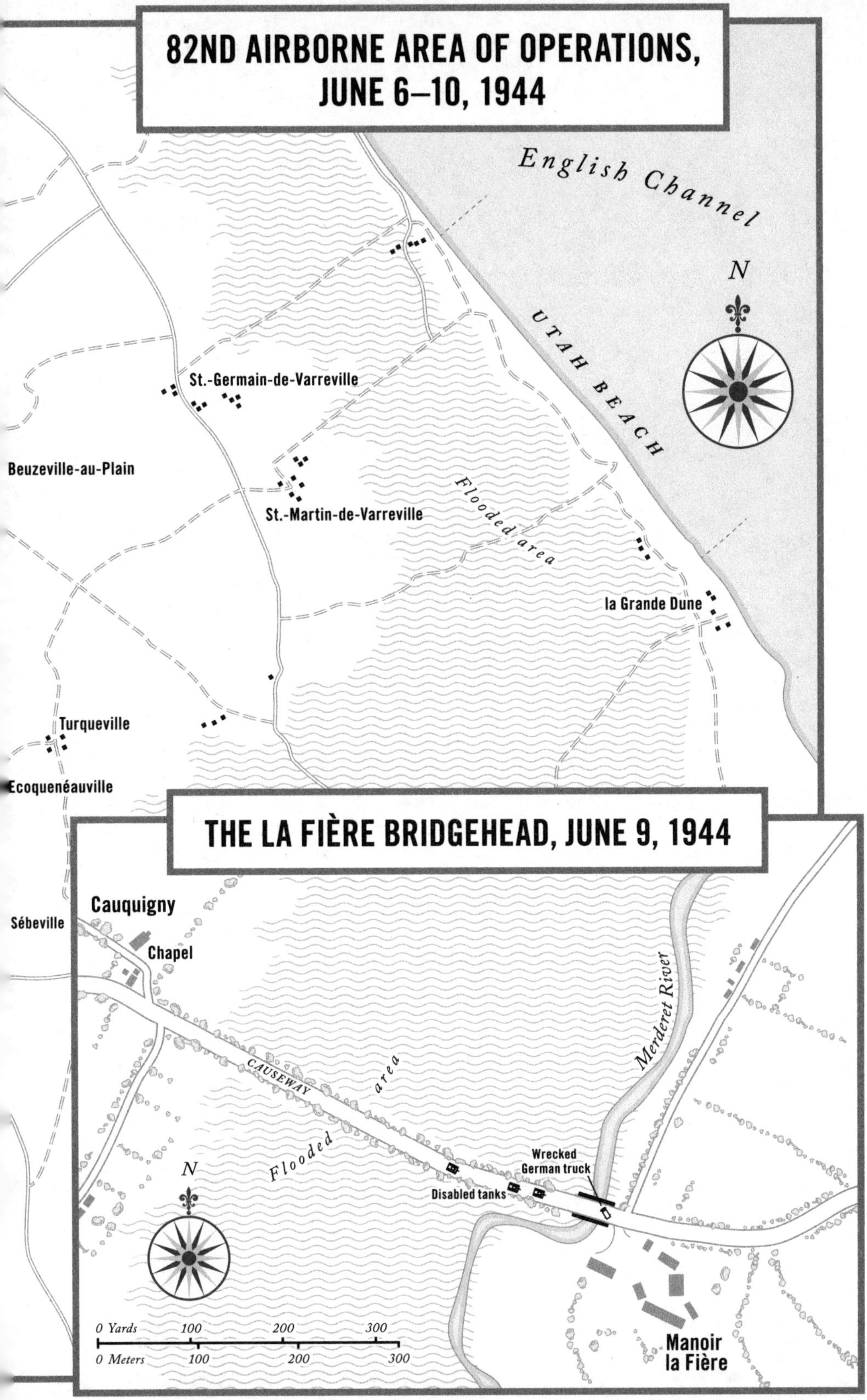

82ND AIRBORNE AREA OF OPERATIONS, JUNE 6–10, 1944

English Channel

N

UTAH BEACH

St.-Germain-de-Varreville

Beuzeville-au-Plain

St.-Martin-de-Varreville

Flooded area

la Grande Dune

Turqueville

Écoquenéauville

Sébeville

THE LA FIÈRE BRIDGEHEAD, JUNE 9, 1944

Cauquigny

Chapel

CAUSEWAY

Flooded area

Merderet River

Wrecked German truck

Disabled tanks

N

0 Yards 100 200 300

0 Meters 100 200 300

Manoir la Fière

PROLOGUE

June 6, 1944

About 2:10 a.m.

When his transport plane emerged from the fogbank around 700 feet over the fields of France's Cotentin Peninsula, Lieutenant Robert Moss of H Company, 508th Parachute Infantry Regiment, was standing in the open doorway at the rear of the cabin. The air rushing by his face was cold, and the drone of the C-47's twin engines deafening.

The moon was near full and high in the ink-dark sky. Red, blue, and green tracers arced up past the plane and black-gray puffs of flak exploded all around, each one sending hundreds of jagged metal fragments in all directions. It was the finest fireworks show any of them had ever seen, beautiful yet terrifying.

They hadn't taken any direct hits yet, but each concussion from the bursting shells rocked the plane, and the seventeen heavily laden troopers standing behind their platoon leader in the dark cabin, left arms raised, their hands gripping the static lines hooked to the metal anchor cable running the length of the cabin's ceiling, held on for dear life. They were getting edgy, pushing and surging against Moss, swearing and urging him to jump. But something was wrong. He couldn't see any other planes, and the red "ready" light next to the doorway had been on far too long—why hadn't the green light next to it come on?

At thirty, Moss was one of his company's oldest men, a Virginian who had enlisted and volunteered for the Airborne. He'd been selected for Officers Candidate School (OCS) after jump training, and graduated as a second lieutenant. In September 1942, he'd used a weeklong furlough to go home to Richmond and marry his sweetheart, Helen. Moss hadn't seen her or their eleven-month-old baby girl in six months. He wanted very much to see them again.

As Moss prepared himself to jump, the ready light still glowing red, the crew chief made his way down the narrow aisle through the scrum of men and equipment and told him the pilots couldn't find the drop zone (DZ)—they were lost. Did the lieutenant want to go back to England? Behind Moss, his troopers were getting louder. He knew they'd throw him out and follow him before they'd return over the Channel or kill him when they got back.

Moss said, "Are we over France?"

"Yes."

"Give us the green light. We're going."

A moment later, he leaped out the door. The static line pulled his chute free, and the jerk when it billowed out and filled was wrenching but welcome. Below him he could see what looked like a large pasture. As a strong wind carried him past it, he realized it was the Merderet River, one of the features they had studied; normally a modest little stream, now it looked flooded over a vast area. Then houses came up, and a few seconds later he slammed through the thatched roof of a stone barn. He hung in a corner, just a foot from the floor, swinging from wall to wall. Oddly enough, in a night training jump a few months earlier, he had dropped through the thatched roof of an English farmhouse into the farmer's bedroom, where he and his wife were in bed.

Now Moss pulled a trench knife from his boot holster and slashed the right suspension lines of his parachute. Hanging by his left shoulder, still banging back and forth, he heard German voices outside, and a Schmeisser machine pistol fired through the open doorway. By the moonlight outside, Moss could see two figures approaching. He grasped his .45 pistol in its shoulder holster but it had a hair trigger and went off, barely missing his arm. He started shooting. A German soldier came in firing his Schmeisser, and one of Moss's .45 slugs hit him and knocked him back against the wall, where he slid to the floor and didn't get up. Moss grabbed his knife and slashed the left suspension lines and dropped to the ground. Still in his harness, he scrambled over to the open doorway and looked out. The other German stood six feet away. Moss shot him and the soldier spun around and fell dead. Moss crawled through the doorway and around the side of the barn, then got to his feet, dashed down a driveway to a road, and ran across it into the dark cover of an apple orchard.

He could hear gunfire in the distance. He stayed in the shadows of the trees to catch his breath and cut away his harness, then spent the next hour reconnoitering. He didn't see a single soul, friend, enemy, or Frenchman, but he found out he was on the outskirts of a village named Chef-du-Pont. He knew where that was and he knew it wasn't where he was supposed to be. He set out west, through the patchwork bocage of small fields and thick hedgerows toward what sounded like M1 rifle fire, in search of his men. They had a bridge to take, and to hold, and they had to do it soon.[1]

INTRODUCTION

The French people are now slaves. Only a successful Overlord can free them.

GENERAL DWIGHT D. EISENHOWER[1]

IN THE SPRING of 1944, the world was at war.

For four long years, Western Europe had abided its Nazi overlords. After swift campaigns in Poland and Scandinavia, Germany had invaded the Low Countries—Belgium, Luxembourg, and the Netherlands—and France. Six weeks later, the Nazi blitzkrieg had overrun all four. Adolf Hitler now controlled the whole of mainland Europe, and every country, save for a few neutral ones, was soon occupied by Wehrmacht troops. Only England across the Channel held firm, withstanding the four-month Luftwaffe onslaught known as the Battle of Britain, which caused Hitler to cancel his planned assault on the island nation. And Germany's invasion of Russia in June 1941—expected to be another lightning-quick victory—had been met by fierce resistance. The Russian bear, awakened, angry, and battered, had recovered and pushed back, and was now steadily advancing westward through Eastern Europe toward Germany's eastern border.

Pitted against the Axis powers of Germany and Japan, after their former ally Italy surrendered in September 1943, were the Allies: the Big Three of the United Kingdom, the Soviet Union, and the United States, with several others. They had successfully invaded North Africa in November 1942, Sicily in July 1943, and southern Italy in September.

But the progress up through the mountainous Italian peninsula against stubborn German troops was slow and costly—anything but the "soft underbelly" of Europe, as described by British prime minister Winston Churchill.

Soviet losses defending their homeland were obscenely massive: by May 1944, sixteen million dead, civilian and military, with tens of thousands more every week. Since 1941, Premier Joseph Stalin had been calling for a western front, to reduce the Wehrmacht's focus on his country. The U.S. agreed that an invasion of Western Europe would present the most direct way to engage German forces, but an exhausted England—recovering from the near calamity of Dunkirk, the stalwart defense against large-scale German air attacks during the Battle of Britain, and the heavy bombardment known as the Blitz—resisted. It was not until May 1943, after the Atlantic Ocean had been largely cleared of German U-boats (allowing the necessary buildup of men and matériel in England), that a cross-Channel invasion of Hitler's Festung Europa—Fortress Europe—was set for the next year, and a date chosen: May 1, 1944.

By early 1944, the plan—code-named Operation Overlord, with its initial assault stages code-named Operation Neptune—had been decided upon: landings by five army divisions on as many beaches along Normandy's Channel coastline, with massive air and naval bombardments to soften up the German defenses. They would be supported by three airborne divisions dropped inland several hours before the early-morning seaborne assault. In charge of what would be the largest amphibious invasion ever attempted was General Dwight D. Eisenhower, the Supreme Commander of the Allied Expeditionary Force. He had never led men in battle, but he had proven himself overseeing the invasions of North Africa and Italy. His directive from the Combined Chiefs of Staff was unequivocal: "You will enter the continent of Europe and, in conjunction with the other United Nations, undertake operations aimed at the heart of Germany and the destruction of her armed forces. . . ."

If the Allies could establish a firm foothold in Normandy and hold it, they could follow with more troops and equipment, then drive through France and into the heart of Nazi Germany to destroy the Third Reich.

But Hitler, and every German, knew a cross-Channel invasion was coming, and he had directed that the defenses along the Atlantic and North Sea coasts—all 2,200 miles of it, which he called the *Atlantikwall*, or Atlantic Wall—be heavily reinforced in anticipation. The Allied assault must be thrown back into the sea, and quickly, insisted the Führer; failure to do so would result in "consequences of staggering proportions."

D-Day, the date on which Operation Neptune would commence, was finally set for June 5, 1944.

The first troops into France—the tip of the spear—would be the three airborne divisions, two American and one British, scheduled to drop behind the Wall into the enemy lines just after midnight of the previous day. One of them, the U.S. 82nd Airborne, was given the especially important job of seizing and securing a few strategically important towns and bridges behind a beach code-named Utah, in order to keep German reinforcements from reaching it. One of those bridges was a small stone span over the narrow, gently flowing Merderet River. The bridge was unnamed, but twenty yards from its eastern end lay an old farm manor house called Manoir la Fière.

PART I

THE PLAN

ONE

A LAST-MINUTE CHANGE IN PLANS

The key to the German scheme of defense is the rapid counterattack of reserves.

TOP SECRET NEPTUNE REPORT, MAY 3,1944[1]

May 29, 1944

SIX DAYS BEFORE D-Day—the commencement of Operation Overlord, the long-awaited invasion of Nazi-occupied Europe—the American airborne's involvement in the plan was in danger of elimination, thanks to an obstinate Royal Air Force officer, Sir Trafford Leigh-Mallory.

He was Overlord's Air Chief Marshal, commander in chief of all Allied air forces involved in the invasion, and he had long resisted the use of paratroops. He was sure that the war would be fought, and won, through air power—not airborne troops. Now, on the eve of the largest invasion in history, he wanted the American paratrooper and glider operations scrapped.

Leigh-Mallory had made his feelings clear almost from the start. On January 21, in his very first meeting with General Dwight Eisenhower and General Omar Bradley, commander in chief of Overlord's

American ground forces, they had expressed their wish to drop two airborne divisions inland from that section of the Normandy coast designated Utah to assist the seaborne troops landing there. It would be wrong, the Air Chief Marshal told them, to use airborne forces—losses would be 75 to 80 percent, a horrific price to pay. His case was supported by the many wayward drops and high casualties sustained by the airborne operations in Sicily in July 1943.

But the unassuming general whom colleagues and friends called Ike—whose chief talent, it sometimes seemed, was wrangling the massive British and American egos involved in Overlord—was adamant. There would be no Utah Beach assault without an airborne component.

In several subsequent meetings with Leigh-Mallory, Bradley explained why. The coastline there was an excellent choice for an amphibious landing: ten miles of wide, gently rising light gray beach, broad and flat, that rose to a low masonry seawall. But it presented more problems than Omaha, the other American beach. Omaha wasn't perfect; a 150-foot-high bluff set back from the beach provided an ideal position from which Germans could shoot down on troops exiting landing craft. But Utah's problems lay behind the beach.

Beyond the seawall were a hundred yards of low sand dunes topped with grassy tussocks, and through them were the only exits inland: four treeless, dirt-and-stone-surfaced roads that were just ten feet wide and spanned almost two miles of flooded marshland that was barely above sea level and full of dead trees sticking out of the greenish muck.[2] The Overlord planners called them "causeways," and they were raised just a few feet above *le marais*, the swamp. Should the Germans retain control of these causeways, they could keep the 4th Infantry Division, part of the first wave hitting the beach at 6:30 a.m., pinned down,[3] bombarding it from a distance while they moved reinforcements—

troops, including elite SS units; more and heavier artillery; and the dreaded panzer tanks—to the area. Artillery and machine guns in pillboxes and casements behind the flooded areas at each exit could also trap any vehicles or troops on the exposed causeways, and a single immobile truck or tank could create a bottleneck and make sitting ducks of anyone on them.[4] A mile or so behind the coast, on solid ground, were at least eighteen heavy guns and dozens of smaller howitzers, all within easy range of the beach, ready to inflict constant and deadly shelling on American troops. It was imperative that the extensively trained but untested 4th Division receive immediate help, and that could come only from behind the beaches. That meant airborne forces.

The potential for defeat was alarming. If the Utah assault failed, so might Neptune, for Utah, on the western flank of the five beaches, and Sword, on the eastern flank, were the most strategically important.[5] And if Overlord failed, there would not be another major invasion of Europe for a long time. Maybe never. That might force a truce, or allow Hitler to get some of his *Wunderwaffen*—the "wonder weapons" then in development, such as the V-1 and V-2 rockets; improved U-boats; remote-controlled tanks; jet- and rocket-propelled fighter planes; massive antiaircraft missiles; poison gases; a V-3 cannon almost 500 feet long that could hurl a 310-pound shell a hundred miles; even nuclear warheads—up and running in time to change the outcome of the war. At the very least, it would release dozens of divisions in the west that could be used to bolster the Eastern Front against the Soviet Union. That might lead to a negotiated peace and a division of Eastern Europe between the Germans and the Soviets; if not, the conflict could continue for several years. In all likelihood, that meant millions more dead and injured soldiers, sailors, airmen, and noncombatant men, women, and children.

Then there was Cherbourg. Thirty-three miles from Utah by road—the two-lane asphalt Route Nationale 13, or N13, which arced up from Paris—and northwest of Utah on the northern coast of the thumb-shaped Cotentin Peninsula, which juts out into the Atlantic, the city possessed the only large deepwater port in the area. The Germans had heavily fortified it with several defensive perimeters featuring large guns, tank obstacles, barbed wire, minefields, and thick cement pill-boxes, and 47,000 soldiers were garrisoned there. Its commander had sworn to Hitler that he would defend it "to the last man."

But the Allies needed Cherbourg to supply the massive invasion and to continue to pour troops into France. Once the seaborne troops landed on the Cotentin's east coast, it would be a race to see which side could bring a stronger force to the point of attack—the Germans, with four panzer divisions just a couple of days away, or the Allies, who would have to transport their men and matériel by sea and somehow land their heavy armor. Unless the Allies quickly choked off German lines to the well-defended city, the enemy could hold out there for months, until the fickle Channel weather turned nasty in the fall—or even before then—and made resupply and reinforcement questionable. "Unless we could soon seize Cherbourg," Eisenhower wrote later, "the enemy's opportunity for hemming us in on a narrow beachhead might be so well exploited as to lead to the defeat of the operations."[6]

For four long years, most of Western Europe had been under the Nazi jackboot. Much longer and a world weary of war might agree to a peace settlement—and who knew what those terms might be and what territories and countries might remain under that boot?

Overlord's planners decided that three airborne divisions were needed to ensure that none of these outcomes came to pass. The two American divisions would comprise about 13,000 paratroopers and another 4,000 men delivered by gliders. It was an ambitious plan, since the few previous Allied airborne drops had involved only one or two regiments. No nation had ever dropped an entire division—three or four regiments—much less two of them. The number of men and planes involved and the logistics of loading, transporting, and accurately dropping them in one massive operation were staggering. A problem in just one area could doom the entire undertaking.

The plan called for the untested 101st Airborne to drop a few miles behind Utah just after midnight, seize the four invasion beach exits, capture a key crossroads village, and take two vital bridges to its west. Its troopers could quickly link up with the Fourth Division, landing on the beach at 6:30 a.m.

The 82nd Airborne, elements of which had been seen combat in Sicily and Salerno the previous year, would follow, and take on the tougher job. Its four regiments—three parachute and one glider—would drop and land much farther inland, near the village of Saint-Sauveur-le-Vicomte and beyond the immediate reach of the seaborne forces. Sixteen miles from Utah and more than halfway across the peninsula, they would choke off its western half and block any reinforcements to Cherbourg by way of the north-south road that ran to the top of the peninsula and then swerved east to the port city. They might have to hold out for several days or more until the overland forces could break through to reach them. It was a dangerous but necessary assignment.

The two division commanders, General Maxwell Taylor of the 101st and General Matthew Ridgway of the 82nd, accepted the plan without a word of protest. They had extra motivation: If the airborne had no part in this great invasion, it was likely that their divisions, and every other airborne unit, would be disbanded and their troopers reassigned to the regular army. They were eager to show what well-trained and properly dropped paratroopers could do.

THE AMERICAN AIRBORNE plans had gone through several permutations. Early on, higher-ups had pushed for a landing near Paris by three airborne divisions that would hold the French capital until they were relieved by the amphibious forces. After that risky venture was canceled, the next plan called for paratroopers to land along the two invasion beaches and attack the coastal defenses from behind. Another called for the 82nd and the 101st to storm the beaches as amphibious assault troops. Then an attack on Bayeux, at the eastern edge of Omaha Beach, was proposed to block German reinforcements. One madly ambitious idea proposed dropping every U.S. airborne unit available—at least 20,000 men—forty miles inland astride the Seine River, where they would block German forces in central France from counterattacking the Allied beachhead in Normandy.[7] The present plan, still quite challenging, had been settled on only in March.

Without Utah and without Cherbourg, the entire assault, spanning fifty miles across five beaches, would be imperiled.

Leigh-Mallory was not persuaded. "I cannot approve your plan," he announced at a planning session that included ground forces commander in chief General Bernard Montgomery, Bradley, and several other high-level commanders. "It is much too hazardous an undertaking. Your losses will be excessive—certainly far more than the gains are worth. I'm sorry, General Bradley, but I cannot go along on it with you."

Bradley was from a poor rural Missouri family, and his high-pitched voice and homely, weathered face belied a sharp mind and a steely spirit. "If you insist on cutting out the airborne attack," the bespectacled Bradley told the air marshal in his Midwestern twang, "then I must ask that we eliminate the Utah assault. I am not going to land on that beach without making sure we've got exits behind it." He had seen with his own eyes, on Sicily, the damage that just half a battalion of the 505th Parachute Infantry Regiment had inflicted on a heavily armored German division.

Across the table, the burly, thin-mustached Air Chief Marshal bristled, staring at Bradley for a moment. "Then let me make it clear," he said, "that if you insist upon this airborne operation, you'll do it in spite of my opposition." He turned to Montgomery. "If General Bradley insists upon going ahead he will have to accept full responsibility for the operation. I don't believe it will work."

"That's perfectly agreeable to me," said Bradley. "I'm in the habit of accepting responsibility for my operations."

Before Leigh-Mallory could reply, Montgomery—an egotist himself and unaccustomed to resolving the disputes of others—rapped on the table. "This is not at all necessary, gentlemen. *I* shall assume full responsibility for the operation."[8] He had often been overly cautious in the past, but during Overlord's planning he'd become a bold risk-taker. Though he believed that thirteen enemy divisions could be approaching the Allied beaches within forty-eight hours of the landings, he was confident of success.[9]

Not that the Air Chief Marshal's objections weren't valid. Everyone agreed that the airborne mission would be hazardous. The route of the slow and low-flying C-47 troop carriers used by the airborne divisions would take them from the west coast of the peninsula to the east under a full moon high in the sky—a full moon necessary for their operations on the ground. German night fighter planes, Leigh-Mallory insisted, "would get in among the slow-flying transport craft and knock them from the sky like hawks attacking a flight of ducks."[10] They would also run into constant ground fire almost as soon as they made landfall, and be even more vulnerable when they approached their drop zones at 110 mph and dropped down to 600 feet, since the planes were without self-sealing fuel tanks or under armor, increasing the odds of fire and damage. If they survived the barrage of antiaircraft fire and flak to reach their drop zones and deliver their paratroopers, those men would be enduring heavy ground fire while they floated down to earth in hostile territory. And gliders would not only face the same antiaircraft fire but would also have to navigate the formidable hedgerows, the bocage that divided the small fields of that part of Normandy and which would routinely grow to solid root-and-soil-entangled heights of six feet or more, with ditches on each side; almost no one planning Overlord knew how formidable they would actually be. That was in addition to anti-glider devices such as thick, ten-foot-high wooden posts implanted in the ground, some of which appeared, at least in surveillance photos, to be connected by barbed wire or booby-trapped with mines or artillery shells.

No, the airborne segment of the Utah assault would be risky. But the invasion of Western Europe—and particularly Utah—demanded audacity, which was always accompanied by risk. The Air Chief Marshal had become excessively prudent, and it seemed apparent he was intent on avoiding responsibility for any risks he hadn't approved of.

Leigh-Mallory had commanded a fighter plane group during the Battle of Britain that had played a large part in the victory over the vaunted Luftwaffe—though not everyone in Fighter Command had agreed with his strategy. He had politicked for the job of Overlord air forces commander and been appointed the previous August, but Eisenhower had refused his demands for control over heavy bombers. The air marshal had little experience in working with ground or airborne troops—or any aircraft other than fighters—and he was in over his head, stubbornly refusing to accede to suggested strategic improvements until forced to. He had become indecisive and pessimistic as the

Overlord plans had expanded beyond his area of expertise, and both British and American senior air commanders distrusted him and refused to take orders from him.[11] Eisenhower finally had to route their orders through one of his deputy commanders, Air Marshal Sir Arthur Tedder.[12] Even Montgomery, who supported the airborne plan, would later call Leigh-Mallory "a gutless bugger who refuses to take a chance."[13] Now the gutless bugger was threatening to derail the Utah assault.

Leigh-Mallory's blithe ignorance knew no limits. A few months previous, Brigadier General James "Jumpin' Jim" Gavin, the new young assistant commander of the 82nd Airborne Division, had been assigned as the American airborne adviser, and he met with Leigh-Mallory at his headquarters in London to review plans for Overlord. Gavin was a mere one-star general in a sea of heavy brass, but he had an ally in Bradley, who appreciated his heroics and leadership in Sicily and supported a strong airborne presence in Overlord.

The Air Chief Marshal made it clear that he did not think too highly of the American airborne forces or, for that matter, airborne forces in general and that he disdained the thought of them using his planes as ferries.

"Now, I want you chaps to tell me how you do this airborne business," he said indulgently.

Gavin patiently explained how airborne operations worked, referencing the 82nd's drops in Sicily and Salerno the previous summer and its accomplishments there. Leigh-Mallory expressed skepticism more than once. When Gavin was finished, the air marshal said, "I don't think anyone can do that."

The normally soft-spoken Gavin exploded. "We just got through doing it in Sicily!" he said.[14] He left the meeting in a foul mood, disgusted with the air marshal's attitude. Leigh-Mallory knew almost nothing of airborne combat, yet he was telling the Americans that they would be ineffective.[15] A few days later Gavin left London for the British Midlands, where the 82nd troops had just arrived. Grateful to be done with the political squabbling, jealousies, and self-aggrandizement—not to mention the tedium of endless meetings of far too many committees—he plunged into their training. When Ridgway asked him to return to London and the planning, Gavin begged off.

At another meeting, the Air Chief Marshal insisted that the drop altitude for any paratroopers be no lower than 1,200 feet to limit damage to his aircraft. But that height would have meant more time drifting to earth, more susceptibility to ground fire, and more risk of wider troop dispersal. When another 82nd officer made an impassioned plea for a lower altitude safer for the paratroopers, Leigh-Mallory dismissed him curtly, though he eventually lost the argument.[16]

Despite Leigh-Mallory's protestations, Eisenhower declared that airborne drops would accompany the Utah landings. Thus far in the war, the jury was still out on their effectiveness. The first large-scale airborne operation, which had been into Sicily, had not gone particularly well; sloppy navigation had resulted in scattered drops, and friendly antiaircraft fire had shot down twenty-three C-47 transports, killing hundreds. Only aggressive, on-the-fly action on the ground that disrupted communications and stopped a panzer division from attacking the seaborne invasion force saved the operation. The mixed result had left Eisenhower, and most of the other top brass, unpersuaded. But Bradley had insisted to him that airborne troops were necessary, and Ike trusted his longtime friend—they had known each other since they'd graduated from West Point together some thirty years earlier.

Then, on May 25, military intelligence from Bletchley Park—the old mansion north of London where cryptographers had been intercepting, decrypting, and analyzing top-level German radio messages since

1941—reported alarming news: The enemy had reinforced the area south of Cherbourg with three units. One of them, the fresh but below-strength 91st Luftlande (Air-Landing) Division, had moved to the sector the 82nd was jumping into, and another, the inexperienced but well-trained Fallschirmjäger (Paratroop) Regiment 6, was not far away. They seemed specifically positioned to anticipate airborne landings.

The next day, the 82nd's drop zones were shifted ten miles east, nearer to the beach but farther inland than the 101st. The division would drop astride the narrow, slow-moving Merderet River, which flowed south into the Douve, which in turn emptied into the English Channel. The 101st would still take control of the four causeways inland from Utah while guarding the southwest, but the 82nd troopers would now seize the nearby village of Sainte-Mère-Église and the two bridges across the Merderet, and guard against counterattack from the northwest. "Our chances of survival are greatly improved," wrote Gavin in his diary.[17]

That wasn't enough for Leigh-Mallory, who still thought the drops were too hazardous. On May 29, at a heated top-level conference in London that Eisenhower didn't attend and at which two British commanders insisted that Utah was essential and the airborne landings an "acceptable risk," he continued to predict disaster, citing the gauntlet of searchlights and heavy flak his aerial armada would endure.[18]

After the meeting, Leigh-Mallory called Eisenhower and urged him to cancel the Utah airborne operations. The losses would be catastrophic, said the air marshal: He estimated that 50 percent of the paratroopers would be dead before the beach landings and 70 percent of the gliders would be destroyed. The result would be "the futile slaughter of two fine divisions."[19]

Eisenhower was alarmed enough to phone Bradley, who told him that he could not and would not order the Utah landing without the airborne drops—the beach forces would be isolated and in great danger from the strengthened German defenses. Then Eisenhower called Ridgway, who would be parachuting in with his men. The 82nd commander echoed Bradley. If the troop carriers could get them to their drop zones without disastrous loss, they could take care of themselves. Ridgway's reassurance was the clincher.[20]

But that night, alone, Eisenhower agonized over his decision. He weighed every factor over and over. Then he called Leigh-Mallory. He told him that the American airborne drops would proceed as scheduled, and suggested that the Air Chief Marshal put his objections in writing.

Leigh-Mallory's letter was hand-delivered to Eisenhower at midday. "I would be failing in my duty to you," he wrote, "if I did not let you know that I am very unhappy about the U.S. airborne operations as now planned for the night of D-1 D-Day." Once more he listed all the dangers and went on to criticize the entire Utah assault as "unsound"—if Utah depended on the airborne drops, it would be "seriously prejudiced." His wording strongly suggested that the letter's real purpose was to avoid personal blame if something went wrong.

At Southwick House, the elegant mansion six miles north of Portsmouth where he had moved his command post a few days earlier, Eisenhower recognized this. But outside the trailer that served as his sleeping quarters, he sequestered himself in the square tent where he held conferences with his staff,[21] and he spent most of the afternoon considering the matter again, going over each step. Another in his place—someone more callous, perhaps—might have quickly dismissed Leigh-Mallory's predictions. But Ike cared deeply about his soldiers, and he took the Air Chief Marshal's forecast seriously. It would be, he wrote later, his most difficult decision of the entire war. If he disregarded the counsel of his technical expert on the subject, "I would carry to my grave the unbearable burden of a conscience justly accusing me of the stupid, blind sacrifice of thousands of the flower of our youth."[22] He finally realized that no one else, British or American, shared Leigh-Mallory's degree of pessimism. The commanders he trusted most believed the air marshal's opinion to be wrong.

He called Leigh-Mallory to acknowledge his letter and give him his answer. The airborne operation, he told him, would proceed. He followed that up with a letter in which he made it clear that he expected the air marshal to keep his doubts to himself—there was no need for such a dire forecast to reach the troops and damage their morale.[23] "If the exits of these causeways should be held by the enemy," Eisenhower would write later, "our landing troops would be caught in a trap and eventually slaughtered by artillery and other fire to which they would be able to make little reply."[24]

The 82nd troopers would be dropped behind—and among—enemy lines. They would be on their own, with no "rear" from which to resupply and reinforce, no rear to retreat to. They would face the grim gauntlet Leigh-Mallory described. They would also encounter unforeseen hazards no one could have anticipated. And against a determined and desperate enemy—the strongest in the world, some claimed—they would need to display courage and know-how and initiative on a scale beyond that which anyone could have imagined.

TWO

JUMPIN' JIM AND HIS ALL AMERICANS

It is a unique characteristic of airborne operations that the moments of greatest weakness of the attacker and the defender occur simultaneously. The issue is therefore decided by three factors: who has the better nerves; who takes the initiative first; and who acts with greater determination.[1]

AIRBORNE OPERATIONS: A GERMAN APPRAISAL

General James Gavin, at thirty-seven the youngest combat general in the U.S. Army, wasn't worried about leading his men into battle—he knew his All Americans were ready for the task ahead of them. It was the drop, with so many things that could go wrong, that concerned him.

The 505th, the parachute regiment he had personally commanded and trained until General Ridgway had made Gavin the 82nd's assistant commander, had proven itself in combat in the Sicily and Salerno drops the previous year. And most of the troopers in the two new parachute regiments, the 507th and the 508th, had been training for at least eighteen months. Almost every day involved endless rounds of push-ups, grueling workouts, rugged obstacle courses, mock battles, long runs and hikes—there was nothing like twenty-five- to forty-mile field marches with a full pack to harden a young body—and the occasional practice jump, usually at night. Every man was in superb physical shape and possessed all the tools and knowledge needed to do the job, which they practiced in field exercises with battle conditions as tough and realistic as possible, sometimes with live ammo. "You will kill or you will be killed," they were told over and over,[2] and they were trained to kill in close quarters in a dozen different ways; the most effective, slitting an enemy's throat from behind, was just one of them. They were also cross-trained on virtually every weapon a trooper could carry besides the standard-issue M1 Garand rifle—bazooka, light machine gun, Browning Automatic rifle (BAR), Thompson submachine gun, various mines and mortars, and more. You never knew when the situation might arise.

Gavin was convinced they would give a good account of themselves, once the untested got over that first heart-pounding shock of receiving fire from an enemy trying to kill them.

Since he'd reunited with the division in mid-February after a frustrating three months in London helping to plan Neptune, the landing phase of Overlord, "Slim" Jim, as his men called him—sometimes it was "Jumpin'" Jim—had thrown himself into its final training. Ridgway was kept busy by high-level planning, and Gavin took to his task with relish, pushing the regimental commanders hard and showing up to see the results for himself. He also placed combat veterans of the 505th with each company of the 507th and 508th for about a week to impart some of their hard-earned wisdom.[3] Training became even more intensive, focusing on battalion-sized jump, assembly, and attack maneuvers—some of them punishing three-day exercises that involved little sleep and ended with a long march back to camp, and that was after a field "problem" such as a bridge to be taken or a position to be seized. A primary tenet was "speed and initiation of combat immediately upon landing"; another was "recognition of isolation as a normal battlefield condition."[4] Besides honing the skills the men would need in combat, and getting them to trust their squad mates before they entrusted their lives to them, the idea was to make combat seem easier in comparison, at least physically.

Overall, Gavin was satisfied with what he saw. Even the 82nd's glider regiment, the 325th, looked impressive and was now full strength—its two battalions had been beefed up with another from the 101st Airborne's glider regiment, the 401st. Their diminutive commander, Colonel Harry Lewis, was a known taskmaster, which helped. Both Gavin and Ridgway believed that the paratroopers' high physical standards should apply to them also,[5] so the glidermen trained harder than other army infantry units. But though they had seen limited action in Italy, Gavin doubted they would ever fight with the "élan and dash" of the volunteer parachute regiments, and he and Ridgway spent little time with them—after all, they wouldn't arrive until D+1. For Neptune, the 325th would be given a reserve role with no specific mission.[6]

Gavin had made sure that the training for the new units, glider and parachute, was especially intense: long marches through the English countryside that ended with the exhausted troops receiving challenging field problems, night jumps, near-constant small-unit tactical exercises, hours on the rifle range, instruction in hand-to-hand combat, and classes in everything from map reading and first aid to language lessons in French and German. And Gavin seemed to be everywhere. He would arrive unannounced at a paratroop unit exercise to observe, add missions, and lead them back to camp, often at a run—and even at thirty-seven he could outrun almost any man in the division.

Soon the new parachute regiments were outperforming the veteran 505th, and at the same time, its discipline problems increased dramatically. After talking to the regiment's enlisted men and officers to find out exactly what was going on, Gavin discovered that, while the 505th was out on field exercises, its new commander, Colonel Herbert Batcheller, a married man, spent almost every afternoon with a local woman at her house right outside the camp's gates. He paid little attention to his regiment, and they had taken their cues from him. Gavin wasted no time in replacing Batcheller with a disciplinarian, Lieutenant Colonel William Ekman. The 505th's new boss had no combat experience, and he was only thirty-one years old, so his veteran troops took a while to warm to him. But he was a sound choice. Raised poor, his father a onetime circus strongman, Ekman had earned an appointment to West Point the same way Gavin had, as an enlisted man. He was smart and sensible, and he immediately began working sixteen hours a day to acquaint himself with the regiment and make it the best fighting unit in the army. "He tightened the screws a little bit but did it in such a sensible manner that I think everyone had begun to respect him by the time of Normandy," observed one of his men. Just as important, he marched with them and showed time and again that he cared for them. Gavin monitored his progress as he pulled the 505th up to the high standards demanded by Ridgway and him both.[7]

The division had changed considerably since the operations in Italy. The 505th's sister parachute regiment, the 504th, had done such a good job there that Lieutenant General Mark Clark, commanding the Fifth Army in its assault on mainland Italy, had, over Ridgway's objections, insisted on keeping the regiment, called "devils in baggy pants" by a Wehrmacht soldier, with him for several more months of hard campaigning. The 504th was utterly exhausted and bloodied with more than 1,100 casualties by the time it was finally relieved and sent to England late in April. It would be too late for the regiment to rebuild and participate in Neptune. Instead, the 507th and 508th were attached.

Gavin knew his men would rise to the occasion. But after dinner on May 30 with General Omar Bradley and all the 82nd's unit commanders, Gavin returned to his HQ with some misgivings about Bradley's bullishness. "He is still confident as ever that we will swamp the Germans," he wrote in his diary. "It is difficult to fully share in his optimism although one really wants to."[8]

Gavin had been informed of the 82nd's changed mission plan only a few days before, and he and his staff had been scrambling to adjust. And though he didn't share Air Chief Marshal Trafford Leigh-Mallory's pessimism, he was fully aware of the many dangers his men would face and how much could go wrong. "Either this 82nd Division job will be the most glorious and spectacular episode in our history," he concluded, "or it will be another Little Big Horn."[9]

The overall mission of the 82nd, along with the 101st, was to protect the right flank of the seaborne assault at Utah Beach and prevent German reserves from reinforcing their coastal units. To accomplish this mission, the 82nd's assignment comprised two main objectives.

The most important was to take and hold Sainte-Mère-Église, a village of a thousand or so that lay six miles inland, and the smaller villages around it, until the 4th Infantry Division reached them from Utah. Sainte-Mère-Église lay on the N13, the main thoroughfare from Cherbourg to Paris, and another six roads radiated from it; any German troops attempting to reinforce Utah would have to traverse the village. That job was given to the experienced 505th, which would drop about a mile west of town.

The 82nd would also seize and secure two nearby bridgeheads over the Merderet that controlled all traffic—particularly armored vehicles—moving east to west or vice versa. The first bridge was near Chef-du-Pont, two miles southwest of Sainte-Mère-Église. The other lay due west, two miles away, and was adjacent to the farmhouse called

Manoir la Fière. Control of the two small bridges was imperative to the success of the seaborne landings at Utah—and to the entire invasion. These two jobs were also given to the 505th.

Each regiment would hit an oval-shaped drop zone two or three miles from one another, close to their objectives. Both the 507th and the 508th would land just west of the Merderet. The 507th would assist the 505th with capturing the La Fière bridge and securing their assigned sector. The 508th, two miles south of the 507th, would assist the 505th with the capture of the Chef-du-Pont bridge and destroy two crossings over the Douve River to the south.

A special armored task force commanded by Colonel Edson Raff—seventeen Sherman tanks, two armored cars, and ninety glider troops—would land at Utah and break through to the 82nd as quickly as possible. The bulk of the 325th Glider Infantry Regiment would land on the morning of D+1 to reinforce the division and fill in wherever needed.

There were any number of dangers. It would be a night drop, with all its inherent difficulties. A nearly full moon would be high in the sky just when the 378 C-47s carrying the three regiments hit the French coast, and Gavin knew the German defenses on the Cotentin Peninsula would be at full alert—especially since the 101st Airborne, also dropping behind Utah Beach but a few miles closer, would precede the 82nd by thirty minutes. Any element of surprise would be theirs only. And everyone knew what had happened in similar circumstances on the Sicily drop, where many of the transport pilots had veered off course, sped up, and gained altitude to avoid flak, making an accurate and safe jump next to impossible. The division had triumphed over the disastrous drops, but luck had been involved, and you could never count on luck—especially since most of the Neptune transport flight crews would be seeing their first enemy action.

In the previous two months, there had been several test runs held in the English Midlands. A couple of night drops in March were encouraging, though some others had been canceled due to bad weather—a factor that turned the first division-sized one, in early April, into a fiasco, with planes flying every which way and at different altitudes through thick fog and light rain. Most of the transports had to be rerouted to aerodromes all over England. The division's final exercise on May 11 and 12, Exercise Eagle, was a full-scale dress rehearsal involving 800 aircraft simulating the flight time, route, and drop of the upcoming assault. Conducted in perfect weather and involving many green pilots, it was only marginally more promising—one-third of the troopers either didn't drop or did so far from the DZ. Despite a midair collision that killed both plane crews, a few paratrooper deaths, and hundreds of ankle, knee, and leg breaks and sprains, it was judged a success—but not by Gavin, whose criticism of the sloppy drops was not received well by the troop carriers.[10]

More troublesome still, for six months Gavin's officers had been studying constantly updated maps and aerial photographs of their objective areas near the west coast of the peninsula, but now they had just a week to prepare for their new objectives ten miles east, nearer the assault beaches. First, the regimental commanding officers had been told, then lower-ranking officers and noncoms, and finally, a couple of days after arriving at the airfields, the enlisted men. They now spent thirty minutes every day in closed tents studying sand tables—roughly six-foot-by-six-foot wooden-sided sandboxes with terrain models of the areas behind Utah, accurately scaled and detailed by modeling experts and including miniature buildings, homes, German gun emplacements, and even trees—in an attempt to burn these new objectives and destinations into their memories. But now there was not enough time to study and fully rehearse their attacks on specific targets and no chance of elaborate tactical preparation. Everything would have to be improvised. Paratroopers were trained for that, but the risk factor was now much higher. There were bound to be snafus and unknowns.

Privately, Gavin thought the revised drops would lead to confusion and chaos, and he fretted that it would be "several days until any semblance of organization or tactical integrity comes out of the mess." Although the men were ready as they could be, that was not a recipe for a successful airborne operation. And by May 1944, Gavin had studied and taken part in more of those than anyone alive.

"JUMPIN'" JIM GAVIN was a different kind of general—and a different kind of man.

He was born in 1907 to an unmarried, newly arrived Irishwoman in Brooklyn who gave him up for adoption. At eighteen months he was adopted by an Irish immigrant family in Mount Carmel, Pennsylvania. Martin Gavin worked the coal mines and provided for young James and the Gavins' young daughter. But like many pre–World War Two families who needed the extra income, they pulled him out of school after he finished the eighth grade—just enough learning to know how to read and write well enough and do basic math. Over the next two years, he worked a variety of full-time jobs—shoe store clerk, filling station manager, Mobil oil salesman—while suffering physical abuse at the hands of his alcoholic mother, who beat him with a heavy leather strap or a hairbrush at the slightest provocation. He found some solace in books; early on, young Gavin developed a passion for reading, and he ran through most of the Mount Carmel public library by the time he was seventeen. He especially liked reading about the acclaimed battle leaders, from Alexander the Great and Hannibal to Napoleon and Stonewall Jackson.[11]

On his seventeenth birthday, he ran away from home to New York City to find a better job. One week later he joined the army, which managed to get around the fact that he was underage by providing an attorney who had Gavin sign a paper declaring him the youngster's guardian, thus providing the required parental consent for an under-eighteen enlistee, to which Gavin eagerly attested. Rather than ask the Gavins, he had claimed he was an orphan.

In the army, Gavin found a new family and sent his old family $10 a month out of his $18.75 pay. He was sent to Fort Sherman in the Panama Canal Zone and learned how to soldier in the peacetime army. He continued to read voraciously, though he tried to hide it from his barracks mates. A tough but kind American Indian sergeant noticed the intelligent youngster and made him his company clerk. He pushed Gavin to apply for an appointment to West Point—but before that, a chance to attend an army prep school designed to find the few enlisted men who might make good officers. He scored poorly on the entrance exam for the course, but was accepted anyway.

After four months of exhaustive studying, reading, and testing, and daily tutoring from a lieutenant who also saw his potential, he took a four-hour written test. He passed, and was allowed to apply to West Point, and was accepted. There he found college to be difficult early on—his first semester was a "nightmare of work," he remembered.[12] But twice a week he woke early at 4:00 a.m. and snuck down to the well-lit basement latrines for extra study time. And by the time he graduated in June 1929 with a second lieutenant's commission, the miner's son who hadn't attended a single day of high school was confident in himself intellectually and socially.

Others besides that sergeant would recognize Gavin's keen mind and perseverance—but not for a decade. After giving him several routine postings, the army sent Gavin back to the Point in 1940 as a tactics instructor. It was there that he developed a fascination with the recent German airborne assaults on Belgium, Holland, and Crete and studied everything he could find on them. He wasn't the only one. The top British and American brass had been so impressed that both armies quickly formed paratroop units. And in August 1941, Gavin, now a captain, applied for and received a position in the army's new airborne force. After he finished parachute school and while he was just in charge of a company, his superiors recognized him for the keen and innovative thinker he was, the one man capable of answering the many questions about how paratroopers should deploy and fight—which needed to be answered quickly, before they were thrown into battle against an enemy. Gavin was promoted to major, made chief of training and doctrine, and tasked to develop the tactics and rules of this new form of combat. He embraced the assignment and quickly wrote the first manual on the subject: *Tactics and Technique of Air-Borne Troops*.

Most Americans had never heard of airborne troops. But it didn't take long for a mystique to develop, even before U.S. parachute troops had been used in combat. That was deliberate—Gavin and his superiors envisioned an elite fighting force, and they knew how to attract the right kind of men. Their recruiters were chosen for having the right look, and the spiel they used was calculated to appeal to those who wanted to be part of something special. "Why walk like regular infantry if you can ride?" was a typical recruiting sergeant's line. For many a poor kid from the sticks, it was irresistible.

The military got plenty of help from the media. The cover of the May 12, 1941, issue of *Life*, the country's most popular magazine, featured a determined-looking "U.S. Army parachutist," and the photo article inside might as well have been a recruitment ad. Soon after America's entry in World War Two that December, the actual ads began appearing, accompanied by posters and more magazine and newspaper stories about a new special force called the Airborne. "Look out below!" read one U.S. Army ad. "Johnny Skytrooper is rough, tough, and nasty. Striking behind lines, he hits hardest where it hurts the most." "They've got the GUTS," screamed another, under a striking color illustration of two paratroopers in action, one brandishing a tommy gun. "They are hand-picked—only the best men can serve with them" was the bold challenge in one brochure, and another went straight to the point: "The Mark of a Man," read the copy next to a paratrooper's badge, "the mark of a real combat soldier—a man among men." Four months later, the movie version appeared: *Parachute Battalion*, a thinly veiled propaganda film that followed three very different young men as they underwent paratroop training at Fort Benning, Georgia. "Thrill to the Drama of Uncle Sam's New Jump Fighters!" and "A New Kind of Courage for Men!" read the movie ads.

Fully outfitted soldiers jumping out of planes into enemy territory and ready to hit the ground fighting—what was this? The public was vaguely familiar with parachutes and parachutists, but an army of them?

It was a new way to deploy troops: vertical envelopment, some called it. The men who signed up had to be intensely trained—not only physically but psychologically in how to jump without hesitation out of a low-flying cargo plane and land safely behind enemy lines. They had to know how to fight in new ways, whether they found themselves alone or able to join up with a squad, a platoon, or a company. A paratrooper had to be taught to display greater initiative than other soldiers, for he might be surrounded by the enemy and have to survive on his own for days until reinforced or resupplied—and, of course, he had to immediately enter combat against any opposition he encountered. Toward this goal, airborne leaders decried the army's "old method of forcing individuals into a mold, while at the same time removing their personal identities as far as possible," wrote Gavin. Instead, they "tried to impress upon them what outstanding individual soldiers they were."[13] The result, they hoped, was a superbly trained and conditioned soldier ready to operate alone, if necessary, under the most adverse conditions—and to think for himself.

A job that dangerous was purely volunteer. Young men throughout America—very young men, most of them still in their teens—responded to the idea of this new kind of soldier and signed up in droves. The extra $50 in jump pay, more than double a buck private's basic monthly take-home of $21, was another incentive, and a powerful one in an America just emerging from the long and painful Depression. Young men from every part of the country and every segment of the population signed up—"farmboys, woodsmen, city boys from the East, rebels from the South, Indians and Mexican transplants from the Southwest," as one trooper remembered. "The officers were mainly from colleges and military schools, many of them from the South."[14] Most of the enlisted men, and many of the officers, had never even been in an airplane before they jumped from one.

Not every volunteer made the grade. The four-week-long Parachute Training School at Fort Benning—200,000 acres of rolling hills along the Chattahoochee River just seven miles south of Columbus, Georgia—was designed to weed out the weaker applicants, and many were. The cadre sergeants who supervised the merciless training seemed to have one goal: to make as many recruits as possible quit. Every volunteer was required to run everywhere; anything more than two walking steps meant a set of push-ups. After the first week, which was strictly physical conditioning, each man was required to run eight miles without stopping, climb a rope thirty-five feet high, and do a punishing series of sit-ups, push-ups, pull-ups, and knee bends.

But the worst tests were the long marches. One 508th officer remembered it vividly more than sixty years later: "One day we marched and maneuvered, had early chow, and slept in our pup tents until 2300 hours when we were awakened, assembled with full field packs on our backs, marched for twenty-four hours, and then tented again. . . . That was one of the few times I went to sleep walking. When I slept, [a friend] steered me and then I steered him while he was sleeping. It is easy to sleepwalk. You just watch the feet of the man in front of you, and when the column stops, you run into him."[15]

These and other rigorous tests ensured that only the toughest and most motivated survived to make the five required jumps and graduate. Many men passed out from heat exhaustion. Officers had it no easier. After just two weeks, one wrote home to tell his family, "We had ninety officers in our section when we started, now we have fifty-five. The rest have been 'washed out,' quit, or injured." Less than half of any jump school class made it.[16]

Then there was the matter of jumping from a height—first from a ten-foot platform, then from a small shed thirty-four feet above the ground, which for many of the men required more courage than much higher elevations. After climbing a ladder up, a man was strapped into a leather harness connected above him to a steel cable that ran down to earth—but he wasn't "caught" until he had jumped out the door and fallen sixteen feet. Then he would slide down the cable to the ground. "What made this intimidating," recalled one trooper, "is that it was so close yet so far from the ground."[17] If he conquered that terror, the next ordeal, a 250-foot-high tower that simulated an actual parachute jump, wasn't nearly as bad. That one pulled up two men at a time in a chair and dropped them. But the worst was the next tower. It was the same height, but an individual was placed in a parachute harness, lying on his stomach, and then raised fifty feet above the tower and dropped. He went into free fall for twenty feet, then came to a sudden stop. If you survived that without quitting, the final high tower, from which a man was released in an actual parachute and floated to the ground, was a breeze. By that time, washouts were few. Each stage was repeated until form was perfected and fear disappeared—or at least subsided.

And finally, the real thing: five jumps from an airplane. When the paratrooper jumped, a fifteen-foot static line clipped to a cable running the length of the plane's cabin ripped the parachute pack cover off and pulled the chute out. The propeller blast blew the chute open and snapped the break cord connecting the static line and the top of the chute. The process took two seconds, tops, and the hard jerk when the chute opened was painful but comforting—it meant the system had worked.

A man who endured the training received his silver paratrooper's wings—and a pair of distinctive calf-length jump boots, which set him apart from the foot sloggers in the army. He was part of an elite fighting force, and the spirit and camaraderie its intense schooling engendered made it a brotherhood. There is no bonding experience the equal of war, but the next most effective thing is preparing for it, and after another year or so of training, when they were judged ready for combat, each man would know and trust with his life every other man in his squad of twelve. They thought of themselves as "the baddest of the bad" and were proud of it. And since their officers shared their hardships—or most of them—the men respected them for it. "In this outfit, you'll jump first and eat last," Gavin told every new officer.[18]

All told, the paratroopers were an outfit whose preparedness and toughness, both mental and physical, outmatched any other in the U.S. military—except, possibly, the army's Rangers, whose live-fire obstacle courses were already legendary . . . though any paratrooper, and many objective observers, would disagree that anyone could match them. According to Gavin, they possessed one more quality that was not just essential but singular. "Parachuting is a good test of a man's courage for combat," he observed. "A man who will jump regularly with equipment will do almost anything."[19]

IN AUGUST 1942, eight months after the Japanese attack on Pearl Harbor that propelled the U.S. into World War Two, the reactivated 82nd Infantry Division—nicknamed the "All American" when it was created in World War One, because its recruits came from every U.S. state, unusual at the time—was converted into the first U.S. airborne division. Gavin was named the commanding officer of the 505th Parachute Infantry Regiment and promoted to colonel. After almost a year of constant training, the 505th was attached to the 82nd and chosen to participate in Operation Husky, the July 1943 Allied invasion of the Axis-controlled island of Sicily, just off the coast of Italy—the first thrust into what Winston Churchill called "the soft underbelly of Europe," with the hope of knocking Italy out of the war. The invasion would also placate Joseph Stalin, who had been calling for a large-scale invasion in the West; Sicily wasn't that, but it would do until the western Allies could gather the necessary manpower and matériel. No less important was taking the island's thirty airfields and landing strips back from the Luftwaffe.

Gavin's new commander was General Matthew Ridgway, West Point class of 1917. Ridgway was a smart, charismatic leader with a hawklike visage often likened to a Roman emperor's, and piercing brown eyes that could make the toughest noncom quiver in his jump boots. If Gavin resembled a Western screen hero, and he did, Ridgway looked like an aristocrat—but a powerfully built one who owned every room he walked into.

Ridgway's background was in many ways the opposite of Gavin's. From an early age, Ridgway felt destined to be a soldier—his father, a graduate of the Point's class of 1883, spent thirty-six years in the coast artillery and retired as a colonel. Matthew was born and raised on army posts. His mother was a concert pianist, and he grew up surrounded by music, books, and culture. Despite that patrician upbringing or perhaps because of it, Ridgway, like Gavin, cared for his men and looked out for them, with high expectations but fair treatment—and he too believed in leading from the front. When another officer asked him why, Ridgway replied, "It won't hurt troop morale to see a dead general from time to time."[20]

Ridgway saw leadership as an almost mystical quality—"the highest service a man can perform is to lead other men in battle," he wrote—and heaven help the officer who didn't measure up to Ridgway's standards. At the same time, he took good care of his men, and wouldn't sacrifice them for a quixotic mission. Even as a young officer, he hadn't been hesitant about standing up to ambitious superiors whose orders he disagreed with. Such an officer was "more butcher than battle leader. . . . I shall go to my grave humbly proud of the fact that on at least four occasions I have stood up at the risk of my career and denounced what I considered to be ill-conceived tactical schemes which I was convinced would result in useless slaughter." He constantly reminded himself that "on the field of battle all men's lives are equally precious."[21] Ridgway loved his men, and they knew it. And, like Gavin, they knew he wouldn't ask them to do anything he wouldn't do first.

He was, if anything, more intense than Gavin; he pushed himself so hard that his staff constantly fretted that he'd have a heart attack. More than once, he drove himself to the point of exhaustion, resulting in a hospital stay. And no one was more disciplined. When he took a seat, he sat so straight, said one of his aides, that "no matter how soft his chair might be, the goddamned chair stiffened when he sat down on it."[22] Even Gavin worried about him, though he marveled at his single-mindedness: "He'd stand in the middle of the road and urinate. I'd say, 'Matt, get the hell out of there. You'll get shot.' 'No!' He was defiant."[23] Ridgway's blithe disregard of enemy fire would become legendary, though few would know the real reason: He was very religious, and he believed that God would not allow him to be killed before Germany was defeated.[24]

Ridgway had just missed out on World War One, and he was devastated that he would have no share in "the last great victory of good over evil."[25] But he stuck with the postwar army, in which promotions were few and far between. After six years as an instructor at the Point, he was stationed in China. There he met and became good friends with then-Lieutenant Colonel George C. Marshall, who became a mentor of sorts to the young officer who seemed to even sit at attention. In 1939, after other postings in Nicaragua, the Philippines, and Brazil, Ridgway was sent by Marshall, now a general and army chief of staff, to Washington, to report to the War Plans Division, which was preparing for the great conflict everyone expected. By January 1942 he was a brigadier general. A month later he was made assistant commander of the reactivated 82nd Infantry Division commanded by Major General Omar Bradley. Six months later, when Bradley was promoted, Ridgway was made a major general and given command of the 82nd, which had just been selected to become the first of the army's five airborne divisions. That same month, Ridgway was elated when the 505th PIR and its commander were attached to the 82nd. He was quickly impressed with Gavin, as was Gavin with his new boss. And like Gavin, he thirsted to lead men in combat.

EARLY IN MAY 1943, Ridgway explained to Gavin his assignment. In two months, on July 9, he would lead the U.S. Army's first regiment-sized airborne landing. It would be a night drop into Sicily, behind the Italian lines, to block counterattacks against General George S. Patton's Seventh Army, which was set to land on the beaches the next morning. Since the bulk of the 82nd's other regiment, the 504th, was still back in Africa, Ridgway would not drop with the 505th, but had arranged to arrive in Sicily on Patton's command ship.

In his nineteen years in the army, Gavin had never led men into combat. This would be his trial by fire—and the 505th's. It would also be the first large-scale test for the Airborne, and the army's top brass was watching closely—not every general was convinced of its worth. If this operation failed, it might be the last, and paratroopers would become ordinary infantry.

Gavin was elated. This was a chance to put his airborne doctrine to the test. He believed it had a role in the modern army, and he believed his men were ready—and after two more months of hard training and preparation in the unrelenting heat and miserable conditions of North Africa, they were. "They will fight as American troops have never fought before," he confided to his diary.[26] Long marches with a full combat load had made them tough, tanned, and bad-tempered—during sniper contests in the last few days, "regrettably . . . they have practiced on some menacing-looking Arabs," Gavin wrote to his daughter. Fortunately, no one was killed.[27] But there had been only one practice night jump involving the entire division, and it had gone so badly that all further ones were postponed. Throw in transport pilots who were inexperienced and undertrained, especially in night operations, and the stage was set for a major snafu.

On July 9 at the airfield in Kairouan, Tunisia, Gavin climbed up on some barrels and addressed his men. *Go kill the bastards,* he told them in language earthier than the more formal printed personal message each man was given. *Stick them with your knife if you can and don't think twice about it.*[28] Near midnight, under a full moon, the 505th took off, flew 400 miles over the Mediterranean, and parachuted onto the island of Sicily. Extremely high winds, inexperienced pilots and jittery navigators, and the inherent confusion of a night drop resulted in widely scattered parachutists, many as far as twenty-five miles from their drop zone, seven miles from the coastal town of Gela, their objective. Some troopers hit the ground nearly sixty miles away. Only one company hit the drop zone.

Just before Gavin climbed aboard his plane, a messenger from base operations ran up and told him that the latest reports showed a thirty-five-mile-an-hour wind over the target area. Training jumps were usually canceled if winds exceeded fifteen miles an hour, but there was nothing to be done—this wasn't a practice drop. To make matters worse, his plane's navigator allowed them to get off course, and just before they hit the coast of what they hoped was the island, Gavin recognized nothing below him. The pilot turned the green light on, and he and his stick (a planeload of about eighteen men) jumped into a strong wind.

He didn't know it at the time, but when he landed, hard enough to slightly injure one of his legs, he was twenty miles away from his objective. He wasn't even sure he was on Sicily, though a great deal of gunfire could be heard. He could walk, though with some pain. He eventually collected about twenty men and set off cross-country in the direction he thought the drop zone was, west through olive groves and over stone walls, all the while following the old West Point axiom to head toward the sound of gunfire. His small band was further reduced to six after an Italian ambush, during which his lightweight M1 carbine jammed; he picked up an abandoned, heavier M1 Garand, which he would carry with him throughout the war. Heavy naval shelling the next morning confirmed that they were in Sicily.

Gavin and his men hid most of that day in an irrigation ditch, then set out again at twilight. About 2:30 a.m., they ran into a 45th Infantry Division outpost, and Gavin finally found out their exact location. He commandeered a jeep, piled his men aboard, and continued northwest toward Gela, now about twelve miles away. At first light they came across the 3rd Battalion, or a good portion of it, about 250 men, just waking in foxholes in a tomato field beside the road.

Their commander, twenty-six-year-old Major Edward Krause, had a fiery temper and a gung ho attitude that had led to the nickname "Cannonball." While training his men he brandished a swagger stick, and he was a fiend for discipline—he was prone to loud tirades at the slightest sign of the lack of it. He had even issued a standing order to all his jumpmasters and assistant jumpmasters to shoot any man who refused to jump.[29] Gavin found him sitting on the edge of his foxhole, dangling his feet. He had not set out perimeter guards or sent out patrols. When a perplexed Gavin asked him what he'd been doing, Krause said he'd been reorganizing his battalion. Gavin asked him about his objective, several miles closer to Gela; Krause said he hadn't done anything about it because there were Germans up ahead. His men had been awake for thirty to forty hours, and he had been told by the 505th's XO (executive officer, second-in-command) to dig in and remain there for the night, but for some reason, Krause neglected to tell Gavin this. Gavin considered relieving him of command, but told him to get his men on their feet and start moving; then Gavin continued west in his jeep.[30] Two miles later he ran into a platoon of 82nd engineers. He ordered them to move west also and drove on.

About 9:00 a.m., less than a mile down the road, he came to a gently sloped hundred-foot-high ridge surrounded by olive groves and dotted with trees. With a low stone wall running across the crest, the hill dominated the surrounding area. *Take the high ground,* thought Gavin, and ordered his men up through the foot-high yellow grass of the ridge, then sent back a runner with orders to move Krause's battalion up quickly. By this time Gavin had collected a diverse group that included engineers, cooks, clerks, orderlies, truck drivers, some riflemen, and several officers without their units—some sixty-odd men. The officers included three lieutenant colonels and several captains and lieutenants, none of them commanding anything but their own rifles. With this lightly armed patchwork platoon, Gavin was taking a huge risk attacking an enemy of unknown strength and size.

As he led them through the trees, machine-gun and rifle fire rained down from on high, sounding like a swarm of bees as bullets sliced through branches and leaves that fell on the men. Several of them fell to the ground, dead or wounded. With their bayonets fixed, the others drove the enemy troops off the summit, sometimes in bloody hand-to-hand combat, but they were soon pinned down by a much larger force below them. Gavin crawled down the rear side of the ridge and ordered the 3rd Battalion, which had just begun to arrive, to the top. They charged up the hill firing their M1s and continued down the front side into the German ranks. As they neared the bottom, heavy machine-gun and rifle fire ripped into them from below. Gavin led 250 men down through the barrage. When mortars and large-caliber artillery, including the fearsome 88mm Flak gun, began shelling them, followed by six Tigers—the most formidable of German tanks at fifty-five tons, with a massive 88mm gun and 100mm-thick armor—Gavin ordered his men back over the crest and had them dig into the hard-shale ground. Besides a few bazookas, ineffectual against the thick frontal armor of the Tigers, he had only two 60mm mortars and two 75mm pack howitzers.

A prisoner revealed that the German element below was part of the heavily armored Hermann Goering Division driving toward the coast to attack the open flank of the recently landed seaborne troops of the 45th Infantry Division. This was a surprise: In briefings, Allied intelligence had reported only Italian forces on the island—"There may be a few German technicians," Gavin and Ridgway were told.[31] The truth was that Eisenhower and the Allied high command had known in advance that two German panzer divisions were there, but had decided not to tell any of the invading troops—even their commanding generals. The reason: Ultra, the top secret Allied project that decoded top-level encrypted communications of the German, Japanese, and Italian militaries. The idea was to protect the secret of Ultra for future campaigns; the result was that no one involved in the assault knew what they were up against.

If Gavin's regiment had landed where they were supposed to, in drop zones north of Gela, the Germans could have smashed into the 45th unimpeded and driven it back into the sea. Now the ragged force he commanded was all that stood between the 45th's exposed left flank and a German armored division with ninety Mark III and Mark IV tanks and seventeen Tigers.

Over the next several hours, Gavin's undermanned battalion withstood a constant artillery barrage and tank assaults. In their desperate scramble to find shelter on the ridge and under thick clouds of smoke and dirt, his men could dig only shallow foxholes in the hard shale. When Gavin's entrenching tool bent, he used his steel helmet to scrape out a small trench barely deep enough to protect him from being crushed if an advancing Tiger's treads rolled over him. The harder the surface, the more damage a mortar shell makes, since its explosion sends lethal rock shards flying in addition to shrapnel, and Gavin was losing men right and left. The panzer machine guns and 88s swiveled back and forth to train their 88mm gunsights on individual troopers. Several two-man bazooka teams were destroyed. But Gavin refused to retreat and surrender the high ground. By flanking the lighter-armored Mark IV panzers on their more thinly armored sides, troopers managed to knock out three of them by firing into their vulnerable gas tanks and ammunition racks. Major Krause had been in the rear getting an injury treated, but he returned to lead his men from the front while manning a bazooka.[32]

In a shallow foxhole nearby, two troopers rose up. One aimed his bazooka at a Tiger 200 feet away, while the other crouched behind him and loaded a rocket. The first man fired and hit the oncoming tank but failed to stop it. He fired a second rocket, which just missed the tank's tread. His loader jumped out of the foxhole and ran but was gunned down instantly. The Tiger rolled over the shooter, its tread crushing him to death. Minutes later, six Wehrmacht soldiers in a German command car drove toward the American lines, their Schmeissers firing. Several machine guns finally stopped it just short of their position. A trooper ran over to it, pulled the dead driver out, and jumped in, then turned and drove straight at an oncoming Tiger. He hit it head-on, with no apparent damage. The tank began backing up, and another Tiger's turret rotated toward the command car and fired one shell at it—a direct hit that destroyed car and trooper.[33]

Gavin, moving from foxhole to foxhole amid constant artillery and machine-gun fire, inspired his men to stand fast. "We're staying on this goddamned ridge," he told his two-gun howitzer crew situated a few hundred yards behind the crest of the ridge, "no matter what happens."[34] At one point he found himself lying flat on the ground and bouncing from the concussion.

With his binoculars, Gavin could see, a half mile away, hundreds of grenadiers and a dozen or so Tigers massing for an assault on the ridge. He sent Captain Alfred Ireland, who had been by Gavin's side since the drop, to find the 45th's command post (CP) some four miles away and summon reinforcements. Ireland had fractured his left kneecap when he'd landed, but he started painfully trotting down the road behind them. About a mile later he liberated a bicycle from an irate civilian and pedaled onward. He eventually found the 45th's CP tent. Inside were Major General Troy Middleton, the division commander, and General Omar Bradley, commander of the II Corps—which included the 45th—and the 82nd's former commander. Ireland showed them on the situation map where Gavin's makeshift battalion was holding off a much larger German force. Bradley told Middleton, "Give him what he wants."[35]

Late in the afternoon, the captain returned in a jeep with a forward observer and a radioman, who began calling in artillery shelling. Then a navy ensign who had parachuted in with Gavin radioed warships offshore for gunfire. More troopers and six Sherman tanks arrived. Ireland had gotten everything he had asked for. At 8:30 p.m., when the sun was low in the west and salvos began to rain down on the advancing Germans, a cloud of smoke hung over the ridge and the enemy below. Gavin turned to Ireland.

"We're going to counterattack," he said.

Ireland was incredulous. "You're going to counterattack the Hermann Goering Division?"

"Yes."[36]

Gavin led his force of exhausted, grimy soldiers over and down the slope. The Goering troops gave way and began to retreat. Soon Gavin's men reached empty machine-gun nests, then mortar pits abandoned by all but a few. The entire German force, including the Tigers, had withdrawn.[37] Afterward, Gavin came upon Krause sitting on the side of the road, sobbing, his head down. At one point that afternoon, he had told Gavin that his thoroughly battered battalion was combat ineffective, and he suggested they retreat—they'd be finished if they stayed. Gavin had looked at him and said, "I don't know about you, Ed, but I'm staying right here." Now, overwhelmed by his men's steadfastness in the face of overwhelming odds, he told Gavin that they would never be as brave again as they had been that day.[38]

Though widely dispersed, other elements of the 505th had assembled in groups small and large and fought well, preventing two armored forces inland from attacking the Allied seaborne assault and leading German General Karl Student, the premier airborne authority, to say: "The Allied airborne operation in Sicily was decisive despite widely scattered drops."[39] Despite an off-target drop, the 2nd Battalion was able to assemble most of its men and clear an impressive part of the 45th Infantry's invasion beaches, and a hundred-man group of 1st Battalion troopers knocked out two separate tank columns on their way to attack the Allied forces on the beach.

The stand on Biazza Ridge, as the hill came to be known, proved to be essential to the invasion's success. The amphibious forces had run into trouble putting their artillery, armor, and anti-tank weapons ashore, and the 505th had prevented a veteran panzer division from striking the 45th Infantry at its most vulnerable point. The victory came with a heavy toll: a hundred wounded and fifty-one dead, who were buried along the ridge with crude wooden crosses fashioned from K ration crates.[40] But the 505th had won its first battle—as had Gavin. For his valor and leadership, he earned a Distinguished Service Cross, given to soldiers who display extraordinary heroism in combat. Three months after the Sicily drop, he was promoted to brigadier general and made assistant division commander of the 82nd. He'd been a captain just two years before.

Before Sicily, Gavin had known that he could lead men. After Sicily, he knew that they would follow him. And after another emergency drop at Salerno, Italy, in September, in which the 82nd turned the tide in the battle there, the division gained valuable experience, learned what worked and what didn't, and ironed out hundreds of small and large logistical problems. Now, with several more months of intense training under their belts, the All Americans of the 82nd Airborne were ready to meet the enemy on the continent: "Troops are in top condition," he noted in his diary on June 5, "and morale couldn't be higher. They are ready, anxious and confident."[41] The division was prepared for its next assignment. They would need to be, for the largest airborne operation in history was coming up.

THREE

ENGLAND IN THE SPRING

So if we assemble swiftly, seize our objective and the seaborne forces come into contact with us on the afternoon of D-Day as scheduled, it will be quite an easy job; and we will have time to taste the apple cider we know they are making a lot of on the Cherbourg peninsula.

505TH PARACHUTE INFANTRY REGIMENT BRIEFING

If paratroopers would spearhead the invasion of Europe, the tip of the spear would be the pathfinders. They began training in the spring of 1944, a few months before D-Day. One of them was Private Fayette Richardson, a twenty-year-old in the 508th who owed it all to Errol Flynn.

He and his regiment hadn't been in England long before he was summoned one day to see his captain. Five foot six, slender, dark-haired, and thoughtful—he had briefly considered a career as a journalist—Richardson reluctantly left the pyramidal canvas tent and the warm coal stove around which he and his bunkmates were huddled making tea. Early April in England could be quite chilly and wet. In late December 1943, the 508th and two other 82nd regiments had been shipped to Northern Ireland, which had proven decidedly unsuited to large-scale airborne exercises. The 507th and the 505th had arrived in

England in mid-February, the 505th settling into their tents at Camp Quorn near Nottingham and the 507th thirty miles down the road near Leicester. In early March the 508th had moved to Wollaton Hall, a large country estate just outside Nottingham in the English Midlands. The grounds of the sixteenth-century manor had been converted into an army camp. The Midlands were much more conducive to training, which even General Jim Gavin had conceded was going well.

In the orderly room tent, the captain and his executive officer asked Private Richardson a few questions. Did he join the parachute troops because it was challenging? "Yes, sir," said Richardson, curious. It was true; when he'd been inducted in November 1942, he'd immediately volunteered for the Airborne. They were the army's elite troops, and he wanted to be part of the best.

The captain got to the point. A "special challenge" had come up—and a new group called a "pathfinder" team was being formed. They would parachute in before the regiment's main body and set up equipment—lights, radar beacons—to guide their assigned carrier planes to the drop zone. It was a new program whose idea the U.S. Airborne had borrowed from the British, and it had shown early promise in the 505th's drop into the Italian peninsula. After the mess in Sicily, General Gavin had insisted something be done to improve coordination of airborne drops.

"What we need is a man from the company to send to train for it, so what we're looking for is a volunteer." The job would require special training to learn the equipment and so on, the captain said. "Are you interested?"

"Yes, sir."

"You can think it over if you want. But we need to know as soon as we can."

Richardson thought of the dashing Flynn in *The Dawn Patrol*, the film in which he played a World War One aviator who volunteered for dangerous missions. Flynn had also played Robin Hood in a recent film, and the 508th was billeted just outside Nottingham, where Robin and his Merry Men had played onscreen havoc with the Sheriff of Nottingham and his constabulary force.

"I'd like to volunteer, sir."

"You sure?"

"Yes, sir."

"That's fine, Richardson. That's just fine."

Richardson was moved to a nearby airfield, North Witham. And for the next two months, as England gradually warmed, he and the other pathfinder trainees learned their job.

A regiment's three battalions would each have its own pathfinder team of sixteen to eighteen men. A half dozen of these were combat-tested riflemen from the 504th who would provide security for the rest of the team, which would set up navigation aids to assist the C-47 transports locating the DZ. The aids included large Holophane lights on metal tripods and a Eureka radio transmitter—a homing beacon that communicated with a Rebecca radar unit, the other half of a transponder system, in the lead airplane of each regiment's thirty-six-plane formation, called a "serial." The signal would guide the plane to the DZ. Each team would include two Eurekas; Richardson would carry the backup set. Seven amber lights (or green for the 505th or red for the 507th) would be set up twenty-five yards apart in the form of a large T for a visual aid. The teams practiced setting up the signals and made many practice night jumps over the British countryside to perfect their techniques. And meanwhile, aerial photographs of the drop zones—new ones almost every day—were studied at great length. Small black specks began to appear in the photos, and they began to proliferate.

They were finally identified as large poles placed in the ground, clearly to hamper airborne and glider operations. Large antiaircraft weapons and parking bays could be seen too. When it was discovered toward the end of May that a German infantry division had moved into the area, and the 82nd's drop zones were moved ten miles to the east, on either side of the narrow river called the Merderet, everyone who was privileged to know breathed a sigh of relief—everyone, that is, except for the officers and enlisted men involved in planning and preparations, since they had to destroy all sand tables, maps, battle plans, and briefings and start their planning over. They worked day and night to redo everything in less than a week. Somehow they got it done.

The men in the pathfinders alternated weeks—one week practicing their pathfinder duties, the other training with their regiments. Each pathfinder unit worked, lived, and ate—very well on steak, eggs, and other foods they hadn't seen during the war—with its C-47 crew.[1] There was even a keg of beer in a corner inside the compound. And maybe the best dividend: no KP or guard duty and a lot more freedom than given to other troopers.

In the upcoming invasion, the pathfinders would be dropped thirty minutes before their units—the first men into occupied territory and among the enemy. Each regiment had its own DZ, an oval-shaped area about a mile east to west and a half mile north to south, and its three battalion pathfinder teams were spread left to right in each DZ. All three DZs were west of Sainte-Mère-Église and separated from one another by a couple of miles. The 505th, on the east side of the Merderet, was closest to the village. The 507th and 508th would drop farther west on the opposite side of the narrow river.

Without the pathfinders, the 82nd drops had a greater risk of being scattered to the four winds, as had happened in Sicily. It might take hours, or even days, for a unit larger than a platoon or company to assemble. That would seriously hamper the accomplishment of its objectives. The pathfinders' job was a dangerous one—some estimates of their survival ran as low as 20 percent. Gavin hadn't sugarcoated the risk: "When you land in Normandy," he'd told them, "you will have only one friend: God."[2] Some called them "suicide troops." But like their comrades in the 82nd, they were young men in the best shape of their lives and superbly trained, and they thought they were immortal.

On May 28 and 29, after three months of hard drilling daily at their camps near the two large English Midlands cities—and hard carousing nightly in the plentiful area pubs and restaurants—the 82nd paratroopers climbed onto army trucks and British buses to be transported to seven airfields in the area. (No aerodrome in the country was large enough to accommodate even a single regiment and the aircraft required, much less the entire 82nd—8,900 men in more than 800 C-47s and 427 gliders.) The glidermen of the 325th moved to the Ramsbury and Aldermaston airfields, closer to the southern coast. All brought only the bare essentials. The rest of their belongings went into duffel bags to be stored in the mess hall until they returned.

They arrived at each field to find its fences topped by barbed wire, with armed MPs guarding every entrance and patrolling the perimeter. Once they were inside, no one was allowed to leave. Storage and repair hangars were packed wall to wall with folding canvas cots, and each unit was assigned an area. At some fields, rows of pyramidal tents handled the extra troops; at others, straw-filled mattresses replaced the cots. On the tarmac, dozens of Douglas C-47 transport planes waited, not the usual trucks. Everyone realized this would not be just another practice jump. This was the invasion. The big question now was: Where were they going? Norway was a popular guess, as were the Netherlands and even Yugoslavia. So was Calais, which lay just twenty miles beyond the White Cliffs of Dover.

Once they settled in, there was little to do after morning calisthenics besides attend the occasional briefing. Finally, a few days after arriving, they were told their destination: Normandy, France—specifically, several miles inland from the east coast of the Cotentin Peninsula, near the village of Sainte-Mère-Église. They began spending hours studying maps, aerial photos, and sand tables in large briefing tents. Some men cut their hair Mohawk-style; most of them just trimmed theirs short in case of a head wound. Friends found one another to shake hands, say, "Good luck—see you in France," or, "See you on the ground," and get autographs on the French paper money they'd been issued. Everyone checked and rechecked their gear, cleaned their weapons, and sharpened their knives and bayonets as if their lives depended on doing so, which of course they did. Those who would be part of mortar or machine-gun squads, or carrying bazookas or the large, limited-range telephones, rolled their equipment and ammo into canvas-wrapped bundles called parapacks to be strapped under their planes—three under each wing and three more below the belly—and then released at jump time by pulling three toggle switches next to the exit door.

When they weren't preparing, many wrote last letters home that would be mailed after their departure. Some men played softball or volleyball. Others read comics or books, and at night projectors and screens were set up in the hangars and recent movies were shown. Small French phrase books had been handed out, and some of the men practiced basic sentences: "*Bonjour, mademoiselle*" was a favorite. Card games and dice games were everywhere, some of them involving huge amounts of money. Many of the men—even the nonreligious—attended services by a priest, minister, or rabbi under bright fluorescent lights.

Every day at 7:30 p.m., men crowded around radios blasting out the daily German State Radio shortwave broadcast of the anonymous woman everyone called Axis Sally. (Though no one knew it at the time, she was an American engaged to a German, and had become indoctrinated into the Nazi effort.) The "Bitch of Berlin," soldiers called her as they wondered whether she was as good-looking as her sultry voice suggested. She played the best Big Band songs in between needling the Americans with propaganda that didn't work and information about their plans, some of it alarmingly prescient. "Good evening, 82nd Airborne Division," she said. "Tomorrow morning the blood from your guts will grease the bogey wheels on our tanks."[3] Had there been a leak? Would the Germans be lying in wait for them? No one seemed too concerned, and some men pointed out that she'd been saying much the same thing for more than a week.

With a year or more of rigorous training behind them, they were finely honed and ready for this day, and they were at a fever pitch—after a week of close captivity, fights were breaking out for little or no reason. If the Germans knew they were coming, that was fine with these paratroopers. They were ready to take on anybody.

PRIVATE KEN RUSSELL, a nineteen-year-old kid from rural Tennessee, almost missed the big show after he fainted in front of General Ridgway.

Like many other boys during the Depression, Russell had dropped out of high school to get a job and help his family out. He was working at a lumber company when war was declared, and he had enlisted in

October 1942. In early 1944, just before he shipped out as a replacement with the 505th, he'd been home on leave when he walked into a five-and-dime store and met a young woman named Dorothy who worked there. They hit it off, and things got serious quickly. After he joined the regiment in Northern Ireland, they wrote to each other often. He had a girl back home, he was part of the best parachute regiment in the army, and he was about to become part of the greatest invasion force in history. He was on top of the world.

Until early May, when the 505th received smallpox vaccinations. Russell's reaction was so severe, he could hardly lift his left arm the next morning. More than a week later, when Ridgway and Gavin arrived at Camp Quorn to review the regiment, he could barely close his left fist, and he was extremely weak. But he lined up, and as Ridgway passed Russell, the young trooper passed out. He was sent to a hospital nearby and was confined for more than a week. Near the end of May, when one of his visitors, a buddy from his own F Company, told him that "big things" were happening back in camp and that the big day was near, Russell told the doctor he was fine. The doctor said he wasn't. That afternoon, out his window Russell saw a jeep being driven by a soldier he knew who was there to bring back recovered soldiers. Russell slipped into the room where the patients' uniforms were kept, grabbed his, and changed in a restroom.

Russell walked out of the hospital and almost ran to the jeep and jumped in just as it was leaving. Back at camp, his comrades were packing their bags—a large one to leave there and a small one of absolutely necessary items they'd bring with them. He reported to his first sergeant, who told him to double to his tent and get his bag packed—they were moving to their assigned airfield, Cottesmore.[4] This time everyone knew it was the real thing.

THIRTY MILES NORTH of Cottesmore, at another airfield, called Fulbeck, the 600 men of the 1st Battalion/507th prepared for the big day. Corporal Earl Geoffrion, older than most of his comrades at twenty-six, was another man who considered himself lucky to be going into France, especially since he'd killed a fellow paratrooper before the regiment had shipped overseas.

Geoffrion was a muscular five foot ten and sported a well-trimmed mustache that lent him a resemblance to actor Clark Gable. Born and raised in Toledo, Ohio, in a family of twelve children, he was twelve years old when his mother died. To help put food on the table, he found work on a farm—six days a week, $15 a month. Wages were low and jobs were scarce in the middle of the Depression, when 25 percent of the workforce was unemployed. Better jobs followed, and Geoffrion was working as an engineer for the Pennsylvania Railroad on the Chicago–Detroit–Cleveland route when he was drafted in 1942. A few months later he was in the infantry, running a train between army camps, when he volunteered for the paratroopers—mostly for the extra $50 in jump pay. After parachute school he was assigned to the 507th as a rifleman and sent to Fort Benning.

One night, while on liberty in a nearby town, he met a young waitress in a restaurant. She told him her boyfriend—another 507th soldier waiting for her outside—was abusive and asked Geoffrion to walk her home. Soon after they left the restaurant, the other paratrooper approached with two of his friends and began insulting her. Geoffrion, who had been a Golden Gloves boxer before the war, suggested he leave, but the man threw a punch. The fight lasted only a few seconds and ended with Geoffrion delivering a right uppercut to the man's head. The trooper fell and struck his head on the curb and died five days later. Geoffrion was jailed. His commanding officer (CO)—Lieutenant Colonel Edwin Ostberg, an officer who truly cared about his men—suggested he plead guilty to a lesser charge. He did and was sentenced to ninety days in a military prison—even during wartime, and even for defending a woman's honor, involuntary manslaughter demanded a sentence. After his release, he was transferred to the 507th's service company, where he became a parachute rigger. The man some of his comrades were now calling "the Killer" might not jump with the regiment into Europe, since some riggers would need to stay behind.

After the 507th was attached to the 82nd and sent in December 1943 to Northern Ireland and then England, volunteers were sought for a two-part mission: to blow up railroad tracks and telephone lines upon landing in Europe, then to proceed to find the 507th's regimental command post and serve as a guard for its commander, Colonel George Millett. Geoffrion, consumed with guilt over the death he'd caused, felt that his penance included taking part in the invasion. He volunteered and was chosen, along with his best friend, Don Cleary. Geoffrion had taken demolition training back in the States, and now he took two months' more. He was just happy he wouldn't be left behind.[5]

Private First Class (PFC) Leslie Cruise, at the same airfield as Russell, still felt like an outsider.

He'd joined the 505th as a replacement only on March 15. Most of the other men in his H Company platoon had already seen action together in Sicily and Salerno, and they were standoffish to him. He knew that was natural. "You probably won't last the first day in combat," one of them told him, only half kidding.

On May 29, Memorial Day, when the 505th had been transported from Camp Quorn to area airfields—in the case of Cruise's 3rd Battalion, Cottesmore Aerodrome, which they would share with the 2nd Battalion and an artillery battery—they'd been told to bring only their combat gear. They had made the same trip several times before for exercises. But this time felt different—the veterans of Sicily and Italy said so, anyway. Some English folks standing along their route seemed to know something was up as they yelled, "Give 'em hell, Yank!"[6] Upon arrival at Cottesmore, the entire 3rd Battalion—Companies G, H, and I—would sleep on five hundred cots on the floor of a hangar, with barely enough room to walk between them. Each company was assigned its own area.

Les Cruise just wanted to finish the war so he could go to college and learn to be an architect—he had turned twenty on May 27. He was color-blind, and when he'd been drafted in January 1943 and applied for the Airborne, they wouldn't take him, so he'd had to settle for the coast guard. But on a furlough home in July, he'd volunteered again for the paratroopers. This time he'd been accepted, and after more basic training and jump school, he'd been sent to Northern Ireland, then assigned to the 505th.

One of his platoon buddies—like most of them, a combat veteran—was a quiet Mexican American named Richard Vargas. The baby-faced Cruise was short, just under five foot six, but Vargas, wavy-haired and good-looking, was only five foot four, one of the shortest men in the regiment. Like every other paratrooper, Vargas was extraordinarily fit; he resembled a trim bantamweight boxer. He kept to himself mostly, but he had a friendly smile; when he talked, he was soft-spoken, and he usually only spoke to his buddies with whom he'd seen combat in Italy. Every night in their pyramidal tent in Camp Quorn, Cruise and his four other tentmates would watch as Vargas knelt beside his cot and prayed his rosary.

Vargas was twenty-three, older than most of his fellow paratroopers. Born in San Antonio, he, along with the rest of his family, had followed his father, a laborer, to Michigan in the middle of the Depression in search of better wages in the sugar beet industry. Even before the move, Vargas had dropped out of school after eighth grade to help support his family—he had worked as a farmhand for several years before he'd enlisted in the army when he was twenty, six months before Pearl Harbor.

When each company had found its area and each man his cot, the briefings began, and a few days after arrival, each battalion was assembled to be informed of their destination: Normandy, France. They were told that the seaborne troops of the 4th Infantry Division would relieve them the day after their drop—D+1. Some were even told that the linkup would happen on the afternoon of D-Day itself.[7] Then it was time to study the sand tables, hidden in canvas-walled tents, which were made mostly of painted foam rubber and plaster of paris. The men were especially interested in the detailed mock-up of a small but key crossroads village almost seven miles inland from the beach designated Utah, where the 4th Infantry Division would land. Each regiment had its own sand table tent with maps and photographs and battalion objectives. The 3rd Battalion's assignment: to seize and secure the town of Sainte-Mère-Église. Les Cruise marveled at the workmanship and details of the tableaux: houses, rivers, fields, and more. Like most of the men, he was bewildered by all the unfamiliar French names and their difficult pronunciations.[8] But he and every other trooper studied the sand tables and hundreds of aerial photographs of the area until they were familiar with the area their unit would be focused on. And until they knew it well, they all studied a large blown-up photo of Sainte-Mère-Église that showed great detail—even Germans loading jerry cans into trucks parked in the tree-bordered town square.[9]

Later, after a low-key but confidence-inspiring speech by General Gavin, Lieutenant Colonel Edward Krause, still the battalion's commander, climbed onto the hood of a jeep. Cannonball's heroics on Biazza Ridge had atoned for his puzzling early-morning bout of nonchalance and helped earn him a promotion—though it hadn't improved his reputation among his men. One described him as a "psycho," and another thought Krause "fancied himself a junior-grade George Patton," who was notorious for his temper.[10] Many of the original members of the 505th had first encountered Krause in their parachute training, where he was known for severe punishments for even the most minor infractions. His style hadn't changed after he was given command of the 3rd Battalion. He seemed obsessed with appearances—parades, inspections, and the like—and he was even known to kick his junior officers from behind while berating them.[11] His men didn't love him—some hated him—but no outfit was better trained or tougher.[12]

What the men of the 505th didn't know was Krause was supremely self-disciplined—and couldn't understand why others weren't. The son of a small-town janitor in Wisconsin and the grandson of German immigrants, Krause had been commissioned a second lieutenant upon graduating from a small college there, where he'd joined the ROTC and worked his way through school as the maintenance man for the women's dorm—and carried a full load of classes, played football, ran the high hurdles, and participated in the Rifle Club, where he met his wife. Soon after war broke out, he volunteered for the Airborne and rose quickly through the ranks. Now at twenty-seven, Krause was one of the youngest lieutenant colonels in the army—and still as gung ho as ever.

Speaking to his men, he held the Stars and Stripes above his head. "This flag was the first American flag to fly over Gela, Sicily, and the first American flag to be raised over Naples," he told the men. "Tomorrow morning, I will be sitting in the mayor's office in Sainte-Mère-Église and this flag will be flying over that office!" The roar of approval, accompanied by whistles, applause, and war whoops, lasted five minutes.[13]

When it quieted down, he said, "You have only one order—to come and fight with me wherever you land. When you get to Sainte-Mère-Église, I will be there."[14] The 505th had its marching orders, and they were simple and direct. The latest intelligence had indicated only a couple of German companies in the immediate area, and with any luck, they could get the job done and hook up with the 4th Division later on D-Day.[15]

In the last few days at the aerodromes, other battalion commanders tried to fire up their men in different ways. Private First Class Nelson Bryant, a lean, intense twenty-one-year-old from Martha's Vineyard with literary aspirations, had been attending Dartmouth when he'd decided to do his part against Hitler. He'd been born blind in one eye, and the ROTC program on campus wouldn't accept him. So he decided to join the army. After basic training, he'd become bored with his stateside position and volunteered for the Airborne. He managed to pass the vision test by using his good left eye both times, but just changing the hand covering his right eye. No one caught on, and they listed him as having 20/20 vision in both eyes.

On June 3, the night before the jump, a colonel with the 508th addressed the battalion in the hangar. "Men," he said, "one thing you've got to realize is, chances are you aren't going to be dropped where you're supposed to be dropped. You're going to be miles off. This usually happens. But don't worry. Because you have one overriding mission. It's to kill Germans. Now get this in your heads. Repeat after me: Kill Germans."

For some reason, Bryant couldn't say it. But the hangar echoed with everyone else saying, "Kill Germans, kill Germans!"

"And if you have to do it with cold steel," the colonel continued, "do it that way, too. Any way you can. But kill, kill, kill."[16]

LIKE THEIR PARATROOPER brethren in the 505th, 507th, and 508th, the two battalions of the 325th had been living and training in and around Camp March Hare since mid-February, after a couple of months in Northern Ireland. Their tent quarters were near the large city of Leicester, the headquarters of the 82nd. For five months they had drilled and practiced and become familiar with their gliders. In March they had been joined by the 2nd Battalion/401st GIR of the 101st Airborne, which became the 3rd Battalion/325th, creating a more standard three-battalion regiment. The 650 men of the 401st, who had been perfectly happy where they were, were still grumbling about the abrupt reassignment. No American glider infantry regiment had entered a battle zone via gliders. And the only Allied glider operation thus far in the war had been near-catastrophic.

Operation Husky, the invasion of Sicily in July 1943, had called for 144 gliders—all but eight of them the smaller but sturdier American Waco CG-4As, not the larger British Horsas—to be released at dusk over the water off the invasion beaches and glide to their landing zones (LZs) inland.

High winds, poor visibility, and a difficult flight path caused immediate havoc. Sixty-nine gliders were released too early and crashed into the sea, drowning at least 252 men. Ten more aircraft and their crews were never seen again and assumed to have experienced the same fate. Those that reached land crashed into stone walls, trees, or the ground. Only about a dozen landed near their LZs.[17]

But the American glidermen were kept largely unaware of the magnitude of those losses. Nor did they know that some of their Wacos were defective or poorly constructed when they left the U.S. assembly lines. And the British gliders in Sicily had not confronted a countryside like that in Normandy, with its small, hedgerow-lined fields made even more perilous by German anti-glider devices and antiaircraft fire. And on top of that were the rifles and machine guns that could cause damage and destruction at the low altitudes the gliders would fly at. The rank and file didn't know Normandy would be their destination, but they would soon be well aware of these dangers.

Two other facts galled the glidermen more than anything else. They were not supplied with parachutes, not even the smaller reserve type like the ones the paratroopers—and the glider pilots—wore. And both those groups received hazard pay. The glidermen didn't, and they would float down to at best a controlled crash in a plywood-and-canvas craft without protection, defensive armament, or an engine. They felt like sitting ducks—"tow targets" or "flying coffins," they called their planes.

But gliders made possible airborne delivery of features that paratroops could not: a combat-trained team, about half a platoon, ready to immediately engage the enemy, and delivery of invaluable larger equipment such as jeeps and light artillery pieces—matériel vital to the success of achieving an objective. Military planners who swooned over the potential benefits both underestimated and minimized the danger to the soldiers who flew into combat in them. Training under controlled conditions—in good weather, on open fields, and without enemy fire—produced illusory positive results.

While in the U.S., the glidermen had trained in Waco CG-4A gliders, which could each transport fifteen men or a few men and a jeep or a 75mm pack howitzer. Each man took at least one flight during which the glider was dragged into the air by a hundred-yard nylon towrope attached to a C-47. After it reached several hundred feet, it was released to circle a landing field once or twice and then glide to a smooth landing. They practiced loading and unloading jeeps, equipment, and smaller artillery pieces. The flights, all daytime, were uniformly safe and smooth. Most of the men were reassured.

They had continued their training over the last five months, and they were also introduced to a new monster—the much larger British Horsa glider. It could transport two pilots and thirty fully equipped men, or a jeep and a 75mm pack howitzer, or two jeeps—up to 7,000 pounds—and it required new and different loading-unloading exercises. Unlike the smaller Waco, the Horsa had no steel frame—it was all wood and canvas. It was also less maneuverable and more fragile.

Despite the glidermen's rigorous training and risky delivery method, they were disrespected by the other Airborne regiments. Back at Fort Bragg during training, the main bar frequented by enlisted men in nearby Fayetteville had been the Town Pump. It was the site of many a donnybrook between the glidermen and the paratroopers, who looked down at anyone without their silver wings. Even after seeing a few weeks of frontline combat in Sicily and Salerno—and incurring as many casualties there as the 505th, the only 82nd parachute regiment to see action thus far—the glidermen had gained little respect.

Nor did they receive much from the division's two commanders, though both men believed that the high physical standards of the paratroopers also applied to the glider infantry. But neither he nor Gavin found much time to spend with them—and since they would have no specific ground mission, only a reserve role, that seemed reasonable.

At least Ridgway had taken a few glider rides and landed in them, and he knew how dangerous they could be. Gavin agreed: He had taken one glider ride and later told Ridgway, "We don't pay these guys enough."[18] On April 18, a dawn rehearsal of forty-eight gliders released over small, unprepared fields went badly. One glider's crew and passengers were killed, and more than half of the others were wrecked or their cargoes disabled. There was not another glider exercise. Ridgway had been petitioning since February for glider personnel to receive an extra $50 just like the paratroopers.[19]

In mid-May, when the 325th's tough daily training regimen was significantly relaxed and became one that consisted primarily of inspections, the men knew it wouldn't be long before they would glide into combat in their tow targets. And when they learned that their chaplains were compiling rosters that would include each man's religion and next of kin, they were certain of it.[20]

Then, in the last few days of May, the soldiers of the 325th—three battalions' worth, about 2,300 fighting men—were moved by truck and then train to marshaling areas at airfields closer to the southern coast of England. They were billeted in conditions similar to those of the paratroopers: confined to the air bases and assigned to tents or to cots in hangars.

Over the next few days, they attended lectures on France, the French, the French Resistance, their weapons and equipment, tactics, and many other subjects deemed vital to their mission. The hours in between they filled with playing sports, gambling, watching movies, reading books, writing letters home (though they wouldn't be sent until after the invasion had begun), and eating the much-improved food—"fattening pigs for slaughter" was the saying making the rounds.

But they were anxious enough. In Italy, they had gone into battle by sea. This would be their first arrival into enemy territory by glider.

Another factor that didn't inspire confidence was the shortage of pilots. Glider pilot school graduated men who had never flown any kind of plane before—and in some instances, the copilot was a glider infantry officer or noncom impressed into service and given a tutorial in how to fly a glider in case the pilot was rendered incapable of doing so. It usually began like this: "Now, if I should get shot or killed on the way over to France, here's what you're going to have to do in order to get this crate on the ground in one piece. . . ."[21]

None of the men knew of Air Chief Marshal Trafford Leigh-Mallory's prediction of up to 70 percent glider-assault casualties, or of the Germans' anti-glider poles and trenches designed to wreak havoc on them in many of their designated landing fields, or of the other dangers they would face. If they did, they likely would have found a way to allay any anxiety or fear through the black humor common to fighting men throughout history. After all, besides their grim nicknames for their gliders, they loved to sing a ditty set to the tune of "The Daring Young Man on the Flying Trapeze":

Oh! Once I was happy, but now I'm Airborne.
Riding in gliders all tattered and torn,
The pilots are daring, all caution they storm,
And the pay is exactly the same. . . .

IN A PYRAMIDAL tent at Ramsbury Aerodrome, the massive feet of Private First Class Charlie DeGlopper, with C Company of the 1st Battalion/325th, hung over one end of his cot. He was six foot seven and 245 pounds and solid as an oak. Charlie—everyone called him that—had lots of friends and family back home, and he sometimes wrote almost twenty letters in a day. One of his favorite correspondents was his cousin Berni. In his last letter to her before leaving Camp March Hare, after she told him she'd gone to a spiritualist, he wrote: "Go back to that spiritualist and find out when this is going to be over. Kinda like to know whether I'll be coming home in the spring, summer, fall, or winter. . . ."[22]

DeGlopper was a twenty-two-year-old native of Grand Island, New York, an island a few miles downstream from Niagara Falls that was half again as large as Manhattan. It was covered by farms, and DeGlopper and his older brothers helped their father work theirs. But there was plenty of time for fun; he had grown up running through the island's fields and swimming in the Niagara River, often with his best friends, Lester Yensen and Jimmy Williams, a Black youngster whose father had been enslaved. DeGlopper's nickname was "Gentle Giant," and it described him well, since he was soft-spoken and nice to everyone. He'd been drafted in 1942 and placed in the GIR. He was also assigned to carry a BAR, a powerful, heavy, fully automatic rifle that was often handled by one of the larger soldiers in each squad of twelve.

He'd been having a grand old time in England—"This nite life has its good points but it is beginning to catch up to me," he'd written in April.[23] But in the most recent letter to his family, he was more reflective than usual: "These boys are going home to see their children if I have anything to say about it."[24]

Seventy miles south at Upottery, Sergeant Bud Olson, Headquarters Company/3rd Battalion/325th, was anxious but fairly happy, all things considered. Twenty-two and already a staff sergeant, Olson had been raised on a ranch just outside Great Falls, Montana. He couldn't wait to get away from it, but now he wanted to return. Before he'd gone off to basic training in 1942, he'd pulled out a ring and asked his sweetheart, Vi, to marry him. She'd said yes. They'd decided to wait until he came back. In the meantime, he and Vi wrote each other almost every day. Vi worked at the town Woolworth's, and they both saved their money—Olson had a dream of buying his own small ranch near Great Falls. Since he didn't smoke, he sold his cigarettes to other troopers, often for a going rate that was surprisingly high.

As a boy, Olson shot snakes and coyotes. In high school, he'd taken typing, one of the few boys in his class, and in the 80th Infantry Division, his first outfit, he'd been made a company clerk and, soon after that, sergeant. The previous September he'd finagled a fifteen-day furlough and trained home, arriving in time to help with the harvesting and spend a lot of time with Vi. In November, he'd arrived in England with the 80th on the *Queen Elizabeth*, the luxury liner turned troop transport, and a week later found out he had been reassigned to the Headquarters Company of the 2nd Battalion/401st Glider Infantry Regiment.

Olson was quiet and unassuming, but his battalion commander was impressed with his smarts—he could type and take shorthand, and he'd studied military law on his own—and in December put him in Intelligence. A week later, he got sick on his first glider ride. In January 1944, Olson had spent six weeks at SHAEF (Supreme Headquarters Allied Expeditionary Force) in London—the only enlisted man to do so and one of the few men in the regiment to know the D-Day invasion site. He'd studied maps and aerial photos of the 82nd's area of operations until he had it memorized. He knew where, but he didn't know when.

Soon after arriving in Upottery, Olson and several officers had begun briefing the glidermen on their mission. Most of them would arrive in France by glider on the morning of D+1, though some artillerymen would fly in on D-Day with their howitzers and jeeps. All three glider infantry regiments would initially be designated the division reserve.[25]

The first few days at the airfields, the weather had been perfect. The sky was clear on the morning of Saturday, June 3, but soon a steady downpour began, accompanied by a cold fog. The next day the men woke to intermittent rain and strong winds, but they had been told that they would depart that evening, so after a morning and afternoon of calisthenics, briefings, and weapon checks, then an excellent meal some men called "the Last Supper," the paratroopers began to prepare. Each planeload of about eighteen men gathered around their equipment, laid out on the ground next to their assigned C-47 Skytrain, the army's workhorse twin-engine Douglas DC-3 painted camouflage olive drab with five alternating white and black stripes on the fuselage and both wings, the inter-Allied recognition symbol of all aircraft involved in Operation Neptune—some 13,000 fighters, bombers, transports, and gliders. The air and ground crews had painted the stripes that day and in the process used up much of the white paint in England. Parapacks were secured on racks underneath the fuselage and would be released with parachutes—red for ammunition, mortars, and machine guns; blue for medical supplies; green for communications; yellow for food and water—at the same time as the men.

Every paratrooper carried eighty to a hundred pounds of equipment, supplies, and ammo—some even more. They might have to spend up to three days in the field before they were relieved by "leg" troops from the beaches, and there would be no rear echelon to resupply or reinforce or retreat to. Each man would carry everything he might need for at least three days, from food and water to ammo and morphine syrettes. One posted general order decreed the basic load of ammunition to be packed or carried for each weapon: 167 rounds for an M1, 680 for a BAR, 270 for a Thompson submachine gun, 12 for a bazooka, 100 for a 60mm mortar, and so on.[26] Each trooper would be well armed, though the mortars, bazookas, and heavier ammo in parapacks would need to be recovered and removed.

Each man's standard load included a haversack (called a musette bag) packed with a ten-pound anti-tank mine; several grenades—fragmentation, smoke, and a British invention, the anti-tank Gammon, about two pounds of plastic explosive in a stocking-like container and armed with a simple impact detonator (thrown closely and accurately enough, it could immobilize a panzer tread); three days of K ration cans and crackers; toothbrush, soap, and a change of socks and underwear; a first aid kit, an entrenching tool, a canteen kit, and a bayonet on his belt; a long trench knife strapped to his right ankle, with a handle molded as brass knuckles; a small jump knife in a small zippered pocket in his jacket, which also had four larger pockets stuffed with letters and photos from home, cigarettes, chocolate bars, a compass, and a flashlight; and more of the same stuffed into six large pants pockets.

He wore a bandolier of ammo over each shoulder; a gas mask strapped over the left shoulder; and his M1 Garand rifle over the right shoulder, muzzle pointed down, unless it was disassembled into three parts and carried in a padded canvas bag on his back. Under his olive-drab jump jacket and uniform—impregnated against gas, and thus uncomfortably stiff and smelly—almost every man wore a wool undershirt and long johns in preparation for Normandy's cool spring nights, which could drop into the forties. Their helmets were covered with camouflage, held fast with netting. Over everything, each trooper draped a yellow "Mae West" inflatable life vest. They were flying over water, and the rules required it.

Officers and some noncoms were given waterproof escape packets that included a silk color map of France, $40 in French money, and a tiny compass. The packet was small enough to be hidden almost anywhere, including inside a man's anal canal if necessary.

A red, white, and blue American flag was stitched on the right upper arm of every man's jump jacket. On the left, in the same colors, was the division's "AA," for "All American." It was a toss-up as to which patch the 82nd paratroopers were prouder of.

Some officers and noncoms carried the shorter M1 carbine or a Thompson M1 submachine gun, the rapid-fire tommy gun made famous in countless gangster movies of the thirties, though the army used box rather than drum magazines. Officers were also issued M1911 Colt .45 automatics, and some enlisted men carried sidearms they had managed to acquire in past campaigns or by other means. One soldier in each twelve-man squad carried the heavier BAR, which was twenty-one pounds fully loaded and could lay down effective covering fire; another carried plenty of ammo for it. Others with specialized jobs—radiomen, machine-gun crews, mortarmen, bazookamen—carried up to fifty more pounds of equipment and ammo, with the heaviest items packed into parapacks.

Every man was checked to make sure that around his neck was a thin chain holding two metal identity tags—"dog tags"—each engraved with name, service number, next of kin, and address. That information would be needed in case of severe injury or death, in which case one would stay with the body for positive ID purposes and the other would go with the Graves Registration personnel for recordkeeping. The tags were taped together to avoid making noise.

After final briefings with their company commanders and platoon leaders, the men lay on the grass near their aircrafts, waiting to board. Every runway was tightly packed with C-47s, each with a tail number matching a manifest listing the troopers and equipment it would carry. When word came down that the bad weather—low clouds, high winds, and heavy seas—had postponed their jump, and the entire operation, till the next day, they unloaded and returned to the hangars. Most of them were so wound up that few got a good night's sleep, and fights and arguments broke out here and there. "Our men were trained fighters who desired to close with the enemy," observed one 82nd captain.[27]

The next morning, Sunday, June 5, was also overcast and unpleasant, with occasional rain. But in the afternoon, the sun came out. After dinner—another fine one at some airfields, basic chow at others that had served their best the previous day—they loaded up again, strapped in, and waited, blackening their faces with burnt cork, soot, or greasepaint. Battalion, company, and platoon commanders gave last-minute talks to their troopers and made sure everyone knew the challenge and response words: "Flash" and "Thunder." "Thunder" had been selected on the assumption that Germans would mispronounce it as "Zunder" instead. Red Cross girls circulated, handing out coffee and donuts, and even men who were full stuffed themselves more—who knew when they'd enjoy such treats again? At one field, a British band in the back of a truck parked near the airstrip and played the latest swing tunes, and many of the men began jitterbugging with one another.[28]

The crews of the troop carrier squadrons had trained for several weeks in night formation flying and night drops—though they could have used more. They had been briefed as thoroughly as the men they would transport, and had spent many hours studying the same sand tables, maps, and aerial photos. From navigation (courses, beacons, turning points, drop zones) and communications (radio frequencies to monitor, the importance of radio silence), to weather (clearing, full moon, scattered clouds), operations (mission objectives, two of the most important being: "deliver your paratroopers to the DZ, and do *not* return with any—all must exit the plane" and "evasive action prior to delivery of troops will not be tolerated"), and intelligence ("You can expect this sort of antiaircraft fire *here*, and *there*, but don't worry about German fighters; there are concentrations of Krauts *here* and *there*; use this road for a checkpoint as you come in to the DZ"), every detail was gone over many times. All this was repeated at their final briefing two hours before takeoff, with one last directive: "If forced down, retain your status as a soldier and fight your way to the Allied lines."[29] And since they would be flying low and slow, without self-sealing gas tanks, armor plating, or mounted guns—sitting, or flying, ducks, and highly flammable and vulnerable ones at that—their minds were eased when they were told that most of the German antiaircraft units (and there were dozens spread throughout the Cotentin Peninsula) had been taken out in the increased bombing of the last month or so.

It was almost dark, about 10:00 p.m., when the order came to chute up. The remains of the setting sun glowed red in the west and a cold wind had come up[30] as they struggled to their feet and selected a camouflage green main chute and a white reserve chute, thirty-five pounds combined, and adjusted the heavy canvas webbing straps as tight as they could stand it—a necessary precaution to withstand the bone-jarring jolt of a chute opening. Then, with the man behind him pushing, each trooper struggled up the portable two-step ladder and through the rear door of the plane, and took one of the aluminum bucket seats lining each side of the bare, metal-ribbed cabin; some had to kneel on the floor and rest the bulk of their load on the seat. An army air forces ground crew member helped the last man on. The door was taken off and stored, and the hinges around the opening taped down so as not to snag a paratrooper on the way out. Men with nervous bladders waddled their way toward the rear of the plane to try to squeeze into the small bathroom there, or climbed back out and relieved themselves on the ground behind it. Most troopers took airsickness tablets, which also induced drowsiness. The air smelled of oil, high-octane gasoline, and hot metal, and the temperature was in the forties.[31]

At Cottesmore, Les Cruise and Richard Vargas found themselves in the same stick as their battalion commander, Lieutenant Colonel Edward Krause, who would act as jumpmaster and jump first. Cruise had spent much of the previous afternoon watching the craps and poker games, and too much time worrying if he would remember the essential information from all the briefings—and if, once they hit the ground, he'd be the soldier he was trained to be. Earlier that evening, he and his comrades had attended a chapel service led by their chaplain, George "Chappie" Woods, who would jump with them. Besides the normal paratrooper's load, Cruise had put his New Testament, a gift from his mother, in the breast pocket close to his heart. He carried so much ammunition—in two bandoliers crossing his chest and in most of his pouches—various grenades, and land mines, he felt like a two-legged ammo dump.[32]

Not far away, where some other 505th troopers were walking to their plane, one nervous replacement said, "Well, I guess this is really it, huh?"

A veteran of the Biazza Ridge battle, his face blackened, looked at him and said, "Now Tarzan make war!" The line was from the latest Johnny Weissmuller movie, in which the ape-man fought the Nazis with help from a machine-gun-toting Cheetah. It was clear from the look on the bewildered replacement's face that he didn't get it.[33]

At Spanhoe Airfield, sixteen miles away, where the 1st Battalion/505th was loading onto its planes, a muffled explosion was heard. A Gammon grenade carried by a 1st Battalion trooper had gone off inside a C-47 fuselage, killing four men, wounding fifteen others, and setting fire to the plane. The only two men who survived unhurt, shaken and with blood and flesh adorning their uniforms, were reassigned to another plane close by and staggered over to it.[34]

At another 82nd aerodrome, an army air forces colonel was observing the takeoff. He chatted with a PFC from Louisiana, his home state, and as the trooper prepared to board, the officer clapped him on the shoulder and said, "Happy landing, soldier!" The young PFC smiled and said, "Some of us won't come back, Colonel, but we're going to win. They can't stop us!"[35]

As the planes filled at each airfield, over near the hangars or lining the runway, hundreds of cooks, bakers, Red Cross girls, ground crewmen, and MPs stood and watched in silence. Outside the airfield fences, crowds of English civilians gathered, some waving white handkerchiefs and cheering, some standing quietly. Many yelled encouragement: "Give 'em hell, Yank!" was the most common.[36]

And then there was the mimeographed piece of paper each trooper had been given (some had it read to them by their officers) with a message from the Allied Supreme Commander, General Dwight Eisenhower. "Soldiers, Sailors, and Airmen of the Allied Expeditionary Force!" it began:

> *You are about to embark upon the Great Crusade, toward which we have striven these many months. The eyes of the world are upon you. The hopes and prayers of liberty-loving people everywhere march with you. In company with our brave Allies and brothers-in-arms on other Fronts, you will bring about the destruction of the German war machine, the elimination of Nazi tyranny over the oppressed peoples in Europe, and security for ourselves in a free world.*
>
> *Your task will not be an easy one. Your enemy is well trained, well equipped and battle-hardened. He will fight savagely. . . .*

I have full confidence in your courage, devotion to duty and skill in battle. We will accept nothing less than full Victory!

The letter was signed, with no rank, "Dwight D. Eisenhower." What the men didn't know of at the time—no one did—was the press release Ike had written by hand a few hours earlier in his trailer at Southwick House, just outside Portsmouth, in case it was needed: "Our landings have failed, and I have withdrawn the troops. My decision to attack at this time and place was based on the best information available. The troops, the air and the Navy did all that bravery and devotion to duty could do. If any blame or fault attaches to the attempt it is mine alone."[37]

OVER THE LAST few days, as the new plans had been finalized and disseminated, Gavin and Ridgway had visited the 82nd's airfields by car or plane and addressed their troopers in an attempt to inspire and reassure them. In his slight New York accent, the 82nd assistant commander had appealed to their sense of patriotism and history: "You men are to take part in a tremendous act in the history of mankind," Gavin told them. "You will be among the first few soldiers to land in the greatest invasion of history. Some of you will die but your missions will be remembered and cherished. Those who live will remember for the rest of your lives your part in this necessary, noble, and historical effort. . . . All I can ask of you is that you do your best, and I will do mine. God be with each and every one of you." Gavin's sincerity and fervor raised their confidence, as did the fact that one of their generals would be the first man out the door of the 508th's lead plane.[38]

On his own, Gavin also had commandeered a small Piper Cub and a pilot to visit each airfield, where he would stand on the hood of a jeep and talk to the men gathered around.[39] "You will feel as though you and God alone are making this invasion," he would tell them. "Remember, you are going in to kill, or you will be killed."[40] He usually finished with "I am not sending you anywhere—I am taking you with me. Happy hunting."[41] His earnest, low-key speeches had the desired effect; the men respected and admired Ridgway, but they worshipped Gavin as a man who had risen from the lowest rank—not only a soldier's soldier but a soldier's general, and the first to jump, a leader in every way that counted. One trooper summed it up after Gavin's talk: "He needed only to lift a finger and say 'Follow me,' and there wasn't a single man who wouldn't have followed him straight to hell."[42]

In the last week, Gavin had put his affairs in order and tied up loose ends—life insurance, letters to his wife and his ten-year-old daughter, Barbara, the apple of his eye. Over the last three years he had made more than fifty jumps without incurring serious injury, and in a recent letter, he reassured Barbara: "I am certain that I have a few bounces left in me."[43] He would jump first out of the lead plane in the 508th's second serial. He was still worried about the drops—and German tanks, even though more than a dozen American anti-tank guns would arrive by glider a few hours later. But overall he felt confident. Not only were his men well trained and ready, but Ridgway had devised an unusual command structure for the invasion that recognized Gavin's expertise and experience. He put Gavin in charge of the three-regiment parachute operation, while he himself would command the 325th Glider Infantry Regiment and supporting units arriving by glider. A third unit comprising Company F of the 325th and twenty-one Sherman tanks would arrive with the seaborne assault and quickly move inland to reinforce the 82nd troops.

Now, early in the evening of June 5, Gavin wrote a letter of several pages to his daughter. Much of it was a summation of his thoughts and feelings about the great undertaking ahead, how necessary it was and how proud he was of the men he commanded—a final statement, if it came to that. But he ended it with a paragraph about her summer camp and her next year of school: "I would like very much to know that you are applying yourself to the best of your ability in everything that you undertake. . . . Love to everyone, Pappy."[44]

Ridgway was jumping now too. He had originally planned to ride into Normandy in one of the 325th's gliders with his division staff—he'd already made several practice landings. He hadn't made his fifth parachute jump, so he was still without his paratrooper wings. He was also worried about his back—he had pulled it severely more than once. But as the big day neared, he decided to jump with the experienced 505th, which would be the first regiment dropped—he wanted to be on the scene as soon as he could. His staff was relieved. Glider night landing rehearsals had not been too encouraging, and some had been disastrous.[45] In his quarters, Ridgway had left a photo of himself with a sentimental inscription to his 82nd soldiers to be read if he didn't return. With him he carried a small GI prayer book in which he'd pressed several four-leaf clovers collected in different places he'd been. He'd taped a hand grenade to a harness strap on his right chest and a small first aid kit on his left. His weapon of choice was a .30-06 Springfield rifle, in his experience more dependable than a carbine. When he settled into his seat on the C-47, with a crew and eleven-man stick specially picked out for him, he found himself almost lighthearted, with his soul at peace and a fatalistic attitude.[46] He could do no more until his unit landed on French soil.

THE DIVISION'S NINE pathfinder planes took off about 10:00 p.m. from North Witham. Thirty minutes later, at each of the 82nd's airfields, a starting signal flare was sent up and the pilots of the 52nd Troop Carrier Wing started their engines. The deafening roar of several dozen aircraft warming up rose through the surrounding English countryside and the sky filled with blue exhaust smoke. A half hour later they taxied into position on the perimeter leading to the takeoff runway, and while waiting for the green light from the control tower, they went through yet another preflight cockpit check—for some of them, their third or fourth. As the line rolled onto the runway, they each ran their engines up to full power, and when the green light appeared, the group leader in first position shoved the twin throttles all the way forward and took off; the rest followed at ten-second intervals, lumbering down the tarmac with their full loads, slowly climbing into the night sky, then circling overhead until every plane was in formation—three planes in a V, nine planes in a V of V's, a hundred feet between each plane and a thousand feet between each V of V's. Then they gathered in serials of thirty-six to forty-five planes, each serial carrying a battalion. They joined hundreds of other C-47s to form an air armada nine planes wide and 150 miles long—fifteen miles between each of ten serials. Then, at a cruising speed of 140 mph, all 369 headed southwest toward the English Channel and France under a nearly full moon high in a clear sky, following the ten serials of the 101st Airborne, which would drop first, by ten minutes: almost 13,000 paratroopers in total.

Fifty-two 82nd gliders towed by C-47s and carrying anti-tank weapons and other heavy equipment joined the massive sky train near the coast. Almost 400 more, transporting the 325th troops, would arrive over the next two days. Each serial would be escorted for most of the way by fighter aircraft on their flanks.

In about two hours, 6,420 men of the 82nd would be dropped on either side of the Merderet River, about seven to ten miles west of the beaches selected for the 6:30 a.m. amphibious assault by the 4th Infantry Division. Each man knew that many of them would die, but as they sat in the darkness, most worried more about failing their comrades than dying themselves. *God, give me the courage to do what I have to do,* prayed PFC Bob Dumke of the 505th to himself. That sentiment was shared by many others.[47] And though each man was alone in his thoughts, he took comfort in those around him and in their leaders—from the lowest three-striper to Gavin and Ridgway, each one respected not just for his rank but for sharing the common soldier's danger to a degree beyond any other military unit's.

They felt honed to a fine edge, ready in every way for the challenge ahead. "Hitler made only one big mistake when he built his Atlantic Wall," paratroopers were fond of saying. "He forgot to put a roof on it."[48]

The long-anticipated assault on Fortress Europe was finally about to begin.

FOUR

THE FORTRESS, THE WALL, AND THE VILLAGE

We have fortified the coast of Europe from the North Cape to the Mediterranean and installed the deadliest weapons that the twentieth century can produce. That is why any enemy attack, even the most powerful and furious possible to imagine, is bound to fail.[1]

JOSEPH GOEBBELS, NAZI MINISTER OF PROPAGANDA

HITLER CALLED IT Festung Europa—Fortress Europe.

Along more than 2,200 miles of Atlantic coastline, from the northernmost cape of Norway above the Arctic Circle through Denmark, the Netherlands, Belgium, and France down to the Spanish border, Nazi Germany had built the Atlantic Wall: a system of fortifications designed to discourage and withstand the anticipated invasion from England by the Allied powers.

Construction of the Wall had commenced in March 1942, in response to Hitler's Führer Directive No. 40, which called for an *Atlantikwall* strengthening the coastal defenses. In France, 600,000 Frenchmen—some forced into labor, some paid volunteers—did most of the work. Colossal gun emplacements, hundreds of thickly walled concrete bunkers and massive pillboxes overlooking the beaches, millions of land mines and anti-tank obstacles on the beaches themselves, and four belts of fiendishly clever underwater obstacles and naval mines in waters just offshore—all these and more were begun. Many of them were topped with touch-sensitive mines to destroy landing craft. Behind the beaches, mortars and heavy artillery, including the dreaded 88mm antiaircraft guns, were ready to wreak havoc on enemy troops, and thousands of ten-foot-high anti-airborne and -glider poles were implanted fifty feet apart in fields—the German soldiers called them *Rommelspargel*, "Rommel's asparagus." By June 1944, there were almost six million mines and 500,000 assorted obstacles in France—and that was just on the beaches.

But the planned works were at most half finished.[2] At some places along the coast—those more likely to be attack points, at least according to the OKW (*Oberkommando der Wehrmacht*), the German High Command—the fortifications were indeed impressive. The Pas de Calais area, separated from England by just twenty miles of the English Channel, was deemed the most likely spot due to its proximity to the German heartland, and it was lavishly fortified and well manned. But there were long stretches of the coast—most of them ill-suited for an amphibious assault—that were essentially unguarded and without defenses. One German general likened the Atlantic Wall to a "thin, in many places fragile, length of cord with a few small knots at isolated points."[3] And by this time, the Allies had made three successful large-scale seaborne invasions in North Africa, Sicily, and Italy, and another, even larger one seemed imminent. Something had to be done.

The man in charge of the *Atlantikwall* was Field Marshal Erwin Rommel, Hitler's onetime golden boy. Unlike most of the Führer's older generals or the younger cronies he surrounded himself with, Rommel had shared with him the experience of fighting in the trenches during the Great War. Both had earned an Iron Cross First Class for courage under fire—Hitler as a corporal, Rommel as a lieutenant. In 1937, Rommel had authored a bestselling book on his wartime experiences, and the Führer had read it appreciatively. For these reasons and others, Hitler in October 1938 had plucked Lieutenant Colonel Rommel from his job as a military academy instructor and placed him in charge of his personal escort battalion.[4]

Fifteen months later, on the eve of the invasion of France, Rommel was made a general and given command of a panzer division. After a steady series of triumphs in France and North Africa due chiefly to his genius as a commander of armored units—particularly in North Africa, where he earned the nickname the "Desert Fox" for his outmaneuvering of the British and the Americans—he was known worldwide. Recognizing his considerable tactical talents, Hitler made Rommel his youngest field marshal in June 1942, and the "Desert Rats" of the British Eighth Army in Egypt referred to him in grudging admiration as "that bastard Rommel."[5] But in March 1943, after sustaining several defeats in Africa at the hands of larger Allied forces and superior air power, Rommel had become pessimistic—in his eyes, realistic—about the eventual outcome of the war, and he had been sidelined in Italy by the Führer for several months.

After two years focused solely on the Eastern Front, Hitler finally recognized that the threat of an Allied invasion in the west was now a stark reality. That realization came only after an alarming report issued in October 1943 by General Gerd von Rundstedt, at sixty-seven the Wehrmacht's oldest field marshal and supreme commander, OB West (*Oberbefehlshaber West*), of the German armed forces on the Western Front. The no-nonsense old Prussian had described the Wall as mere propaganda. "It must not be believed that this wall cannot be overcome," he had written after detailing its many deficiencies.[6] Military units stationed in the west had been steadily stripped of all their younger and higher-quality men and matériel to be sent eastward. Cement, steel, and construction workers designated to build the Atlantic Wall fortifications were diverted to Germany to repair the mounting bomb damage to industry. The work on the Wall was woefully behind schedule; barely half of the construction originally ordered by Hitler was complete. Von Rundstedt was even critical of the *Atlantikwall* strategy: "it doesn't suffice to build a few pillboxes—one needs a defense in depth," he pointed out.[7]

Hitler responded quickly. On November 3, he issued his Führer Directive No. 51, which called for even stronger efforts in strengthening the coastal fortifications. Two days later, he gave Rommel his assignment: a thorough assessment of the Wall's defenses. The field marshal's candid report delivered six weeks later was no more encouraging than von Rundstedt's and echoed its lament over the lack of depth. The Wall was "an enormous bluff,"[8] he wrote, and in need of serious reinforcements in both troops and fortifications. Many of the strongpoints had no overhead cover, or concrete shelter, at all—some only consisted of sandbags and trenches with a few strands of barbed wire. In fact, the engineer general in charge had made no serious attempt at putting large stretches of French coastline that lay outside the main ports into a state of defense against invasion.

Hitler's response might have been predicted. In mid-January 1944, he assigned Rommel the responsibility of improving the Wall's coastal defenses. Hitler also gave him command of the armies manning them in France and the Low Countries—Army Group B, comprising the Seventh Army, defending Normandy and Brittany, and the Fifteenth Army, manning the coast north of the Seine River. Rommel would be nominally subordinate to von Rundstedt but have autonomy—of a sort—over his forces. He was also given operational control of three panzer divisions, though they couldn't be moved without Hitler's express permission.

That gave Rommel twice the incentive to make the Wall as impregnable as possible. (Another was the drafting of his only child, fourteen-year-old Manfred, on January 6.) He brought his usual vigor to the job, and over the next several months, he strengthened the fortifications significantly. The invasion, he knew, would include airborne troops, and he stressed the importance of disrupting them.[9] Rommel was not only a great battle tactician but also an excellent engineer, and a great believer in mines; he had used them extensively in North Africa with success. He designed mines no one had ever seen before—even one detonated by the interruption of a beam of light. Not all of them would come to fruition, but the ones that did were impressive. The six million mines were just a fraction of the fifty to one hundred million he planned for the Wall.[10] And Rommel knew only too well that he was racing against time; with every passing day, the invasion grew closer. There was not enough concrete or other materials, or guns, or workers—even with paid or forced-labor French, German soldiers, and slave labor—to finish his plans in less than a year, and any Allied invasion would surely come before then.[11] His efforts were also impeded by the intensive Allied bombing of the French rail system, which had begun in late 1943 and which seriously hampered the delivery of needed materials.

Nevertheless, over the first five months of 1944, Rommel spent more of his time visiting various parts of the Wall—encouraging, goading, and inspiring his troops to construct and prepare—than he did at his headquarters in La Roche-Guyon, on the banks of the Seine forty-five miles west of Paris, where he resided in a château below an abandoned twelfth-century castle overlooking the river. Von Rundstedt, who was in Paris, was not particularly impressed with either Hitler or Rommel—the first he called "the Bohemian corporal"; the second, the *Marschall Bubi* ("Marshal Laddie"). The two field marshals talked frequently and got along well, even if they didn't see eye to eye on everything.

Rommel doubted the coastal defenses alone would stop a formidable invasion, but he did think they would slow it down. And if the Allied assault managed to establish a beachhead, it would all come down to a swift German counterattack—and that had to include some of the ten panzer divisions stationed in France and the Low Countries. Three well-trained armored divisions, more than 500 tanks, were stationed no more than a hundred miles—a drive of a day or so without enemy interference—from the east side of the Cotentin. One of them, the 21st Panzer, lay just fifty miles away, around Caen, with 140 Mark IV panzers and forty assault guns; even if the Allied air forces dominated the skies, the Germans expected their armor to make sixty miles per night—and move swiftly enough to wipe out one beachhead after another.[12]

But every hour, every minute would matter, and Rommel had ensured that the 21st Panzer practiced a swift counterattack in the event of a seaborne invasion.[13] If even one of these armored divisions reached the beaches before enough Allied troops and artillery could be brought ashore and a beachhead established, the enemy might be driven back into the sea and the invasion repulsed. Victory would mean that Germany could shift most of its fifty-eight divisions in the west to the east to fight the Russians with renewed vigor. The Third Reich would survive and if necessary might negotiate a peace with the Allies. Some German leaders even hoped a united Europe would emerge to fight a common enemy: Bolshevism, the communist form of government of the Soviets, now getting the best of the Wehrmacht near Germany's eastern border.

Some of those German units in Normandy were "static" (nonmobile) divisions—like the 709th Infantry Division manning the coastal defenses of the Cotentin Peninsula's east side, one of the locations thought to be conducive to a cross-Channel assault. Except for its anti-tank battalion,[14] it had very little or no transportation, save for a few bicycles, because they weren't intended to go anywhere. In an army that still depended to an alarming degree on the horse to transport artillery and supplies, the 709th had none of those, either. Not that it mattered to its directive. In May, the *landsers*, enlisted men, in Normandy were ordered directly by Hitler to hold their ground to the last man and the last cartridge; under no circumstances would retreat be acceptable. To their advantage, most of them were deployed in concrete strongpoints and the rest in entrenched field positions. But many of the troops in these units were older, unhealthy, or convalescing—soldiers injured in the meat grinder known as the Eastern Front, where Germany's war against Russia had incurred more than a million Wehrmacht casualties over the previous twelve months.

Quite a few of them, at least 2,000, were an unreliable mix of conscripts and *Osttruppen*, "Eastern troops": POWs and defectors from occupied Soviet territories, Russia, and other countries overrun by the Wehrmacht. When tall, cleft-chinned, and hawk-nosed General Karl-Wilhelm von Schlieben—who had led an infantry company in World War One and a panzer division on the Eastern Front—was given command of the 709th in December 1943, he almost immediately requested reinforcements; four battalions of *Osttruppen* were sent to the Cotentin. Von Schlieben was dubious: "We are asking rather a lot," he observed, "if we expect Russians to fight in France for Germany against Americans."[15] How hard they would fight, no one knew for sure, but their German commanders made it very clear to them that any sign of retreat or desertion would result in a bullet in the head.

These coastal units were seriously undermanned, undertrained, undersupplied, and underequipped. "Our best weapons are old corporals, sergeants, and NCOs" was a quip heard frequently.[16] But their officers, who knew better, lied to them, insisting that panzers from behind, aircraft from above, and U-boats from below the waves would help them deter the invaders before they could establish a beachhead.[17] Few officers believed the Allies could actually be driven back into the sea; they were expected to make some progress inland until a German counteroffensive. Many of them even preferred that outcome. "It would be better if it did progress some small distance," an officer involved in the fortifications revealed later. "This would bring large volumes of troops and armor into a prepared zone where they could be surrounded and ground down." Needless to say, the *landsers* were not told that their sole purpose was to slow the enemy's progress.[18]

Most of the German static units hardly trained at all. In fact, Rommel had ordered training to be limited to one day a week so they could focus on the Wall.[19] With the shortage of manpower from both the French civilian force and Germany's Todt engineering and construction organization, soldiers were tasked with constructing the new fortifications, such as beach obstacles and *Rommelspargel*. So demanding was the labor, they had neither the time nor the energy for much else.

Both Rommel and von Rundstedt—and most of the German High Command—thought the cross-Channel invasion would come near the Pas de Calais coastal area. It was much the shorter distance, and a secure beachhead there gave the Allies the shortest path to Germany itself.

But in late April 1944, Hitler—who fancied himself a superior military strategist but often relied on intuition that led to bad results—looked at his maps of the French coast, listened to the latest intelligence noting the heavy concentration of Allied troops in southwestern England, and decided that the Cotentin Peninsula needed troop reinforcements. He ordered two units moved there—the inexperienced 91st Luftlande ("Air-Landing," because they were trained and equipped to be transported by aircraft though they would be deployed throughout the war as a standard infantry unit) Infantry Division and, attached to it, the youthful but fervent Fallschirmjäger Regiment 6.[20] Both units shared the same mission—to defend against airborne landings, which would likely be a part of the Allied invasion.

The 91st comprised a pair of 2,000-man infantry regiments, the 1057th and 1058th; artillery, anti-tank, and antiaircraft regiments; and a tank battalion—with only one Panzer Mark III and two dozen French-made light tanks captured during the invasion of France four years earlier and used as simple trainers until posted to Normandy.[21] The division was specifically trained and equipped to deter and destroy enemy parachute and glider actions. The 91st arrived May 1, after a march of 200 miles—there was no transport for enlisted men—and immediately began dispersing most of its 8,000 troops throughout a swath of the Cotentin from just below Cherbourg south to Carentan, a span of thirty miles. The twelve-man squads erected their tents and settled into the peaceful bocage countryside of irregularly shaped small fields bordered by thick hedgerows, and the tanks were deployed between Sainte-Mère-Église and Carentan, eight miles to the south.

One 1057th *landser*, twenty-three-year-old *Unteroffizier* (Sergeant) Rudi Skripek, had spent four and a half years in the Wehrmacht. Like nearly every other schoolboy in Germany, he'd spent time in the *Hitlerjugend* (Hitler Youth, a paramilitary Nazi organization for boys aged ten through eighteen), though he was no fan of Hitler and his methods. Skripek had been drafted into the German Army and had been working with a bomb-disposal unit in Brittany. But the pressures of that job had been taking their toll, so he was glad to be transferred to the 91st Luftlande, thanks to a cousin pushing paper who spotted his name on a list of men destined for the Russian front. He'd moved cousin Rudi's name to a list of troopers bound for France to join the 1057th.

In mid-May, Skripek had arrived in Normandy with his regiment. He was a squad leader, and he and his dozen men set up their tents in the sector assigned to them west of the Merderet River, and prepared for their assignment—repelling enemy airborne landings. They became familiar with the area and, like many of their comrades, spent the mornings planting *Rommelspargel*, the afternoons on exercises, and the nights on patrol and guard duty. Their everyday food was meager, usually thin soup and hard black bread. To supplement it, many soldiers bought or bartered for milk, butter, and eggs from nearby farms. They had been thrilled to receive a visit from the Desert Fox himself on May 17 on one of his frequent inspection tours of the Cotentin Peninsula. Skripek had stood just yards away from the short, stocky legend in the long leather greatcoat as he waved his marshal's baton.[22]

Rommel's star had dimmed somewhat since his defeats in North Africa at El Alamein the previous year at the hands of General Bernard Montgomery. But he remained enormously popular with the German people, and more important, Hitler still thought well of him. His appointment as commander of the coastal forces inspired soldiers manning the Atlantic Wall, and their confidence increased considerably. Some of them were ardent Nazis and would fight to the death for their Führer. Others—most of the *landsers*—would fight for other reasons. President Franklin Roosevelt's announcement at the Casablanca Conference in January 1943 that Joseph Stalin, Winston Churchill, and he would accept nothing less than the unconditional surrender of Germany, Japan, and Italy meant that even those soldiers opposed to Nazism felt they had no choice but to fight fiercely for themselves, their comrades, and their beloved Deutschland.[23]

The reserve units deployed behind the beach—the units that the

82nd Airborne would face—were in better shape than the static coastal units: younger, healthier, and more loyal to the cause. A case in point was the 3,457 men of Fallschirmjäger 6, led by Major Friedrich August von der Heydte, hero of the 1941 German parachute assault on Crete, where he had commanded a battalion. A Bavarian aristocrat with a law degree, von der Heydte had once been a fervent Nazi but now had nothing but disdain for the Party. By this time, he was fighting for the Fatherland and his soldiers.[24] Aside from the regiment's noncoms and officers, the average age was seventeen and a half years old. Raised as *Hitlerjugend* and fully devoted to the Führer, the young volunteers had spent no time in combat on the Eastern Front—no time to develop any disillusionment, just four months of intensive and effective training. And they had been further hardened toward the enemy just a few weeks before moving to the Cotentin Peninsula, when they were tasked to recover civilian corpses in Cologne for a full day after heavy bombing by the Allies. It was a shock, especially to the youthful enlistees, to see such destruction in their homeland.

Fallschirmjäger 6 was a parachute regiment in name only. After the heavy airborne losses involved in the invasion of Crete, Hitler had declared that there would be no further large-scale airborne operations. But the Fallschirmjäger was still an elite, well-trained, and highly motivated arm of the Wehrmacht, on an equal status with the Waffen-SS, and excellently equipped for land fighting. A full 30 percent of the men—the officers and noncoms—were combat veterans of Russia, Crete, or Monte Cassino, in Italy.[25]

One of the regiment's cadre, Fifth Company *Oberjäger* (Corporal) Eugen Griesser, was thirty-seven, ancient for an enlisted man—at least in any other army besides Hitler's depleted Wehrmacht. The teenage *landsers* in his company called him Opa—Grandpa. He had fought as an infantryman in Russia. While recovering in Germany from an injury, he had seized a chance to transfer to the Fallschirmjäger. It would mean better food, jump pay, shorter missions, and no Russia. He loved his country, but he wanted to return to his wife, Emma, and their three children, and he did not worship Hitler as his teenage comrades did. But he and his fellow veterans, including their 2nd Battalion commander—*Hauptmann* (Captain) Rolf Mager, recipient of the Wehrmacht's highest honor, the Knight's Cross—felt confident they could withstand the enemy's airborne troops.

Upon reaching the Cotentin by train in mid-May, the men of Fallschirmjäger 6's three battalions were dispersed throughout a section of the peninsula southwest of Carentan in an area roughly twelve miles by nine miles—and south of the 91st Luftlande's units. Each of the battalions was assigned a subsector and proceeded to secure its area against enemy airborne operations. Company headquarters were established in farmhouses, smaller units deployed throughout the countryside in tarpaulin- and plywood-covered ditches, and observation and sniper posts set up under camouflage nets in tall poplar trees. Alarm exercises were conducted night and day. In some areas, positions were connected by narrow trenches so that guns could be quickly moved to an Allied landing area.[26]

Fallschirmjäger 6's dispersal throughout the countryside would make it difficult to gather its scattered units for rapid deployment.[27] The regiment's deficient transportation, which plagued most of the German Army by this point in the war, would complicate things even more. Each company had only two trucks, and they were from various countries and mostly without replacement parts. Many of them were out of commission. When the invasion came, motor pools would be supplemented by horses requisitioned from local farmers and marked for use by each unit, or at least that was the plan; most likely they would move on foot.

But the troops were provided with plenty of effective light machine guns—the MG34 and MG42, two per each rifle squad instead of the standard one—and other weapons such as mortars, rocket launchers, submachine guns, and flamethrowers. Thus equipped, the men of Fallschirmjäger 6 felt ready for the enemy—no matter where the Allies landed, they would be met by well-trained soldiers, even if many of them were still boys.

They too had been visited by Field Marshal Rommel on May 17, a few days after their arrival. His presence had both bolstered the spirits of the young Fallschirmjäger troops and alerted them to their new responsibility. He cautioned them against complacency, especially during foul weather: "They will fall suddenly from the sky," he said of the enemy airborne, "during a rainstorm in the middle of the night."[28]

By the end of May, three divisions—the 91st Luftlande; the 709th Infantry; and the 243rd Infantry, another static division that fortified the Cotentin's west coast—were firmly installed in the peninsula, outside of the Cherbourg defenses. Combined with Fallschirmjäger 6 and another unit relocated at the last minute—the Seventh Army Sturm (Assault) Battalion, 1,106 infantry shock troops with four field howitzers situated west of Cherbourg—the German Army in this part of Normandy totaled about 40,000 men available to be thrown into battle against any invading force. The 709th and 243rd were stationed along the coast to defend against amphibious landings, but the other units, tasked with the specific mission of stopping an enemy airborne assault, comprised about 12,600 troops—roughly the same number as the 13,000 men of the two-division American airborne attack planned for the early hours of D-Day. The men of the 82nd and the 101st would have their hands full even if their drops went smoothly.

MORALE MAY HAVE been a problem, and transportation a larger one, but in one area the Germans had an advantage. The Wehrmacht's weapons were generally superior to those of the Allies, who had nothing to compare to the fearsome, high-velocity 88mm Flak 18 cannon, which could be trained to devastating effect on both aircraft and ground targets, or the 37mm Flak 36 and Flak 37, single-cannon antiaircraft guns with a range of three miles, or the antiaircraft Flakvierling 38, with its four 20mm cannon that could fire an ungodly 880 rounds a minute more than a mile into the sky. One 82nd trooper described it as sounding "like a jet plane five feet off the ground."[29] Or the MG42, nicknamed "Hitler's buzzsaw," a durable light machine gun that could spit out 1,200 rounds per minute and paralyze with fear almost any Allied soldier within hearing distance of its instantly identifiable "ripping" sound—at twenty-six pounds, it could be carried easily by one man and moved quickly. By contrast, the American light machine gun, the M1919, weighed thirty-one pounds and required two men to carry the gun and the unattached fourteen-pound tripod. And at its highest rate of fire—450 rounds a minute, less than half that of the MG42—the barrel overheated quickly, causing the gun to malfunction.

A new German weapon called the *Panzerfaust* was gaining a reputation—a yard-long tube that could be used by one man and required no special training. A disposable, one-shot, recoilless anti-tank grenade launcher, it had an effect similar to that of the American "bazooka" anti-tank rocket launcher. The *Panzerfaust* could take out a Sherman, and even tanks with heavier armor, at short range, and the *Panzerschreck*, an even larger version, could penetrate thicker metal yet. The bazooka, by contrast, required a trained two-man team, and was too underpowered to penetrate a panzer's thick frontal armor.[30] And the Allies had nothing to match the six-barreled German 150mm Nebelwerfer 41 rocket launcher in effectiveness and nimbleness. Its two-wheeled carriage could be moved by truck, by horse, or even if necessary by troops, and it had a range of more than four miles. The loud shriek emitted by incoming Nebelwerfer rounds led Allied soldiers to call it the "Screaming Meemie." Even the German anti-tank mine was much better than the Americans'. And though the Wehrmacht's standard medium mortar, the Granatwerfer 34, was no better intrinsically than its Allied counterpart, its better-trained crew could lay down a more accurate and persistent barrage. The Germans had an even larger and more devastating mortar, the Granatwerfer 42.

No one pretended that the Sherman, the American medium tank, was superior to a German tank in any area except reliability. The massive Panthers and Tigers were overdesigned and overengineered, with intricate suspensions and drives liable to break down—though that was cold comfort to Allied troops facing a phalanx of approaching panzers. The thinly armored Sherman was on a par with the Mark IV, the mainstay of the German armored corps, but it had half the firing range and twice the vulnerability of the larger Mark V Panther and Mark VI Tiger. There were panzers in the north part of the Cotentin, but the only tanks the 82nd was liable to tangle with on D-Day belonged to the battalion attached to the 91st Luftlande. Until it was sent to the Cotentin in May, it had been a training unit only. The Allies' major advantage was a simpler and far more common weapon: the American semiautomatic Garand rifle, the M1. Reliable, accurate, and gas-operated,[31] and using an eight-round clip that enabled a soldier to fire as fast as he could pull the trigger, it was the best rifle in the war, and far superior to the Mauser Karabiner 98K, a five-round bolt-action that required all but the best shooter to move his face away and re-aim after every shot when he chambered another round. The M1 almost never jammed—unlike its shorter and lighter carbine version, which was sensitive to dirt and dust and lacked the range of its sibling.[32] And the American M1911 pistol, also known as the Colt .45 automatic, was the superior sidearm—though adequate, neither the Luger nor the Walther PPK measured up to the Colt, which was more durable and had far better stopping power.

Two other American hand-carried weapons proved effective. One man in each rifle squad of twelve carried an M1918 BAR. With its twenty-round magazine attached, the BAR was almost twice as heavy as the M1 rifle. The original idea was to have a soldier carry it on a sling and shoot it from the hip as he advanced with his platoon and lay down suppressive fire, a practice known as "marching fire," but it was often used with a bipod as a light machine gun. And the Thompson M1 .45-caliber submachine gun was reliable and effective at close quarters—one airborne trooper likened it to a garden hose that you just had to wave back and forth and you would be guaranteed to hit something[33]—though the German MP40 Schmeisser submachine gun was comparable and lighter.

But the Americans were at a disadvantage in one important area. The German rifles and machine guns used smokeless and flashless gunpowder. American gunpowder was neither, so their weapons emitted a brief flash and a puff of light blue smoke, which allowed the Germans to pinpoint their enemy's location and pour MG42 fire into it, causing all but the bravest or most foolish GIs to stay flat against the ground until it ended. The Americans had to locate firing positions by sound, a much more difficult and inexact method.

Each side also had effective light and heavy artillery, though the 91st Luftlande and Fallschirmjäger 6 were both weak in heavy weapons. The 82nd Airborne would have twenty-four 105mm howitzers and

57mm anti-tank guns, and thirteen 75mm pack howitzers—the latter effective and maneuverable, if they could be landed safely by glider and retrieved by troopers, two big ifs.

By the spring of 1944, Germany was losing the war of materiél, thanks to relentless Allied bombing of manufacturing plants over the past year. The thus far less important units—in Normandy, the static units along the coast—were the first to feel the pinch, and some of them supplemented the shortage with a wide range of captured small arms, which of course led to an ammunition resupply problem. But the better units, like the Fallschirmjäger 6 and the 91st Luftlande in the Cotentin, were usually furnished with good German weapons and an adequate supply of ammunition.

German weapons and armor may have held an advantage, but the factor that tilted the table toward the Allies was air power. Heavy and continuous bombing over the last year had devastated the Luftwaffe, the German air force, and the result in the skies above most of Europe—everywhere except Germany itself—was not merely superiority but supremacy. Allied fighters and bombers virtually flew at will over German territory, and they were fully expected to be the decisive factor in an Overlord victory—not only raining death on any troops below but preventing the feared panzer divisions from rushing to the invasion sites. At least that was the Allied plan.

For the German soldier, duty on the Western Front was paradise compared to any time spent on the Eastern Front. That didn't mean that the reserve troops stationed in Normandy, behind the coastal static units, had just been living the easy life in rural France. They fully expected airborne drops in the impending Allied invasion, and they were preparing for them in several ways. *Rommelspargel* was one deterrent.

The goal was a hundred poles per square kilometer. Though few areas reached that saturation point, 900,000 poles had been planted behind the coastline. They would tear up gliders and impale paratroopers, or at least that was the idea, though the mines and wires that were to be attached would not arrive till early June. Wide trenches were also dug in some fields to disrupt the glider landings, and machine-gun nests were set up on the edges of many of the Cotentin's small fields.

In April 1944, copies of an illustrated handbook entitled *What Every Soldier Should Know About Airborne Troops* were distributed to troops in the most likely target areas. In May, two thorough memoranda were published with more information about the tactics the German units should use in dealing with Allied airborne troops.[34] The units conducted frequent anti-airborne training alerts, exercises, and lectures, and began regular anti-airborne patrols. The *landsers* were told that many of the American paratroopers were hardened criminals released from their sentences to serve their country, and that they would take no prisoners. That seemed outlandish to few; after all, half of one of Germany's own parachute battalions, a Waffen-SS unit, had consisted of imprisoned German soldiers. If they needed any additional motivation to fight besides love of country and Roosevelt's insistence on unconditional surrender, that was it.

Too young, too old, too ill or injured—aside from the 91st Luftlande, the Fallschirmjäger 6, and the recently arrived Sturm Battalion stationed in the fields surrounding the small village of Le Vast, seventeen miles north of Sainte-Mère-Église, the Wehrmacht troops in the area were not of high quality. But they would be ready, and their seasoned officers and noncoms would lead them, or force them, to engage with the enemy whether he landed from the sky or the sea. And panzers, U-boats, and bombers and fighters of the Luftwaffe—a thousand planes, they were told—stood by to help them hurl what was left of them back into the English Channel. The fate of the Fatherland itself, and their loved ones, depended on it.

A PROBLEM EVEN greater than the deficiencies in men, fortifications, and transportation was the Wehrmacht's cumbersome command structure in the west. Unlike the Allies' in Overlord—and in virtually every other inter-Allied operation of any kind, which were simple and practical, with clear responsibilities at every level—Nazi Germany's was chaotic and impractical. Most of the problem lay with Hitler. As the war dragged on, the former World War One corporal had become increasingly distrustful of his generals and more and more convinced that only he could make the right decisions in times of crisis. *Divide et impera* became his guiding principle. The result was entire divisions hamstrung by their inability to take instant action unless it was approved by the Führer, who was usually hundreds of miles away from any front.

In March 1942, Hitler had appointed von Rundstedt, a veteran of fifty years' service in the German Army, as commander of the German forces in the west (OB West), assigned to defend the coasts of France and Belgium against attacks by the Allies. The field marshal's health was deteriorating—he'd suffered a mild heart attack in November 1941—and so was his energy. He was also frustrated at the limitations placed on him; OB West had no control over the Luftwaffe (air force) or the Kriegsmarine (navy) in his area of command, and he now had to ask first before making the smallest decision. And even after Rommel's unceasing efforts to strengthen the Wall, von Rundstedt was under no illusions about its impregnability. He was from the art of war's old school of mobile defense, and his preferred strategy was to keep his armored reserves inland, back from the coast and out of range of the

Allies' large naval guns, for maximum maneuverability. He believed in what one historian termed the "crust-cushion-hammer principle": a crust of infantry troops manning the coastline, a cushion of infantry divisions in reserve behind them, and a hammer of armored forces still farther inland.[35] When the Allied invasion came, he planned to use the last in a decisive counterattack away from the beaches as soon as the exact location of the attack became clear.

By contrast, Rommel wanted a strong belt of reserves and armor along the coast, just a few miles inland. He believed that unless the Allied invasion was met at the beaches or right behind them and thrown back into the sea in the first twenty-four to forty-eight hours, Allied air superiority would guarantee an eventual German loss. Their fighters and bombers could roam at will, preventing armor, troops, supplies, and fuel from moving toward the beachhead during daytime. In North Africa he had experienced their overwhelming power firsthand. Von Rundstedt and other Wehrmacht generals—especially General Leo Geyr von Schweppenburg, the commander of armored forces in France who had spent much of the last two years in the east—had not. Rommel wanted most of the ten panzer divisions in the west, about fifteen hundred tanks, stationed close to the coast. He petitioned Hitler for control of some of them and was denied. Then he asked for an entire flak corps, its twenty-four batteries at that time scattered over much of central and northern France, to be transferred to his command. That was denied also, as was his request that the Luftwaffe, and then the navy, lay mines along possible invasion routes.

Instead of committing to one strategy or the other, Hitler compromised. Half of the panzer divisions would be under von Rundstedt's control, and half would be kept in reserve under von Schweppenburg—though von Rundstedt's panzers could not be deployed without Hitler's approval. This decision meant that neither Rommel nor von Schweppenburg had enough panzers to carry out their respective plans.

In mid-May, after constant petitioning from Rommel, Hitler reassigned three of the six panzer divisions in northern France to Rommel's Army Group B. But only one was moved closer to the Normandy coast, southeast of Caen. The other two were stationed east of the Seine—a long day's march away, or more likely two nights', since Allied fighter-bombers were likely to attack any daylight movement with impunity. Rommel could still not move them, even in the most extreme circumstances, without a direct order from the Führer himself.

The Allied air forces hadn't been idle during this time. Throughout May, they had stepped up their attacks on bridges, rail yards, railways, and coastal fortifications, and the reconnaissance runs by fighter planes probed deeper and more frequently. But the Germans could discern a pattern to them; they ranged from Holland in the north through Belgium and France down to the Cotentin Peninsula. Activity by the French Resistance groups intensified, and German intelligence reported a marked increase in coded radio messages from London.

The cross-Channel invasion seemed imminent—probably in the next couple of weeks or not at all. The big question was whether the Germans had correctly anticipated where.

At 7:00 a.m. on Sunday, June 4, Rommel left his headquarters at La Roche-Guyon in his black convertible Horch to drive home to Herrlingen, 490 miles and about eight hours away in southern Germany, for his beloved wife Lucie's fiftieth birthday on Tuesday. With him he carried a box containing a pair of handmade gray suede shoes he'd bought for her in Paris the previous day. He sat in the front seat next to his driver, Karl Daniel; his aide, Captain Hellmuth Lang, and his chief operations officer, Colonel Hans-Georg von Tempelhoff, sat in back. The field marshal planned to visit Hitler at the Berghof, his alpine retreat in Berchtesgaden, near the Austrian border, on Wednesday or Thursday, as soon as he could secure an interview in the Führer's busy schedule. He intended to ask him to move two more armored divisions, the flak corps, and a Nebelwerfer brigade closer to the coast.[36] Rommel felt sure Hitler would agree if he could just see him face-to-face. Although the high command had refused almost all of his recent demands for aid and reinforcements, chiefly in the Normandy sector, he knew how susceptible the Führer was to in-person persuasion: "The last one out of his door is always right," he had written his wife.[37] The trip, all of it by car since the Allied air forces controlled the skies, would probably take at least six days total.

After three days of beautiful weather, June 4 had dawned with thick clouds, occasional rain, and conditions in the English Channel rough enough to confine all German naval craft to their ports and all surveillance aircraft to their fields. Despite the gray skies, Rommel was feeling particularly confident. "I'm convinced that the enemy will have a rough time of it when he attacks, and ultimately achieve no success," he had written his wife just a few weeks earlier.[38] The forecast handed to the field marshal earlier that morning, from the meteorological station at Cap de la Hague, on the northwest tip of the Cotentin Peninsula, called for these conditions to continue for several days, and naval intelligence had declared that the weather was highly unfavorable for an amphibious landing. The Allies would have to wait at least until the skies cleared, and it was more likely, Rommel was convinced, that the required combination of tide and moon conditions would put off the invasion for a couple of weeks, a conclusion affirmed by both Luftwaffe and OB West meteorologists. When it did come, it would be at the Pas de Calais—at high tide to minimize the ground the attackers would need to cover while under fire, he had said more than once. He had even put his prediction on paper in his most recent weekly situation report to von Rundstedt.[39]

Even more assurance had come the day before, when Rommel had seen his old Afrika Korps comrade, General Hans Cramer. The general, recently released from a British POW camp in Wales and repatriated to Germany for health reasons, had assured Rommel that the Allies would land near Calais—he had been driven through southeast England, he told him, and had seen all the troops, armor, planes, equipment, and other evidence of the massive invasion buildup directly across the Channel from the French port city. What Cramer didn't know was that he had actually been taken through south-central England and the genuine assembly areas there. But all signs denoting road, town, and railroad names had been taken down years ago in anticipation of the German invasion that had never happened, and during the drive, Cramer's escorts "let slip" that they were going through the Dover area of southeastern England. After reaching Germany a few days later, Cramer had told his story to the German High Command in Berlin and then the Führer in Berchtesgaden.[40]

The subterfuge was just one part of a massive deception strategy, Operation Fortitude, that had been going on for several months. Its chief aim was to mislead the German High Command as to the location of the invasion, and it included phantom field armies to be led by Lieutenant General George Patton, who was greatly respected by the Germans. The plan included false information leaked through double agents and diplomats, false radio transmissions, simulated large-scale troop movements, mock staging camps and equipment dumps, a Montgomery look-alike masquerading as the general, and dummy tanks, planes, and landing craft made of inflatable rubber or wood. The operation had been spectacularly successful. The German High Command believed that the Allies had twice as many divisions preparing for the invasion than they did—eighty-nine, plus twenty-two other brigades, instead of the actual thirty-five divisions—and that the phantom army would either lead the seaborne assault in the Pas de Calais area or follow up there after a diversionary attack somewhere else. They also were under the illusion that the Allies had enough landing craft to transport twenty divisions across the Channel in a first-wave attack when it was all the Allies could do to deliver five.[41]

Von Rundstedt, at his headquarters in Paris, was similarly reassured. He had been studying the enemy's bombing patterns—Allied air forces had been dropping two bombs on the Pas de Calais area for every one dropped in Normandy. A week ago he had notified Berlin of his conclusion: Pas de Calais.[42] And at noon on June 5, he signed the weekly report to be sent to the Führer, which concluded: "There is no immediate prospect of an invasion." Then he had lunch at one of the city's finest restaurants, the Coq Hardi, with his son, an army lieutenant. After returning to his château, he went to bed early. He planned on taking his son on a tour of the *Atlantikwall* the next day.[43]

Rommel wasn't the only Seventh Army field officer who would be away from his post on June 6. A Seventh Army map exercise was scheduled to take place in Rennes, the capital city of Brittany, a three-hour drive south over bomb-pitted roads from the eastern coast of the Cotentin. Rennes had been picked because everyone agreed that it was a bad idea to collect so many high-ranking officers at the Seventh Army HQ in Le Mans—one Allied bomb would devastate the Seventh Army high command. This *kriegsspiel*—"war game"—would focus on the destruction of any airborne landing in the peninsula. It was scheduled for 10:00 a.m. on June 6, and it would involve the commander of each division in the area and two subordinate commanders. They were ordered not to leave for Rennes before sunrise—that way, in case of a dawn attack, they would still be with their units.[44]

Many of them had departed the night before anyway—or even earlier. Von Schlieben, commander of the 709th Infantry, had left his headquarters ten miles north of Sainte-Mère-Église the previous afternoon; Major Hugo Messerschmidt, commander of the Sturm Battalion, accompanied him.[45] The 91st Luftlande's commander, General Wilhelm Falley, whose headquarters were in a château near Picauville, a few miles west of Sainte-Mère-Église, decided to leave about 1:00 a.m. Falley, at forty-six young for a lieutenant general, was admired by his men and even liked; he was known to stop his car on the road and give a soldier a ride on a warm day.[46] Von der Heydte, commander of Fallschirmjäger 6, felt the invasion could come at any time, so he elected to spend the night at his headquarters south of Carentan and hit the road at 5:00 a.m. with another general.

Another map exercise was carried out on the afternoon of Monday, June 5, this one by the battalion officers and company and platoon leaders of Fallschirmjäger 6. They too ran through the various scenarios of an airborne landing by the enemy. Upon finishing, the officers and noncoms laughed as they left for their posts. They felt prepared for any eventuality.[47]

In the village of Sainte-Mère-Église, six miles from the coast, a 1058th Regiment observation squad of eight German soldiers led by twenty-three-year-old Sergeant Rudi Escher was quartered in the bell tower of the ancient church, just below the bell chamber and above the right transept. They had been there for only six days: tomorrow they would move to another location for a week, and one of the two other observation units would bicycle into town and take their place. They slept in their field gray uniforms on the floor and urinated in a bucket, and they had to send one of their men a half mile south to their company command post for their meals. But they were happy to have a roof over their heads—most of their comrades were in tents or trenches out in the country. A telephone had been installed in the bell tower. It connected them to their combat unit command post a half mile south in a château near a hamlet called Fauville, and also to Cherbourg to the north. Two guards were posted on the roof of the tower, one on the north side and one on the south, around the clock—they had to climb a rickety twelve-foot ladder and squeeze through a small window to reach their stations behind a low balustrade, but the view in all directions was commanding.

The six other *landsers* had spent the evening of June 5 having a great time racing their bikes around the town square adjacent to the old Gothic church, under the large chestnut trees with their cone-shaped flowers. They had the place all to themselves. After supper, the men stowed their bicycles in a nearby shed and retired to their quarters in the tower. By 10:00 p.m., as the last light faded in the west, the town was quiet and still.[48]

THE MARKET VILLAGE of Sainte-Mère-Église had existed for almost two millennia. Early settlers were likely attracted by the terrain, since it was situated on ground slightly higher than the large flood plain around it and commanded every approach. A Roman military milestone on the town square gave evidence of Caesar's legions marching through during their pacification of the Gauls. The Cotentin Peninsula was conquered and explored by the Vikings in the tenth century, and intermarriage and assimilation with the Franks of the area followed over many generations. Viking blood ran through the veins of most Normans, whose name derived from their Norsemen forebears. The Cotentin soil was fertile, and the grass grew thick and green year-round.

Just six miles from the Normandy coast and its wide white beaches, Sainte-Mère-Église, like almost every other town on the peninsula, was surrounded by hundreds of irregularly shaped fields owned by families that had for centuries pastured their livestock there, cows legendary for their milk and Thoroughbred horses celebrated for their winning ways at racetracks throughout Europe. They tended their apple and pear orchards and distilled the strong apple brandy called calvados, and generally kept to themselves as long as strong authority kept its distance.

Thursday had always been market day in Sainte-Mère, as the locals called it. Farmers would drive their cows and horses into town to sell them at the cattle market on the town square, the center of market day. Under the chestnut trees lining the square's western edge, merchants set up booths along the Rue Cap de Laine, the main thoroughfare, where the farmers would barter their milk, cream, butter, and eggs for necessities and indulgences, and catch up on the news of the world and their neighbors. Overlooking the square on its north side was the Catholic church of Sainte-Mère-Église, for which the village was named. Begun in the eleventh century in the simple, bulky Romanesque style and finished four centuries later in the more ornate Gothic, the church was the heart and soul of the townspeople. A thousand or so Normans lived in the village,[49] and all but three families were Catholic. Surrounding the church square were a couple dozen shops that every decent-sized Normandy town offered, among them a butcher, baker, barber, pharmacist, electrician, mechanic, cobbler, blacksmith, and tobacconist—though there had been no tobacco for a long time, only artichoke leaves to roll into cigarettes and smoke unsatisfactorily.[50] There were clothing, hardware, furniture, and grocery stores, a few small restaurants and cafés, even a beauty salon and a small cinema.

Sainte-Mère-Église—with its two hundred or so houses and shops, almost all made of the grayish yellow limestone found in the region—was little different from hundreds of other small rural towns throughout France, except for two things. It was the only town of any size close to Utah Beach, and five roads passed through it. Most were narrow and macadamized, with a light asphalt covering, and used by country folk to bring produce and livestock to market. But one, the asphalt-paved two-lane N13, ran from Paris west to Caen and Bayeux and Carentan before becoming Sainte-Mère's Rue Cap de Laine, and then continuing north to the port city of Cherbourg. If Allied forces landed almost anywhere on the Cotentin's east coast, any German reinforcements would need to go through Sainte-Mère-Église. Control the town, the Overlord planners understood, and you controlled the German counterattack—and there was always a German counterattack. It was as predictable as the sunrise.

The town had been occupied since June 18, 1940, the day that the gray-uniformed German Army had marched into town along the N13, officers on horses followed by goose-stepping soldiers. For Sainte-Mère's residents, it had been four long years of tolerating their Nazi occupiers, of having their autos, their horses, their cattle, their hunting rifles, and other belongings requisitioned or confiscated, and their gasoline and much of their food rationed. Food stamps were distributed according to occupation and age. Four years of lodging German officers, one per house, and of having their municipal buildings and even some businesses taken over. Four years of obeying the evening curfew imposed on them—9:00 p.m. in the summer, even earlier in the winter. Four years of enduring countless indignities, such as having to give way to a German soldier on the sidewalk. Four years of suffering many of their young men being rounded up and sent to prison and forced labor in Germany, leaving few available to maintain the region's farms. And of knowing that their country, their land, and everything they owned were no longer theirs and might never be again. But they would survive. They had survived Edward III's English invaders in July 1346, during the Hundred Years' War, when they had landed on the northeastern Cotentin coast and embarked on a total-war mounted raid through the countryside in a frenzy of burning, destruction, pillage, rape, and murder, and they would survive these invaders too.

That first day, the Germans had raised the Nazi flag above the town hall entrance on Rue Cap de Laine and set the clocks ahead an hour to Berlin time, though most of the area's residents continued to use French solar time. Soon, posters pasted up all over town warned that anyone found guilty of sabotage against the occupying army, or even of trying to escape by boat across the Channel to England, would be executed. Fifty-one-year-old pharmacist Alexandre Renaud, white-haired, mustachioed, and always well dressed, was the newly elected mayor. He did his best to protect his citizens and resist the more outrageous demands of his German overlords, not an easy task. He had largely succeeded, and the town had avoided the harsh, often deadly measures exacted upon their countrymen elsewhere. Still some demands could not be avoided. Horses, automobiles, and men were requisitioned and usually supplied—and then the large, brutish Nazi lieutenant named Zitt, who was in charge of the area, summoned Renaud to his headquarters in Gambosville, a mile south. He usually tried to bully and threaten, though neither tactic had much effect on the mayor, a veteran of the Great War. Now he made a new demand.

"We need twenty-five young girls placed at our disposal—it's your job to order this done," he told the mayor. What they would be used for was unspoken but clear.

Renaud flatly refused. "I cannot do that," he said. "You have force on your side, but I cannot order such a thing." He turned away to leave. "Goodbye," he said in English instead of *"Auf wiedersehen."*

"Ah, you like the Tommies," Zitt said, using the nickname for British soldiers. "We've known for a long time that you like the English. Well, when they land, we'll hang you from one of your own trees." But the request was dropped.[51]

For four years, the German Army had been a constant presence. Troops marched or drove through, their equipment and supplies often on horse-drawn carts, and some remained for months bivouacked in town or on its outskirts. In March 1944, a flak supply–repair platoon arrived. Mostly older Austrian soldiers, they were commanded by fifty-eight-year-old *Oberfeldwebel* (Master Sergeant) Werner Kassel, who was less interested in his military duties than in living the easy life in France—he had been a music critic in Vienna before the war. They parked their dozen or so trucks under the chestnut trees bordering the square and billeted in the two- and three-story buildings near it, most of them storefronts on the ground floor with shopkeepers' homes above. Aside from the observation squad in the church, Kassel's men were now the only German soldiers in Sainte-Mère-Église—though it was hard to miss the several thousand soldiers who had arrived in the area in mid-May. The officers lodged in neighboring villages and châteaus, and most of the enlisted men in dozens of squads set up in tents and trenches throughout the countryside. Other troops just moved through town up the N13 toward Montebourg, Valognes, and Cherbourg.[52]

Despite the buildup, few Normans believed that *le débarquement*—the landing that had been promised for so long—would happen, if it ever did, anywhere near them. So most of the residents just tried to get along with their lives and endure their Nazi occupiers. The Germans in the region were fairly well behaved; Rommel had issued edicts stressing that. The French "bore their four years of occupation as they would have borne any other unwelcome visitation," wrote one war correspondent, "with patience and a good deal of phlegm."[53]

A few did not. In a three-story stone house on the Rue Cap de Laine less than a hundred yards south of the town hall lived electrician Pierre Maury. His family and he occupied the two floors above his repair shop. Tall, slender, bespectacled, and often wearing a black beret, Maury was the coordinator for the local Resistance efforts—specifically, the *Organisation Civil et Militaire* (OCM), one of the eight major groups in France doing undercover work against the Germans. He had no hand in sabotage—his specialty was intelligence, chiefly German defenses and troop movements. (Besides, the Cotentin's flat, unforested terrain did not suit groups of armed men hiding, as did the Alps.) Maury's wife, Simone, a schoolteacher, prepared false identity papers for Resistance fighters at night when she wasn't insulting a German in rapid French, delivered with a warm smile. Their four children, three teenagers and a younger sister, attended school.

The Gestapo and the Abwehr, German military intelligence, had been systematically rooting out and rounding up OCM members, and by May 1944 most of its leaders were under arrest or dead. Maury and a few others under his direction had avoided detection. One of his confederates was a twenty-year-old named Raymond Paris, who worked across the street as an assistant to the town notary. He obtained much valuable intelligence from the many Germans who were in and out of the office—at one time it was the area headquarters for the Todt Organization, which was in charge of the Atlantic Wall construction. The notary's office was on the ground floor, and the Germans on the second; but the pre-1920 archives were stored in the attic, and the young notary clerk frequently found reason to walk through the Reich office on his way to the archives. Sometimes he got to work early, before the Germans, and looked through their desks; anything of interest, he told Maury about. He also helped prepare false identity papers and ration cards. For an entire month, Paris and his family had hidden a Resistance fighter in their house across the street from the town square, right under the Germans' noses.[54]

Toward the end of 1943, when Paris had gained Maury's full trust, the electrician confided in him: "If you hear on the BBC 'the dice are on the table,' the landing will be imminent." In his upper-floor bedroom at his parents' house, Paris began listening every night on his crystal radio set, which he kept hidden from the Germans. But by early June, after six months, his hopes were flagging.

Just before the war had begun, Maury with the help of his friend Charles Deloeuvre, the EDF (French Electric) district chief, installed an electrical test bench, cutting-edge technology at the time, in his workshop. It enabled him to diagnose and fix almost anything electrical quickly. The Germans, with their smorgasbord of captured international transport vehicles and paucity of knowledge and parts for them, kept him busy and allowed Deloeuvre and him the freedom to bicycle all around the area. On their far-ranging trips, they would take note of the locations and movements of German troops, batteries, and artillery, Todt construction projects, and anything else of interest to the planners of the Allied invasion. Back at home, Maury wrote precise reports that would be delivered to Cherbourg or Caen, then to London.

Early in 1944, the OCM smuggled a radio transmitter to Maury by train, and he bicycled south to pick it up in Carentan, eight miles south of town and the closest station. He hid it in the family's attic. Once a week a report was transmitted directly to London.

One day at Madame Maury's school, Sergeant Kassel told her that the Wehrmacht knew there was an illegal radio transmitter in the town—and that a car specially equipped to locate a radio signal would arrive that afternoon to find it. As soon as he left, she ran to the house and told her husband. The Nazis had already executed thousands of OCM members. But Pierre Maury had been an officer on a French submarine during the Great War, and he was no stranger to pressure. He quickly found a friend who took the transmitter away on his bicycle just before the car showed up—even if it was never used again, the risk of its discovery was too great. Then it was back to clandestine deliveries of all messages.

Maury's two eldest daughters, teenagers Claudine and Monique, attended boarding school in Valognes, ten miles north. But lately there had been too many Allied bombings and observation flights and German counterattacks, and their parents sent word for them to come home. On Monday, June 5, they arrived by train at Chef-du-Pont, two miles south of town—the closest station. Their train had been bombed and strafed by Allied planes, but they were unhurt. Allied air attacks had been occurring sporadically for weeks. A few days previous, several large formations of Allied planes had flown over the Cotentin, followed by bombardments to the north of town that made the shop windows along the N13 rattle. That was enough to convince some residents to pack their bags and leave town to stay with family or friends in the country.[55]

Dinner that evening was late and a meager one: black bread with cream that was going bad. Monsieur Maury often bartered his services to farmers for food, but everything had been hard to come by recently. Six weeks earlier, on April 17, all the radios in town had been confiscated and locked up in the attic of the town hall. That meant no one could listen to the BBC's evening broadcast in French, the only Allied source Normans had for news of the war—and sometimes coded messages to the Resistance fighters. *"Ici Londres, les Français parlent aux*

Français!" it would begin: "London here, the French speak to the French!" But a few radios had been hidden, and the word had spread that the invasion was imminent. That impressed few residents of Sainte-Mère-Église, since such rumors of *le débarquement* had been circulating for months. Besides, no one thought it would happen there—surely it would take place in the north, around Dieppe, Boulogne, or Dunkirk, hundreds of miles away.

Eighteen-year-old Claudine's seat at the dinner table faced the window, the fields beyond, and the western horizon. The family had just sat down to dinner when she said softly, "The sky is full of airplanes."[56]

Gen. Dwight Eisenhower (left, addressing members of the 101st Airborne on June 5), Supreme Commander of the Allied Expeditionary Force in Europe, was not a true believer in the Airborne before D-Day. But his old friend and West Point classmate Gen. Omar Bradley (right), former commander of the 82nd and commander of Overlord's U.S. ground forces, was, and campaigned for the Airborne's use in Operation Neptune.

Air Chief Marshal Sir Trafford Leigh-Mallory opposed the use of U.S. Airborne troops in Neptune and pressed his case with Eisenhower to the end.

(ALL PHOTOS FROM THE AUTHOR'S COLLECTION OR THE LIBRARY OF CONGRESS, UNLESS OTHERWISE NOTED.)

By the time Airborne recruits shipped overseas, they had been trained and honed to a fine point through constant exercise and long runs such as this, at Fort Benning, Georgia.

Ads and posters like this one inspired thousands of young men to apply for the Airborne.

Gen. Matt Ridgway (left), the 82nd's charismatic commander, stood and sat so straight that "the chair stiffened when he sat down on it." His deputy commander, Gen. James Gavin (right), a "ranker" who had enlisted at seventeen as a buck private, was worshipped by his men.

Col. William Ekman, commander of the 505th

(Left) Col. George Millett, commander of the 507th; (right) Col. Roy Lindquist, commander of the 508th

Lt. Col. Mark Alexander, executive officer of the 505th

Lt. Col. Edward Krause, commander of the 3rd Battalion/505th

Lt. Col. Benjamin Vandervoort, commander of the 2nd Battalion/505th

Lt. Col. Charles Timmes, commander of the 2nd Battalion/507th

Lt. Col. Herbert Batcheller, commander of the 1st Battalion/508th

Lt. Col. Arthur Maloney, commander of the 3rd Battalion/507th

Lt. Col. Thomas Shanley, commander of the 2nd Battalion/508th

Lt. Col. Louis Mendez, commander of the 3rd Battalion/508th

Maj. Teddy Sanford became commander of the 1st Battalion/325th after Lt. Col. Richard Klemm Boyd was injured on June 7.

Lt. Col. Edwin Ostberg, commander of the 1st Battalion/507th

Col. Edson Raff, commander of Task Force Raff

Col. Harry Lewis, commander of the 325th Glider Infantry Regiment; Maj. Gen. J. Lawton Collins, VII Corps commander; an unidentified officer; and Gen. Ridgway inspect a 57mm antitank gun of the 325th two weeks before D-Day.

Maj. Fred "Jack of Diamonds" Kellam, commander of the 1st Battalion/505th

Maj. James "Black Jack" McGinity, executive officer of the 1st Battalion/505th

Gavin's temporary HQ on Biazza Ridge, in Sicily. Elements of the heavily armored Hermann Goering Division are just beyond the trees in the distance.

Camp Quorn, just outside Leicestershire, England, where the 505th was billeted for almost four full months before D-Day

Gen. James Gavin speaks to paratroopers at an airfield in England just before D-Day.

Field Marshals Erwin Rommel (left) and Gerd von Rundstedt. They disagreed on the placement of troops along the Atlantic Wall, but they respected each other.

Gen. Karl-Wilhelm von Schlieben, commander of the 709th Infantry Division

Maj. Friedrich August von der Heydte, commander of Fallschirmjäger 6

Gen. Wilhelm Falley, commander of the 91st Infantry Division

Sgt. Eugen Griesser, Fallschirmjäger 6
(courtesy of Volker Griesser)

Sgt. Rudi Skripek, 91st Infantry Division (courtesy of Chris Skripek)

A fully loaded 82nd trooper struggles up into his C-47 transport plane.

82nd Airborne troops awaiting takeoff on the evening of June 5

The pathfinder team of the 1st Battalion/505th just before boarding their C-47 on the evening of June 5. Pvt. Robert Murphy is standing third from right, wearing a cap.

Lt. Robert Moss, 508th

Pvt. Fayette Richardson, Pathfinder, 508th
(courtesy of Nancy Richardson)

Cpl. Earl Geoffrion, 507th
(courtesy of Jason Lohner)

PFC Leslie Cruise, 505th
(courtesy of Leslie Cruise)

PFC Richard Vargas, 505th
(courtesy of Leslie Cruise)

The flooded Merderet swamp was a surprise to everyone, and the cause of at least three dozen 82nd Airborne drownings.

PFC Tom Porcella, 508th
(courtesy of Christine Fleming)

PFC Bob Nobles, 508th
(courtesy of Bob Nobles)

Lt. Neal Beaver, 508th
(courtesy of Kevin Beaver)

Sgt. Ed Jeziorski, 507th

PFC Tony DeMayo, Pathfinder, 505th
(courtesy of Anthony DeMayo)

Sgt. James "Buck" Hutto, 508th

Aerial view of Sainte-Mère-Église a short while after D-Day, looking south down the N13

PART II

THE DROP

FIVE

JUMP INTO DARKNESS

Wherever the Allies might land, they will be given a suitable reception.

ADOLF HITLER, DECEMBER 1943[1]

FAYETTE RICHARDSON COULDN'T get Tommy Dorsey's "What Is This Thing Called Love?" out of his head. Armed Forces Radio had been playing it every evening at chow time, and the catchy tune had conjured images of home.

He put down the paperback copy of *Oliver Twist* he'd been trying to focus on and reached down to his leg holster and pulled out his .45 automatic. It was the only weapon he carried. He wasn't allowed to carry a rifle—the twenty-eight-pound Eureka radio transponder strapped to his chest precluded that—but he hoped to pick one up on the ground. The .45's heft was reassuring.

"For Christ's sake, Richardson," said one of the other 508th pathfinders. "Quit waving that goddamn thing around and give me a hand here." He was trying to fit a large land mine into his musette bag. Finally he stuffed his K rations into his side pockets and squeezed it in.

They were in their tent waiting for the arrival of the trucks that would take them to their planes. Their faces were blackened, their tin-clicker "crickets" pocketed, their gear checked and rechecked. Like the rest of the 82nd paratroopers, their loads made it difficult to walk.

When the trucks arrived, they waddled out to them, and cooks and maintenance men helped each of them up and into the canvas-covered back of a vehicle. When they drove away, the maintenance men waved and shouted, "Good luck, fellas! Give 'em hell!" The troopers waved back. At the field, they dumped their gear beside their olive drab C-47 transport plane and waited, drinking coffee. After a photographer took a shot of each of the nine teams—three for each 82nd parachute regiment, one for each battalion—they waited again. Then it was time to board, and again they needed help, this time up the two-step ladder and through the cargo door at the rear of the thirty-foot-long cabin.

The sun was just setting in the west. Richardson plopped down onto one of the bare aluminum bucket-seat benches lining each side of the six-foot-wide cabin and tried to get comfortable, finally resting the weight of the Eureka pack, the size of a double-thick attaché case, on the edge of the seat across from him. About 10:15 p.m., the engine coughed into life, and the roar of the C-47's twin Pratt & Whitney engines filled the cabin and every man felt their vibration. The crew chief walked through the cabin and slammed the door shut, and at full throttle the plane roared down the runway and became airborne. By 10:30 p.m., all nine of the pathfinder sticks were aloft and headed southwest in a V of three V's, following the 101st pathfinder serial.

Before takeoff, the team leader, a lieutenant, had offered Richardson a Dramamine tablet, but he refused it—he never got airsick. Now he felt nauseous; he got one and swallowed it dry. It didn't help, and moments later he barely got to his feet in time to puke over the radar set. When he sat down, he felt better.

The engine drone made it almost impossible to talk in the dark of the cabin. Next to him tall, steady Francis Lamoureux, the other Eureka operator, nudged him and pointed to the rectangular window behind them. Richardson twisted around and looked out. There had still been light in the sky when they'd left, but now it was dark and a nearly full moon was shining on the sea just a hundred feet below—they were flying "on the deck" to avoid detection by German radar. Earlier, while passing over the vast invasion armada in the Channel, the plane had barely cleared the masts of some of the larger ships. Less than an hour later, they made landfall over the west coast of the Cotentin—the "back door" to Normandy, the route chosen to avoid the heavy German defenses on the east coast with their massive guns aimed toward the Channel—and the crew chief made his way down the middle of the crowded cabin and pulled off the cargo door and stowed it. The cool air and the full roar of the engines poured in. Then there was a flash of light—antiaircraft fire—and moments later, as they passed over the village of Saint-Sauveur-le-Vicomte, it came fast and thick, going by the open door like Roman candles on the Fourth of July. The flak put the lie to the claim by Allied intelligence that most of the anti-artillery units in the Cotentin had been bombed out of existence. At least they weren't jumping near Saint-Sauveur-le-Vicomte anymore—the relocation of their drop zones ten miles east had come as a welcome relief to the pathfinder leaders, who had become increasingly concerned by reports of the recently arrived anti-airborne forces in the area.[2]

The red "ready" light on the right side of the exit went on, and the men struggled to their feet and reached up to hook their static-line fasteners to the steel anchor cable that ran the length of the cabin, fastened to the ceiling above their heads. When a man threw himself out the door, the strap buckled to the cable would rip the cover off a man's parachute pack and then, by a thinner cord attached to the canopy, pull it out of its pack, opening the chute immediately and deploying the rigging lines. Gravity, and the prop blast, would do the rest. The resulting shock when a body dropping at more than a hundred miles an hour was jerked to a virtual stop by canopy and lines could "pop lights in the back of your eye-balls" and tear off anything not tightly secured.[3] The plane swayed as each man checked the equipment of the one in front of him and they counted off from the back. Richardson was fifth in line from the door in a stick of eighteen men. He pulled down his helmet, an illusion of added safety, and pressed against the back of the trooper in front of him. The plane slowed, fishtailing as it dropped to 300 feet, and when the green light came on, someone yelled, "Let's get the hell outta here!" and the lieutenant jumped out, and everyone followed him as fast as they could.

Richardson's parachute opened with a hard jerk and he swung clear. Machine guns fired at him from below, their colorful tracers arcing past. He looked down to see an orchard coming up fast and let up on the risers and, swinging, just missed a tree as he crashed into the grassy earth. The time was about 1:40 a.m.

He lay on his back until his ears stopped ringing; then he grabbed hold of his .45 and aimed it at the darkness in front of him. He could hear gunfire in the distance, but around him it was quiet. He put the pistol away, pulled his knife from its boot scabbard, and sawed through his leg straps. Then he pulled out his cricket, stood with the Eureka still strapped to his chest, and started walking through apple trees in search of the DZ, a rough oval of fields and orchards. He came to a moonlit clearing where other men on his team were gathering. Soon there were nine of them, half their stick: two Eurekas, one of them a backup, but only one light man. The other six were nowhere to be seen.

The main body of their regiment would be dropping soon—it was thirty minutes behind them. Colorful tracers began zipping over their heads, and they could hear German voices in personnel carriers going by on the dirt roads bordering their field beyond the hedgerows. Enemy soldiers were looking for them.

No one had told them about the hedgerows—these hedgerows, anyway. They'd heard there were such things in this part of Normandy, built up over centuries to mark boundaries and to keep livestock from wandering out of family pastures. But they looked nothing like the ornamental hedges in the U.S., lines of low bushes in a front yard a man could jump or step over.[4] Especially in the shadowed moonlight, these resembled something out of the Brothers Grimm: thick, six-foot or higher embankments of soil and rock and roots, with gnarled trees that reached up as much as fifty feet. Near impenetrable, they bordered every field and made it almost impossible to follow a compass heading, or move in a straight line in the dark, or find a landmark that had looked so prominent on a map or sand table. Who knew where the rest of their team was?

The lieutenant appeared out of the darkness—he'd gone looking for a farmhouse that marked their DZ, but he was not successful. "We're not going to find any place better than this," he said. "We don't have time to move anyway. Start sending the signal."

Lamoureux pulled out his olive drab Eureka transponder, laid it flat on the ground, and fastened the tall antenna to it. He turned it on, and a few seconds later, when the tubes warmed up, he began tapping out the code signal. He nodded at Richardson. "It's working all right."

That meant Richardson's transponder was now surplus and a liability, and they could destroy it. Orders were to do it by 6:30 a.m. to prevent the Germans from finding out the frequencies they were using. Lamoureux pulled the self-destruct handle that activated the internal detonator and there was a low rumble inside the Eureka. They buried it, and then the night was silent except for the sound of small-arms fire far away beyond the looming trees. Richardson walked over to the security team facing one of the roads beyond a hedgerow and lay down in the grass and held tightly to his .45. They waited for the sound of the planes.

Minutes later someone whispered, "There they are!" and on the dark western horizon above the trees, they saw small sparkles of light that eventually came closer and became larger as the German anti-aircraft flak burst around them. Then they could hear the drone of the planes as they approached, and they could see the blue, green, red, and yellow of the tracer bullets as machine-gun fire soared up at them. The Eureka's signal would become ineffective at a range of about two miles, and without guiding lights the pilots would have to make last-second guesses as to the DZ location. The sole light man turned on his amber Holophane light, set up on a metal tripod, and Richardson and five other men took spots in the T formation ten yards apart and turned their flashlights on, pointing their beams west toward the planes that seemed to be moving in slow motion. Richardson tried to will them to move faster.

As they came overhead, Richardson and the others flashed their lights on and off, and from one C-47 a stream of men poured out and their parachutes filled up. Some of the pathfinders gave a soft cheer. Less than a minute later, a trooper thumped onto the ground nearby, and Richardson ran over and helped him out of his harness and to his feet. They shook hands and the trooper raced off across the field.

But the next group of planes passed over them, and no one jumped. The expected third serial, with Richardson's H Company buddies, never arrived—at least, not that they could see. After Richardson watched a lone C-47 with fire streaming from an engine pass right over their heads and disappear over the eastern horizon, all was silent again. Only one stick had jumped on the DZ. What happened to the other 131?

"Let's get the fucking bastards on those guns!" somebody said, and that seemed to pluck an angry chord in the men, who milled about. But an officer told them to start digging in, and Richardson suddenly felt tired, sleepy, and drained. He grabbed his shovel and began to dig. When he had a shallow hole he sat in it, waiting to be told what to do, and when he leaned his head against its side, he fell asleep.[5]

THEIR EUREKA WOULD be the only one operational that night in the 508th, whose DZ was the southernmost, just west of the Merderet. Richardson's pathfinder team, and the other two from the 508th, all landed one to two miles southeast of the DZ—and, they would find out later, smack in the middle of an area infested with soldiers of the 91st Luftlande. German machine-gun fire and the hedgerows kept the pathfinders separated and unable to move far from where they landed. None of the teams reached the DZ, and only one managed to set up their amber lights. When the 508th pathfinders' numbers were totaled a few days later, two-thirds of them were missing.[6]

Without the pathfinders' directions, and because of fog and antiaircraft fire that dispersed the serials, only twenty planes dropped their 508th troopers on the DZ—and fewer than half the regiment's 132 planes deposited their sticks anywhere near it. Richardson's team had been too far away and too hemmed in by hedgerows to see any of them. The rest were scattered widely across the peninsula, over an area roughly fifteen miles wide by twenty miles deep—some of them a good distance from their DZs, with the hedgerows and German emplacements and patrols between them. They were all on the ground by 2:20 a.m., twelve minutes after the first stick landed.

Several planes carrying the 508th's G Company dropped their sticks just seconds before reaching the English Channel. Just before dawn, almost the entire company assembled on a piece of high ground about a thousand yards north of Utah Beach. They would stay long enough to watch the initial stages of the 4th Infantry Division landing at 6:30 a.m., then head west to cross the Merderet and find their regimental command post (CP).[7]

Startled by the thick fogbank and heavier-than-expected ground fire, most of the planes carrying 507th pathfinders unavoidably veered off course.[8] At 2:02 a.m., they dropped onto or near their DZ a mile north of the 508th's, and also found themselves in the midst of enemy troops—only sixteen of the fifty-one troopers avoided death, capture, or injury. They came under machine-gun fire the minute they hit the ground, and only a few members of each of the three teams found one another. No one dared turn their green assembly lights on, but two Eurekas were activated—only one of them on the DZ. That meant the 507th pilots had to find the DZ by dead reckoning. Since the Eureka signal on the Rebecca receiver on each serial's lead plane dropped off as it approached the DZ, and the Holophane lights could be seen only if approached head-on or nearly so, few of them were able to find the DZ, and the four pathfinders on the DZ watched as their 507th comrades dropped well beyond them.[9]

Few of the 82nd planes following them continued straight on when they hit the clouds; most broke formation and either descended below them or climbed to about 1,500 feet. When the clouds began to break up just a few miles west of the Merderet, there was little time to adjust speed and altitude. An airplane didn't have brakes. The C-47s dived down to the preferred jump altitude of 600 to 700 feet—or didn't. Many pilots cut back the throttles, extended flaps and lowered landing gear to produce drag, and even jerked the elevator and aileron controls around to help. The rough ride down angered some paratroopers who believed their pilots were scared and taking evasive action to avoid flak, which they weren't supposed to do.[10]

2:14 a.m.

In the lead plane of the 508th's second serial, Jim Gavin stood in the rear doorway watching the flak come up from the Channel Islands and "burst in plumes of smoke and flame just short of the plane," as he'd anticipated they would.[11] Their air cover had increased when they'd left England, and fighters had been weaving back and forth above them. Then the flak was behind them, and about twelve minutes later, he looked down to see the countryside of the Cotentin Peninsula as they reached the French coast. By the light of the nearly full moon high in the sky, the land appeared reddish brown, and roads and houses shone white in the moonlight as the plane and the others behind it dropped to 600 feet. He had just given the order to stand and hook up when they entered a dense cloud bank and visibility dropped to zero. Gavin couldn't even see the wingtips of his own plane, much less any others. His first thought was *Is this a smoke cloud put up by the Germans?* But as they continued to plow sightlessly through the fog, he realized it wasn't. He felt as if he and the men with him were entirely alone.

Like every other jumpmaster, he knew the exact time between landfall and his drop zone—theirs was eight and a half minutes. He also knew that if twelve minutes passed, they would have overshot the DZ and be over the east coast—and seconds later over the English Channel. There seemed no end to the fog. He checked his watch and soon checked it again.

Seven minutes after landfall, the fog began to break up. Gavin looked out and saw not one other plane—just moonlight reflecting off a river straight ahead. Was it the Douve, several miles south of Sainte-Mère-Église? Or the Merderet? He wasn't sure. Then machine-gun fire from the ground began peppering the plane, and the pilot started "a lot of jinking around," Gavin remembered.[12] Directly ahead a few miles, he could see a lot of small-arms fire and buildings burning—it had to be Sainte-Mère-Église, and that meant the 505th was already fighting the Germans for the town. Then the green light came on, Gavin took one last look at the land below, yelled, "Let's go!" and plunged out the door into the slipstream amid thick tracer fire.

He landed hard but unhurt in an apple orchard. Cows grazing among the trees continued, unfazed. The general's aide, Captain Hugo Olson, hit the ground nearby. They got out of their chutes and began rolling up the stick, following a narrow tree-lined dirt road east in the direction the rest of the men had dropped, and in a few minutes, all but a few of the troopers were with him. Four hundred yards on, the lane ended at a large body of water glimmering in the darkness that seemed to stretch to the horizon. He had no idea where he was—though, unlike the Sicily drop, this time he was sure he was in France. They watched as a C-47 in flames skirted low over the water. *We're in for a hell of a night,* he thought.[13]

After jumping from a plane in the same serial, Colonel Roy Lindquist, West Point class of '30 and commander of the 508th, landed in two feet of water. Machine-gun fire and tracer fire were coming across the swamp and he lay prone while he got out of his harness. He had just freed himself when someone said, "Halt!" It was the colonel's orderly, who had forgotten the challenge word "Flash."

Some of his men thought the bespectacled Lindquist pompous, and Gavin had little respect for him as a leader; he didn't think he spent enough time with his men.[14] Unlike Gavin, who always wore his fatigues in the field, Lindquist would go out to check on his regiment's training in his Class A uniform. But Lindquist had high standards, and he picked good people—and didn't hesitate to replace officers who didn't measure up.[15] This operation was a chance for Lindquist to change Gavin's opinion.

The colonel and his orderly waded through the swamp, twice stepping into water over their heads, which forced them to swim twelve feet—the worst way to encounter the drainage canals that ran through the fields and into the Merderet. Finally, exhausted and completely soaked, they saw an amber light—the 508th's assembly beacon, where his 2,000 troopers were to assemble. A few minutes later, they reached the light. Twenty men were there. Lindquist sent out runners to round up others in the area and to retrieve parapacks. They returned with only a handful of troopers—some of them from the 507th—and almost no equipment bundles. They managed to find one of the few that hadn't sunk in the marsh, and pulled a radio out. They couldn't raise anyone on it.

Lindquist was uncertain what to do and where he was. Then someone said, "While in the water I'm sure I saw a railroad bank to the west of us," and then the colonel knew his location and his course of action.

2:10 a.m.

Private First Class Harold Kulju was a slender twenty-year-old from California's San Joaquin Valley, where his Finnish grandparents had settled at the turn of the century to farm. He was in the California State Guard when war broke out, and when the Guard was activated, he volunteered for the paratroops—he'd never heard of them until another draftee told him about them, and they sounded like a good idea. The doctor who examined him thought he was a bit scrawny to be a paratrooper—Kulju was five foot ten but only 123 pounds—and wasn't inclined to accept him, but after some discussion he relented.[16] Kulju made the grade and became a radioman in the 508th.

Now he was number six in his stick, part of the 2nd Battalion's HQ company. As his C-47 made landfall on Normandy's west coast, the antiaircraft fire started up. He had never felt so helpless. Then the jumpmaster yelled, "Stand up and hook up!" and he and the other men staggered to their feet and hooked up and checked their equipment. A few minutes later the green light went on and the jumpmaster hurled himself out the door. He was followed by the next four men, and as Kulju stepped to the door, a shell exploded and the top of the plane disappeared.

While the plane dipped to the right and headed toward the ground, Kulju grabbed the outside of the door with both hands as they had been taught. It was all he could do to drag himself over the threshold and roll over it and fall out at about 500 feet. No one followed him. When his chute opened a second later with a hard jerk, Kulju looked up to see tracers ripping through it. He heard what sounded like a Gammon grenade explode below him; then he oscillated twice and hit the ground seconds later. Thirty yards away was a German bunker. Another trooper must have just thrown in the grenade he'd heard, and knocked it out. He tore his trench knife free—he had taped it to his boot sheath—sliced through all his chute straps, picked up his carbine, and stood up. He looked around the field, but he had no idea where he was. He ran for the closest hedgerow and threw himself against the solid earth. He lay there for a while, gathering himself. Then in the moonlight he saw two Germans approaching on the other side of the embankment. He hadn't loaded his carbine, and he hoped they'd go by, but he unscrewed the cap of his Gammon grenade just in case and waited. When they reached a point just opposite him, they saw him and ducked down. He waited. One of them rose slowly, and he tossed the Gammon over the hedgerow. The German lifted his rifle and fired, and the bullet zipped harmlessly through the crotch of Kulju's pants, but the rifle's muzzle blast was so close, it knocked him senseless. When he recovered, his face was in the dirt embankment and his mouth was open and drooling blood and saliva. He tasted gunpowder.

He couldn't hear, and he thought he was dead. Then his hearing returned, and he heard moaning on the other side of the hedgerow.

Soon the moaning stopped. Kulju began to move. He thought he heard two troopers approaching on his side of the hedgerow. One shouted, "Thunder!"—that was actually the counter reply. Kulju said, "Flash," but not loudly enough, for a bullet hit his helmet and ricocheted off. He rolled away and started swearing. Another round was fired and barely missed him, going through papers in his left hip pocket. He swore louder, which seemed to work better than the password. The two men came over and they all talked for a while and decided to wait there. Kulju must have dozed off—when he looked up, he was alone again. He ran for a brush-filled gully he could see and jumped into it and lay on his back.

He heard the creaking of leather and knew it was Germans. He reached for his carbine but it was off to his left somewhere. He lay still and closed his eyes. He heard them approaching through the grass until they stood over him. He felt the need to urinate and did so. He hoped that in the dim light, they might think it was blood.

After a while Kulju heard them move away. He slowly opened his eyes. They were gone. He crawled down into the gully as deep as he could and fell asleep, exhausted. Just before he did, he heard a glider approach, crashing through the trees.[17]

2:22 a.m.

Twenty-three-year-old PFC Bob Nobles of C Company/508th had volunteered for the Airborne after seeing the 1941 movie *Parachute Battalion.* At the airfield, even though there were only two short steps up to the C-47 Skytrain's rear door, he couldn't climb them by himself. He'd been an athlete in high school, average-sized though strong and fast enough to win most of his high school track races, but now the

120 pounds of gear he carried, nearly doubling his weight, were holding him back. The man behind him gave him the boost he needed up into the open cabin. Nobles was number fifteen in this sixteen-man stick, the second to board, so he made his way down the inside of the cabin and fell onto the last aluminum bucket seat along the left side. The other men followed.

Nobles patted his front left jacket pocket. Inside were the last four letters he'd received from Bette, his high school sweetheart back in Ithaca, New York, where he'd been born and raised on a farm. They'd been together for six years and had finally gotten married in April 1943, on Easter Sunday. After a brief honeymoon, he'd returned to his regiment, the 508th, for several months of war games and training. Then it was off to Northern Ireland in late December, and then Nottingham in March. Now, after five more months of intensive exercises and small-unit training, he felt he was as ready as he'd ever be. But Nobles had never experienced actual combat, and like many of the men, he wondered if he'd get out of it okay—and if he'd be more coward than hero when it came down to it. He prayed that he wouldn't. Just in case, he'd written a last letter to Bette earlier that day telling her he loved her and how much she meant to him.

An hour after takeoff, when they'd joined the 300-mile-long air formation, they left England behind and flew over the red-and-white lighthouse at the tip of the narrow promontory known as Portland Bill, heading south over the Channel for France. Most of the transport planes were seriously overloaded, between 1,000 and 4,000 pounds too much, and as a result their cruising speed was only 140 mph, 20 mph less than normal. The noise of the C-47's twin engines was deafening, even more so with the open door at the rear of the plane, and it was dark inside. There was little conversation. Some men smoked, and that, combined with the tight quarters, made the cabin feel stuffy. A lieutenant walked up and down the aisle, talking to the men, trying to lighten the mood. Nobles was one of the quieter guys in his company, but now he almost told the lieutenant to go sit down.

The man to his right nudged him, and Bob turned and peered out a window behind him. They were flying at 500 feet, and the moon reflected silver off the water below. Although the weather had been overcast and raining for the past few days, the sky was now clear, and he could see fighter escort planes off to their side, not too far away. The only visible lights were sets of three small, dimmed blue ones on the tops of the wingtips and fuselage of the planes ahead; they could be seen only from directly behind or above—it took full concentration for a pilot to follow the lead plane. Even the wispiest cloud was enough to cause the pilot to lose sight of the tiny blue dots, so it was the copilot's job to look everywhere else.[18]

Nobles looked down at a sea filled with ships and their white wakes—hundreds, thousands, of all sizes, from behemoth battleships to small landing craft: the largest armada ever assembled—and for the first time, he felt the full magnitude of Operation Overlord. He was proud to be part of it.

Fifty-seven miles south of the English coast, where a surfaced British submarine with a blinking light could be seen below, the planes made a hard ninety-degree left turn, ascended to 1,500 feet, and flew between the German-occupied Channel Islands of Guernsey and Alderney, thirty miles off Normandy's west coast. The sky erupted in an explosion of searchlights and the dull pounding of Krupp 88mm Flak guns, which could hurl a twenty-pound shell as high as 25,000 feet, where it would explode into sharp fragments of steel in every direction. Nobles's heart felt as if it might burst out of his chest. He and his comrades had made many jumps. Heavy artillery fire with the specific aim of killing them had not been a part of those.

But the flak didn't reach them, and the barrage faded away as they left the islands behind. Twenty minutes later they reached the French coast and descended to 600 feet. Below them they could see the water crashing into the rocks offshore and turning to white foam on the light gray sand. They were less than ten minutes from their drop zone, which was six miles inland from Utah Beach, where the Fourth Infantry would arrive at 6:30 a.m.

Within seconds they entered a thick cloud bank. Due to strict air silence, none of the pathfinder pilots who had flown into it had been able to warn the armada. The planes around them vanished and again there was the pounding roar of the 88s, accompanied this time by the glare of huge searchlights and the bright trails of tracer rounds, blue, red, yellow, green, all around them. The C-47 shuddered and dropped as flak exploded nearby, and men were thrown to the floor. Machine-gun fire hit the plane, sounding like a heavy hailstorm on a tin roof. A few minutes later they broke through the fog and some of the pilots, few of whom had ever done a combat drop, sped up to 150 miles per hour and descended even lower—much too fast and low for a safe jump. The usual drop speed was about 95 mph, but the overloaded planes would have stalled at that speed, so tonight it was 110 mph.[19] In their briefings, when the flight crews had been ordered not to take evasive action, they'd also been assured that most of the German antiaircraft batteries had been put out of commission by bombing runs in the weeks previous. That was clearly not the case, and none of them had expected the hellish gauntlet they flew into. For many pilots, the only way to survive until the drop zone was to disobey orders, and sometimes that meant speeding up to avoid other planes or a deadly stall.

The jumpmaster—the lieutenant—stood at the open rear door. When the red light went on, he shouted, "Stand up and hook up!" When all sixteen men did, he shouted, "Sound off for equipment check!" and each trooper checked the parachute gear of the man in front of him, then counted off with his number in sequence from the rear: "Sixteen, okay!" "Fifteen, okay!" The plane bounced and bounced again. Bob Nobles and his comrades gripped their static lines, each pressing against the man in front of him, right hand on his back. Then the red light went off and the green one next to it lit up, and the lieutenant yelled, "Let's go!" and threw himself from the plane. The men followed, almost running out the door less than a second apart, and when it was his turn, Nobles jumped into the darkness.

He and the other men in his stick would land twenty-five miles from their DZ. Few of them would make it back to their lines alive.[20] Thousands of other misdropped paratroopers would meet the same uncertain fate. And many of them would wonder what had happened to all their meticulous plans.

SIX

THE SWAMP

All I saw was water. . . .

SERGEANT RALPH BUSSON, 508TH[1]

The Merderet River was normally a fifteen-yard-wide, softly flowing waterway with well-defined banks that flowed through dry fields on its way to the Douve River, below Carentan. Aerial reconnaissance photos taken from straight above had failed to reveal the true situation: What appeared to photo analysts to be thick pasture grass was actually tall and heavy underwater vegetation that prevented a reflection from the water. Their conclusion: "Ground here probably soft."[2]

More than a year before the invasion, the Germans had closed the locks at high tide at La Barquette, where the Douve emptied into the Bay of Seine; this closure prevented drainage and backed up both rivers. The result was a swamp almost a mile wide and less than four feet deep in most places, but in some as deep as six feet or more. The 82nd's three drop zones lay adjacent to the flooded area, and the paratroopers' wide dispersal resulted in hundreds of very surprised men dropped into water where there should have been dry land. Loaded down with heavy packs and entangled in chutes and riser lines tightly strapped in several places to their torsos, they struggled to free themselves while trying to keep their heads above the water and stay on their feet in the ooze. Chutes would often remain full of air or catch enough wind to drag a struggling trooper below the surface for some time. Dozens drowned, and many others barely avoided watery deaths.[3]

2:24 a.m.

Private First Class Tom Porcella of Company H, 508th, a first-generation Italian American from Far Rockaway, New York, had been working as a mechanic at Republic Aviation on Long Island before he enlisted. He was of average height, sturdy and good-looking, and he had been seeing a nice English girl in Nottingham named Molly. They'd fallen in love, and the last time he saw her, he told her that if he were lucky enough to survive, he was coming back to marry her. Raised a Christian, Porcella had been agonizing over what he'd been trained to do—kill people. He was having a hard time trying to reconcile that with the Sixth Commandment.

Now, as he floated down to French soil with luminous, multicolored tracer rounds flying all around him—and he knew that in between each tracer round were three or four bullets that couldn't be seen—he saw nothing but blackness below. *It's like the Fourth of July,* he thought, and then: *All those machine guns down there are shooting at* me. Porcella released his reserve chute and let it drop, then opened his harness chest strap, leaving just his leg straps secured.

His descent lasted only a few seconds. Then he got the shock of his life as he plunged straight into water. His heart pounding, he was entirely submerged when his boots hit the mucky bottom. He jumped up, broke the surface, took a deep breath, and fell underwater again. He realized that if he stood on the bottom, the water was just below his eyes. He stretched on tiptoe, gasping, and took another breath. He held that one as he ducked down and tried to remove his leg straps. He couldn't—they were too tight. He straightened up for another breath, praying to God: *Please don't let me drown in this damn water in the middle of nowhere.*

Porcella calmed down some, then went under again and felt for his trench knife in a scabbard attached to his right boot. It was still there. *Now I have a chance,* he thought. He pulled it free, jumped up for another breath, then went below again and started to work on the strap. Nothing happened. He began to panic and came up for another breath. He said a Hail Mary to himself as he tried again with no luck. He finally realized that his razor-sharp blade was upside down. He craned up for another gulp of air, submerged, and tried again. This time, with a few pulls of the blade on each strap, he freed himself of the heavy chute.

He took off his helmet and let it float upside down in front of him; then he cut loose a ten-pound land mine, emptied his musette bag, and rearranged his ammo bandoliers and rifle. He looked around as best he could. He was in almost total darkness now in water up to his neck, and he couldn't tell which direction dry land was in. All his thorough training hadn't prepared him for this. It was only then that Porcella became aware of the rifle and machine-gun fire in the distance. He was starting to shiver from the cold, and his teeth began to chatter. He put his helmet back on and started working his way away from the gunfire and, he hoped, toward shallower water.[4]

Many of those who dropped into the flooded lake that was once the modest Merderet River barely escaped with their lives. One 82nd trooper didn't realize until after he had used his trench knife to slash through his harness straps that he had sliced off the top of his thumb. Another frantically cut completely through his jacket pocket into his skin, while one man jabbed into his own thigh and another hacked up his own wrist.[5] Private James Blue, Company A/508th, thought he was about to land in a dark meadow and was pleased, since he could see no signs of the enemy in it. But when he splashed down into three feet of cold water instead of solid earth, he fell sideways and underwater. Blue was a fit and strong six-foot-three North Carolina farm boy, but he was terrified and started thrashing about. He finally struggled and got his feet on the muddy bottom and came up for a breath. Then his chute caught some wind and dragged him and his seventy pounds of equipment backward and under again. He fumbled with his harness for what seemed forever and finally got free of it and managed to stand in the waist-high murk, coughing up water and shaking, drained from the ordeal. He looked around and felt lost and alone. Then he heard a familiar voice swearing. It was a buddy who had jumped with him, and suddenly he didn't feel as scared.[6]

Others weren't so lucky. Weighed down by their equipment and strapped so tightly into their harnesses they couldn't quickly escape, some couldn't get to their feet and manage to grab a breath before expiring. German soldiers killed even more troopers as their parachutes pulled them helplessly across the swamp or as they waded toward dry land. Hundreds of equipment bundles with ammunition, radios, and other supplies were lost. Few of them could be retrieved.[7]

2:26 a.m.

At Folkingham Aerodrome, as the 508th's Third Battalion serial had begun moving down the runway, the men of the Third's HQ mortar platoon were in a panic. They were loaded into three C-47s, but their lead plane's port engine wouldn't start, even after an attempt to hand-crank it.

Lieutenant Neal Beaver, just twenty years old but married with a little boy, was the jumpmaster. He was another "ranker"—as an enlisted man he'd been recommended for OCS; then, as a new second lieutenant, he had transferred to the Airborne. After he had conferred with the pilots, they quickly decided to switch everyone and everything—crew, stick, and parapacks—to an empty C-47 200 feet across the airfield. The crew of that plane was reluctant to hand it over to another crew, but after an animated discussion—the pilot of Beaver's stick was the senior officer, which helped—they were persuaded. The troopers "fell out of that plane like bloated frogs," Beaver remembered later. Dragging their 250-pound parapacks with them, they quick-waddled across the runway between aircraft taxiing by. When one parapack containing mortar ammo burst open, they left it behind. Twenty minutes later, by the time the crew had checked out the plane, men and bundles had been loaded on, and the three planes had taken off, they were far behind their serial.

Beaver stood in the rear doorway as they flew across the Channel. Except for the other two planes, one on either side, there were no other aircraft in sight. When they reached the French coast, they were the only C-47s in the sky. No cloud problems for them, just some occasional ground haze. Beaver could see the Merderet and Douve rivers, shining like silver ribbons in the moonlight up ahead, but he couldn't see any sign of the 508th's LZ. He had studied the sand table for hours, and he knew they were flying too far south. The pilot took them down to 600 feet and turned the green light on, but then they flew over the east coast and back over the Channel, and Beaver told the crew chief standing next to him, "We're not jumping. There's nothing but water down there. Tell him to turn left—turn left!"

As the plane made a steep left turn and passed back over the waves breaking on the wide white beach, machine-gun fire came up at them from the German fortifications below. The first burst of tracers arced by them in a curve to the east, but the next one ripped into the plane front to rear. The plane lurched, lost some altitude, then increased speed. The pilot had taken a round in his left leg, and the copilot, the only one of the five crew members who wasn't hit, took over the controls. A glancing blow from a tracer round smacked into Beaver's chin and knocked him back into the cabin, but he bounced back into the doorway, and as the green light flashed on again at 2:26 a.m., he kept going out of the plane at about 350 feet. His chute opened and he oscillated once or twice, then hit the ground hard, right in front of a German pillbox.

Beaver saw it and froze. Feeling vaguely silly, he raised a hand and slowly waved it to see what would happen, but there was no one in the pillbox. He lay there sore as hell, cursing the War Department and everyone else responsible for putting him there, and finally stood up. He was about four miles south of his DZ, and he'd never felt so alone in his life.[8]

2:27 a.m.

In a plane in the same serial and just behind Beaver's, Sergeant Dan Furlong, Company H, 508th, stood with his back to the C-47's cockpit as it neared the DZ. He was the assistant jumpmaster, the "pusher"—the last man to jump. Something slammed into the plane, and Furlong looked out to see that a flak shell had taken off the last three feet of one of the wings. Another shell hit near the rear door and sheared the light panel off. The next one came straight through the floor, ripping a foot-wide hole in it, and then exploded, killing three troopers and wounding four others, and leaving a four-foot hole in the roof that almost sliced the plane in half. Inside the cabin it was complete chaos as men, opened parachutes, and tangled static lines were in disarray in the darkness and the smoke. The lieutenant at the rear door seemed to be in shock, still waiting for the green light that was no longer there to go on, and Furlong began pushing the man in front of him and screaming to the lieutenant to jump; the pilot yelled at him too while trying to keep the shattered plane steady as it nose-dived toward the ground. They were only a couple hundred feet above some treetops when the lieutenant finally went out the large opening where the door used to be, and the men followed him, clambering over the three bodies. Three of the wounded troopers made it, but the fourth just lay on the floor. As Furlong climbed over him, he stepped into the hole in the floor and had to pull himself out. He made his way through the dead men's static lines and opened chutes, finally reached the door, and fell out headfirst at about 200 feet.

The chute popped open and he smashed into the trees on the edge of a field. A tree limb caught under a leg strap and almost impaled him as it thrust under his reserve chute and reached past his ear, then broke. Furlong fell from the tree into a cement cattle trough full of water.

He heard the hobnail boots of German soldiers running in the road on the other side of the hedge, just ten feet away—they had seen his chute, still up in the tree, and were looking for him. Furlong pulled his knife from his boot and cut his chute loose and took off.[9]

2:30 a.m.

As he floated down, Sergeant James "Buck" Hutto, a Company I mortar squad leader from South Carolina, watched as machine-gun tracers rose from a farmhouse and a barn in a corner of the field below him, while a white pony galloped in circles. As soon as he hit the ground, he saw a black donkey also running, terrified. Hutto was so frightened that he lay as still as possible in his harness. His chute fluttered in the wind and pulled his lines to their full length.

When the last of the 508th's planes disappeared in the east, the Germans stopped firing and the horse and donkey stopped running.

The donkey turned toward the barn and crossed the field—and ran across the chute lines and got tangled in them. He started dragging Hutto toward the barn. The roof had been knocked out, and two MG42s were in it shooting up at the planes above.

Hutto held his risers with his left hand, and with his right, he pulled out the trench knife strapped to his boot and started frantically cutting the risers. When he sliced through the last one, he was fifty feet from the barn, lying in the grass in the bright moonlight. As quietly and carefully as he could, he slipped out of his harness and musette bag and slowly crawled to the opposite corner of the field and into a hedgerow.

Hutto breathed easier until he heard, to his left around the hedgerow, the sound of the feed lever of a machine gun pulled back. Expecting the MG42 gunner to open up into the hedgerow at any minute, he lay there hardly breathing until dawn, when the Germans evacuated the barn and the machine gunner left with them.[10]

THE LAST OF the division to be dropped were the men of the 507th, starting at about 2:32 a.m. Their drop was almost as bad as the 508th's, and most of the regiment's 2,000 troopers were scattered miles from their DZ—only one stick landed on it. The 507th dispersal covered sixty square miles, and a few wound up even farther away.

Just like the 508th's, most of its transport pilots were facing enemy fire for the first time. When they hit the cloud bank, they changed direction and altitude, then changed again when they finally emerged from it. The flak and machine-gun fire from the ground were relentless and spurred more evasive action by some pilots—even though they had been ordered not to. And since only one pathfinder unit had set up its Eureka transponder and it was off target and there were no lights, the transport pilots were almost flying blind, navigating by ground features. Antiaircraft fire brought down several C-47s, sometimes before a stick had made it out the door. More than one plane climbed to 2,000 feet to avoid the antiaircraft fire and turned its green light on without descending. Some troopers jumping from that altitude saw C-47s below them.[11] One plane's engine took heavy fire and burst into flames that quickly spread to the fuselage. Most of the men got out the door, but some had to climb over the lifeless bodies of their comrades. Then the plane's surviving crew started jumping. The last man left was the pilot. He climbed through the escape hatch above the cockpit of the burning plane and threw himself off, pulling the rip cord on his chute. He and three of the four other crew members survived. The plane somehow stayed in the air for a few more miles before it crashed into the ground.[12]

As the rattled pilots dropped their sticks, flak exploded around them, searchlights illuminated them, and tracers arced up through the sky, the colorful streaks enabling their gunners to adjust their fire in the dark more accurately. The noise was deafening. Most of the pilots were new to combat, and no training could have prepared them for this. Somehow most of the planes survived, but rare was the one that didn't incur damage. But the C-47 was a tough and resilient bird, and most that didn't receive direct flak hits would make it back to base.

Some of the 82nd's demolition specialists carrying the C-4 plastic explosive composition faced even more dangerous odds than their comrades. One 507th trooper heard an explosion moments after his chute opened, and he turned his head to see the remnants of a man from his stick floating down. He had been blown to bits when a German bullet ignited the demolition charge carried in a hip pocket.[13] Another trooper somehow got hung up on the wing of his plane. Only when the pilot slowed down and dipped his wing did he slide off.[14] One man, Sergeant Thomas Rogers of the 505th, stood in the cabin hooked up and waiting, and his reserve chute opened. He gathered it up and held it bundled to his waist. When he jumped, he got only a short distance before he stopped—the reserve chute had caught on one of the aluminum seats. As he hung there, each of the next six troopers dived down onto him, trying to break him loose, before their own chutes opened and they fell away. Only when the seventh man landed on him did the reserve chute's suspension lines break. His static line snapped tight and ripped open his main chute, and Rogers floated to the ground safely, if somewhat battered.[15]

2:30 a.m.

As his plane passed over the Cotentin west coast and ran into heavy flak, Captain Leroy "Dave" Brummitt, operations officer for the 3rd Battalion/507th, stood in the open rear door. He noticed that his C-47 and nine others in his serial had veered off course, each pilot following the lead plane. He peered down into the darkness, then checked his wristwatch—it was about 2:30 a.m.—then looked out again. He saw nothing there he recognized, though he too had spent hours studying sand tables, maps, and aerial photos of the DZ area. When the red light went on, he had his men stand and hook up. Four minutes later, when the green light was supposed to go on, the red light continued to glow.

Men were leaving the other planes around him. Nothing on the ground below matched anything he'd studied, but he shouted, "Go!" grabbed each side of the doorway, and threw himself out. The other seventeen men followed him, and as they drifted to the ground, their C-47 disappeared toward the east with the others.

Most of the ten sticks fell into marshland, muddy and shallow. Separately, the men began slogging toward a prominent church on a hilltop not far away, and they continued to do so as dawn arrived. By midmorning, Brummitt and twenty-five other tired and wet troopers had assembled in the village that surrounded a twelfth-century stone church. Its name was Graignes, and it was seven miles south of Carentan—and eighteen miles southeast of their drop zone. Eventually 182 men would gather there—and remain there for almost a week fending off German forces.

2:40 a.m.

One 507th plane was so overloaded with equipment bundles and sixteen heavily laden jumpers that it barely got off the ground at Fulbeck, the northernmost 507th airfield. Soon after passing over the French coast, it was droning along at about 125 mph and an altitude of 800 feet when its red light went on. The jumpmaster was Captain Chester Bailey "C.B." McCoid. When he was sixteen, he'd lied about his age to join the Connecticut National Guard. After Pearl Harbor was bombed and his Guard unit was activated, he was promoted to sergeant. He applied for OCS and was accepted—even though, unbeknownst to his superiors, he was a high school dropout and younger than he claimed. Seventeen weeks later he was a commissioned officer and still a teenager. He volunteered for the Airborne—he'd seen his first parachutist at a 1928 state fair when he was six and had been fascinated ever since—and was assigned to a 507th artillery unit. Now, at the ripe old age of twenty-one, he commanded B Company. During the regiment's brief stay in Northern Ireland, he'd met an Irish lass, Dorothy, whom he planned to marry.

Standing at the open rear door, McCoid yelled, "Stand up and hook up," when the red light came on, and the troopers struggled to their feet and hooked up. The plane passed over a bank of white fog for thirty seconds. As soon as they cleared it, ground fire erupted from below, and colorful tracer rounds flashed by with a cracking noise.

Machine-gun fire seemed to be coming from everywhere. It was the first experience he and his men had had with the MG42 and its terrifyingly rapid rate of fire.

Below him the area was lit up by fires—it looked to McCoid like ten downed aircraft were burning. He looked for recognizable features denoting their landing zone, about a thousand yards north of the small village of Amfreville, west of the Merderet. Then there was a loud explosion beneath them and McCoid felt a sharp pain in his right knee and fell to the floor. Every trooper in his stick did the same. The plane began to lose altitude, then leveled off at about 200 feet and sped up—far too fast for a safe jump.

McCoid and his men pulled themselves to their feet. He knew they'd soon be over Utah and then the English Channel. He salvoed the six parapacks, shouted, "Let's go!" and jumped out at what seemed to be treetop level. His men followed him.

Their chutes opened in the plane's prop blast so fiercely that most of their gear not fastened tightly to their bodies ripped away. Everything in McCoid's jump pants pockets burst through the reinforced seams—K rations, ammo magazines, grenades, his entrenching tool, even his musette bag and everything in it. He was left with little but his M1 carbine under his reserve chute—the carbine had been specially modified by a 507th armorer to be fully automatic—and a few other items. Seconds later he crashed down on his knees onto a stone road. The right kneecap that had been shot was crushed. When he finally disentangled himself from his harness and chute, he grabbed his carbine. The fifteen-round magazine in it was his only ammunition. Several low-flying C-47s flew over at high speeds and in all directions. In the tree-shadowed darkness, McCoid saw a shadowy figure approaching on the side of the road. When he recognized the coal-scuttle-shaped helmet, he got up on his good knee and shot the German dead. He had no idea where he was, so he crawled over a berm and began hobbling through a field of cows.[16]

2:48 a.m.

McCoid wasn't the only 507th trooper lost—there were many of them. Sergeant Ed Jeziorski, C Company/507th, a twenty-three-year-old from Long Island's North Shore, was in charge of a machine-gun squad. Just before he'd climbed into his plane, he'd taken his fiancée's photo from his wallet and taped it inside his helmet—he figured it would be safer there. He landed in an open field close to the burning wreck of a crashed C-47. When he stood to free himself of his parachute harness, he was silhouetted by flames and a German machine gun began shooting at him. He dropped to the ground and stayed there. But his harness straps were so tight that he couldn't get enough slack to unhook them. Every time he moved, it seemed like the machine gunner fired another burst just inches over him. He decided to cut himself out and managed to slowly move his right leg up close enough to pull his trench knife from his boot holster. He cut all the chute straps, wiggled free, and rolled over into a slight depression. He was just low enough to reach his M1 and then squeeze a few rounds in the general direction of the machine gun. The firing stopped.

He looked around. There was no one in sight. He began crawling in the dark along a hedgerow until he heard something moving toward him through the underbrush. Jeziorski lay flat and aimed his rifle toward the sound. He called out, "Flash," and someone in front of him said, "Thunder." Jeziorski breathed easier. The trooper who emerged from the darkness was Private Grover Boyce, his assistant gunner. With a buddy, the world seemed a better place.

They were soon joined by two privates from the regiment's medical detachment. The four men kept moving, and about 4:00 a.m., they found a parapack with a .30-caliber machine gun and two boxes of ammo. They took it all. There had been eighteen men in their stick. The four men wandered through the mazelike bocage for a few more hours without meeting anyone, friend or enemy. After the sun rose, they decided to set up a defensive position along the side of a narrow road and dug in around the machine gun. They had no idea where they were, but would find out later they were ten miles southeast of their drop zone.[17]

3:10 a.m.

Earl Geoffrion, the 507th corporal who had killed another trooper with his fists, jumped second out the door of his C-47 at about 400 feet, terrified. He was heavily laden with the usual equipment and also with dynamite sticks, C-4, and several grenades, and he felt like a walking bomb. With all the flak and machine-gun fire around him, he knew that if just one round hit any of his explosives, he'd be obliterated. The chute's opening jerked him hard enough to smash his helmet down over his eyes. Just as he lifted it up, he landed in a couple feet of water. Geoffrion cut his lines, got out of his chute, and looked around. No one from his stick could be seen, and that included Private Don Cleary, his mission partner. He started wading through the water toward dry ground. He hadn't walked more than fifty feet when he ran into General Gavin standing on a small knob of a hill surrounded by some men.

"What outfit, trooper?" Gavin said.

"507th, sir."

"You guys, over that way," Gavin said, pointing to the 507th gathering point.

"I jumped with explosives. I'm a demolition expert," Geoffrion said. "I'm supposed to blow up the railroad." He told Gavin he couldn't find his partner.

"Well, then, get another trooper and go down the railroad that way and blow it up." Gavin gestured in the direction of the elevated railway to the east across a wide expanse of water.

Geoffrion picked a man nearby from the 508th. They waded through the swamp to the double-tracked Cherbourg-Paris railway, climbed onto the embankment, and headed south. Where two rail lines converged, they stopped and Geoffrion set dynamite charges while the other trooper stood watch. The explosion ripped the tracks apart and left a large hole underneath. Then they blew up a telephone pole and cut all the communication wires in sight and continued south down the tracks.[18]

By 3:15 A.M., the 6,400 paratroopers of the 82nd—except for seven who refused to jump, a couple dozen others who were dead or badly injured by flak or machine-gun fire, some uninjured men who for various reasons were unable to get out the door, and a plane that dumped its troopers into the Atlantic, all of whom drowned—were on French soil.[19] But like the leaves of a tall oak tree on a gusty late-fall day, many of them had been scattered far and wide. Few of the 507th or 508th had hit their drop zones.

Nothing like the "futile slaughter" predicted by Air Chief Leigh-Mallory—50 percent of the U.S. Airborne troops dead before the amphibious attack—had come to pass. But there were a few hours left before the seaborne forces hit Utah Beach. And no one had reckoned with the hedgerows. Or the flooded Merderet. Or the cloud bank, the heavy antiaircraft fire, and pilots whose only recourse was evasive action that scattered thousands of men far from their DZs.

For hundreds of individual troopers, pairs, and small squads, their first order of business was not the completion of their mission but simple survival. As the cloud-covered moon dropped in the western sky and the troopers slowly made their way in the increasing darkness through the labyrinthine bocage countryside bordered by sunken dirt roads and thick hedgerows anchored by trees that grew fifty feet or more, thousands of German soldiers awaiting just such an assault were sent out in search of them. And because most of the American radio sets were dropped in parapacks, not with their operators and scattered who knew where, officers in rank from lieutenant to general were unable to communicate their situations or location to others. Half the division's men were lost, and almost no one—even those who knew where they were—knew where anyone else was.

The small fields and high hedgerows made it difficult for troopers to assemble. The result was hundreds of skirmishes with the enemy. As Sergeant D. Zane Schlemmer put it, "Each field became a separate battleground." Their mission, their job, was made even more difficult by the scarcity of anything but handheld weapons. "We had no mortars," recalled Schlemmer, "few machine guns, few bazookas, fewer radios, little medical supplies, few medics."[20] They also lacked the means to communicate with anyone not within shouting distance, since most of their bulky Signal Corps Radios, or SCR-300 radios—thirty-two pounds with a five-mile range at best—had been damaged or lost, mostly in the Merderet swamp. Outside of his immediate area, Ridgway at his command post just west of Sainte-Mère-Église had little knowledge of where his men were, how they were organized, or what they were doing. It was only a command post in the most primitive sense.

Walking through the dark, shadowy maze of fields and hedgerows, any one of which might have been hiding German soldiers, most troopers fought back upon coming into contact with the enemy. Some were killed; some were taken prisoner. Hundreds of men injured in the drop—bad sprains if they were lucky, or broken or busted ankles, pelvises, hips, clavicles, ribs, shoulders, and wrists—were treated and either managed to accompany their comrades or were left behind in hedgerows, farmhouses, and barns, with or without friendly Normans watching over them. Until daylight, most of the French hunkered down in their basements or beds throughout the drop, unwilling to risk their lives to offer aid and assistance that might lead to their executions by the Boche. And who knew if those small groups of Allied invaders would succeed or be driven out to leave them with the vengeful Germans again?

There were curious encounters with the enemy. A few miles to the north of his drop zone, Lieutenant Jack Tallerday led a half dozen of his C Company/505th men toward the bridge at La Fière along a hedgerow, this one with thinner foliage than most. They heard a group of men approaching from the opposite direction on the other side of the hedgerow. Tallerday put up his hand to signal halt, then clicked his tin cricket. No return click. He snapped it a second time and thought he heard the sound of a cricket in response. Both groups resumed walking until only the thin five-yard-thick hedgerow separated them; through it, in the patchy moonlight, could be seen the distinct outlines of German helmets on the men opposite the Americans. Tallerday and his men, surprised and frightened, kept on walking. So did the enemy soldiers. Neither group spoke a word as they continued on their way.[21]

Between the darkness, the alien landscape, and nerves, sometimes the enemy took strange forms. Two 508th men from the regimental HQ company landed near each other and quickly linked up. In the darkness they began moving in the direction they hoped would lead them to friendly troops. Then a shadow loomed up ahead. They stopped, and one of them whispered, "I think I can make out the barrels of a double-mounted machine gun. Cover me and I'll crawl up closer and knock it out with a grenade." He dropped to his belly and quietly inched his way toward the gun emplacement, which soon was outlined against the night sky. When he was just a few feet away, he pulled the pin on his grenade, reared back with it, and raised himself to his knees for a better throwing position. That was when he saw the lower part of the gun mount and realized that he was about to attack an upside-down wheelbarrow.[22]

Another 508th trooper deployed outside a hamlet heard what he was sure was a German tank coming up the hill. He grabbed several land mines and ran out in the darkness and laid them across the road. As the tank approached, it turned out to be a milk cow with a large bell around her neck. She walked through the minefield without setting off a single one.[23]

Most of the men tried their best to make their way to their mission objectives, finding others and banding together in small groups. Alone in the dark, afraid for their lives, surrounded by the towering bocage and gunfire close or far away, ignorant of where they were or which direction they should move, overwhelmed or exhausted after landing, often drowsy from the Dramamine still flowing through their veins, and hyperaware of the imminent threat of death everywhere—some troopers facing all this burrowed into hedgerows or brush-covered ditches and went to sleep.

One trooper summed up the chaos and the seeming futility of the plans and preparation: "Instead of a regiment of over fifteen hundred men carefully assembled on a well-defined drop zone, D-Day was one man alone in an old swamp that the Air Corps said didn't exist."[24]

SEVEN

THE GOOD DROP

It seems that yesterday's map assignment has become the real thing.

OBERLEUTNANT MARTIN PÖPPEL, FALLSCHIRMJÄGER 6[1]

JIM GAVIN HAD been right. The small-arms fire he'd seen just before jumping did indeed involve the 505th and Sainte-Mère-Église.

The regiment's pathfinders had had the best drop—all three teams landed accurately at 1:21 a.m. in an area with little enemy opposition. All three Eurekas were activated, and two lit T's were set up.[2] The fields in the area, just north of the D15 road and west of the town, were called La Vallée de la Misère—the Valley of Misery—for a good reason. It was the first place Sainte-Mère-Église had been settled, just an abbey and a winding lane of thatch-roofed cobhouses. One day in the winter of 1346, during the Hundred Years' War, English troops fell upon the village, torturing and killing the inhabitants and slaughtering the friars in the abbey. The few survivors moved to the town's present site and rebuilt.[3]

Tony DeMayo, a twenty-five-year-old pathfinder with the 505th's Second Battalion, had felt sick to his stomach when he and the rest of his team were told on Sunday, June 4, that they'd be dropped into France that night. The weather had been miserable—cold, overcast, and rainy. At 8:45 p.m., just as they were preparing to leave their hangar, word came down: The invasion had been postponed for twenty-four hours. *Boy, what a relief,* thought DeMayo. *Twenty-four more hours to live.* He was pretty sure everyone else felt the same way.

DeMayo—a slim six-footer from Far Rockaway, New York, with a wide, ever-present smile and a sense of humor that made him the life of every party—had another reason to stay alive and return to England in one piece. A few weeks before, he'd gotten engaged to a dark-haired young woman from Loughborough, just three miles from the 505th's camp at Quorn. They planned to wed when he returned. DeMayo had slept well the night of June 4, and he felt good upon waking Monday morning. The weather was fine—perfect for a jump. Everyone prayed it would stay that way.

It did, and by 10:50 a.m., all nine of the 82nd pathfinder teams were aloft. Most of the men in DeMayo's plane were laughing and joking as if no one realized what was about to happen. It was only when the pilot turned off all their lights except the small blue ones on the wings and fuselage that things got quiet. By the time the antiaircraft fire started up and flak began hitting the plane, they were up, hooked up, and itching to get out. The green light next to the door went on, and out they went. It was 1:21 a.m.

In a few seconds DeMayo hit the ground in the middle of a field. As he got out of his harness, he saw some of the other boys doing the same, and felt better. It was quiet except for the rustling they made.

They were in the center field of three that made up their DZ. His team had been told to look for a barn and a haystack on one edge of the field. DeMayo stood up and looked around and was surprised to see a barn and a haystack. Their drop had been on the nose.

The men assembled quickly and set up their equipment and light; then they retreated into the shadows of the closest hedgerow. The security troopers set up a defense perimeter. The team waited near a hedgerow and the trees that lined it.

Someone said, "God help the glider boys with those trees."

Almost thirty minutes after their drop—it felt like thirty hours to DeMayo—they heard the low drone of far-off planes, many of them. DeMayo and the other light men ran out in the middle of the field, turned on their lights, and ran back to cover.

As the serials came closer, tracers of all colors lit up the sky and the sound of antiaircraft guns was deafening. Then about 1:51 a.m., the planes were overhead and men from the 2nd Battalion started to pour out. To DeMayo, it looked like a mushroom crop had suddenly bloomed. He could hear men on the way down talking to one another: "Is that you, Joe?" Then an equipment bundle crashed to the ground nearby and exploded with a tremendous roar.

"Now we're going to get it," said DeMayo.

But no Germans appeared, and soon hundreds of 505th troopers were moving through the dark fields toward the assembly area marked by a green light on a seven-foot-tall pole. The pathfinders stayed where they were. The first group of gliders, fifty-two of them, was scheduled to land a short distance away at 4:00 a.m., and the pathfinder team had to follow the same procedure for them but with orange lights.[4]

The two other 505th pathfinder teams had almost as easy a job. They had each landed about a half mile from the DZ and managed to set up some lights and Eurekas without enemy interference. Their battalions, the 1st and the 2nd, largely landed near their DZ. About a thousand of the regiment's 2,200 men dropped there, and many others landed close by.

Matt Ridgway had flown with the 505th's 2nd Battalion HQ company[5] in the regiment's third and final serial. The number-two man in his stick, he sat across the aisle from the open rear exit and looked past the jumpmaster lieutenant out the door. He remained silent during most of the two-hour flight. Most of the other men did too, though an occasional joke generated nervous laughter. When they passed the French coast, the bright moon high in the sky illuminated the farms and fields, the houses and the hedgerows, the paths and streams of the countryside below. Ridgway was struck by how peaceful it looked. Then they hit the dense cloud bank and the plane yawed and dropped, and there was nothing to see outside. A few minutes later, they broke through to smooth air and clear skies.

The men were standing now, their static lines hooked to the anchor cable above, and after someone shouted, "Are we downhearted?"—a line from a popular World War One song—and the other men roared, "No!" the green light came on and the jumpmaster poised in the doorway yelled, "Let's go!" and leaped out the door. Ridgway was right behind him.

The general made a soft landing in the middle of a grassy field. He grabbed his .45, spilled the air from his chute, and shucked his harness. In the process his pistol slipped from his hands, and as he knelt to look for it in the grass, he saw out of the corner of his eye something moving in the dark shadows. He said, "Flash."

There was no answer. On his knees, still groping for the .45, he recognized the shape of a cow. He breathed easier, not just because it wasn't an enemy soldier. The presence of a cow meant the field wasn't mined or staked with those ten-foot wooden stakes that had shown up on so many reconnaissance photos. Not even the constant gunfire and explosions everywhere around him and the rockets and tracers streaking through the sky above could dampen the exhilaration he felt at being part of a great adventure. His back hadn't gone out, he was uninjured, and he was on the ground with his men.

Ridgway found his .45 and made his way toward the closest hedgerow. There was another movement in the shadows. This one was a captain in his stick. As planes continued to fly over them, the two met up with men of the 505th's 2nd Battalion. Soon they found Lieutenant Colonel Benjamin Vandervoort, the battalion's commander.[6]

Vandervoort, twenty-seven, had been in charge of the 2nd Battalion since Italy, but had only been promoted in rank just before takeoff. Following in the footsteps of his father, who'd been an army colonel in World War One, Vandervoort had earned his commission in 1939 after graduation from college. He'd volunteered for the Airborne the next year and had been with the 505th since its creation. He'd been Gavin's right-hand man in Sicily at Biazza Ridge, but that was as a staff officer. Though Ridgway and Gavin believed in Vandervoort, some of his men didn't, suspecting him of putting personal gain ahead of their welfare. He'd trained them hard, and he was a strict disciplinarian, but many of the 2nd Battalion vets weren't convinced he was the right man to lead them in combat. Vandervoort knew this and was determined to show them he was.

He had been the jumpmaster in the lead plane of the 2nd Battalion—the very first of the 82nd Airborne's 369 planes. When he landed on a slight slope in a cow pasture and heard his left ankle snap, he knew it was broken. After crawling to the nearest hedgerow and injecting himself with a morphine syrette, he loaded a Very pistol and shot up green flares, the visual assembly signal for his battalion. It was about 2:15 a.m.[7]

While men from Vandervoort's battalion and other misdropped troopers assembled, Ridgway and Vandervoort conferred while Vandervoort's staff set up the division command post nearby under a tree in an apple orchard. A few hours later, they would move into a small abandoned farmhouse about a mile west of Sainte-Mère-Église and a hundred yards north of the D15, the road to the La Fière bridge. Though they appeared to be surrounded by the enemy and had no functioning radios, Ridgway was pleased. They had been dropped exactly where they'd been told they would.[8]

Third Battalion Commander Lieutenant Colonel Ed Krause and his stick were only five minutes behind the 2nd Battalion serial, which crossed the French coast in perfect order. He stood at the rear doorway, his hands on either side of it bracing him. He leaned out and looked back at the following planes. He said to his pilot on the interphone, "It looks like a good show if we can just hold her in." Moments later they ran into the cloud bank and Krause couldn't see another plane. Then a C-47 loomed out of the fog just thirty feet below them and he shouted at the pilot to take evasive action. They barely avoided hitting the other plane, and his hopes for a good drop seemed dashed. Though Krause's plane rocked and swayed and the troopers behind him struggled to stay on their feet, the formation somehow kept to its course, and after about five minutes, they emerged from the fog to see German fighter planes zooming past them. Flak exploded around them and tracers shot past. Some of the men in the stick were hit. Then, far below, Krause saw one of the 505th's green T's and was encouraged. He yelled, "Let's go!" and plunged out the door at about 2,000 feet. Four C-47s passed close beneath him as he floated down. Tracers from three different flak ground locations were streaming up toward him. He reached up to his risers and slipped the chute to descend more quickly.[9]

Private First Class Leslie Cruise was the ninth man out. His chute opened and he began a descent that seemed entirely too leisurely to him as tracers and rounds whistled by. There was the unmistakable sound of a German machine gun to his left—or was it to his right? He was turning under his chute and couldn't tell. He heard a huge explosion close by: an ammo bundle without a chute slamming into a field.

Then he hit the ground, just missing a twenty-foot hedgerow, and tumbled backward, hitting his head and jamming his helmet over his eyes.

His heart pounding, Cruise struggled to adjust his helmet and get out of his chute harness; then he assembled his M1 and slapped in an eight-round clip. He looked around. He was in a three-acre pasture, and troopers were landing in the field or crashing into the hedgerows around it, swearing as they did. Soon he could see them emerging from the shadows. They headed in his direction, and he remembered that he had been number nine, in the center of the plane, and they were rolling up the stick—the men in front of him and behind him moving toward the middle man. A trooper said, "Flash," and someone answered, "Thunder." Soon his platoon had assembled, along with men from the other 3rd Battalion companies. Some of them arrived carrying equipment from the parapacks and distributed it; Cruise grabbed two boxes of machine-gun ammo.

He could hear rifle and machine-gun fire in the distance but not in the vicinity. He moved closer to an opening at the end of a hedgerow and looked out onto a sunken dirt road. A group of officers, including Lieutenant Colonel Krause, was talking to a Frenchman who was waving his arms in several directions and appeared inebriated.

By this time several hundred men had gathered—most of 3rd Battalion's three companies along with some from other regiments and even a few with the 101st Division. Word was passed down that they would move southeast toward Sainte-Mère-Église, about a half mile away, and take the town. Led by the Frenchman, who had been walking home after a late night of calvados at a friend's house and who had told Krause that there was just a small company of Germans there, they moved out, with Cruise's H Company in the vanguard. There was a red glow in the sky—something was burning in the town. It was about 3:00 a.m., three hours before sunrise.

They moved quickly down the sunken lane. It was so dark that Cruise almost lost the man in front of him—he seemed to vanish, though he had only turned onto a cattle trail three feet lower than the lane and fresh with cow manure. It was almost like a tunnel through the brush hanging close over their heads, and the men stumbled along it, muttering softly. Then they were back on a road, and Sainte-Mère-Église lay close ahead, and they paused to reconnoiter. Everyone knew it wouldn't be long. Cannonball Krause had a flag to raise.[10]

Other members of the 3rd Battalion were making their way to Sainte-Mère-Église. But none of the men headed toward the village would be the first troopers to arrive there.

FACED WITH UNTOLD numbers of enemy paratroopers falling out of the sky, the German forces stationed inland from Utah Beach—the 91st Luftlande and Fallschirmjäger 6 farther south—reacted with what was to be an unforeseen advantage for the Allies: confusion.

AT MIDNIGHT (GERMAN time, one hour behind the Allies' British Double Summer Time) in a field south of Carentan, a town larger than Sainte-Mère-Église and nine miles below it on the Cotentin Peninsula, *Obergefreiter* (Corporal) Rudolf Thiel of the Fallschirmjäger 6 combat platoon relieved his bunker mate, Arthur Völker. Thiel hadn't been able to sleep, and even when he tried to read by the small tin-can candle of a Hindenburg light, he couldn't concentrate. They had drawn duty on the high lookout post. Bombings had been particularly severe the last few nights, but tonight was calm—too calm—and Thiel, like another veteran in their bunker, felt sure something was coming their way.

He dressed, checked his MP40 submachine gun, and crawled out of the bunker. He walked over to the observation perch and called up into the tree, "Arthur, come down! I can't sleep and will relieve you now!"

Völker climbed down. "Shitty wind, the damned cold, nothing particular to report," he said, and walked away.

Thiel climbed the ladder and tried to get comfortable. A few minutes later, he heard the distant drone of airplanes approaching—and there were a lot of them. With his binoculars he looked to the northwest and saw red flares and white lights. It was the invasion, he was sure.

He cranked the field telephone connected to the regimental HQ at a house in Gonfreville, eleven miles southwest of Carentan. A clerk answered.

"*Obergefreiter* Thiel reporting, combat platoon, red and white light signals sighted direction northwest, loud airplane noise, the enemy is attacking!"

He heard someone yell to get the major right away—von der Heydte had not left his regiment yet for the *kriegsspiel* in Rennes. Then the major was on the phone. "Combat platoon, report!"

Thiel repeated his message, then asked, "Should I sound the alarm?" He looked at his watch. It was 12:11 a.m.

"Sound the alarm," the major said.

Theil hung up and started yelling, "Alarm! Alarm!" and shot off two full magazines. He climbed down to find sleepy comrades approaching. Most of them didn't believe it was the invasion, but they took to their positions and foxholes and prepared to meet the enemy.[11]

IN A FARMHOUSE near Carentan, *Oberleutnant* (First Lieutenant) Martin Pöppel, in command of Fallschirmjäger 6's 12th Company, had set up his command post. Pöppel was only twenty-three, but he was a grizzled veteran despite his still soft face—he'd been with the Fallschirmjäger since 1938 and had jumped into Holland and Crete, fighting there and on the Russian front and in Sicily and Italy, earning an Iron Cross First Class along the way. As a younger soldier, he'd been as eager to fight as his Hitler Youth comrades, and he still lionized the Führer. But he had become weary of war and mostly just wanted to get his men home safely.

It was almost midnight and cool outside. Inside, Pöppel and his staff luxuriated in the warmth of a fire. He was about to retire when his aide, an older *feldwebel* (sergeant) named Behne, asked permission to open up another bottle of champagne to ease his nerves. Behne had been on edge all day, feeling that something big was going to happen. Pöppel told him to go ahead. They could hear bombings in the distance and planes passing overhead. The bombings had been going on for days.

Then a call reporting loud explosions about five miles away came in from Pöppel's observation post. He gave up trying to get some sleep and went outside with Behne, but they saw nothing besides the distant blasts on the northeast horizon. The phone rang again. It was von der Heydte calling from his Gonfreville HQ: Could the lieutenant make a more precise report? No, Pöppel told him, he couldn't. After he hung up, more aircraft could be heard even closer. Just in case, Pöppel ordered his company to be ready for action. More calls came in. They reported bombings throughout the area and massive enemy air formations, some of them very close and very low.

At 2:00 a.m., alarm signals started going off, and all through Fallschirmjäger 6's area, observation posts were calling in and reporting enemy paratroopers. Pöppel called regimental HQ, thinking, *It seems that yesterday's map exercise has become the real thing.* But so far, it was only individual parachutists.[12]

Von der Heydte had the alert order transmitted to all elements of his regiment. Soon reports came in of the first captured prisoners. They were Americans.

The major began telephoning adjacent regiments, and General Falley's 91st Luftlande Division HQ west of Sainte-Mère-Église, and the next organizational level up, the 84th Corps HQ in Saint-Lô, with no luck. Someone, either the Resistance or the paratroopers, was cutting the lines, and when linesmen were sent out for repairs, they were being attacked. Finally, using the private telephone of the woman who owned the house, von der Heydte was able to get through to 84th Corps HQ and talk to General Erich Marcks, who gave him his orders: find the enemy paratroopers and eliminate them.

Throughout a large swath of the lower-southeast Cotentin, the story was the same. Observation posts reported paratroopers dropping everywhere, it seemed, and patrols were sent out in search of them, sometimes in trucks and sometimes on foot. Some came back with prisoners—Americans with huge pockets stuffed with food, chocolate, cigarettes, and mines. They were captured in small numbers—singly or a few at a time, occasionally more. But the widespread sightings seemed to paralyze the command staffs. They didn't know where to send their troops. They rightly had expected the airborne landings farther inland with specific strategic points as objectives. But they didn't have the vehicles or the fuel to go chasing small groups of paratroopers all over the countryside, and many did little or nothing in response.

Staff officers continued to wait for more, and more accurate, information before issuing orders. "Single reports arrived in rapid succession, contradicting or confirming each other. Our staff could do nothing but wait," remembered one intelligence officer, Major Friedrich Hayn. "Wait until the confusing situation could become somewhat clearer; until the centers of attack of the paratroops" could be pinpointed.[13] Was this the beginning of a full-fledged invasion or merely a diversionary attack for a larger assault on some other part of the *Atlantikwall*? Or were these just scattered groups of enemy paratroopers dropped to support Resistance forces? There had been skirmishes at Montebourg and Valognes, and several prisoners, Americans, had been taken. If the port at Cherbourg was the objective, there would likely be more airborne drops. After all, seven or eight airborne divisions were said to have been massed in England.[14] No one knew for sure. And there had been many false alarms in the last few weeks—just a couple of nights ago, an American bomber had been shot down and its crew captured after they'd bailed out.

At 2:15 a.m. German time, a general at Seventh Army HQ in Le Mans called Rommel's HQ at La Roche-Guyon. The field marshal's chief of staff, Major General Hans Speidel, picked up. Speidel had hosted a party the night before for some other officers, and he had stayed up late drinking. The general told Speidel of the widespread enemy airborne sightings in Normandy. "These actions point to a major action," he said. Speidel, a career staff officer with no combat experience, disagreed. "They're still localized encounters," he replied, and hung up. He didn't bother to notify Rommel at his home in Herrlingen.[15] To complicate things further, almost every division and regimental commander in the region had left for the *kriegsspiel* in Rennes.

One commander, General Wilhelm Falley of the 91st Luftlande, had departed at 1:00 a.m. with two regimental commanders, but told his driver to turn around when he heard airplane motors and explosions behind him. He was on his way back to his HQ at the Château de Bernaville. In his and their absence, inexperienced staff officers were reluctant to make hasty decisions that they might regret later—or they were incapable of the boldness required to do so.

By 2:30 a.m., the situation had become a bit clearer. From maps taken from prisoners, it was evident that Sainte-Mère-Église was the focus of their operations. A short while later, about twenty miles north of Sainte-Mère-Église at the command post of the 1058th Regiment, an order was received from corps headquarters. Two battalions of the regiment, reinforced by the Sturm Battalion, were to immediately march south toward the village. They had one task: "annihilating the airborne enemy and pushing on to the east to throw the enemy who had landed on the east coast back into the sea." With a unit of self-propelled anti-tank guns attached, surely 2,500 Wehrmacht troops could do the job—the Allied paratroopers must be lacking in heavy artillery themselves.[16] Without means of transportation, it would take the Germans several hours to assemble their scattered forces and march down the N13 to the outskirts of Sainte-Mère-Église. But the battalion deployed in the hills north of Montebourg, just six miles of there, could surely be there by 6:00 a.m. German time at the latest.[17]

FARTHER NORTH AT his command post in a barn a mile west of Valognes and twelve miles up the N13 from Sainte-Mère-Église, *Hauptmann* Willi Hümmerich, commander of the 709th Infantry's anti-tank battalion, had a premonition. He was only twenty-six, slim, and bespectacled, but his age and looks were deceiving, for he had earned a Knight's Cross of the Iron Cross in Russia, where his unit had destroyed twenty-one tanks in thirty minutes. Now he commanded the 709th Infantry's anti-tank battalion: one company of nine 75mm tracked assault guns, one company of twelve carriage-mounted 57mm anti-tank guns, and one company of nine half-track-mounted 37mm antiaircraft guns. They had been training constantly since

March, when the battalion was organized. Hümmerich felt he could depend on them when the invasion came.

On the evening of June 5, after making a careful inspection of his three discretely deployed companies and returning confident in the readiness of his men, he'd driven into Valognes to dine at the 709th's officers' mess. There he'd heard that his commanding officer, General von Schlieben, had already left for a Seventh Army map exercise in Rennes. Other officers interpreted this as a sign that the invasion would not happen in the next twenty-four hours.

But Hümmerich felt nervous. Back at his CP, he telephoned his three companies and ordered them to make a test run of their engines. He was attending to a pile of paperwork when, at about 11:00 p.m., he heard the sound of enemy aircraft overhead. An hour later, his flak company near the coast called to report strong numbers of low-flying fighter-bombers—they'd downed one. Over the next hour his other two companies reported that they were capturing Allied paratroopers in their areas.

Around 3:00 a.m., he heard the rumble of aircraft again and stepped outside to see men jumping out of planes right over his head. They were followed by aircraft towing gliders, which were set free and soon made loud crashing sounds when they landed. While the paratroopers in the immediate area were still struggling out of their harnesses, they were surrounded and taken prisoner by the battalion staff. There were about twenty of them—heavily armed men with blackened faces and with knives and cartridge clips sticking out of their many pockets. When they were brought in front of Hümmerich, they refused to reveal anything but their names and serial numbers; he admired them for that. They were marched off to a central POW collecting point to join other paratroopers for interrogation.

Over the next few hours, Hümmerich could hear small-arms fire all around him. Mopping-up operations seemed to be in full swing, though reports coming in indicated that the Americans were putting up stiff resistance. About 6:00 a.m., an infantry regiment a mile from the coast called with an urgent request: They needed assistance fighting off American tanks just landed on the beach and making their way inland. Hümmerich quickly sent off six 75mm guns towed by half-track trucks. The company commander was away on a training course in Germany, so a young *leutnant*, Hermann Seidel, was put in charge.[18]

Seidel carefully avoided Montebourg on the N13 and took narrow tree-lined roads around it. As his column approached the small village of Saint-Floxel and came around a bend, enemy soldiers armed with bazookas and flamethrowers ambushed it from both sides. In a matter of minutes, Seidel's entire detachment was put out of action. Besides Seidel and the occupants of his car, only one other man survived—and he died shortly afterward from severe burns. But Seidel didn't have a radio transmitter with him, so Hümmerich wouldn't find out the details until later that day. The young lieutenant claimed the soldiers were American paratroopers.[19]

SOUTH OF CARENTAN, Colonel von der Heydte's eager young Fallschirmjäger 6 troopers were beginning to assemble. Their orders were much the same: March north and clear the Carentan area of enemy paratroopers, then attack those to the north at Sainte-Mère-Église and destroy them.[20] That key crossroads town was not to be taken by the enemy. An hour later, communication with Sainte-Mère-Église was cut off.[21] But the German counterattack was about to begin.

Just before dawn, von der Heydte's 2nd Battalion, including Eugen Griesser and his comrades in 5th Company, gathered on a road in their subsector. The two other battalions did the same. At the 1st Battalion assembly point, a company commander looked around at the young Fallschirmjäger surrounding him, each one wearing on his left breast his gold parachutist's badge, the diving eagle with a swastika in its claws, and the commander said to them, "Well, it's started. Now we are going to see who are men."[22]

EIGHT

OBJECTIVE: SAINTE-MÈRE-ÉGLISE

Oh Lord they're jumping us into hell.

PRIVATE KEN RUSSELL, 505TH PIR

IN SAINTE-MÈRE-ÉGLISE, ON the second floor of the Maury house on the Rue Cap de Laine, the family of five looked out the window at dozens of planes emptying their contents into the night. The small dots bloomed into parachutes of different colors, mostly green. Then they heard them falling outside on the cellar roof and in the neighbors' garden. Gunfire and rockets arced through the cloudy sky. The fire alarm bell began to sound.

Pierre Maury turned to his family. "Go down to the workshop," he said. "Hide under the workbench and wait. There's a fire and I'm going. Do not move from here!" Then he descended the stairs and walked out into the chilly darkness. His wife and three children did as he instructed and hid under the long oak bench fixed to the wall.

Maury hurried down the N13 and turned onto the Rue des Écoles, the east-west street that ran behind the church. Eight doors down on the left was the pharmacy owned by the mayor, Alexandre Renaud. Opposite it and farther down the street, in a recess of the church, he saw five paratroopers hiding. He knew they weren't Germans. Maury said nothing and continued on around the church into the square.

Across from the church, just beyond the southeast corner of the square and the row of chestnut trees bordering it, a large house was ablaze.

A FEW MINUTES after 10:00 p.m., Renaud and his wife, Simone, had just fallen asleep in their bedroom above his pharmacy when they heard a persistent banging at their front door. Earlier that evening, there had been a heavy bombardment several miles to the northeast, and the sky in that direction was lit up for a long time—probably, they suspected, an Allied air attack on the Germans' massive coastal battery at Saint-Marcouf. Every house shook, and mirrors and windows rattled and threatened to break.

Renaud had fought the Germans in the long and bloody Battle of Verdun, and he knew something was up. Over the last few weeks there had been many planes flying overhead and occasional bombings on the flak units dotting the Cotentin and on the Cherbourg-Paris railway line, with searchlights sweeping the night sky and antiaircraft shells exploding among the planes. But nothing this massive and persistent.

The knocking continued. Renaud went downstairs, walked through his pharmacist's shop, and opened the door. It was the chief of the volunteer fire brigade, a man named Mayer in his shiny brass helmet, and behind him Renaud could see an orange-red light silhouetting the trees across the street that lined the square. Mayer told him that the elegant two-story villa owned by Madame Julia Pommier, an elderly woman who took care of the village children, had caught on fire—maybe started by a stray incendiary from a plane. The firemen couldn't get it under control. Would the mayor ask the German *Kommandantur* to relax the nine p.m. curfew[1] so they could call the village's residents out to help?

Renaud went upstairs and dressed quickly, then put on his coat and hat. He brought his wife and three sons down to the living room behind the pharmacy, away from doors and windows—the safest place in the house in case of bombing, he thought—and hurried across the square to the large home of the town's veterinarian, Georges Monnier, where the garrison commander, *Oberfeldwebel* Werner Kassel, was billeted. The former Viennese music critic gave permission for the curfew to be lifted. Then the mayor walked to the presbytery next door and told white-haired Abbé Louis Rouland, who immediately had the sexton ring the church bell to summon the townspeople. Soon sixty or seventy had reached the square. Few of them were fully dressed, and some were in their nightclothes. They were organized into two lines and began passing canvas buckets of water from the cast-iron hand-operated pump in the cattle market area near the church to the firemen at the burning Pommier house.

Earlier that evening, just after eight o'clock, in his bedroom in his parents' house across the street from the southwest corner of the square, Raymond Paris had been lying on his bed, listening to the BBC broadcast on his crystal set. When he heard the words "the dice are on the table," he tore his earphones off, jumped up from his bed, and ran into his parents' bedroom.

"That's it! That's it!" he told them.

"What?" said his father.

"The landing!"

After much discussion—Where? When? How?—his parents went back to sleep. Raymond couldn't. He returned to his bedroom and lay on his bed fully clothed. At ten o'clock, the church bells chimed ten times. Their echoes had barely faded away when Paris heard through the open window someone outside calling his name.

"Raymond! Raymond!"

He ran to the window and looked down. Two of his friends stood there.

"Come quickly," one said. "There's a fire at Julia's house."

The trees lining the square hid the house 200 yards away, but the light from the fire glimmered in the darkness. Paris woke his father, a volunteer firefighter, who alerted other volunteers. Five of them hurried to the hangar where the firefighting equipment was stored on the Rue des Écoles opposite the church, and they wheeled out the brass hand-powered pump on its four-wheel wooden cart and began hauling it with hoses along the streets that led to the Pommier house.

Now, as the townspeople poured water into a metal tub mounted on the cart, four men, Raymond Paris and his father among them, worked the pump like a railroad handcar and supplied pressurized water to the two hoses manned by other firemen.

About thirty Germans from the flak supply unit who had been summoned by Kassel also turned out to watch over them. They stood around the square holding their Mausers and Schmeissers at their sides. A few of them hefted MG42 machine guns on their shoulders. The firemen did their best but the two hoses had little effect on the conflagration, and soon the strong wind carried embers twenty yards away from the burning house to a small barn, which also caught fire. From behind the church balustrade almost seventy feet above the square, two young *landsers* leaned back against the sloped slate roofing of the bell tower with their feet in the gutter and looked down on the spectacle below.[2]

A FEW HOURS earlier, between bouts of airsickness, Ken Russell—the private in the 505th's F Company/2nd Battalion who had slipped out of a British hospital to join his platoon just in time to leave for the airfield—looked around the dimly lit C-47 cabin at the other fourteen men in his stick. Most of them had blackened their faces. There was Sergeant John Ray—"Big Ray," they called the tall, good-looking twenty-year-old from Louisiana who had joined the Airborne after quitting school in his senior year at Gretna High School, where he'd starred in football. In May 1943 he had gone home on a furlough and married the girl next door—the next block, actually. They'd honeymooned for a week. Then he'd returned to the 505th, they'd shipped out, and he hadn't seen her since. There was also "Big Ass" John Steele, who wasn't called that for his height since he was only five foot nine. The old man of the stick at thirty-one, PFC Steele was the company barber and one of its biggest cutups. Standing at the rear door was another recently married man, Lieutenant Harold Cadish, the jumpmaster who had just joined the 505th a few days ago. He was a tough, powerfully built thirty-year-old from Massachusetts, the son of Jewish Lithuanians who had escaped anti-Semitism in the old country for a better life in America. Before the U.S. had entered the war, he'd tried unsuccessfully to enlist in the Canadian army to "join the fight and kill Nazis," he told his family, and he chose the Airborne because they'd be in the thick of things.[3] He'd married a young woman whose parents were also Lithuanian Jews. Near Russell was nineteen-year-old Charles Blankenship, a good buddy and a devout Christian whose father was a minister—early on, he'd arranged with regimental HQ to take his tithe out of his earnings and send it to his church. At the airfield, he'd tried to cheer up Russell by assuring him, "I'm going to raise the chickens to pick the grass off of your grave." He'd become engaged to a Belfast girl in the brief time the 505th had spent in Northern Ireland. Russell himself had written a letter while at the Cottesmore Airfield to his girl back home, Dorothy, whom he planned to marry. He told her to ignore anything she heard about him and Louise, an old girlfriend.

Ray, Steele, Blankenship, a new man from Texas named H. T. Bryant, and baby-faced PFC Ladislav Tlapa were members of the platoon's mortar squad. Early in the flight, somewhere over the Channel, Tlapa—whose parents were Czech immigrants and whom everyone called "Laddie"—said loudly over the roar of the engines, "Hey, guys, I made it!" When there was no response, he pointed to his wristwatch, which indicated it was just after midnight. He said, "I made it! I'm twenty-one years old. I'm legal to drink and vote." There were shouts of "Happy birthday," then the plane returned to silence.

Russell dozed until the antiaircraft fire coming up from the Channel Islands woke him.[4] Then Cadish gave the order to stand up and hook up, and a few minutes before 2:00 a.m., with flak exploding around them, the fifteen troopers jumped from their plane at about 1,500 feet, much higher than was ideal. They were not over a lit drop zone. Seconds later they looked down to see a town where no town should have been.

BELOW THE PLANE, the fire continued to blaze and the townspeople continued to pass the water buckets to the house and back. When a low drone began in the west and became louder, and a huge phalanx of planes appeared from that direction and flew just a few hundred feet over the town, everyone stopped what they were doing and looked up, half afraid that bombs might fall. Some of them ducked out of instinct.

Along with flak batteries across the peninsula unleashing artillery barrages on the armada as it came into range, the roar was deafening. There were white and black stripes on each plane's fuselage and wings, and some were so low that the people in the square could see figures standing in the open doors. Then men poured out and began floating down under green camouflage parachutes, almost horizontal in the gusty wind. The townspeople watched as the Germans began shooting up at them with machine guns, Schmeissers, and Mausers, the red, blue, and green machine-gun tracer rounds stitching the cloudy sky. A half dozen paratroopers in olive green uniforms with black faces dropped into the square or onto trees around it to cries of *"Parachutistes! Parachutistes!"* Raymond Paris stood near the pump shouting, *"Ça y est, c'est l'invasion!"* ("That's it, it's the invasion!") When one fell into a lime tree near the church, Paris and a few others helped him down and out of his harness, and he ran out of the square.

A parachutist fell on Maury in the bucket brigade. A nearby German lifted his rifle toward them. Paris ran over and tapped the soldier on the shoulder and said, *"Ne tirez pas—civils!"* ("Don't shoot—civilians!"). This distracted the *landser* just long enough for the paratrooper to run toward the church and around it. A few seconds later, when another landed in an ivy-covered lime tree near the church and hung there helplessly, a half dozen German soldiers shot at him, their Schmeissers almost cutting the man in half. Seconds later another got tangled in the chestnut trees lining the south side of the square and was also shot dead. One paratrooper fell directly into the Pommier house, his chute sucked into it by the raging heat. Sparks flew as he crashed into the burning roof and screamed once before succumbing to the flames. In the middle of the Rue Cap de Laine, a German shot a paratrooper who crumpled to the ground, dead.

Over the rumble of the airplanes above and the roar of the fire and the acrid smell of smoke, the bursts of automatic gunfire and the crack of Mausers, the screams of women and the shouts of men in German and French, the church bell continued to toll. Raymond Paris would always remember the scene as "Dante-esque."[5]

WHEN RUSSELL SAW the house on fire below, his first thought was *Oh Lord they're jumping us into hell.* Their drop zone was about a mile west, not right over the village. Floating down seemed to take forever. Below him he could see what appeared to be a town square, with a large church on the north side and a lot of people running around. Some of them were German soldiers firing their rifles up at him and the others. He felt like an open target in the light from the burning house. He tried to scrunch down behind his reserve chute above his stomach. A round hit the back of his left hand, slicing between his knuckles, and he could feel others hitting his chute. He could hear the church bell ringing.

He looked to his right and saw a trooper not too far away. He turned to the left and saw another one, then heard an explosion and snapped his head back to the right to see an empty chute. The trooper was blown away, most likely from his Gammon grenade taking a hit and exploding. He watched as Cadish, Bryant, and Tlapa all came down onto utility poles along the street and were shot to death, left hanging by their risers. As Russell neared the ground, the heat from the fire began to draw his chute toward it. He pulled on his risers with everything he had and heard a scream and looked down to see a trooper land in the fire—a recent replacement named van Holsbeck, he thought.

Then he hit the slate roof of the church's transept, slid across it, and fell over the edge. Some of his risers caught on something above him and jerked him to a stop. He found himself hanging against the side of the church in the shadow of its south transept, his bootheels almost twenty feet above the ground. He looked up to see another man's chute snag on one of the bell tower's corner gargoyles. The trooper went limp—*Probably dead,* thought Russell.

He looked down just in time to see another trooper drop into the square near the church. It was Sergeant John Ray, and before he could get out of his harness, a German without a helmet—Russell thought he was a redhead, but it could have been blond hair reflecting the firelight—ran from the left side of the church and shot Ray twice in the torso. The German turned and looked up toward Russell and the other trooper hanging above him. He raised his rifle toward them, but Ray managed to pull out a .45 pistol, shot the German in the head, and collapsed.

The church bell continued to ring. Russell grabbed his trench knife from his right boot scabbard and cut his suspension lines and fell to the ground. Still in the shadows, he looked up at the trooper hanging from the bell tower. He was missing his helmet, but with his face blackened, Russell couldn't tell who it was. There was still no movement or sound from him. Russell stood up and sliced himself from his harness, then shed most of the hundred pounds of equipment he was carrying, except for his M1 and ammo. As he finished assembling his rifle, Germans began firing at him from across the square. Russell turned and ran in the opposite direction, around the church's front entrance and down the street and then into a grove of trees. He made his way away from the center of town and across a field. He heard a noise ahead and dropped to the ground and started crawling toward it. He got close and snapped his cricket. He heard two snaps in return and felt a tremendous sense of relief—he wasn't alone.[6]

Ernest Blanchard had jumped right after him, and floating down he too heard the trooper explode—except Blanchard actually saw the man as he was blown into bits. Then Blanchard fell hard into one of the trees lining the square. He could hear Germans machine-gunning his comrades, and they were getting closer to him. Blanchard grabbed his knife and got to work on his harness. His heart pounding, he sawed through the straps and then fell from the tree and ran into the shadows. It was not until later that he would realize he'd sliced off the top of his thumb.[7]

KNEELING BEHIND THE three-foot-high stone balustrade on the south side of the gabled bell tower, *Obergefreiter* (Corporal) Rudolf May watched the chaotic scene in the square. May was twenty-two and looked even younger, but he had spent eighteen grueling months on the Eastern Front, and only a serious injury in July 1943 had delivered him from that freezing hell. His watch partner, nineteen-year-old *Grenadier* (Private) Heinz Strangfeld, had come over from his station on the other side to join May.

About forty-five minutes before the house had caught on fire, their squad leader, *Unteroffizier* (Sergeant) Rudi Escher, had taken four men and gone in search of eight or ten of the American parachutists who had been seen dropping on the eastern edge of the village; several others had landed in the park south of the square and been killed.[8] Since then, May had descended from the bell tower to talk to his NCO, who told him to get back in the church and climb back up and continue his observation, and use the telephone in the tower to call regimental HQ to find out what to do. But the telephone had been disconnected—probably cut by the Resistance or paratroopers—and now May and his inexperienced comrade were beginning to worry. Many of the flak supply unit's trucks had already left for their regimental command post in a wood near Fauville, a half mile south.

In the tower behind them, the bell still clanged, and planes continued to fly over the village. Then the light from the burning house across the square was momentarily blocked out. May realized that a camouflage green parachute had snagged on the pinnace to his right and dropped over the balustrade . . . and an enemy soldier was hanging just below it, his back against the gray brick wall.

The trooper was Private John Steele. He'd lost his helmet as soon as he had hit the prop blast and his chute opened. Then a flak shell fragment smacked into his left ankle—"like the bite of a sharp knife," he recalled later—and after he fought wildly to avoid being sucked down into the burning house, he slammed into the church bell tower and seconds later found himself dangling above the square, his chute caught on something above. As Germans, French civilians, and fellow paratroopers ran around below in the orange light of the fire, he tried to reach his knife in his boot but fumbled it away and watched it drop to the cobblestones below. With a throbbing, bloody ankle, he decided to play dead and tried to remain as motionless and quiet as he could, hanging twenty-five feet above the south transept's steep slate roof and sixty feet above the ground.

To Rudolf May, the soldier appeared to be dead. A while later May heard him make a noise. Next to May, Strangfeld raised his Karabiner and suggested they shoot him.

"Are you crazy?" May said. "If you shoot, everyone among them will know we are here, and we'll never get out of this place alive." It was becoming increasingly clear that a large number of enemy paratroopers were in the area and would soon take the town.

Below them the soldiers of the flak supply unit ordered the Frenchmen in the square to return to their homes, then began loading their trucks and leaving down the N13. May and Strangfeld crouched behind the balustrade and stayed as still and quiet as possible.

BACK AT 10 Rue Cap de Laine, Maury's wife and their three daughters stayed huddled under the workbench. The noises they heard were scattered and faint, but then there was a startling round of machine-gun fire, and another one, and another. They could hear men walking carefully outside, breathing heavily as they stopped to reload their guns. Then someone kicked in the shop's front door. A large man dressed in green walked in and saw them under the workbench. He took off his helmet, which was covered in a net with leaves and twigs stuck in it, and wiped his face.

He turned to leave. A German stood in the doorway. As the Maury family watched, the two men attacked each other with their bayonetted rifles, the only sounds their ragged breathing and frenzied struggle. The German won. He dragged the dead soldier to the doorway and dropped him there, then left.

The family, terrified, didn't move from their hiding place until Maury returned to tell them that the paratroopers were Americans. And that an American officer had asked to see him and told him, "Thank you, Mr. Maury, for all that you've done. We'll meet again." Then the officer had left.

Sporadic gunfire continued outside. Maury joined his family under the workbench. They remained there until dawn.

AS ALEXANDRE RENAUD hurried across the square to his house, a German pointed to a dead soldier still harnessed to his green camo parachute and said to Renaud, "Tommy parachutists, all *kaput*!" Renaud knew better. When he got home, the mayor said to his family, "It's too many! It's not commandos. It's the liberation!" They listened as German trucks and motorcycles roared down the N13. Then he took his family out back to their garden to a covered ditch he had dug away from the house to prepare for the artillery bombardment that was bound to come. He knew that all through the village, his people would be doing the same—leaving their houses for makeshift air-raid shelters in their gardens or out in the fields, or hiding in the safest parts of their basements.[9]

IN A FIELD east of town, Rudi Escher and his patrol were still looking for the American paratroopers who had dropped earlier, when a wave of planes passed overhead and men began falling out of them. Moments later one landed right in front of the Germans. Before Escher could tell his men to try to take him alive, they shot the soldier dead. Other parachutes were descending in the area. Escher told his men to double-time it back to the church. They reached it to find a house and a nearby barn afire and illuminating the area and American parachutists lying dead on the N13 and in the square and hanging from trees, utility poles, and even the church. Another 1058th observation squad of seven soldiers had arrived on their bicycles from their camp at the railway level crossing near the Merderet. The flak supply company was still in town, though most of its soldiers had left with all but a few of the trucks. Escher yelled up at May and Strangfeld to come down. They untangled the lines of the parachute below them and slowly lowered the paratrooper to the ground. Both men knew some English, and they talked to the paratrooper as they did. He was loaded into a truck heading south on the N13 toward Fauville.[10]

The fifteen *landsers* assembled outside the church in the relative quiet—the church bell had finally stopped ringing, and the members of the flak unit who hadn't left town had returned to their billets and beds. The disconnected telephone line was worrisome, and they could hear scattered gunfire on the outskirts of the village. As Escher and the other noncoms debated what to do, the men rifled through the pockets of the dead paratroopers for cigarettes, chocolates, rations, and other treasures and divided them up. One of the Americans was near the front door of the church, not far from a flak soldier with a bullet hole in his head. The American, apparently dead, was covered with blood. He was still barely alive, though the Germans didn't know it. It was almost 3:00 a.m. German time.

A shot echoed through the square and a nineteen-year-old grenadier named Alfons Jakl fell to the ground near Escher, shot through the chest, dead. The rest of the Germans scattered and took cover, their Mausers at the ready. Resistance? An American parachutist? A stray bullet from the flak unit? There were no more shots, but that was the deciding factor—it was time to leave. The burning house and barn had been largely consumed, and the smoke-diffused light from the fire was dim and the shadows dark. Escher led the men across the N13 and down the sidewalk. In the road lay a dead paratrooper, his body crushed by one of the trucks. They passed American soldiers huddled in the shop doorways, but neither Germans nor Americans were inclined to open fire. When the fourteen *landsers* reached the wooden shed, Escher's men pulled out their bicycles, and in single file, they all cycled down the N13 toward Fauville.[11]

WHILE KRAUSE'S 180 troopers were following the Frenchman down a winding path through the dark night, other men of the 3rd Battalion were making their way toward the village.

Bazookaman Bill Dunfee, a former truck driver from Ohio who had dropped out of school after the ninth grade to help his family, was a twenty-one-year-old sergeant with I Company and a veteran of Sicily and Salerno. He jumped out of his own plane moments after Krause did and looked down to see a similar sight: C-47s flying below him. He started swearing at them—he didn't want to be turned into hamburger by his own air forces. Then he looked around and saw his buddy and ammo bearer, Jim Beavers, close to him and their equipment bundle descending off to one side. He breathed a sigh of relief once the planes below him disappeared into the east. He yelled over to Beavers that he'd meet him at the bundle.

Dunfee and the bundle dropped on one side of a hedgerow, Beavers on the other. Beavers found his way up and through the embankment and helped Dunfee unroll the bundle and pull out their bazooka and ammo. They loaded up and headed toward Sainte-Mère-Église; that was where most of the firing was coming from, so it was easy to locate. It was also their regiment's objective. On the way they saw two gliders come down—one in an orchard, the other on the porch roof of a farmhouse. On the northwest outskirts of town, they ran into Krause's group and joined them.[12]

At the HQ of the 91st Luftlande, in the château outside Bernaville, there was still no concerted action, much less a counterattack. Standing Wehrmacht doctrine called for one, but where? The reports coming in from battalion, company, and smaller unit commanders indicated American airborne troops dropping over a large swath of the southwest Cotentin Peninsula. Other connections were lost, clearly due to lines being cut, though whether by the paratroopers or the Resistance, no one knew—since the Occupation had begun four years ago, there had been few acts of sabotage in the area. That didn't matter now. The result was paralysis and indecision. And without orders from above, most subordinates out in the field decided to remain in their positions rather than do the wrong thing. Initiative took a back seat to caution. Staff officers were operating without their commander. Where was General Falley? He had left with his adjutant just a few hours ago.

At 3:30 a.m., just a few hundred yards away, a short thirty-three-year-old American lieutenant named Malcolm Brannen, commander of the 3rd Battalion/508th's HQ company, stood in the doorway of a large stone building, talking to its owner. The house was on a one-lane dirt road lined with tall trees that made the dark night even darker. With Brannen were thirteen other troopers surrounding the house. The windows upstairs were filled with wide-eyed children looking down at the Americans, while adults looked out of the ground-floor windows. Using his map and French phrase book, Brannen, his cheeks blackened, had just found out that he and his men had landed near the HQ of the 91st Luftlande, just down the road—the stately Château de Bernaville, named after a tiny hamlet nearby that was just north of a village called Picauville. Now that they knew where they were, they could start moving in the right direction—west, toward a larger village called Étienville, the 3rd Battalion's objective.

They heard a vehicle approaching from the west, and lights flashed down the road as a large, open automobile—a Duesenberg or Mercedes Phaeton, thought Brannen—rounded a curve. He said, "Here comes a car—stop it!"

The troopers near the house moved toward the road, and the Frenchman ducked back into the house and slammed the door. The heads in the windows disappeared. Brannen ran toward the side of the road and put up his hand and shouted, "Stop!"

The car accelerated, and as it passed Brannen, he ran to the other side of the road. His men, some of them behind him, opened fire on the open car. Brannen fell to the ground and watched as bullets shattered the windshield and the driver hunkered down and the car swerved and crashed into the stone wall of the side of the house at an angle, and the driver was thrown from the car.

Brannen jumped up and climbed up the side of the six-foot earthen hedgerow next to the road and watched as the driver staggered toward a cellar window. Brannen fired his .45 at him, grazing his right shoulder. The German stopped moving and sat down next to the house.

The officer in the front passenger seat was slumped on the floor with his head and shoulders hanging out the open door. He was dead. An officer in the back seat had been thrown into the road five yards from Brannen. He started to crawl toward his Luger several feet away. As he neared it, he said in German and in English, "Don't kill! Don't kill!" Standing on the dirt above him, Brannen hesitated—*I'm not a cold-blooded killer,* he thought—but when the man's hand touched his pistol, he pulled the trigger, and the bullet hit the German in the forehead and knocked him on his back as blood spurted into the air and then subsided.

They took the driver, a corporal, prisoner. In the car was another officer slumped in the back seat, dead. From his uniform and insignia they knew he was a general. Brannen picked up his hat and looked inside it. There was a name printed there—Falley. After examining the contents of two briefcases in the car, they realized whom they had just killed: the commander of the 91st Luftlande Division and a major on his staff.[13]

A FEW MINUTES after 4:00 a.m., fifty-two C-47s began releasing their Waco gliders over the 505th's drop zone, "O," at about 500 feet. It was still dark. They carried a total of sixteen 57mm anti-tank guns, twenty-two jeeps, and several tons of ammo, all desperately needed by the lightly armed 82nd troopers. Gavin knew the Germans would send tanks against them soon, and without artillery, they'd be helpless. The gliders also bore 220 infantrymen and artillerymen whose jobs would be to unload their planes and get the artillery to where it was needed.

The serial, following the same route as the paratroopers had, approached the DZ from the west. The C-47 towplane pilot would look for the 505th's Holophane lights—not every pilot saw them—and then it would be up to him to decide when to break free. Once he reached up over his head and pulled down the large lever that released the 300-foot nylon towrope and cut his plane loose, the C-47 would bank and begin climbing as it flew back east toward the Channel, and the glider pilot would circle, looking for a good place to land in the darkness below; the only sounds would be the air rushing around the canvas sides, the flak explosions and machine-gun fire outside, and the loud pop when a German bullet punched through the canvas.

The cloud cover and flak and machine-gun fire scattered the serial just as it had the paratroops earlier. After releasing from their towplanes at 400 or 500 feet, the glider pilots could circle only one or two times before they had to pick out spots and aim for them, and finding the lit DZ was a lot harder when the fields were small and ground fire was coming up at them. About twenty gliders managed to land on the DZ, and almost all were destroyed—most of those were the flimsy British Horsas, almost completely plywood and not very maneuverable in the air. The rest set down, or crashed, somewhere else. A skilled glider pilot could hit the ground and stop within 200 feet, but the high, dew-covered grass failed to provide the friction needed to do so.[14] The result should have been predictable. A few that found longer fields in the darkness slid into safe landings on their two wheels and skids, but most smashed into obstacles—trees, farm buildings, swamps, the ditches the Germans had dug or the poles they'd implanted, or the high, solid hedgerows bordering every field.

Tony DeMayo was still at the 505th DZ with his fellow pathfinders and watched as the gliders came down: "There was just one crash after another as they hit the hedgerows. It was just like crumbling wooden matchboxes in your hand." Men in the fragile planes were crushed by loose jeeps, anti-tank guns, and other objects hurtling toward them. The pathfinders spent a long time pulling injured men from the wrecked planes. Like many other paratroopers who witnessed the landings, DeMayo felt his respect for the glider infantrymen increase dramatically.[15]

Two gliders came down in Sainte-Mère-Église itself—one into a building on the western edge of town, the other just twenty yards away. Another came in too low on its approach and hit some trees that tore off the right wing and flipped the glider, which hit the ground upside down. Somehow everyone in it survived—seat belts helped—with no injuries except a sore knee and a couple of scratches despite the heavy anti-tank gun it was carrying, which had been well secured with chains; most were tied down with ropes.[16] Another glider ran into a herd of cattle.[17] Broken artillery, jeeps, trailers, ammunition, and supply bundles lay strewn about the countryside. No more than a dozen avoided significant damage. Half the jeeps and eight of the anti-tank guns were unsalvageable. But if some of the anti-tank guns could be found, extricated, and dragged to where they were needed, they would be of tremendous help, whether they were hauled by jeeps or men. Somehow there were only twenty-six serious casualties—three dead and twenty-three wounded.[18]

One glider pilot laid his Waco down gently in a 600-foot-long field and coasted to a stop just short of the high embankment at its far end. After unloading, he and his copilot decided to remain near the glider till daylight. A couple of hours later at dawn, they started walking down a road. The two got separated when a Messerschmitt strafed the road and the pilot dived behind a stone wall and remained there, shaking, for a half hour. When he got up and started moving, some Germans threw grenades at him. He ran and hid farther down the wall, and when he heard some paratroopers talking on the other side, he found an opening and walked through it to them. There were twenty 505th men. He asked if he could stick with them, and they took him along. Their confidence reassured him, and he felt safe with them. "They were veterans of North Africa," he remembered, "and didn't seem scared or worried about anything."[19]

Flight Officer Cyrus Carson, a skinny twenty-two-year-old from North Carolina, hadn't finished high school, but he was piloting one of the Wacos that morning. When the C-47 towing his glider hit the fogbank and then banked hard to the left, the towrope snapped, cutting his glider loose. Carson swung right to avoid being hit by the C-47 behind him, and he began losing altitude. When he came out of the fog, he was fifty feet above the ground. He had only a few seconds to decide where to land. The nearest field was too small, and to slow down, Carson decided to hit a tree with his right wing just as he landed. Somehow there were no injuries, and the five men inside the Waco ran to a hedgerow. A few hours later a truckful of German soldiers arrived, and the Americans divided into two groups and left. Carson soon found out that he was twenty miles north of the DZ. After five days of evading the Germans with and without other lost and misdropped American soldiers, Carson and another soldier were captured by the Wehrmacht. The next day the two men were left in an abandoned house with a German sergeant and two grenadiers. In the afternoon, while the sergeant watched over them in the house, they looked out a window to see the grenadiers digging two holes in the yard. The other

American took out a photo of his wife and two young daughters and showed it to the sergeant, who took out a photo of his own wife and children of similar ages.

When the grenadiers came in, the sergeant told them to leave—he'd do the dirty work. After they left, he brought the two Americans up to the straw-filled loft. He dug out two holes in the straw for them to hide in, left them a bottle of wine, then shook hands with them and left. A few minutes later they heard two shots. After several more weeks of hiding in different places, the two men would reach American lines and safety.[20]

IN A FIELD near Sainte-Mère-Église, G Company/505th Platoon Sergeant Ron Snyder, just twenty years old but a three-year veteran, had landed and set to work rolling up his stick. With bewildered cows roaming around and troopers clicking, whistling, and yelling, and several other mixed-up companies doing the same, it appeared it would take some time. His lieutenant told him to take a few of his men and do some reconnaissance of a group of Quonset hut–like buildings on the west edge of town and clear them of enemy soldiers. Snyder took two riflemen with him. They walked off and came to a fence, and as they crawled under it to reach a road, they froze when they heard a large number of troops marching rapidly. They sounded like they had German hobnail boots. The three troopers stayed hidden in the shadows and held their fire.

After they reached the buildings and found no Germans there, they picked up a half dozen straggling troopers. C-47s roared over their heads, and machine-gun fire from somewhere in town streaked through the sky. They watched as tracers reached the fuselages of some of the planes.

Snyder decided to go into town and silence the antiaircraft fire. He led his makeshift squad past the darkened houses along the Rue Chef du Pont, the road that ran west to the village of the same name. It was still dark, but just ahead, they could see German vehicles heading south through the intersection with the N13, a block away. One truck screeched to a stop to let soldiers in the back shoot down the street at them. The troopers flattened themselves into doorways to escape being hit. Snyder ordered his men to withdraw. He left two riflemen to keep firing on the truck to keep it occupied while he and the other six men ran south down a narrow street and turned east at the first corner. As they ran toward the N13 up ahead, more German trucks roared by, some with headlights on, some without.

When they came to the N13, they found themselves across from the northwest corner of the town square. By the light of a burning house beyond it, they could see German soldiers loading several trucks. Snyder and his men opened fire on them until they too drove south out of town.[21]

Several hundred yards to the northwest, the now fairly sober Frenchman, wearing a white coat and carrying an American mine forced on him, led Krause's two half-strength companies into the outskirts of Sainte-Mère-Église. In the half hour they had spent following their guide, mostly down sunken paths along hedgerows, there had been no sign of the enemy—yet. Heavy clouds hid the moon, now dropping toward the east and the coast, where a faint light presaged the dawn.

When they reached the N13, Krause sent detachments north, south, and other directions to set up roadblocks at the six main roads entering town. Then he led the rest of his men quietly down the street, sticking to the buildings on each side. Krause had told them to use only knives, bayonets, and grenades—no guns—so that enemy small-arms fire could be spotted by sight and sound.[22] They didn't search the houses—Krause wanted to get the town encircled and roadblocks established before daylight. The landings were scheduled for 6:30 a.m., a half hour after sunrise, and who knew when the Germans would become aware of the seaborne forces and order reinforcements into Sainte-Mère-Église and the beach area? There was no time to lose.

"There is only one German company in the town," the Frenchman had said. "Service troops, company headquarters, motor park and supply dumps. One infantry battalion was quartered here until a week ago. Now it is camped on high ground south of town."[23]

Krause's luck was continuing to hold.

Then they heard rifle and machine-gun fire emanating from the south end of the village—the last of the Germans escaping the steady fire from Snyder's squad. With them they took John Steele.

When Krause reached the church square, his men and he found a sobering—and infuriating—sight. A half dozen of their comrades hung lifeless from the trees and power lines around it, and a few others lay dead on the ground, one of them charred and still steaming near the smoldering ruins of a house at the southeast corner. But they would have to wait. Krause walked into the building across the N13 that housed the Germans' main communications cable to points north—Valognes, Montebourg, and Cherbourg at the tip of the peninsula. He cut the cable himself.

As more men reached town, he sent bazooka teams and reinforcements out to the roadblocks. He had his men roust the last of the German soldiers billeted in the village. Most were in houses on and near the square, including several in the presbytery and more in a large home next to it; they had either slept through the din or returned to their beds unconvinced that this truly was the invasion they had been preparing for. They rounded up thirty German prisoners—including their commander, a sergeant named Kassel, who had surrendered to a 505th trooper earlier in the garden behind the Monnier house, then donned his dress uniform.[24] They also killed eleven more who resisted. Near the church, they found one trooper still alive, Sergeant John Ray, and transported him to the aid station set up in a large building on the N13 north of the square.[25]

Krause walked back up the street to the Hôtel de Ville—the city hall. He had a trooper walk in and up to the second floor, open a window, and pull in the large red-and-black German swastika from the flagpole hanging over the entrance. The trooper then hoisted the Stars and Stripes Krause had carried in his musette bag.

Then Krause sent a runner just west of town to find the regimental CP, Colonel Ekman, to tell him Krause was in the village. A short while later, he sent another message: "I have secured Sainte Mere Eglise."

On the eastern horizon, dawn's first light could be seen. The time was 5:00 a.m., ninety minutes before the Fourth Division was to land on Utah Beach, six miles distant. Krause knew that there were large Wehrmacht units a short distance south of town and somewhere to the north—and even more on the west side of the Merderet. Whatever happened on Utah, they had to hold the town from the counterattack that was sure to come.

Ninety minutes later and 120 miles to the north across the English Channel, the phone rang in the tent of General Eisenhower's aide, Captain Harry Butcher. It was an ebullient Leigh-Mallory, who wanted to speak to the general. Butcher told him Eisenhower wasn't awake; could he take a message? The air marshal had good news. Of the 860 C-47s carrying the two airborne divisions, only twenty-one were missing and only four gliders unaccounted for. The ratio was similar on the British side. Nowhere near the slaughter of American paratroopers Leigh-Mallory had predicted. "Grand," Butcher told him, and hung up to go tell his boss. When he reached the trailer that served as Eisenhower's sleeping quarters, Butcher found him awake and reading a western. The general greeted him with a smile and lit a cigarette. Admiral Bertram Ramsay had just called to inform him of the good news. The airborne divisions had been successfully dropped into the Cotentin countryside. But what had happened to them after that, no one knew.[26]

At the Paris headquarters of OB West, Gerd von Rundstedt was awakened at 1:30 a.m. German time with news of the widely scattered airborne drops. His first thought was they were feint attacks for an invasion elsewhere; after all, seaborne landings had not occurred. But as reports of paratroopers in Normandy piled up, it became clear that they were a prelude to a larger invasion—paratroopers alone, no matter how many, made no sense, since their lack of heavy weapons and support would doom them. A short while later he was convinced. He left the 21st Panzer alone but ordered parts of his other two panzer divisions to reconnoiter in force toward Lisieux, thirty miles east of Caen, to investigate airborne landings there. Those "paratroopers" were actually half-sized dummies dropped to confuse the Germans, and they did. That order was soon canceled by OKW, the German High Command, who admonished OB West for arbitrarily taking charge of the formations. At 4:15 a.m., when it became clear that a full-scale invasion was imminent, von Rundstedt called the OKW to secure permission to move the two panzer divisions toward Normandy. He was told by General Alfred Jodl, chief of staff at OKW, that only Hitler could make that decision, and the Führer, who habitually stayed up late, had gone to bed just two hours ago at his Berchtesgaden mountain retreat three miles away; Jodl would not awaken him unless von Rundstedt explicitly asked him to, which only a *feldmarschall* could do. Besides, Jodl and the OKW were still skeptical—this could be part of the Allies' deception plan. The old Prussian, furious at such ridiculousness, hung up.

A few minutes before 6:00 a.m.—a half hour after the Allied seaborne forces began landing on the east coast of the Cotentin Peninsula—von Rundstedt's chief of staff, Major General Günther Blumentritt, called OKW again. This was it, he insisted—the real invasion. The panzer divisions must be brought up with all due speed to the coast to expel the Allied landings. General Walter Warlimont, the staff officer who took the call, relayed the message to Jodl, who remained unconvinced.

"Are you so sure of this?" he said to Warlimont. "I am not sure that this is *the* invasion. According to all the reports I have received, this could be part of the Allies' deception plan. In my opinion it is necessary to wait for more information."[27]

Warlimont was shocked. Yes, the panzer reserves were under the Führer's direct authority, but he'd understood, like von Rundstedt, that in case of enemy attack the panzers would be released immediately, whether the attack was diversionary or not. But he did not argue with Jodl and called Blumentritt back and told him of Jodl's decision.

Officers at OB West continued to call OKW and plead for the release of the panzers—all to no effect. Hitler awoke late, had lunch while hearing the news, and only released the two panzer divisions at 2:00 p.m.—far too late to reach the beaches and make any difference. As he stood in front of the maps, he chuckled and acted as if this was the opportunity he had long awaited, and said, "So, we're off."[28]

Twenty minutes later, Seventh Army HQ in Le Mans, 150 miles

south of Sainte-Mère-Église, sent a summary of the situation to Rommel's Army Group B:

> . . . There is no immediate danger at this time, since the forces on the east coast of the Cotentin Peninsula have not linked up, which is necessary to cut off Normandy. The Cotentin Peninsula is supposed to be cleared [of enemy paratroopers] by the troops already allotted to its defense. . . . There is a possibility of an advance action to sap our strength.

The situation, it appeared, was well in hand—at least to Seventh Army HQ—though no one was sure that this was *the* invasion and not a feint. Just to be overly cautious, Seventh Army ordered elements of two infantry divisions protecting the Brittany shoreline to move by train the next day to the battle areas near the Cotentin's east coast.[29]

THE ONLY PANZER division in Normandy, the 21st—the unit that had been directed by Rommel to practice a swift counterattack with its 127 Mark IV panzers and forty assault guns—was commanded by Lieutenant General Edgar Feuchtinger, a favorite of Hitler's who had neither armor nor combat experience. Like many other Normandy-based commanders, he was absent from his post, having decided to visit his mistress in Paris and spend the night there. He and other Wehrmacht officers first heard of the Allied airborne drops a little after midnight, and they waited hours for orders from Rommel's headquarters at La Roche-Guyon. Finally, at 6:30 a.m., he decided to take action. He ordered his armored division to attack British airborne and glider troops east of the Orne River—and east of the assault beaches. Thirteen panzers were lost in the operation. At 10:35 a.m., Feuchtinger received new orders to redirect two-thirds of the division westward toward the landing sites on the other side of the Orne. But circumstances—narrow and sometimes blocked roads, detours, rubble-strewn streets in Caen, bombardment by Allied naval artillery and fighter-bombers—delayed any semblance of a swift advance. By 4:20 p.m., when elements of the 21st finally reached a point six miles from the coast, the British were ready for them. Anti-tank guns and Sherman Fireflies—specially equipped with a powerful seventeen-pound anti-tank cannon—knocked out thirteen panzers in as many minutes. A few tanks pushed through and reached the coast at 7:00 p.m., the only armored units to do so. But they too ran into formidable resistance, and soon what was left of the division, which had lost 25 percent of its tanks, pulled back in disarray and retreated to its original position.[30]

Rommel, if he had been present at his headquarters, would doubtless have handled the panzer divisions differently, even without authority to move them. He would almost surely have insisted on speaking to Hitler and likely persuaded him to release the panzers early that morning in time to reach the Allies' beachheads that day. But Rommel was not at his château in La Roche-Guyon.

Four hundred forty miles west of Paris, a phone rang at 7:20 a.m. in the foyer of the Rommel villa in Herrlingen. The *feldmarschall*, always an early riser, answered it, still in his dressing gown. He'd been arranging his wife's birthday presents on the drawing room table, with the handmade gray suede shoes from Paris featured in the center.

It was his chief of staff, Speidel, the career staff officer with a brilliant mind but no combat experience, who had finally decided that the many sightings of enemy paratroopers all over the Cotentin Peninsula were worthy of his superior's attention. Speidel still wasn't sure whether it was the prelude to a full-scale invasion or just scattered commando operations.

"Well, find out—now!" Rommel told him, and hung up. He changed into his uniform and waited for Speidel to call back, pruning roses in the meantime. Three hours later, at 10:15 a.m., Speidel confirmed that it was indeed the invasion—besides the thousands of American and British troopers dropping chiefly into the southeast base of the Cotentin, formidable seaborne assaults had happened at five coastal sites along more than fifty miles of Normandy coast—and the beachheads were already fairly well established.

The Allies had finally invaded, but not at the Pas de Calais. Rommel paused to absorb that fact, then told Speidel he'd leave immediately, and hung up.

Lucie by now had come downstairs to stand next to him. He shook his head and muttered over and over, "Normandy! Normandy! How stupid of me. How stupid of me . . ."[31]

The *feldmarschall*, his aide, and his driver left less than fifteen minutes later. By the time they reached La Roche-Guyon at 9:00 p.m., the complete failure by the 21st Panzer to push back or impede the Allies' beachhead, and Rommel's deepest fears, had been confirmed.

PART III

THE BATTLE

NINE

LE MANOIR LA FIÈRE

The specific mission of Company A was to seize and defend the bridge. . . .

LIEUTENANT JOHN DOLAN[1]

THE MANOIR LA Fière was the only home nine-year-old Jeannine Leroux had ever known.

Her parents, Louis and Berthe, had rented the *manoir* since 1929. The family made a modest living as dairy farmers, selling the milk of their forty-five cows and some crops, mostly wheat. Early in the war, Louis had been sent to a labor camp in Germany, and life on the farm was difficult for Berthe and their three children until he returned home in 1943.

Jeannine was the youngest. Dark-haired and small for her age, she helped with the milking. She'd grown quite attached to some of the cows and the few horses they owned. One of them would pull the family's two-seat carriage into Sainte-Mère-Église when they went to shop or to attend mass on Sunday. Jeannine also helped with the cider press, making the cider and calvados for the family and their three employees, a maid and two laborers.[2]

The *manoir* comprised seven buildings. Several were centuries old.

Six of them—the two-story farmhouse, a bakery, a cidery, two stables, and a long shed—surrounded a narrow courtyard. A large cow barn sat thirty yards away, closer to the Merderet. Arcing around the *manoir* on the east for hundreds of yards, and just beyond the wooden gate at the south end of the courtyard past the two stables, were the *buttes féodales*—feudal mounds—as the locals called them. These long, ten-foot-high, grass-covered embankments dated back to the Middle Ages and gave evidence of the strategic importance that the location had had for a millennium. A modest castle of stone and wood had once perched on and inside the *buttes féodales*, overlooking—and guarding—an old ford on the river. All that was left of the medieval settlement were the mounds, the long ridges, and a turreted cylindrical staircase incorporated into the rear of the main house.

Just outside the wooden front gate, at the north end of the courtyard, was the reason that the *manoir* was important to both the Germans and the Allies. The *manoir*'s drive let out onto the D15 road and, twenty yards along, to a short two-lane bridge over the small Merderet River, which doglegged sharply west a hundred yards as soon as it flowed under the arched stone bridge and then turned south again. The shallow river was normally fifteen yards wide here, and the bridge, built in the mid-1700s,[3] was not much longer—sixty-four feet from one end to the other. Lining each side of it was a stone parapet less than three feet high. The bridge was unremarkable in every way. But it was asphalt-paved and strong, and offered one of only two river crossings that could handle large vehicles—tanks, anti-tank guns, trucks, and the like. The bridge at Chef-du-Pont, almost two miles south, was the other.

The Germans would need the La Fière bridge to rush reinforcements to the assault beaches and destroy the Allies before they could gain a foothold. The Allies needed it to move west quickly and seal off the Cotentin Peninsula across its base. The job of the 4th Infantry Division if and when it arrived from the beach code-named Utah was to prevent German reinforcements from hindering its drive to seize the deepwater port in Cherbourg, thirty-two miles north. And now that the extensive flooding of the Merderet was known, control of the bridge was even more important. Troops could have easily crossed a shallow fifteen-yard stream almost anywhere along its length, but not a half-mile-wide swamp.

Six hundred yards west of the bridge, at a fork in the D15, lay a hamlet barely worthy of the name. Aside from a few houses spread around the intersection, Cauquigny's defining feature was a small twelfth-century stone chapel named after Saint Ferréol, though people in the area just called it la Petite Chapelle. An air bomb had left little of its dark gray shingled roof intact, but its three high, arched clerestory windows on each side and the tiny cemetery of a couple dozen graves next to it were unscathed. The D15 continued west past the chapel to Amfreville, and a smaller road split off to the village of Étienville, a stronghold of the 1057th Regiment of the 91st Luftlande Division, two miles southwest. On the chapel's western side, a narrow dirt lane ran north through a checkerboard of fields and hedgerows until it was subsumed by the swamp.

The 600-yard stretch of road from the bridge to the chapel was now a narrow causeway only a few feet above the flooded marsh. There was little cover along the expanse—only low, sparse bushes and small trees on either side. And twenty yards from the bridge's east end was the wooden swing gate that led to Louis Leroux's farmhouse.

On Monday, June 5, Jeannine had gone to bed late, around ten o'clock. That was because around sunset Monsieur Genêt, the veterinarian in La Haye-du-Puits, eleven miles to the southwest, had been returning from a late farm call with his son when their motorbike ran out of gas near the Leroux *manoir.* They procured enough gasoline from the Lerouxs to get them home and then left, as darkness descended on the countryside.

Jeannine and her siblings—Geneviève, twelve, and Louis, eleven—had not attended school that day. Usually, every Monday the three children walked the two miles east to Sainte-Mère-Église and Madame Angèle Levrault's private *académie*, and they slept at a teacher's house until they walked back home on Wednesday afternoon. There was no school on Thursdays. Friday morning, they would walk back into town and stay until Saturday afternoon, when school let out.

It had been gray and cold most of the day. The family had eaten their dinner and then listened to the BBC French broadcast on the radio they had hidden when the Germans confiscated everyone else's. About ten o'clock, soon after the Genêts had puttered away and while it was still light, the Allies had started bombing the bridges over the Douve, two miles to the southwest. To better see the barrage and the responding German flak from Picauville, near the bridges, the family walked through their courtyard, past the sheds, and out the small gate at the south end, where they climbed to the top of one of the ancient *buttes féodales.* They soon returned to the main house, and the children and their parents, the young maid, and the two farm workers, who roomed above the bakery across the courtyard, retired to their bedrooms.

They had been asleep only a short time when the roar of hundreds of airplanes could be heard, and Louis and Berthe looked out their window to see parachutists falling from them. "Look, it looks like mushrooms falling from the planes!" Berthe said. They were landing in the flooded marshes and in fields and trees. Colorful tracers arced up at them, lighting up the night, and flak exploded in black clouds that hung in the sky. The Lerouxs could hear shrapnel and bullets falling on their roof. They woke up the children, and with their three employees, the family took shelter in the thickly walled stone stairwell. Jeannine had few toys, and the only one she took with her was Mimisse, her favorite, a foot-high teddy bear stuffed with straw and covered in thick brown cloth. After an hour or so, when there were no more planes, they went back to their beds.

ABOUT 3:00 A.M., Sergeant John Hardie, a mortarman with A Company/508th, landed with another member of his mortar squad in a field and started moving west, following a hedgerow bordering a road. Forty minutes later, they found themselves at the top of a gently sloping hill with a dozen or so apple trees on it. Fifty yards down the slope was a large stone building with a steeply pitched roof and a silo-like structure with a turreted tower jutting out of the back roof, like something out of the Middle Ages. Farm outbuildings, what looked like stables or sheds, extended to the left.

The two troopers walked down to a rickety wooden gate between one of the stables and the large farmhouse—for Hardy could now see, by the moonlight that occasionally broke through the cloud cover, that it was a three-story house. They could hear gunfire in the distance, but it was quiet inside the farm complex.

They lifted the latch, pulled open the wide gate, and entered the courtyard, the only sound a soft crunching their boots made on the dirt and fine gravel. They walked past the darkened farmhouse on the right and between other buildings on each side of the yard and went to its end, where there was another wooden gate. Ten yards beyond was the road they had been paralleling. They walked back to the farmhouse and up the twelve wide stone steps, and Hardie knocked on the front door.

No one answered. The two men decided to leave and look for more of their comrades. After all, more than 6,000 of them had just dropped down.[4]

THE LEROUX HOUSEHOLD was up early, before sunrise. No one had gotten a good night's sleep, though the explosions had died down soon after the last of the planes disappeared eastward. Just before dawn, there was banging on the front door of the farmhouse. When Louis Leroux opened the door, he found a platoon of German soldiers come to defend the bridge, their ammunition-carrier open truck sitting on the side of the road outside the front gate.[5] He, his family, and his three employees were told to remain inside the house.

Unlike American infantry, the Germans built their rifle companies around their superb machine guns, and each platoon had three or four, one for each squad. Unlike his American counterpart, the German rifleman's job was to support his squad's MG42 by covering the crew, carrying ammo for the machine gun, even digging foxholes for it. And once the enemy was engaged, the machine gun—at twenty-six pounds, heavier than a Mauser but light enough for one man to easily carry it and set it up in seconds—was shifted from one position to another to confuse enemies and keep them from locating and attacking it, a tactic called *stellungswechsel* ("change in position"). The Germans "were masters of making one man appear to be a whole squad by moving rapidly from one concealed position to another," an American infantry major would observe two weeks after D-Day.[6] So the positioning of the machine-gun crews to maximize each one's field of fire and the ability to move at a moment's notice were of critical importance. Even *Feldmarschall* Rommel was known to advise a squad leader in the disposition of his MG42s.

Now the sergeant in charge deployed his machine guns around the *manoir*, including one by the bridge just twenty yards from the main gate, one up beyond the slope on the east, one on the west side, and one on the east side. Then he directed his best shots, his snipers, into trees and hedgerows away from the buildings—they too would move after firing if they could. After these outposts were established, he set up the rest of his *landsers*, a dozen or so, inside the *manoir*'s grounds. Then they waited.

He hadn't enough men to hold out indefinitely, but he had a decent fortress to defend, with its walled—for the most part—courtyard and the medieval tower in the rear, with its thick stone walls and a few small square windows that could defend the eastern approaches. The enemy would need a large force to take it, and he and his men could do a good bit of damage before that happened. They might be able to hold the position until reinforcements arrived. Their regiment, the 1057th, was no doubt assembling at that very minute, and the two dozen or so tanks of the Abteilung 100, though mostly old light French tanks, did include a Panzer III, and they were spread out in the area, with its headquarters in a château just two miles south of Sainte-Mère-Église. They too would be mobilized and moving to the bridge at La Fière soon if they weren't already.

First Lieutenant John Dolan hadn't been given the nickname "Red Dog" just for his red hair—it was also for his toughness and tenacity. The barrel-chested Dolan, a Boston native from a large Irish family, had been in the Massachusetts National Guard while attending law school. He'd just finished his first year when his unit was activated, and he was quickly selected for OCS. His desire to be a fighter pilot was scuttled by color blindness, so he'd volunteered for the Airborne, mostly for the extra pay to send to his family—he was the eldest of eight children. When the commander of A Company/505th was injured in Italy, platoon leader Dolan got the job. A lieutenant rarely led a company, but when he did, it was for a good reason. Not only was Dolan well regarded by his superiors, he had the respect of every man under him. He was an aggressive combat leader who led from the front. And he didn't waste words—when he said something, his men paid attention.[7]

The company had had a good drop, on or very near their DZ "O" east of the Merderet at 2:00 a.m. There seemed to be no Germans in the vicinity, and almost all of the company's 176 men assembled fairly quickly—only a couple were missing. Over the next two hours, while they searched out bundles and secured machine guns, mortars, bazookas, and ammunition boxes, Dolan conferred with a 505th pathfinder about the terrain, the railroad line, the bridge, and the east-west road from Sainte-Mère-Église to the bridge. Then he grabbed another pathfinder who spoke fluent German and gathered his lieutenants to coordinate his three platoons.

Dolan's immediate superior, 1st Battalion commander Major Fred Kellam, was a twenty-nine-year-old Texan—and a character. While at West Point, he was the plebe that other plebes had told stories about; he loved to belt out country and folk songs, especially one called "Jack of Diamonds." He had not one but two middle names, Caesar Augustus, so of course he was called Caesar. Kellam was newly married, and his wife had given birth eight months before to a son he'd never seen.[8] He had recently been disciplined for being drunk and disorderly, but when the former commander of the 1st was injured during a test jump, Ridgway gave him the battalion. Kellam was eager to redeem himself and to prove he could lead men in combat—he'd missed out on the 505th's two earlier jumps in Sicily and Salerno. His executive officer,

Major James McGinity, a former seminary student from Detroit, was a ranker like Jim Gavin; he had earned a senatorial appointment to West Point after three years as an enlisted man in the army. He had been a champion boxer at the Point, and he still looked the part: muscular, dark-haired, and handsome. He'd led a company through Sicily and Italy, and his men held him in high regard; he'd been promoted and named 1st Battalion XO in the spring.[9] While the 505th was stationed at a wretchedly hot base in North Africa, Kellam and McGinity had commandeered a C-47, flown it to another base, loaded it with booze, and returned to share it with his three companies. That kind of act and others like it—they occasionally served as altar boys during Catholic masses in the field—had endeared the two to their men, who nicknamed Kellam "Jack of Diamonds" and McGinity "Black Jack" and painted white diamonds on the sides of their helmets.[10]

At the 505th drop zone, Kellam was nowhere to be found, but McGinity was wandering the DZ in search of the engineers who were to accompany Dolan and make sure the bridge wasn't mined—and destroy it if need be. He found none. By early light, soon after 5:00 a.m., Dolan ordered his three platoons to move out toward their objective, the La Fière bridge, about a mile to the west. McGinity joined them soon after they set out. The 2,000 men of the 507th had been scheduled to drop on the western side of the river, and one of their objectives was to establish a position to control the river crossing at Cauquigny, near the west side of the bridge. The 1st Battalion/505th would secure the east side.

After the adrenaline rush of dropping into enemy territory and surviving, the men were "exuberant, high-spirited, and ready for action," noted one of the 505th pathfinders, eighteen-year-old Private Robert Murphy, who accompanied the group as they made their way through the fields under a partly cloudy sky. "Hey, Murphy," said one trooper as they trudged through the wet grass, "have you seen any of those voulez-vouz cooshares tonight?"[11]

That attitude lasted about thirty minutes. The 1st Platoon had left first and flanked to the right, hitting a north-south road bordered with hedgerows and trees that ran along the east side of the swamp and sloped down to the bridge. Just before sunrise, when Dolan, McGinity, and the other two platoons got within 300 yards of the bridge, they stopped alongside a hedgerow where it ended at a dirt road joining the D15, the main thoroughfare from Sainte-Mère-Église. Beyond the D15 to the west, they could see a flat open field. To the left of the D15, they could see the upper story of the *manoir* farmhouse. This meadow, thought Dolan, would be the perfect place for a German defense of the bridge. There was only one way to find out.

He summoned 2nd Platoon leader Lieutenant Donald Coxon, a former factory worker from Peoria, Illinois, to send his scouts forward. In Sicily and North Africa, Coxon had become a seasoned combat officer admired by his men. A couple of days before the jump, he had told two friends that he didn't think he was coming back from this one.[12]

"Well, sir," he told Dolan, "if I have to send them out into that, I'll go myself."

He and two scouts crossed the road and crept forward along a hedgerow. They got about a hundred yards when the unmistakable sound of a German machine gun broke the early-morning silence and rounds ripped into them, killing one scout and injuring Coxon and the other man. Coxon, badly hit, started back, but another bullet ripped into his stomach and he fell to the ground and quickly bled to death.

Second Lieutenant Bob McLaughlin—a thirty-two-year-old from Missoula, Montana, who before enlistment had been living with his widowed mother—moved up and took over the platoon. Almost immediately, his radio operator, Corporal Frank Busa, was hit in the abdomen by a sniper's bullet. Although the small-arms and machine-gun fire was thick, McLaughlin thought Busa was alive and he ran to him and began dragging him back, but a bullet smashed into one of McLaughlin's legs and went through his stomach and into his buttocks. Dolan spotted the sniper and killed him with a burst of fire from his tommy gun.[13] He crawled up to McLaughlin. The radioman was badly injured, and the lieutenant was in excruciating pain and begged not to be moved. Dolan left him there and returned to the platoon. When a soft rain began to fall a little after 10:00 a.m., he grabbed a raincoat and took it to McLaughlin, but he had died. Busa was carried to the rear, but he would expire two days later.[14]

The enemy automatic fire increased in intensity. Dolan and McGinity left a few troopers there to return frontal fire, sent the 2nd Platoon around the right along the river, and took the 3rd Platoon on a flank to the left. With Dolan a few paces behind him, McGinity led his men along a high, thick hedgerow on their left. They were about two-thirds of the way along the hedgerow when Germans well hidden around the bridge and *manoir* opened fire with rifles and Schmeissers. A sniper's bullet smashed into McGinity's skull and he fell to the ground. Dolan returned fire with his Thompson where he saw leaves moving in the hedgerow, and killed the German. He crawled forward to McGinity and dressed his wounds as best he could, then moved back and dived into a German foxhole on his left and continued firing. Several more troopers were killed. They were under fire from two directions—the *manoir* and the bridge. Dolan told his men to keep down and stay where they were until the machine gun was taken out. He lay in the foxhole listening to rifle and machine-gun fire from down by the bridge area. Every time he tried to move, he was shot at. Ten of his men were dead and another twenty wounded, almost a quarter of his force, and he had no idea how they'd take the *manoir*, much less the bridge.

THE LEROUXS COULD hear the battle being waged outside. Despite the gunfire, they decided to descend to the kitchen and restart the fire in the fireplace to prepare breakfast. Their two laborers were already there. One of them ventured outside to fetch a canister of milk and quickly returned with it. Soon coffee was reheating to go along with their bread.

They were just starting breakfast when the front door burst open. It was two German soldiers helping another one in great pain—he had a deep wound in his neck. They carried him to an armchair in a corner of the room opposite the dining table. One of the others left and one stayed.

Outside, the gunfire increased, and grenades began exploding. Another soldier was helped into the room. His legs, shredded by bullets, were bleeding heavily, and his clothes were in tatters.

Berthe Leroux said, "We're not staying down here." The family ascended the old stone spiral staircase to their bedrooms, and huddled on the floor, but when rifle and machine-gun fire began smashing the windows, they returned to the staircase and descended to the bottom, near the door to the kitchen, where they crowded together under the stairs. The automatic gunfire and grenade explosions were relentless and made the air in the house thick with smoke and dust. Jeannine was terrified, but a small part of her was also happy that the British had finally invaded.

Two German soldiers standing at two of the small windows in the stairwell were shooting at Americans on the back slope. One of them, a half dozen steps up, said to the family in crude French, "Are you afraid? Have you never seen war? Me neither." Then he resumed firing. Some bullets entered the windows and slammed into the stone wall, and the air was soon thick with gun smoke and dust. Between bursts of gunfire, he told the family that he was a student from a region of Germany near France. "The war is very sad," he said.

DOLAN'S A COMPANY wasn't the only American group in the immediate area. Captain Ben Schwartzwalder, commanding G Company/507th, was a successful West Virginia high school football coach whose leadership skills weren't limited to the gridiron. He'd dropped on the east side of the Merderet—the 507th's drop zone was on the west—but managed to gather a third of his company, about fifty men, and move out toward his battalion's objective, the nearby village of Amfreville. The troopers moved down the Cherbourg-Paris railway tracks to the D15 and climbed up to the road. They turned right, toward the Merderet and Amfreville almost two miles away, making their way through the fields and around hedgerows south of the road as the sun came up behind them.

Lieutenant John Marr and his four point men were 150 yards in front. As they approached a group of farm buildings, one of them with a turret jutting out of it, a German machine gun opened up on them from a hedgerow about fifty yards ahead. Marr and his men all dived for cover, and no one was hit. Marr carefully made his way back to Schwartzwalder, who decided to move their force off the road just west of the *manoir.* It was about 6:30 a.m., right when the seaborne forces were set to hit Utah, but no one had a radio or any idea whether the assault was underway or how successful it was.

Schwartzwalder, still hell-bent on reaching Amfreville, sent Marr and his scouts left around the *manoir* to see if it could be bypassed to reach the bridge. After working their way among two large grassy mounds thirty yards from a cattle gate leading into the courtyard, they had just reached the south side of the farm buildings when another machine gun—or perhaps it was the same gun quickly moved—in a hedgerow ten yards ahead fired on them, injuring two troopers. This time Marr's men took the gun out, killing one German and taking two others prisoner. Marr started to move back. One of his wounded men was shot through the legs; he fell to the ground still firing his Thompson. Another German stood and cocked his arm about to hurl a "potato masher" grenade, but the other injured trooper shot him with his M1. The German staggered but remained standing, trying to throw the grenade. Marr's two uninjured men both hurled grenades that killed that German and the other two men in the machine-gun nest. A Schmeisser behind the hedgerow kept Marr and his scouts down, but they managed to crawl back through a few hedgerows to Schwartzwalder's position with the two injured troopers. Marr carried one of them on his back.[15]

Close behind Dolan's group was Colonel Roy Lindquist, commander of the 508th, with a hundred or so men. As a forward squad of his troopers started moving down the road toward the bridge a half mile away, a machine gun opened up on them as well. All twelve men dived into the ditch alongside the road. After a runner found Lindquist and told him what had happened, the colonel pulled the point squad back and moved his group south into the fields and then west, not far behind Schwartzwalder's group. When they reached a point south of the *manoir*, they came upon the mounds, but machine-gun and sniper fire stopped them.

Not so coincidentally, the fire pinning down Dolan's position on the east side of the *manoir* finally ceased after about an hour.[16] It was now around 10:00 a.m. Dolan moved down to the bridge at its eastern end. He was repositioning his platoons when the 505th's commander, Lieutenant Colonel Bill Ekman, arrived with most of his command post unit. Ed Krause's runner had never reached Ekman, so he was unaware that the 3rd Battalion had taken Sainte-Mère-Église. He'd radioed Vandervoort and told him to turn back from Neuville-au-Plain and capture the village; then he moved west to the bridge. The two were casually looking over the situation when gunfire erupted from the upper floors of the *manoir* farmhouse.

What Lindquist a half mile to the southeast didn't know—what none of the different groups knew—was that at that moment there were other groups of 82nd troopers in the area around the *manoir.* None of them had one of the backpack-mounted SCR-300 two-way radios—the "walkie-talkies" with a three- to five-mile working range—or the smaller handheld "handie-talkies" with a range of a mile at most. The radios had dropped in bundles or they arrived in gliders, but they had been either lost in the dark or submerged in the swamp. Without those, the peculiar characteristics of the Normandy bocage—the thick, tree-topped hedgerows bordering small, irregular fields that limited sight and muted and distorted the sound and direction of gunfire and movement—severely hindered communication and knowledge. Without realizing it, about 500 troopers would soon converge on the *manoir* area and, in a largely uncoordinated assault, battle the platoon of Germans defending it.

About 10:30 a.m., Kellam arrived in the area—east of the bridge, near the railroad crossing a half mile away; he was with a large group of men whom he had sent to reinforce A Company. Dolan sent his 3rd Platoon under Lieutenant William Oakley to clear out the *manoir* buildings—they had been receiving fairly constant sniper and machine-gun fire from there. Soon after Oakley's patrol moved around the *manoir* in a large circle to avoid the machine guns and somehow avoided making contact with Lindquist's men, Gavin arrived at the D15 with 300 men.

It had been a long morning for the 82nd's assistant commander. At about 3:00 a.m., when he and his stick had reached the edge of the swamp, they could see equipment bundles in the water. The bundles contained everything necessary for survival. A lieutenant volunteered and stripped to wade out through the cold water, his pale skin a bright target in the moonlight. But there was no enemy fire in the area.

Then a red light on a tall pole appeared on the eastern side of the swamp about a half mile away—the 507th's assembly light. A green light, the 508th's, followed it. Gavin sent his aide, Captain Hugo Olson, to cross to the other side and find out what was happening there.

Olson returned an hour later soaking wet with bad and good news. The swamp was shoulder deep and looked to be 1,000 yards wide, with occasional depressions that were even deeper and thick grass that could entangle a man. But he had found the Cherbourg-Paris railway line a few hundred yards beyond the water, and it was on an elevated bed above it. Olson had run into a group of 508th troopers headed south along the embankment toward the La Fière bridge. Gavin consulted his map and figured he was about two miles north of the bridge—far from the 508th DZ.

Soon after first light, the men could see great flashes on the eastern horizon and hear what sounded like distant thunder—the start, they knew, of the heavy naval shelling of the German casemates on Utah Beach. "The tanks have actually landed," men were saying, though the seaborne assault wasn't scheduled to begin until 6:30 a.m. Troopers had continued to drift into Gavin's area, and he now had more than a hundred with him, mostly from the 507th. But after three full hours, as the moon dropped closer to the western horizon, they still had almost no luck recovering bundles from the swamp—just a few machine guns and a bazooka.[17] A patrol sent out to a glider that had landed just a quarter mile away found an anti-tank gun still in it but ran into heavy enemy fire and returned with nothing.

Gavin considered moving south along the western edge of the swamp to the La Fière bridge to attack the enemy from their rear, but enemy fire was increasing and coming closer—patrols sent out reported German units of considerable strength to the north, west, and south. Gavin and his men would have to withdraw across the swamp, and they would have to leave their injured comrades. At 7:30 a.m., Gavin waded into the frigid water. The troopers, following him along a front several hundred yards across and ten to twenty-five yards apart, held their rifles and some equipment above their heads. As they moved slowly through the thick muck, the knee-high grass wrapping itself around their legs, German soldiers moved to the edge of the swamp and began firing at them, hitting some troopers, who then disappeared beneath the surface.

Thirty-four-year-old William Walton, a correspondent for *Time* magazine who had gained fame as the first newspaperman on the spot when gangster John Dillinger had been gunned down before a Chicago movie theater in 1934, had parachuted in with the 82nd in Gavin's stick—Walton's first jump. He held his Hermes Baby portable typewriter above his helmet. He'd already tossed away two heavy cameras a photographer had asked him to carry. Walton and the waterlogged troopers continued to slog across the swamp—"water filled our pockets and every ounce became a pound," he remembered.[18] Sometimes they plunged into deep spots thick with black mud, bullets from machine guns and Mauser rifles zipping past them and into the water. Once Walton looked to his right and saw Gavin ten yards away disappear under the surface, but a few seconds later, he came back up and continued forward. It took thirty minutes, but Gavin, Walton, and most of the men made it, finally dragging themselves out of the swamp and over a thick barbed wire fence, then up and onto a steep six-foot-high gravel railway embankment, where, exhausted, they flopped to the ground on the other side as water slowly drained from their clothes and packs.[19]

Gavin allowed the men a few minutes' rest, then got them up and began moving south along the railway line—six feet separated the two tracks. Others who had dropped in and around the flooded Merderet had also made their way toward the railway line, the only high point in the area, and as Gavin moved south, they attached themselves to him. One group of 507th men was led by Lieutenant Colonel Ed Ostberg, the 1st Battalion commander; he was the son of a Swedish immigrant who had enlisted in the army during World War One and was killed just two weeks before the war ended. Ostberg's mother became a switchboard operator in Brooklyn, raised her son alone, and scrimped to send him to a private Catholic high school. Ostberg had applied for a position at West Point and gotten in, graduating in 1939. He hadn't seen his wife or two-year-old daughter in almost a year. He was a shade under five foot seven and known for his bravery and his devotion to his men.

By the time Gavin reached the D15 road running from Sainte-Mère-Église to the bridge a half mile away, there were 300 men with him. He turned west and ran into Kellam and some of his 1st Battalion/505th troopers. Kellam, green to combat, had only just found out that "Black Jack" McGinity—his XO, friend, and fellow altar boy—was dead. But there was no time to mourn McGinity or anyone else. To Gavin's great relief—because he'd had doubts about the major as a combat leader—Kellam seemed to have things well in hand. He reassured Gavin that the bridge would be theirs in an hour or two; Dolan's A Company was lightly opposed and would take control without much trouble. Gavin left half his men there and continued south toward the other bridge over the Merderet, at Chef-du-Pont.[20]

But Kellam was mistaken. Neither the bridge nor the causeway beyond would be theirs in a couple of hours—or even a couple of days.

A FEW HOURS earlier, Lieutenant Colonel Charles Timmes, commanding the 2nd Battalion/507th, had landed in water up to his knees close to the regiment's DZ. But that was only the beginning of a protracted struggle to free himself from his harness as his half-collapsed chute dragged him along the marsh mud on the swampy bottom. He finally surfaced on a drainage ditch embankment and was able to cut his harness away.[21] On the fringes of the swamp over the next hour, he managed to gather 150 men, a company's worth but less than a third of his own force. In another hour, just before sunrise, he wandered into Cauquigny, quiet as the graveyard there. The sound of gunfire from the northwest led him to believe that Amfreville a mile away was already under attack by some unit of the 82nd. That was his destination, and as the sun rose, he led his men cross-country toward it. When they reached the outskirts of the village, heavy German fire, including MG42s, greeted them from the church steeple, rooftops, and hedgerows on high ground. His troopers sought cover, but eight were hit, four of them fatally. Timmes was mistaken—there were no other Americans there. Threatened with being outflanked and sustaining heavy casualties, he gave the order to fall back to the east. With the Germans pressing them all the way and an MG42 advancing from one hedgerow to the next, his men reached an apple orchard, and by 9:30 a.m., they began to dig in, their backs against the Merderet swamp and less than a mile north of Cauquigny. They quickly set up a machine gun and trained it on the road to the orchard, barely holding the Germans back.

Before Timmes cleared the area, he ran into a group of men under First Lieutenant Louis Levy of the 507th, a twenty-nine-year-old former truck driver from Yuma, Arizona, and a newlywed who kept his wedding band in his pocket. He had seventeen troopers under his command. Timmes told him to move them south and seize and secure the west side of the bridge at La Fière. They too headed out.

BY MIDMORNING, SOME 500 men from all three regiments had reached the area between the bridge, the *manoir*, and the railroad-D15 junction. The problem was, not all of them were in contact. About 10:00 a.m., while Lindquist was trying to figure out a plan of attack, Ridgway drove up in a jeep—one of the few salvaged from the gliders.

His CP had been moved to an abandoned farmhouse close to the apple orchard.[22] He still had no workable radios, but he was well aware that the drops had been near-disastrous, except for that of the 505th, whose CP was near his. He had a working command post of a sort but not much of a command. With little information about the drops of the 507th or 508th or about their operations, he could do little to oversee or control his division's activities. "I could only be where the fighting seemed the hottest, to exercise whatever personal influence I could on the battalion commanders," he wrote later.[23]

He conferred with Lindquist and made his intentions clear. "I want this area cleared of all Germans and the bridgehead secured," the general told him. "I want that bridge taken." Then he left to return to his command post.

Lindquist—like Kellam, green to combat—wasted little time. He set a combined attack by all forces in the area for noon, then sent a runner to Dolan. Red Dog never received the order. But on his own, he had sent a patrol around the east side to attack the last Germans in the *manoir.* Somehow the patrol leader, Lieutenant William Oakley, made a wide clockwise circle around the *manoir* and its feudal mounds all the way to the southwest side without making contact with Schwartzwalder's group. When Oakley and his men reached the Merderet, they quietly made their way up along the side of the river and then began moving around the large outlying barn. Schmeisser and machine-gun fire erupted less than twenty yards away behind the six-foot stone wall around the courtyard. The patrol hugged the embankment, and no one was hit. Oakley and Sergeant Oscar Queen—a big Texan who, along with another sergeant, was called by one of his privates "the toughest, meanest human beings I ever met in my life"[24]—used their rifles to kill two grenadiers and another German who charged toward them a moment later firing a Schmeisser.

Then Oakley and his men jumped up and ran for the stone wall. They made it and opened fire on an MG42 north of the main road. While the others covered him, Queen scurried to a gate and ducked through it into the courtyard. A grenade exploded about five feet away, knocking Queen to the ground, stunned. From behind him he heard small-arms fire. He saw a figure moving in the branches of a tree above him; he fired his carbine at it and a dead German sniper fell out of the tree to the ground beside him. Queen ran back to Oakley, and he found another officer, a captain, who had been firing his .45 at a German throwing grenades at Queen from a window in the main house.

A machine gun was sent for. When it eventually arrived, it was set up near one end of the stone wall. The machine gun, trained on the MG42 on the other side of the main road, quickly knocked it out.

By then it was noon—the time set by Lindquist for the attack. Schwartzwalder approached again from the south side and found the enemy forces weakened, partly due to Oakley's patrol. His men swung open the gate and entered the courtyard.

THE LEROUX FAMILY was still sheltering at the bottom of the circular staircase when ten or twelve more Germans burst into the house. When there was a pause in the noise, Geneviève clutched her communion crucifix and said, "I don't want to stay here. We need to go downstairs!" Then she opened the door to the kitchen. The rest of the family followed her, stepping over several wounded soldiers on the floor outside the small door that led to the cellar.

They descended the stone stairs and walked through the room where the cider and calvados were stored, and then they went into another room—at the end of it was a door into the farmyard. Behind them a German clambered down the stairs and pointed his rifle at them. Everyone in the family screamed, *"Français! Français!"* until the soldier turned and climbed back up and out of sight.

The family pressed their bodies against the walls near the door. The gunfire outside had resumed. The door flew open, and an American paratrooper appeared. His face was painted black. The family again screamed, *"Français! Français!"*

"Restez là où vous êtes," the soldier said—"Stay where you are"—and left.

Fifteen minutes later he returned and gestured at the family to follow him. They emerged into the sunlight to see two lines of soldiers leading fifty feet away to the stable, where more of them were kneeling against the wall with their rifles trained on the windows above.

The family followed the first paratrooper toward the stable. *"Vive les Anglais!"* shouted Berthe Leroux. "No, Americans," said the soldier. *"Vive l'Amérique!"* responded the family, though not too loudly.

The animals were all gone. Some cows and horses lay dead. Through the French-speaking trooper, the family told the soldiers how many Germans were in the house and where they were, and then the family huddled in a corner of the stable.

The Lerouxs stayed there in the corner of the stable for more than an hour. The French-speaking paratrooper told them to hold their noses and open their mouths so the noise would not be so hard on their ears. Outside the door, a half dozen Americans fired continuously at the staircase tower and the attic windows with two machine guns and rifles.

But it was not until 1:00 p.m., when a 508th trooper attached a grenade launcher to his M1 and fired a grenade into a *manoir* window and it exploded in the house, that the Germans hung a white bedsheet out the window.[25] When a trooper stepped out into the courtyard, a German unaware of the surrender opened fire on him from another window and killed him; two others were wounded. That triggered a furious barrage of small-arms fire. Then someone sent a sergeant with a tommy gun into the basement, where he began firing up through the floorboards. That ended the resistance, and a few minutes later, a dozen or so grenadiers walked out the front door and down the stairs, some of them helped by their comrades, their hands raised over their heads. The young German student was one of them.

The Leroux family talked to the Americans for a while—the paratroopers drank some of the *calva* stored in the cellar, but only after Louis Leroux drank it first.

Soon the family was told to leave the *manoir*—there would certainly be a big battle, the paratroopers told them. They packed some clothes, blankets, and food and set off north through the fields to go to Louis Leroux's brother, Jean, who lived on a large farm less than a mile upriver. Their farmhouse was half destroyed, and the outbuildings were almost as bad. Only the medieval staircase tower was relatively unscathed.

It wasn't until they reached Uncle Jean's place that Jeannine realized she had lost Mimisse. She would never see her bear again.[26]

GAVIN, OSTBERG, AND the seventy-five men of the 507th followed the railway into Chef-du-Pont and to the bridge over the Merderet beyond it. The village was even smaller than Sainte-Mère-Église; its chief feature was a large creamery on its western edge, along the road to the bridge. Gavin had the idea that he could find something that could float—a small boat, a barn door, even a large piece of wood—on which he could ferry his men over the swamp, and then they would attack the German forces on the west side of the La Fière bridge. Along the way he sent out a patrol but nothing could be found, which led Gavin to the conclusion that the Germans had deliberately cleared the area of anything larger than a stick that could float.

When Gavin and his men reached the town's northern outskirts at 9:30 a.m., they saw a train leaving the station and heading toward them. German troops aboard fired their rifles at them, then jumped off and scattered. The train screeched to a halt. Troopers boarded to find it empty except for a shipment of cheese, a deserted antiaircraft battery on one flatcar, and six boxcars of empty bottles.

But the Germans who had jumped off the train ran into and among the buildings on the north side of town, and they fired on the 507th men, injuring four of them. Ostberg sent a patrol to clean them out. Gavin told Ostberg to organize an attack across the river when feasible, probably after dark, then left with a few troopers to return to the La Fière area.[27]

It took two hours to clear the area of Germans. Then Ostberg led his men down the road that led southwest out of town, a straight shot toward the Merderet a half mile away. The last of the Germans had withdrawn in the same direction just ten minutes before, and Ostberg decided that now was the time to attack, before they could organize their defense. He led his men at a trot down the road past orchards, empty pastures, and a few houses. When they reached the gabled three-story creamery on the left with its tall smokestack, they saw the Merderet swamp fifty yards away. The two-lane road continued down a bare, narrow causeway that cleared the water by about five feet and offered no protection to anyone venturing along it. Two hundred yards beyond the edge of the water was a low, tri-arched stone-and-brick bridge that was about thirty yards long and arched slightly over the Merderet.

Past the bridge, the elevated causeway continued through what had been fields and was now the Merderet swamp. A half mile down it, on a piece of slightly elevated ground made an island by the floodwaters, lay the Isle Marie, an elegant, four-turreted seventeenth-century château built on the ruins of a tenth-century Viking fortress that, like the Manoir la Fière, spoke to the location's strategic nature. On the northern edge of the island, the Germans had organized a stout defensive position, and their MG42s, with their 2,000-yard effective range, controlled the entire length of the causeway.

Ostberg was fearless in combat, and now another officer and he ran ahead of about fifty troopers toward the bridge. But the Germans had prepared foxholes lining the causeway on both sides of the bridge, and they were now each occupied with at least one machine gun. The Germans opened fire on the men moving toward them.

The two officers ran down the narrow causeway firing at the entrenched Germans. Several of the troopers behind them were shot, and the attack fizzled. But the two men continued forward. Ostberg had just made it onto the arched span when a machine-gun burst hit him several times and he toppled over the metal railing onto the ground near the abutment and rolled into the water. He lay motionless, only his head above the surface. The other officer was shot just before he reached the bridge and fell onto the road, dead.[28]

AROUND THE SAME time, while making their way through fields and around hedgerows, Levy and his seventeen troopers ran into Second Lieutenant Joe Kormylo of the 507th with about twenty men near some houses two hundred yards north of the church. Kormylo was a tall twenty-year-old from Alabama whose parents were both Polish immigrants. He too had married recently—he'd eloped the previous September with a young woman from Columbus, Georgia, while in training at nearby Fort Benning. Since he'd landed, Kormylo had been roaming the area, collecting a patchwork unit of riflemen, glider pilots, and anti-tank personnel; when he walked into Cauquigny, he understood its importance and set up a defensive position at the farmhouses just north of it. Now he asked if he could join Levy, who welcomed the additional men—and told Kormylo that they had better try to get to the church as quickly as possible. Kormylo sent all his men except his machine-gun crew north to Timmes and joined Levy.

At noon, when they reached Cauquigny 600 yards west of the La Fière bridge, they heard sporadic gunfire from the east side of the swamp—some of it zipped around them and clipped branches. They set up a defensive position around the church on the north side of the road, with the machine gun facing the river, then broke out some C rations. From one of the nearby houses, a Frenchman walked over to bring them milk and cider. They were soon joined by thirty-seven men from the 508th led by two lieutenants; those men had gathered on the west bank south of Cauquigny. They set up at the church too, strengthening Levy's force to about sixty-five. Levy felt confident enough to send a runner to Timmes with a message: "We have secured the bridgehead."

At about 2:00 p.m., Kormylo was scouting toward the bridge when he noticed an increase in mortar and small-arms fire around the *manoir.* He ran back and told Levy, who walked onto the causeway with a pair of binoculars and peered in that direction. He yelled, "Kormylo! Damn it, come and see! Here's a paratrooper coming across the bridge."

Kormylo threw an orange smoke grenade out into the middle of the road. Immediately an orange flag could be seen on the other side of the river. Levy and Kormylo yelled at their men to hold their fire, and began walking toward the bridge. Water lapped up close to the causeway on either side. The point man was John Marr, and 150 yards behind him were Schwartzwalder and his eighty 507th men.

Lindquist had told Schwartzwalder to move to the Cauquigny church. A few minutes before 2:00 p.m., Marr got the order to start across the bridge with his scouts. A captured German NCO told them that there were fire positions strung out along the causeway.

Marr's lead scout, Private Johnnie Ward, took the point, followed by Private Jim Mattingly. Ward had walked a hundred yards beyond the bridge, and Mattingly, behind him, had just stepped off its far end when Marr, behind Mattingly, saw a German in the tall grass and bushes on the north side of the causeway just twenty yards from Mattingly rise up and take aim. Marr yelled, and Mattingly swung his M1 around and emptied its clip in the German's direction. Then he threw down his rifle, grabbed a grenade, and hurled it toward the German. It was on target. Four Germans stood up with their hands in the air, an MG42 and a dead comrade at their feet. One of them was badly wounded, and the others had only minor injuries. Mattingly picked up his rifle and stood up, and as he did so, five others in an emplacement on the south side of the road, close to Mattingly and on his left, jumped up, hands held high—they too had an MG42. With his emptied rifle, he covered the nine men and sent them across the bridge, then turned and continued to lead Schwartzwalder's men across the causeway.

When Schwartzwalder reached Levy and Kormylo about 2:30 p.m., they pumped his hand, glad to see him. When he asked about other friendly forces in the area, Levy told him about Timmes's group to the north. With Schwartzwalder's G Company—actually, only about a dozen troopers were from G, the rest being from the other two 2nd Battalion/507th companies—there were now between 150 and 200 men over there. Levy walked over the bridge and reported to Lindquist, who told him that a battalion of the 508th would be coming over the bridge soon to fortify the position. Levy returned to his unit at the Cauquigny church to find that Schwartzwalder, determined to find his battalion, was planning to head north in search of Timmes. The bridge was captured, he told Levy, and the west side appeared secured.

"I was sent to hold the bridge," Levy told him, "and I think I'd better stick here."

All the 508th enlisted men, including the only bazooka team, went with Schwartzwalder. Through a series of misunderstandings, that left Levy, Kormylo, two 508th officers, and eight enlisted men—twelve paratroopers—to hold the west side of the causeway, instead of the 160-odd men who had been there a few minutes ago. They spread out along the road in front of the church, facing west, dug in at ten- to fifteen-yard intervals. One of them wielded a BAR.

Lindquist walked across the bridge to assess the situation himself. He stayed only a moment. When he returned to the *manoir*, he ordered an undermanned company of stray artillerymen and riflemen, mostly from B Company/508th—forty or so—to cross over and reinforce Levy. That would not be enough.

Before Schwartzwalder's men left, they had deployed along a hedgerow facing the river, and while Levy and Schwartzwalder were talking, a German ambulance drove up the road that had veered south at the church. The vehicle turned west on the main road, then stopped. A German waved a Red Cross flag from the door and poked his head out and looked around—just enough to see that there were American troops on this side of the bridge. Then the ambulance drove away west toward Amfreville.

Three minutes later, an artillery shell landed at the intersection where the ambulance had paused. Several others followed, then more shells that seemed to search northward along the hedgerows where Schwartzwalder's men were. He gave the order to move out fast, and with the scouts leading, the eighty men jogged north past a half dozen fields and hedgerows. The shelling stopped. Then Marr on the point heard the word passed from the end of the line: "Tanks!" That only made Schwartzwalder push his men north even harder.

At Cauquigny, Levy and his eleven men had just dug in near the chapel. It wasn't long before they began to sustain rifle fire from the south. Soon machine guns joined the din. Then came the deep roar of powerful diesel engines and the clank and squeal of metal tracks moving along metal wheels.[29]

TEN

THE BATTLE FOR THE BRIDGE

Why we were not injured or killed only the good Lord knows.

PRIVATE MARCUS HEIM[1]

WHEN KORMYLO HEARD the approaching screech of metal on metal and the rumble of diesel engines, he yelled, "My God! Tanks! That's German armor."

He knew they couldn't last long against tanks, but they decided to get in a few licks before they had to retreat. From their positions near the chapel, Levy, Kormylo, and a young private worked their way out on the right flank, walking alongside the road to Étienville that split off from the D15. When they reached an indentation in an embankment, Levy stayed there to cover the other two as they continued forward. The tanks were moving along the road—Kormylo could see their turrets above a hedgerow fifty yards away. A moment later he saw a group of German infantrymen in their gray-green uniforms behind the tanks. Kormylo and the private fired a few rounds with their M1s and then beat it back to Levy.

As they reached him, he said, "Keep going!" and they did. Levy stayed there as they ran down a ditch toward the church, then stopped and turned to cover him.

But Levy held his ground, and a few minutes later, some Germans set up a machine gun just ten yards from where he hid behind an embankment; the Germans trained their machine gun on the troopers in the churchyard. Over the clamor of the tanks, Levy could hear the Germans talking and laughing just around the corner of the embankment. Levy took one of his fragmentation grenades, pulled the pin, counted to three, tossed it, then burst through the hedge and finished two Germans with his Thompson. He turned toward the lead tank and sprayed it with his magazine's last rounds and ran back toward the church as a grenade exploded near him.

Kormylo couldn't see Levy, but he heard a grenade go off, then another—this time, a German potato masher, he could tell from the sound. Then Levy appeared, helmetless and laughing like a maniac—a reaction of Levy's that Kormylo had noticed before when things got hot. Levy's shoulder was bleeding and his jacket had almost been torn off. He didn't say anything about the grenade, but Kormylo figured it had come close to killing him.

They ran back across a field to the chapel and settled behind a hedgerow near it and a few other troopers. The tanks were already firing at the chapel, and the German infantrymen had almost reached the D15, with only the edge of a hedgerow separating them from the Americans by about ten yards. Each side began throwing grenades at the other, but in no time, there were only six troopers left, more grenadiers were joining the attack, and ammunition was running low. A German came over the embankment a few feet from Kormylo, who emptied his M1 at him and blew off the top of his head. Kormylo looked around and then over to where Levy had been, but he had disappeared—no, he had only moved down the hedgerow and was hurling grenades at the tanks. There was only one other trooper, the private, left. Kormylo yelled to him, "Come on, let's get the hell out of here!" They sprinted for the rear of the church, but the private was cut down before he could make it.

Three tanks rattled up to the D15 and turned right toward the bridge. The private with the BAR—a Wichita, Kansas, native named Orlin Stewart—had dug in at the edge of the road in front of the church to cover the bazooka team; he was the last man on the line. Like most troopers assigned the heavy automatic rifle, Stewart was on the large side, six feet tall and solid. After the bazooka team had left with Schwartzwalder, Stewart stayed there behind a small hedge, a bit annoyed at their departure, and he was still there as the tanks, French Renaults, slowly came up the road toward him. Then a rocket hit the lead tank and knocked it out of commission, courtesy of some bazookaman south of the chapel near the river. That emboldened Stewart, who ran to the intersection and dropped behind a hedgerow thirty yards from the tank. He was having second thoughts about his move when a sergeant and a private, each carrying several Gammon grenades, crawled down the ditch he was kneeling in and joined him. The sergeant said only, "Hi!" before Stewart gave them his Gammons, and as two more Renaults slowly moved past the burning tank, Stewart stood and gave the other men covering fire as they heaved their Gammons, and he heard one of them yell, "Take that, you sons of bitches!"

After the explosions, both tanks rolled on a little more and stopped. One of the crews jumped out. The sergeant and the private threw fragmentation grenades that killed both tankers. The other crew ducked back into its Renault. When another tank—a larger, German one—came into view on the road, moving toward the chapel with a large group of grenadiers trailing it, the three men hightailed it to the back of the chapel, where Levy, Kormylo, and the others joined them, and they all made their way north along the hedgerows to the apple orchard where Timmes was.[2]

THE FIFTY MEN of B Company/508th sent over by Lindquist had just reached the western end of the causeway and turned south through the fields along the edge of the swamp, aiming to reach Hill 30, a low knoll about a mile south of Cauquigny that had been designated the 508th's reserve assembly point. They hadn't gone more than a half mile before German tanks, mortars, machine guns, and riflemen came into view on their right rear; the Germans were from the same group that had just dealt with Levy's squad. Most of the troopers were in single file behind a hedgerow. The lead tank on the road came around the edge of the hedgerow and opened fire. Several men were killed or wounded, and the others were cut off from the bridge.

Lieutenant Homer Jones yelled, "Every man for himself," and most of them ran toward the swamp and splashed into it. Two men ran down a long ditch that led to the river; fire from machine guns, tanks, and rifles went over their heads. One of them, a young soldier from the 101st, said he wanted to surrender. Private First Class Jim Kurz, a tall twenty-year-old from Maryland, objected. *This is combat,* Kurz told him. *They're shooting real bullets.* The 101st trooper fixed a white piece of cloth to his rifle, held it high, and stood up with his other hand raised. He was hit several times and fell to the ground, dead.

Kurz moved on toward the river channel, where he found nine men standing in the swamp on the Merderet's west bank; most of them were buddies from B Company. One of them said the river was deep and moving fast, but Kurz said he was going to swim over, and jumped in. He lost his helmet and rifle, but he made it across the twenty yards to the east bank and stood up. Two men followed him. When Kurz saw one of them starting to go under, he jumped back in and helped him reach the safety of the east side. The other seven men were still on the west side and taking fire. Kurz and the two others found a parachute, cut the risers, and tied them into a line. They tossed it over the water and pulled all the men across. The troopers continued east toward their lines, wading and crawling to avoid enemy fire. With a hundred yards to go, they were so exhausted that they stood up and walked the rest of the way. No one got hit.

Some of their comrades in B Company made it through the swamp and over the river. A tank on the causeway near the Cauquigny chapel trained its machine gun on them and opened up. A radioman named Bill Dean waded through the swamp, got to the river's edge, and decided he could swim underwater to the other bank. He leaned down, took a deep breath, ducked under, and pushed off. With all the equipment he was carrying, he sank to the muddy bottom. He thought, *This is it—I'm never going to get out of here.* But then he started crawling along the bottom. Soon he could feel he was slowly ascending the side of the river. He lifted his head, helmet and all, took a deep breath, and lay on the bank, exhausted.

Jones, the lieutenant who had shouted, "Every man for himself," was one of the last to cross. He waded through three-foot-deep water hidden by bulrushes that thrust three feet above the surface. Germans on the west shore saw the bulrushes move and started firing at him every time they shook. He stopped moving and hunkered down in the cold water until just his head was above water; he sat there for several hours until, soaking wet and shivering but alive, he could cross under cover of darkness.[3]

LEVY'S SMALL FORCE hadn't slowed the lead element of the 1057th much, maybe fifteen minutes, but it was just enough time for Dolan—and "Jack of Diamonds" Kellam, who had just arrived—to place their men where they wanted them. It was too late to seize the bridge, but the German forces heading east toward Utah Beach had to be stopped, and the bridge seemed to be the right place. It was a defense in depth, with Dolan's A Company dug in at the east end of the bridge in a line of foxholes about seventy-five yards long, and the other two companies of the 1st Battalion, B and C, situated behind A on a slight rise from which they could support Dolan's men. About 150 yards behind A Company on one side of the D15 where it rose slightly before bending to the left, a group of engineers manned a 57mm anti-tank gun, one of the few salvaged from a glider, and sighted it straight over the bridge. Closer to the bridge, another unit of engineers was also on hand, ready to destroy it in case it couldn't be held. But that was the final option.

Dolan had done most of the deploying—the men were his. He put a two-man bazooka team in foxholes the Germans had dug earlier on either side of the bridge where the road shoulders fell off toward the river; another was closer to the *manoir,* where better cover was available. The teams at the bridge would have to stand up to shoot across the river. North of the Merderet, two of his platoons manned foxholes in a line seventy-five yards long. He kept his third platoon behind them in reserve. His men managed to push and drag the German truck, now disabled, from the *manoir* and over the bridge, where they overturned it, then placed anti-tank mines around it and past it on the road.[4]

On the south side of the bridge was bazooka gunner PFC Lenold Peterson and his loader, Private Marcus Heim. They'd had little time to work together. Peterson, a talkative farmer from Minnesota whose father had emigrated from Norway as a young boy, was battle-tested after Sicily and Salerno. But Heim, a short, brown-haired kid from Buffalo, New York, was a recent 505th replacement. After he'd dropped into a field just twenty-five feet from the D15 and was still struggling to assemble his rifle, he heard a vehicle approaching. He shrank to the ground and remained as still as possible, watching as two German soldiers on a motorcycle passed by. Then he met up with other troopers from his stick, including Peterson, and found their equipment bundle. The two had unpacked their rocket launcher and bags of rounds and moved east toward the bridge behind Lieutenant Dolan.

The bazooka team across the road, PFC John Bolderson and Private Gordon Pryne, had had even less practice. Pryne had jumped as a rifleman, but when Bolderson's loader broke an ankle upon landing, Pryne was given the job. He didn't want it, but he was told, "You got it."[5]

About 4:00 p.m., Dolan had just finished his final inspection of the defense and moved back with Kellam when a trooper could be seen running down the causeway and across the bridge. It was PFC Francis Buck, Kellam's runner. Buck was a resourceful Kansan who'd been on his own since the age of fourteen, when he'd left his parents and twelve siblings to make his own way.[6] Since no one seemed to have a radio, Kellam had sent him across the bridge to collect any 505th men he could find and direct them back to the *manoir* area. He'd passed Levy's squad at the chapel and continued west for a stretch, but at the sound of tanks, he about-faced and ran back, warning Levy along the way.

Kellam spread the word to Dolan and the other 505th officers: "Dig in deeper, and get ready."

Buck had barely made it across the bridge when a barrage of German artillery and mortar fire began, shells exploding all around the *manoir* area and fragments flying in every direction. Some burst at tree height, raining shrapnel and jagged wood down into foxholes and on the men in them. Then three tanks came into full view as each emerged around the road's slight curve 200 yards away. They could be seen moving slowly down the narrow causeway from Cauquigny. About 200 German infantrymen walked behind and beside them. A dozen or so captured American paratroopers walked ahead of the lead tank, whose commander stood in the hatch directing them to remove mines on the road's surface and throw them into the swamp on either side of the road.[7]

Two of the tanks were small French Renaults. But in the lead was a twenty-three-ton Panzer Mark III, a medium tank with a crew of five, a 50mm cannon, and two machine guns. Twice as fast as a Renault and three times as heavy, the Mark III was formidable to a ground unit without armor.[8]

The three tanks and the German soldiers began firing on the Americans on the east side of the bridge with cannon and machine guns, and the American prisoners dived to the road's shoulders. When the panzer was forty yards from the bridge, the two bazooka teams stood up. On the left, Peterson and Heim tried to use a concrete telephone pole in front of them as cover. Peterson steadied the long tube on his shoulder, sighted on the tank, and pulled the trigger. Heim loaded another of the nineteen-inch finned rockets into its rear opening, and Peterson fired again. Less than ten yards away on the other side of the road, Bolderson and Pryne stood and did the same.

Then the machine gunner in the *manoir* courtyard let loose a burst that killed the panzer's commander. From its position on the side of the road, the 57mm anti-tank gun went off, and another machine gun across the road opened up. The 505th riflemen dug in along the eastern shore of the swamp also began firing. German mortar rounds from the Cauquigny area began dropping on the east side. The roar was deafening.

Under a hail of cannon, mortar, rifle, and machine-gun fire, both bazooka teams near the end of the bridge continued to stand in their foxholes as each loader shoved in a rocket and each gunner aimed at the lead tank and fired "with the precision of well-oiled machinery," remembered Dolan. The panzer started to turn sideways, but its turret swung around and its cannon continued to fire. A round hit the concrete pole in front of Peterson and Heim, sending shards of concrete flying, and as the pole toppled toward them, they jumped out of the way and continued firing at the panzer until its tracks fell off and it stopped moving and began to burn. A mortar shell exploded in front of them and another eight feet behind them. The shrapnel missed the four men.[9]

The tank behind the panzer managed to push it partly onto the side of the road. The bazooka teams went to work on that tank, firing as quickly as they could. Peterson and Heim moved forward to get a better shot, and in less than a minute, that tank caught fire too. They moved back and jumped into their foxhole.

They had only a few rockets left. Peterson told Heim to run across the road and see if Bolderson had any extra rockets. Heim scurried through heavy fire to find one dead soldier near the foxhole and Bolderson and Pryne gone. Their bazooka lay on the ground with several bullet holes in it. Heim scooped up the few rockets he could find and sprinted back across to Peterson. They stood up again and fired at the third tank until it too was put out of action with the help of the 57mm.

The surviving grenadiers retreated back down the causeway to the shelter of the Cauquigny chapel and farmhouses. Near the bridge, they left dozens of dead or wounded comrades who had been raked by rifle, BAR, and machine-gun fire from the A Company troopers across the Merderet.

Peterson and Heim yelled for more ammunition. Kellam—fifty

yards from the bridge with Dolan and his operations officer, Captain Dale Roysdon—ran forward carrying a bag of rockets. Roysdon was close behind him. They were fifteen yards from the bridge when a mortar round exploded and knocked them to the ground, killing the 1st Battalion commander instantly. Roysdon would die the next day.[10]

That left a lieutenant, Dolan, as the ranking officer in charge of the battalion. He sent a man two miles east to the 505th's regimental CP in a field about 200 yards west of Sainte-Mère-Église. Ekman, the 505th's commander, was nowhere to be found, but the regimental XO, Lieutenant Colonel Mark Alexander, was there, and the runner told him of the attack and the deaths of Kellam and McGinity. In Sicily and Italy, Alexander had proven himself a smart and brave leader in battle. His job as XO was to run Ekman's CP, but he decided that a senior officer's presence was required at the bridge, so he took his orderly and headed west along the D15. Along the way, they ran into two Germans, and in the brief skirmish, his orderly was shot in the kneecap. When the Germans cleared out, Alexander ordered his limping aide back to the aid station in Sainte-Mère-Église and continued on alone.

He arrived to find the situation under control; the Germans had been hitting the bridge and *manoir* area with mortar, artillery, and machine-gun fire from the west side of the causeway, but their attack had ceased—at least for the moment. Dolan's A Company had received the worst of it, with a few dozen dead or wounded. Three disabled tanks were on the far side of the causeway along with an overturned truck near the bridge. With his binoculars Alexander could see two more tanks sitting behind some buildings 600 yards away in Cauquigny.

He found the 57mm gun in a ditch on the side of the road, back near where it had been during the battle. There were two holes in the metal shield, evidently from the duel with the tanks. He organized a makeshift crew and ordered the gun pulled back into position and loaded. The sight was missing, so they'd have to boresight it—look down the barrel and line the shot up.

But as he walked the area, he realized that the few men Dolan had were well deployed, and he liked what he saw of the other officers and noncoms. He walked back to the railroad crossing to find Gavin arriving from Chef-du-Pont. The general had returned with some men after hearing that it was going badly at the bridge.

After Alexander reassured him that the German attack had been repulsed and the east side of the bridge was secured, Gavin told him to take command of the position.

"Do you want me on this side," said Alexander, "the other side, or both sides of the river?"

Gavin thought for a minute. If they attacked the Germans massed on the west side of the causeway and things went badly, the Germans might mount one of their predictable counterattacks, and the Americans might lose the bridge altogether. He said, "You better stay on this side because it looks like the Germans are getting pretty strong over there. Hold fast." Then he took a group of unattached troopers and left for Chef-du-Pont again.

The incoming ordnance would continue throughout the rest of the day and deep into the night, killing and injuring more men. When B Company was taken off the line and moved to Sainte-Mère-Église to reinforce the 2nd and 3rd Battalions, that left Dolan's battered A Company, along with an incomplete C Company, some 507th troopers under Captain Robert Rae on the hill behind the *manoir*, and a platoon or two back at the railroad crossing—a few hundred sleep-deprived and weary men. As they burrowed into their foxholes as deep as they could to withstand the steady mortar shelling, broke out their C rations and washed them down with water, and wrapped themselves in any parachutes they could find to ward off the cold, they wondered what had happened to the invasion forces.

THE DAY HAD been hell on field officers. Amid the chaos, all three of Lindquist's battalion commanders had landed south of the 508th DZ. The 3rd Battalion's Lieutenant Colonel Louis Mendez had found himself several miles away, and with fifteen other troopers, he spent three days and four nights working his way cross-country through and around elements of a 1057th Regiment battalion, losing men and picking up others until they reached safety the morning of June 9. Colonel Herbert Batcheller, the former 505th commander whom Gavin had demoted and put in charge of the 508th's 1st Battalion, landed several miles south near the Douve River. He would be shot in the neck and killed later that day. His executive officer, Major Shields Warren, would assume command and move north with fifty troopers. Lindquist's executive officer, Lieutenant Colonel Harry Harrison, dropped several miles north of his DZ, joined a group of 508th men, and inexplicably refused to take command when he met up with a captain leading 300 troopers. A West Pointer, Harrison would continue to avoid responsibility and a few weeks later would be reduced in rank to major.[11]

The 2nd Battalion's commander, Lieutenant Colonel Thomas Shanley, assembled about thirty-five men soon after landing. But after spending much of the day trying to gather more troops, his mission to destroy two bridges over the Douve and hold that river line had to be abandoned in the face of heavy German resistance and a lack of demolitions and heavy weapons. But he did have two working radios, and after contacting two other groups, he rendezvoused with them at the low knoll labeled Hill 30 on the map, meaning it was thirty meters above sea level. Warren and his group arrived soon after. Hill 30 lay just west of the Merderet and halfway between the La Fière and Chef-du-Pont bridges; it was a mile from each and overlooked the river area in between. During briefings in England, Hill 30 had been pronounced a commanding elevation a few hundred yards west of the Merderet from which a force could control both bridges.

What was on the map was wrong. Shanley and Shields were shocked to find that the superior elevation—the "high ground" that every military leader from time immemorial had headed for in combat—was closer to half the height they'd expected and the commanding view was virtually no view at all, thanks to the high hedgerows and trees in the area, all in full summer leaf, including an apple orchard that circled the crest. Little could be seen beyond their immediate area. But Hill 30 did back up to the Merderet swamp just a few hundred yards to the east, which at least eliminated one angle of attack.

Without enough manpower, heavy weapons or artillery, ammunition, and supplies to carry out their mission, they decided to hunker down and hold out until they could hook up with the rest of the 82nd. Shanley ordered his men to dig in around the hill, and he directed a platoon to move down and establish a roadblock on a rough road that ran along the water south toward the Chef-du-Pont causeway. As the day wore on, more troops made their way to Hill 30.

The rest of the 508th was badly scattered, most of the men to the west and south of Hill 30. Soon after midnight, about 400 troopers had reached the area. Men from every 82nd and 101st regiment, all six, were there. Besides M1s and Thompsons, Shanley had only one small mortar, one BAR, one bazooka, and three light machine guns. They were also desperately low on food, ammo, water, and medical supplies, especially blood plasma, and there were quite a few wounded lying head to toe along a ditch a hundred yards long by a hedgerow. The uninjured men spent most of the night digging foxholes. Shanley ordered the men to pair up—one man would sleep at a time.

Some had parachutes to wrap themselves in for warmth. Tom Porcella, the 508th trooper who had almost drowned, did not. With a friend, he dug a two-man foxhole, and while his buddy slept, Porcella shivered in the predawn hours. His teeth could not stop chattering. All he could think about was England and the mess hall, hot food and coffee, and the warm stove in each tent. When it was his turn to sleep, he couldn't. He didn't sleep all night.[12]

When PFC Harold Kulju awoke in the gully, he moved out and found four other men, and they began moving toward Hill 30. On the way, they helped destroy a German machine-gun nest that was pinning down a small group of troopers on a tiny island in the Merderet swamp. Kulju borrowed a pair of binoculars, located the machine gun, and moved around to its side. He fired at the gunner, who returned fire. It took two magazines, but he finally killed the German. The two groups joined forces and continued on. A few exhausted men dropped out, and eventually even Kulju and another trooper lay down to sleep. They awoke the next morning within a hundred yards of Shanley's perimeter defense and joined him.[13]

It took days for some 508th groups to battle their way through the German positions to reach Hill 30 after their drops. Soon after sunrise, Edgar Abbott, a short, bespectacled 508th lieutenant, was leading a column across a field toward Hill 30. They were about two miles north when a machine gun opened fire on their right flank and every one of the thirty-seven men dived into the foot-high grass.

Corporal Ken "Hard Rock" Merritt, leader of a heavy-machine-gun squad, was right behind Abbott. *That's got to be a Mauser MG34,* thought Merritt as he lay in the wet grass, *or maybe an MG42.* It didn't matter, since both could blast more than a thousand rounds a minute.

It was about 7:00 a.m., and the air was still cool. The troopers had been walking single file. Now, as bullets zipped over them, they were lying as flat as they could in the grass, cool and wet from the early-morning dew. *You couldn't squeeze a cigarette butt under us,* thought Merritt.

The lieutenant twisted around. "Corporal, take two men and knock out that machine gun." He said it as calmly as if he were asking them to go fill up the water cans.

"Yessir."

Merritt was only twenty years old, but it had been a hard twenty. Born and raised in the tiny town of Warner, Oklahoma, he'd worked on the family farm from a very young age. When Merritt was five, his mother died. His father lost the farm and their house in the Depression; they lived in a tent for six months, while Merritt, the eldest boy, helped his father build another house. He dropped out of school after seventh grade to help support the family, planting corn and cotton and picking potatoes for twenty-five cents a day. When he turned seventeen, he left home to join the Civilian Conservation Corps, in which he earned his nickname for the many fights he got in—he was only five foot seven, but he could hold his own. Merritt sent $25 of every month's $30 paycheck back home.

After the CCC camps closed in January 1942, he visited a recruiting office in Muskogee, intending to join the Marines. An Airborne poster on the wall showing a paratrooper and the question "Are You Man Enough to Fill These Boots?" got his attention. The recruiter suggested he was too small to make the cut, but Merritt had made up his mind and eventually persuaded the recruiter. The extra $50 a month a paratrooper got was the deciding factor. The arduous Airborne training hadn't seemed very tough to Merritt, and his maturity had gotten him promoted to corporal and then squad leader.

Now he had been given his first combat order.

Merritt turned around. Right on his tail was Private Wilbur James, a wiry kid from Ohio who had been an athlete in high school and had enlisted two weeks after graduation. He'd just turned twenty four days ago. He was the only man there who was part of Merritt's squad. Behind James was Delbert "Pappy" Fairbanks, a quiet former supply sergeant with a pencil-thin mustache who was nicknamed for his advanced age—he'd be twenty-eight in two weeks if he lived that long. He was short, only five foot six, but he had boxed for the regiment before they'd shipped out. In England, he'd been busted from sergeant to PFC for his part in an interservice bar brawl.[14] Merritt told them to crawl up near him.

He said, "Got any ideas?" He had his own—he'd spent many hours back at Camp Mackall in North Carolina training on how to knock out pillboxes and machine-gun nests—but he figured every man should have a say if he was going to risk his life.

The nest was almost two hundred yards across the field. Every so often there was a rapid-fire burst from the machine gun and everyone tried to squeeze closer to the ground.

"Hard Rock," James said, "remember that demonstration the Brits gave us on the Gammon grenade a couple of weeks ago?" Unlike the American hand grenades, the Gammon had no timer—it exploded on impact once the protective cap was removed.

"Yeah?"

"I can run fast. Give me your Gammons. I've got one too. Let's crawl up there. When we get about seventy yards from it, you two go left and right and lay some cover down. The Jerries will jump in their hole. I'll run up and throw these in. I'll leave my rifle here."

Merritt looked at the two men. "Okay. Sounds good. Fairbanks?"

Fairbanks nodded, and they gave the kid their Gammons. They moved out, slowly crawling through the grass, Merritt and Fairbanks cradling their rifles; Merritt's was a tommy gun. Within minutes the men were soaked in dew.

It felt like it took hours to get within range of the machine-gun nest. Merritt veered off to the right, and Fairbanks went left. Another agonizing fifteen minutes later, they were in position, each about seventy yards from the Germans.

Merritt yelled, "Now!" and he and Fairbanks got up on their knees and began firing. He saw three Germans duck down. James jumped up and sprinted through the grass toward the machine gun as fast as Merritt had ever seen anyone run. When Merritt's twenty-round magazine was finished, he quickly popped in another and continued to fire. James got to within ten yards of the Germans and threw both grenades toward them and fell to the ground. The Gammons exploded and there was a burst of smoke, then nothing but silence.

The three men walked back across the field to the column. They had taken forty minutes to take out the machine gun.

Abbott said, "Good job," and they resumed the march. A short while later they were crossing the road between Chef-du-Pont and Pont l'Abbé when two truckloads of Germans came down the road. The trucks swerved into a field and unloaded, and on both sides of the road, a short, fierce firefight at close range began. It ended when the remaining Germans jumped into the trucks and roared away. Staff Sergeant John Boone trained his Thompson on the two vehicles and fired, and the second truck crashed into the ditch on the side of the road. The troopers had just resumed their trek north when another German attack commenced, and they were pinned down by fire from three directions. They pulled back to a safer area and established a perimeter defense. They would remain trapped there for three days until they were finally able to break out and reach Hill 30.[15]

ON THE EAST side of the Merderet, James Gavin had been walking almost constantly for hours between his CP at the railroad overpass and the two bridges. Carrying only his M1 rifle and accompanied by his aide, Olson, he'd made three trips down to Chef-du-Pont alone, trying to organize and direct his patchwork command in their attempts to fulfill their missions. The La Fière bridge situation seemed to be a standoff for the moment, though the fairly constant German barrage on the area was building in intensity: Artillery, machine-gun, and small-arms fire on the division's exposed positions on the ground that sloped down toward the bridge was "untenable," in the words of one field officer there. Just as serious, there was a severe lack of medical supplies and personnel, ammunition was rapidly dwindling, and officers were dying at an alarming clip. Fortunately, the lieutenants and noncoms, like Dolan, seemed to be doing a good job. And when 200 more men under Lieutenant Colonel Arthur Maloney arrived from Chef-du-Pont, he was put in charge and told to hold the position. By darkness it had been stabilized.

Two miles south, the Chef-du-Pont bridge was still held but barely—the German forces at the far end of the causeway, on the Isle Marie and on the far side of the Merderet swamp, prevented any Allied forces from using the bridge to proceed west. There was a shortage of men and ammo there also, and though troopers from the reserve units had been sent out to find ammunition bundles and bring back their contents, they were having limited success.

No one knew yet if the seaborne forces had landed that morning on Utah or anywhere else—and if they had, their fates were unknown. All the paratroopers could do was try to reach the locations of their objectives and, if they did, to accomplish them. At the two bridges over the Merderet, in Sainte-Mère-Église, and in countless other places on the Cotentin Peninsula, exhausted men continued to battle the enemy, the terrain, and the fear that the members of the 82nd and the 101st comprised the only Allied troops in France.

All Gavin knew to do was try to take the two bridges before the Germans rushed up reinforcements and overwhelmed his meager forces. If they did, he'd pull back his men to Sainte-Mère-Église and hold out there until the invasion troops reached them—if the invasion had been successful.

AT 6:30 GERMAN time that morning, waiting at his hotel in Rennes for the map exercise to begin, General von Schlieben had received a message by orderly from the Rennes *Kommandantur*: "The war game has been canceled. You are requested to return to your unit." The orderly could not supply a reason for the sudden change in orders. Von Schlieben sent the Sturm Battalion commander, Major Hugo Messerschmidt, to find out. He returned quickly with the news that the invasion had begun at 1:00 a.m.; exactly where, no one knew.

They set out immediately, headed north, and stopped at Avranches, fifty-three miles away, to fix their second blown tire of the day. Von Schlieben managed to get in contact with his headquarters by phone and found out more. He was advised to continue driving north along the Cotentin west coast and then proceed east toward Bricquebec. As they drew closer to the east coast, they saw increasing signs of the invasion: vehicles disabled by bombs along the roads, and empty villages with their inhabitants in hiding. On the outskirts of Valognes, just a few miles from von Schlieben's command post at the Château de Chiffrevast, a castle three miles north of town, they stopped to pick up a badly wounded *landser* who told them that he had been under fire from a hedgerow just moments ago. They dropped him at an aid station in Valognes and drove to the command post, arriving at noon. Messerschmidt continued on to his command near Cherbourg.

The briefing from von Schlieben's second-in-command was grim. Thousands of enemy paratroopers had been landing all over the eastern part of the peninsula since 1:00 a.m., though mainly in the Sainte-Mère-Église area. Entire grenadier battalions were out of contact, probably due to cut telephone lines. No one at the 91st Luftlande's HQ knew where their commander, General Falley, was. Worst of all, a massive fleet of fighting and transport craft lay off the eastern coast, where a successful beachhead had been established hours ago after Allied naval guns had delivered a heavy barrage on the German coastal batteries.

But there was some good news: Corps HQ had committed the 1058th Grenadier Regiment, less one battalion, and the Sturm Battalion—in corps reserve near the village of Le Vast, ten miles north of Valognes—to a counterattack. They would proceed south along the N13. Their mission: "to advance via Montebourg and to annihilate the enemy who has landed from the air in the area of Sainte-Mère-Église, then to push on to the east and throw the enemy landed on the east coast back into the sea."

The thousand men of the Sturm Battalion, who had farther to march, had made good progress so far. Not so the 1058th, which had not moved beyond the southern edge of Montebourg—and, alarmingly, had no artillery attached. Falley, von Schlieben was certain, would surely have seen to it that artillery and perhaps motorized units of his division were assigned to it.

Von Schlieben called General Marcks at Corps HQ and made sure that two artillery battalions were ordered to report to the 1058th. Then he prepared to drive to Montebourg to goad the regiment's commander into moving faster. If that could be done, and Sainte-Mère-Église could be taken, and the 1058th and other support divisions could reach the coast soon, von Schlieben believed the enemy could still be defeated.[16]

AT 10:00 A.M., Captain Willi Hümmerich's artillery battalion headed for Fresville, a small village a mile north of Neuville-au-Plain where he was to meet up with two battalions of the 1058th Infantry Regiment preparing to move south and attack Sainte-Mère-Église. His job would be to destroy any enemy artillery there. With a driver and his adjutant, a radioman, he'd jumped into his armor-plated reconnaissance car with an MG42 mounted on the turret and led his remaining artillery east. Between attacks by more paratroopers, field cannon, and Sherman tanks and a naval artillery barrage, his artillery didn't reach Neuville-au-Plain till 6:00 p.m.; units of the 1058th had stopped there because of the heavy naval barrage.

While Hümmerich was regrouping his artillery forces south of the hamlet, a staff car drove up and stopped in front of him. Out stepped General Erich Marcks, commander of the 84th Corps, which manned the western sector of the peninsula. A slender, bespectacled intellectual, Marcks had lost a leg in the invasion of Russia but refused to let that keep him from command. The Allied invasion that day had interrupted a celebration of his fifty-third birthday at his headquarters in

Saint-Lô, thirty miles south; he had just driven up the coast to inspect his units.

After reviewing the situation, Marcks told the young captain that the success or failure of the Allied invasion depended on the German counterattack on Sainte-Mère-Église—unless the village could be conquered that night, the battle, at least in that area, would be lost. Then he climbed back into his car and sped off. He had several more units to inspect and, he hoped, inspire. The battle could still be won.[17]

ELEVEN

COUNTERATTACK

Captain Hellmuth Lang, adjutant to Feldmarschall *Rommel:*
"Sir, do you think we'll be able to manage it, hold them back?"
Rommel: "Lang, I hope we can. I have always succeeded up to now."[1]

THE SEIZING OF Sainte-Mère-Église had gone well—better than anyone could have expected. The 82nd's other goals had not. Due to the scattered drops, the confounding bocage country, and the darkness, none of them had been attained by 6:30 a.m., when the seaborne assault on Utah began.

That operation also went exceedingly well—though for unexpected reasons. Due to strong tides, wind, the loss of three of the four control boats to mines, and large clouds of smoke that were produced by the pre-landing bombardment and that obscured coastal reference points, the landing occurred 2,000 yards south of the intended site. But the luck that dusted Ed Krause's 3rd Battalion also fell on the first wave of assault forces. When the 620 men of the 4th Infantry Division's first wave churning toward shore in twenty Higgins boats landed on the wrong beach, the fortifications they faced were significantly less formidable, and were cleared in a matter of hours. That was chiefly due to the heavy air and sea bombardment on the closest coastal batteries preceding the assault.

The *landsers* of the 709th Infantry manning the trenches in the sand dunes behind the seawall greeted the Americans with small-arms fire, and 88mm shells rained down from a strongpoint north of them, but by the time the first wave of soldiers covered the long distance from the water's edge to the seawall, they found that most of the German troops—a good portion of them *Osttruppen*—just wanted to surrender, and many of the rest had fled inland.[2] Within a half hour, four waves of troops, tanks, and artillery had landed, and naval demolition teams proceeded to blow up the many obstacles at the water's edge as quickly as possible before the tide came in. By 8:00 a.m., besides the heavy artillery fire bombarding the beach for most of the day from enemy batteries a mile or so behind the shoreline, the biggest problem was one of congestion: getting men and vehicles off the beach as engineers worked to create exits in the beach barriers and the seawall, and then moving them across the one-lane exits as key points became blocked and minefields behind the dunes slowed movement.[3]

By 11:00 a.m., as follow-up waves continued to arrive on Utah, men of the 4th Division had already linked up with 101st Airborne troopers. At least one of the four exits behind Utah had been secured, and the others would soon follow. Despite the calamitous drops of four of their six regiments, the men of the 101st and the 82nd were preventing German reinforcements from reaching the coastal units.

But no one with the 82nd knew what was going on elsewhere. Scuttlebutt was that the invasion had been postponed due to bad weather. Whatever the case, it didn't look like they'd be finished with their mission by early afternoon, as some troopers had hoped.

As dawn neared in Sainte-Mère-Église, residents began venturing out of their houses and garden shelters into an eerie quiet. They were astonished to find the village occupied by black-faced soldiers—but from where, they didn't know at first. The flag on each man's shoulder was unfamiliar to most, and it was only when someone ran to their house to consult a dictionary and came back with the news that they knew these were Americans. Their baggy, huge-pocketed uniforms, bowl-shaped helmets covered in camouflage, odd-looking boots with rubber soles, and cartridge belts slung over shoulders and across chests were different from anything the residents had seen before. Almost every man had a dagger sheathed on his right leg and a pistol strapped to his thigh. They looked wild and unkempt, especially compared to the impeccable appearance of the Germans. To Mayor Alexandre Renaud, they "reminded us of Hollywood movie gangsters."[4]

Some were sleeping or smoking in doorways or under trees, their rich tobacco wafting through the village. Raymond Paris and his father brought out some calvados to toast the Americans. The soldiers insisted that a townsman drink first, but after several tasted the liquor, they started spreading the word. In no time a queue formed.[5] Other residents began mixing with the soldiers, who gave American cigarettes to the adults and chocolate and chewing gum to the children.

One Frenchman left his house and began talking to Lieutenant Jim Coyle. Each spoke very little of the other's language, but after several exchanges, Coyle understood the man's concern: He wanted to know if this was just a raid or if it was the full-scale invasion the French had been promised for years. "*Nous restons ici,*" Coyle told him—"We are staying here."[6]

Renaud walked around the square with his two young sons. Dead soldiers still hung from trees and electric wires. There was a pool of blood under one tree. Renaud looked up to see a paratrooper fifteen feet above it. The dead man's eyes were wide open and staring down "as though looking at the bullet holes in him."[7] Two Germans also lay dead, one in the middle of the square and one near the church. Scattered here and there and connected to large packs of supplies were silk parachutes, some of them green camouflage and others different colors. Just beyond the line of trees bordering the southeast corner of the square, the house, barn, and stable were still smoking. The firemen's wooden cart with its pump still sat nearby. Close to it lay the half-charred body of the American paratrooper who had fallen through the blazing roof—it was clear he had made it out of the blaze before he'd died.[8]

But through the rest of the village, people were celebrating—draping their French flags outside their houses, singing "La Marseillaise," and bringing more calvados out to the soldiers. Someone told Raymond Paris that everywhere from Cherbourg to Bayeux, forty miles to the east, had been liberated, though no one knew for sure. The optimism and joy lasted until about 9:15 a.m., when the Americans spread the word that they were expecting a counterattack by the Germans, and a few minutes later when the first shells began to fall, townspeople began gathering food, blankets, money, and valuables and retreating to outside shelters or to the safest parts of their houses. Because of the high water table, there were few basements in the village, and most of the residents left their homes for safer places—in their backyards, where some of them had dug and fortified trenches, or in the fields around town, where they had done the same, often near a thick hedgerow. Others sought refuge with friends or relatives at farms outside town.[9]

One of the first shells exploded between the town's hardware store and a hairdressing salon on the N13, destroying storefronts and killing both shopkeepers and a young woman. Down the street, the baker had just finished his first batch of bread when a shell hit his bakery. Neither he nor his wife, sheltering under a table with their son, was injured. But he packed the still warm loaves into a large bag, placed the bag on a wheelbarrow, and took his family to his brother's farm just outside town, where they found dozens of other refugees.[10]

Mayor Renaud and his family left their house for a ditch about a hundred yards from his house; the ditch was near a small fountain, and they had lined it with parachutes. They were soon joined by a few neighbors. It wasn't perfect, but it would do, the mayor thought. But the German artillery fire intensified and seemed to be focused on the road to the sea thirty feet away. Just before midnight, a shell exploded above the mayor and the others, showering the ditch with branches, dirt, and leaves. Six feet from Renaud, a young mother of three who was sharing her food with those around her yelled that she had been hit. A few minutes later, she was dead. She was one of twenty-two residents of Sainte-Mère-Église who died that day. More would die the next.[11]

A BATTALION SURGEON found Lieutenant Colonel Ben Vandervoort about 3:00 a.m. sitting near a small farmhouse on the 505th DZ. After a quick diagnosis—a broken ankle, though fortunately a simple fracture rather than a compound one—they replaced the boot and laced it as tightly as possible, and the surgeon administered a morphine syrette. Then Vandervoort stood up, picked up his rifle to use as a crutch, took a tentative step, and looked at the men around him.

"Well," he said, "let's go."[12]

Ed Krause's two runners to Colonel Bill Ekman hadn't found him.

Lacking knowledge of Krause's location and disposition, both Ekman and Ridgway told Vandervoort to stand by with his 430 men—more than two-thirds of his battalion's 603.[13] It wasn't until 6:00 a.m. that Ekman gave him the okay to move out. With the sun in his face, Vandervoort led his three companies cross-country through fields and hedgerows to the N13, a mile east; then they began moving up the two-lane blacktopped road toward their objective a mile north of Sainte-Mère-Église: the tiny village of Neuville-au-Plain, with its hundred or so residents. There was no traffic in either direction. The battalion's task was to secure the hamlet and to turn back German troops—and there were many between Neuville-au-Plain and Cherbourg twenty miles north—when they made the inevitable counterattack from that direction. Vandervoort and his men were just south of the hamlet when he received a new order by radio from Ekman: turn south and capture Sainte-Mère-Église. Ekman still hadn't heard from Krause and had to assume the worst—and the crossroads village had to be taken.

Vandervoort changed direction. Just before he started south, he called for 3rd Platoon/Company D leader Lieutenant Turner Turnbull—"a hard-ass lieutenant . . . the best I had," Vandervoort would recall.[14] Just twenty-two, Turnbull was a leader who constantly pushed and trained his men. He was a tall, lanky, dark-haired half-Choctaw from Durant, Oklahoma; in the 1830s, three of his great-grandparents had walked the Trail of Tears from Alabama to what was then Indian Territory. Before enlisting, he'd been attending college to become an architect. Badly wounded in Sicily, he'd returned to his company just in time for D-Day. Like many other soldiers of Native American ancestry, he was nicknamed "Chief," which was typical at the time. His men respected him and didn't dare call him that to his face.[15]

Vandervoort decided he needed a screening force to the north, so he ordered Turnbull to take the forty-two men of his platoon to Neuville-au-Plain and hold it against any German forces attempting to move down the N13. "If there are Germans in the village, mop them up," he told Turnbull. "Mine the road north of it. Set up a defensive position on the most favorable ground. Then hold."[16]

No one in the 82nd knew that two battalions of the 91st Luftlande had already assembled and were moving south on the N13. Somewhere behind them was the thousand-man Sturm Battalion and three artillery units that included ten self-propelled assault guns and several armored cars—about 2,500 troops, all told. Their objective was Sainte-Mère-Église too.

By 5:00 A.M., the roadblocks had been set up at the five main roads into town, with at least one machine gun and BAR at each block. As individual troopers and small groups filtered into town, Krause and his officers sent them out to reinforce the roadblocks. Bazooka squads were distributed evenly.

As the 2nd Battalion moved south, two misdropped sergeants from the 101st fell in with it; the sergeants were towing a two-wheeled ammunition cart retrieved from a glider. Vandervoort asked if they'd give him a lift into Sainte-Mère-Église. One of them said, "We didn't come to Normandy to haul any goddamned colonel around." Vandervoort disabused them of that notion with a direct order. Shortly after they reached town and he clambered out of the cart, an elderly Frenchwoman who saw him hobbling around with his rifle went back in her house and came out with a pair of homemade crutches that she gave him. Not long after that, a couple of jeeps pulled from gliders arrived in town. Vandervoort commandeered one.

When his 400 men and he arrived at the northern edge of town, they ran into the 3rd Battalion roadblock and were told that Krause had secured the village a few hours earlier. Vandervoort found him at the church square, and the two conferred. They didn't like each other—a junior officer often had to separate the men when they would start arguing during an exercise.[17] But now they were all business. Vandervoort suggested they divide the defense of the village: His 2nd Battalion would defend the north and east approaches, and Krause's 3rd Battalion those to the south and west. Krause would oversee the defense from their joint CP near the church. Fortunately, two 75mm pack howitzers delivered in the predawn glider operation had been pulled into Sainte-Mère-Église, and Krause had sent one south and one north. An aid station was set up in a two-story hospice for the elderly north of the square on the N13 near the town hall, and casualties, both American and captured Germans, began flooding in.

THE FIRST GERMAN *Gegenangriff*—counterattack—on Sainte-Mère-Église came from the east at dawn.

Lieutenant Charles "Pinky" Sammon, a tall, slender San Franciscan, had been instructed to place his F Company/2nd Battalion light-machine-gun platoon on the northeast edge of the village, just off the road that led to the coast. He set up his CP behind his three machine-gun emplacements, then wrapped himself in a parachute for warmth and finally got about an hour of sleep. As the sun rose, he took his runner and walked up to check his men to see if they needed any equipment or food. There was only sporadic firing in the distance.

He approached his most forward position and called out to one of his corporals. A long burst of fire erupted from an MG42 and a Schmeisser. Sammon and the runner dived into the ditch beside the road. As they lay there with bullets whizzing over their head, he realized that the Germans had infiltrated their position and killed his forward machine-gun team, and they were now behind a hedgerow directly ahead of them. His runner and he turned around and crawled back up the ditch on their stomachs. After they made some distance from the Germans, an American machine gun began firing at them until a German mortar barrage caused the troopers manning the machine gun to run for cover. Sammon and his runner got up and ran to the machine gun just as its gunner returned.

No one seemed to know what was going on. Sammon gathered what was left of his platoon, then set up the machine gun to resume firing and had a rifleman start shooting grenades into the German position. He also found a mortarman with a complete mortar and a good supply of shells and got him firing rounds. The Germans began retreating from their protected position over the top of the embankment and into a ditch behind them. About twenty men tried to make it. Half of them escaped.

Sammon decided to flank the Germans and throw grenades into the ditch, where he could see tall grass moving. He looked around—none of his men were in sight. But there was equipment scattered all over. So he picked up ten ordinary fragmentation grenades and one Gammon grenade.

He waited until he saw the grass move again, scrambled up and over the embankment, then ran across fifty yards of open ground. When he reached the edge of the ditch and saw the Germans moving toward his men, he tossed the Gammon grenade into the ditch and sprinted back, dropping over the embankment just as a German fired at him with a Schmeisser. He ducked down and waited for the explosion. It never came. And now they knew where he was.

He was trying to work up the nerve to move when a lieutenant from the 82nd's engineering battalion ran up the road toward him. He told

Sammon he had a few men and wanted to help. The two crawled up the tall embankment and cautiously poked their heads up over the top. An MG42 opened up, and they quickly slid back down. When Sammon stood up, the engineering lieutenant didn't. Sammon rolled him over. He was dead with a bullet hole through his face.

Sammon could see from the shifting of the grass that the Germans were moving closer. He pulled the pins on two grenades and threw them. The firing stopped, and Sammon again looked over the embankment. A white flag was waving on the end of a tree branch. Then the German soldier holding it climbed over the embankment and started walking forward. Two of the dead lieutenant's men near Sammon wanted to shoot the German, but Sammon refused to allow them to do so—the man was unarmed. When the German reached them, he began speaking in fluent English. He was a doctor, he said, and many of his remaining comrades were wounded, and they all wanted to surrender. He looked around and seemed surprised that there were only three Americans there.

Sammon told the doctor to go tell his comrades to come out with their hands up. The German left. A few minutes later, a heavy mortar-and-artillery barrage began from the German side and forced Sammon to move back. Finally, the fire eased, and Sammon gathered a dozen men and led them in a counterattack on the Germans, who were now occupying the platoon's original forward position. When they got close to a ditch where the Germans were, they lobbed grenades into it. A few of the Germans made a run for it but were cut down by machine-gun fire from the platoon's main position. When the firing stopped, fifteen dead and wounded Germans remained—many of them, the Americans found out later, "fierce Georgian-Russian" fighters they had been told about in England. There would be no more assaults on the eastern side of the village.[18]

On the southwest edge of town, where an H Company platoon had been assigned to the road leading to Chef-du-Pont, PFCs Leslie Cruise and Richard Vargas and Private Larry Kilroy—who like Cruise was from Philadelphia; his twin brother was serving, coincidentally, on the cruiser USS *Philadelphia*—stood in a slit trench and strained to hear or see any enemy action ahead. Earlier, they had laid their mines in three rows on the asphalt road surface—some defense, they hoped, against tanks. They were glad to be rid of the bulky mines, which they'd been carrying since England. Then in the darkness they dug a foxhole and climbed into it. Their foxhole was about four feet long, two feet wide, and four feet deep. It was about fifty feet off to the right of the road and behind a three-foot embankment perpendicular to the road. Troopers also dug in on the other side of the road and out on the flanks.

No one slept and not just because they stood in a hole in the ground and leaned forward on its front edge. Everyone had been told to expect a quick German counterattack, so they tried to stay alert. Cruise himself was still cold and wet from a dunking he'd taken in a stream while rounding up other 505th troopers after reaching the DZ; he'd had no time to pull off his sodden boots and socks and try to dry them out. The men had gotten only a few minutes' rest when, just before sunrise, they heard a vehicle approaching from Chef-du-Pont; seconds later, they saw two troopers barreling down the road in a jeep towing a 57mm gun. Some of the men near the road shouted warnings, and someone yelled, "Hit the ground!" Cruise and the other two buried themselves in the dirt of their foxhole as the jeep hit the mines and exploded in the air. When the rain of jeep and mine parts stopped, the two men were dead.

Soon mortar fire began hitting their area. About 6:00 a.m., as the sun rose behind the troopers, they could hear rumblings like distant thunder from the same direction—the naval barrage preceding the landings at Utah, they figured. They were six miles inland, but the ground under them still shook. Then some large-caliber shells began dropping among them—miscalculated bombardment from the invasion fleet, no doubt.

When a Frenchman walked up to the roadblock and tried to communicate that a German soldier was in his house and wanted to surrender, a trooper of French descent who could speak some of the language finally understood. The squad sergeant ordered Cruise and Kilroy to go get the German. They followed the farmer to his house and found a young, unarmed grenadier there. They took him back to the roadblock, where Cruise was told to escort the prisoner into Sainte-Mère-Église. After he had done so, then returned, dropped into the foxhole, and opened a K ration box, the full German attack began with artillery and mortar fire. Amid the roaring explosions, the zipping shrapnel, and the falling trees and branches, the three men hugged the bottom of their hole, wishing they'd dug deeper. Rifle and machine-gun fire out on their flanks meant that German infantrymen were attacking through the fields, but there were none at the roadblock.

Then the artillery barrage let up, and a runner appeared and told them to move across the road *now*—several of the men on the left side had been killed or wounded, and the gaps needed to be filled. The three men strapped on the equipment scattered around them. Kilroy still had his BAR and some ammo to gather, but Cruise and Vargas were ready, so they grabbed their rifles and started to run across the open ground toward the road. At the edge of the field, they ran into a cattle fence at the top of the five-foot embankment. Each man held the barbed wire down while the other climbed over, then they slid down to the road gutter. Kilroy hit the fence seconds later and got tangled in the barbed wire. As he struggled to get over it, Cruse and Vargas got to their feet and ran across the road.

They heard the shriek of artillery shells coming in, and as he disentangled himself and slid down to the gutter, Kilroy yelled, "Hit the dirt!" Cruise and Vargas dived through the open wooden gate in the hedgerow along the road and landed in the dirt on their bellies, shoulder to shoulder, as shells burst all around them and fragments flew through the air. The noise was deafening but Cruise could hear moaning from Vargas lying against his right side. Cruise raised himself on his elbows and looked over. Vargas was in great pain. His right pant leg was red with blood.

Cruise shouted, "Can you move?"

Vargas could only shake his head. Cruise got to his feet and grabbed Vargas and dragged him behind the hedgerow as shells continued to explode. He turned the other man on his back. Vargas's jump pants were shredded and his right side, from thigh to ankle, was covered with a mix of dust and blood. Cruise knelt over Vargas and pulled off his own belt, grabbed his trench knife from his left ankle scabbard, and sliced the trousers down the leg and pulled them away. He almost fainted when he saw several large holes all along the leg. He muttered, "Tourniquet! I've got to get one on," and wrapped his belt around Vargas's upper thigh and tightened it.

Kilroy crawled through the gate opening. Over the roar of the mortar fire, Cruise yelled at him to get a medic right away—he'd stay with Vargas. Kilroy took off in a crouching run through an adjacent hedgerow toward Sainte-Mère-Église.

Cruise found a morphine syrette and injected Vargas in his arm. The drug didn't help much—Vargas continued to moan and sob. Cruise applied sulfa powder from their two first aid kits, then tried to cover the wounds with the few bandages in the kits.

Vargas grabbed Cruise's arm and gasped, "Pray for me." Cruise was shaking but he began to recite the Lord's Prayer unsteadily, remembering Vargas on his knees praying his rosary every night in their tent at Camp Quorn. When he finished the prayer, he told Vargas that help was on the way.

Kilroy finally appeared with a medic. Cruise told the medic what he had done as the other man took over. Kilroy said they had orders to move to a new location right away. They left, but before they did, Cruise begged the medic to see that Vargas got to an aid station.

Sometime later, after they'd settled into a new foxhole, Cruise took his musette bag to pull some K rations from it. The bag was full of holes, and inside there were several pieces of jagged shrapnel that had ripped through Vargas instead of him. He managed to mechanically down the food, then told his squad sergeant that he wanted to go into town to see how Vargas was. Things had quieted down some, so the sergeant gave him the okay.

Cruise found the aid station in a large building up the N13. When he asked about Vargas, a surgeon told him that his buddy had died before he'd reached the station—he'd lost too much blood and the shock had been too great for him to survive. Cruise felt in shock himself—he thought the medic had arrived quickly enough. He continued to ask questions: What had happened after he'd left? But no one had any answers, and the staff was very busy with other emergencies.

Cruise walked out of the building, crossed the street, sat down with his back against a stone wall, and began to cry while the occasional artillery shell exploded nearby. After a few minutes, he got up and walked back to the roadblock.[19]

By 9:00 A.M., more than 600 men—most from Krause's 3rd Battalion and Vandervoort's 2nd Battalion but also from the 507th, the 508th, and even the 101st Airborne—had reached the village and been incorporated into its defense. One of the first things Vandervoort had done after arriving was order that the six troopers still hanging from the trees and wires around the square be cut down—it was affecting morale. A detail of a half dozen was assigned the task. By 9:30 a.m., they had cut five down, but then an artillery barrage began and the men were ordered back to their units.[20]

The Germans' bombardment was accompanied by an attack from the south. The 3rd Battalion/1058th Regiment was located on high ground near Fauville, a mile down the two-lane N13—the two observation units had bicycled down there just a few hours before. Now two German grenadier companies, about 200 men with two self-propelled guns, moved up through the fields on either side of the road toward the southern edge of the village—and the roadblock manned by G Company. The 75mm pack howitzer stopped the two guns, but the grenadiers, accompanied by mortar and machine-gun fire, advanced on either side of the N13 along hedgerows.

The men in one G Company squad outpost realized they were in danger of being outflanked and decided to withdraw, but in doing so, they ran into two trucks loaded with Germans. When PFC Dominick DiTullio, a twenty-eight-year-old from Pittsburgh whose parents had emigrated from Italy, opened fire on the trucks, the Germans jumped out and scattered before they could realize how few Americans they faced. DiTullio killed one grenadier and captured two others, then affixed his bayonet and advanced across the road to make sure that the enemy had completely withdrawn. He remained behind to cover the retreat of his unit, then followed them back.[21]

But the Germans had only pulled back to reorganize. Mortar and artillery fire from Hill 20 continued to hammer G Company's position. One mortar round exploded in the midst of a mortar squad, killing two troopers and severing both legs of another and one leg of yet another. Both died a short time later.

Krause showed up in a jeep and ordered I Company, formerly in battalion reserve in an apple orchard near town, to attack. When he got out of the jeep, one of his legs was dragging from a shell fragment in his ankle.[22] Before he returned to town, another piece of shrapnel smacked into his leg, but he ignored it; his leg felt numb, but he could still get around on it.

Company I's eighty-five troopers moved south along a dirt road parallel to the N13. But in following the zigzag course of the protective hedgerows, the point men lost their sense of distance and direction. Ninety minutes later, when they finally turned east and reached the N13 a mile south of town, they ran into the German force. Soon they were under fire from both sides of the road. As they tossed Gammon grenades at several trucks, three of the four scouts were killed. The rest of the company took cover in the ditch by the side of the road and began firing at the Germans in the ditch on the other side just ten yards away and in the field beyond. A machine gun kept them pinned down as the Germans tossed grenades over at them. All they could do was crawl down the ditch north toward Sainte-Mère-Église.

When they reached the edge of town, they were near a farmhouse, but still trapped in the ditch. Twenty-two-year-old squad leader Sergeant Charles Matash stood up in the open and fired his Thompson down the road as the rest of the men dashed across into a sunken orchard near the house. A mortar shell fragment slammed into his shoulder, but he managed to follow the others to safety at the roadblock.[23]

That show of force convinced the Germans that the south side of town was too strongly held for another attack. There would be no more assaults from that direction, though the Germans would continue to shell the village from their position south of town with mortars, Nebelwerfers, 88mm guns, and other artillery.[24]

NORTH OF TOWN, Lieutenant Turnbull led his forty-three troopers—all riflemen, except for a few BARs, one bazooka, and a few machine guns—at a half trot in two parallel columns along hedgerows on either side of the N13. About a mile north of Sainte-Mère-Église, they moved through a cluster of a dozen-odd houses and farms that flanked the road, most of them on the right side, including the centuries-old Gothic church and an elegant château across the street and 300 yards to the east. Turnbull halted his men about fifty yards past the château where the land and the road began to fall off slightly. They would deploy on this high ground or what passed for it.

On the right side of the road, behind a hedgerow that ran northeast and provided a clear field of fire about 600 yards in front of them over a large, open pasture, he positioned two squads with machine guns; a large orchard with hundreds of apple trees spread out to the east. For some concealment, Turnbull placed the bazooka team fifty yards to the rear and next to the last house on the right side of the road. Behind another hedgerow on the left side of the road, he deployed his third squad, which had two machine guns and a BAR. That squad was commanded by Sergeant Bob "the Beast" Niland. From upstate New York, twenty-five-year-old Niland had three brothers, all of whom were also in the service—one of them was with the 101st.[25] On the other side of the hedgerow was a dirt road, and about a hundred yards down it to the left was a two-story *manoir* with outbuildings.

As the three squads dug into the embankments, they noticed farmers gathering their cows and a few people walking along the roads. There were no planes in the sky and no artillery or gunfire anywhere near them. It was so peaceful, remembered one corporal, that "it certainly did not seem like we were at war."[26]

Then they waited. But not for long.

An hour later, about 1:00 p.m., the platoon noticed a Frenchman riding a bike down the N13 toward them. When he reached their roadblock, Turnbull had him stopped. In broken English, the Frenchman told them that not far behind him were several American paratroopers guarding a large group of German prisoners. They let him continue south.

He passed Vandervoort just as the colonel arrived in his jeep, with a 57mm anti-tank gun towed by another jeep behind him. Vandervoort directed the gun to the east side of the road next to a house near the bazooka. A wire team had followed the colonel and laid a field telephone line from his CP near the northern edge of Sainte-Mère-Église.

As Vandervoort used his crutch to walk around the platoon's position with Turnbull, a long column of troops began to crest a ridge about a mile north. Vehicles could be seen scattered in their ranks. To Vandervoort peering through binoculars, it looked to be a battalion's worth of men—500 or so. They wore the field gray uniforms of the German Army. On their flanks were U.S. paratroopers carrying guns and waving orange panels, the Allied recognition symbol.

Something about it seemed wrong. When the front of the column was only a thousand yards away, Vandervoort told Turnbull to have one of his machine guns fire a burst into the field to the left of the oncoming column. The German "prisoners" and their "captors" immediately scattered to each side of the road and the leading vehicle—a tracked, self-propelled gun—opened fire.

Turnbull's anti-tank gun returned fire, and an accurate hit set the German gun ablaze. Another pulled up behind it. The anti-tank gun took that one out too. The German grenadiers, screened by smoke shells fired into the road by another gun, began to move forward on both sides of the N13. After Vandervoort told Turnbull to delay the enemy as long as possible and then withdraw back to Sainte-Mère-Église, he sped off in his jeep.

Mortar fire began falling in the platoon's position. Turnbull's well-disciplined platoon fired at the Germans as they made their way through the fields. But as the afternoon wore on, the Germans ranged farther out on the flanks—and out of range. The steady and accurate shelling and MG42 fire, deafening when combined with Mausers and Schmeissers, began whittling down Turnbull's men—about half of them were dead or injured, mostly from the constant mortar fire. The German self-propelled gun closed to within 500 yards and took out the Americans' only bazooka, then drove the crew away from the 57mm gun. But those men returned and resumed fire until they destroyed the German gun, and when someone with binoculars spied a moving vehicle that looked to be a Mark IV tank in the distance, the crew fired at it until it stopped.

By 5:00 p.m., the Germans were close to outflanking the troopers on the west side, and when they reached the *manoir* and began sniping from there, the few men left in the squad on that side hustled across the road. The Germans had begun the same tactic to the east through the orchard and had almost reached the château and the church, just 300 yards away. Once there, they could more quickly surround the platoon and leave no escape route south. Turnbull's medic was administering to twelve wounded men incapable of walking. Nine others lay dead.

As the battle continued, Turnbull shouted over the din to his radioman—the phone wasn't working. The private pulled up the wire and started following it south alongside the ditch on the east side of the road. He hadn't gone far when he glanced across the road and saw Germans moving toward the road—and him—to cut off the platoon. It wouldn't be long before his comrades were surrounded. He found the cut in the wire and continued south to Sainte-Mère-Église—he had no other choice.

The private could still hear the heavy fire from Neuville-au-Plain as he reached the edge of town and passed 2nd Battalion men digging in and camouflaging primary and alternate positions in the hedgerows on each side of the N13. Small groups of troopers had been sent out to comb the countryside for supply parapacks with their color-coded parachutes, especially those containing much-needed ammunition and anti-tank mines. Others were looking through resupply gliders that had crashed around the town; they salvaged anything that might prove useful. Fired by German coastal units swiveling their guns inland, artillery shells landed here and there or whooshed overhead. Vandervoort had installed his mortar observation post in the attic above the second floor of the town's city hall, which had a good view of the northern approaches. Krause's American flag still waved above the entrance. Vandervoort's mortarmen had wanted the flag taken down—they were sure any German mortar or artillery sighters would be aiming at it—but Krause had insisted the flag stay up.[27]

Back in Neuville-au-Plain, the Germans on the east side of the N13 were only seventy-five yards away, and Turnbull's men on that side had pulled back to where Turnbull was. He yelled to his troopers, "Boys, there's only one thing left we can do—we can charge them."

One private said he was ready. Another who had just returned from reconnaissance to the rear, and who had also heard from a corporal on the right flank, spoke up. "I think we can still get out."

Turnbull looked around at his men. "What's your judgment?"

To a man, they supported falling back. Turnbull told them to get ready for a run. They'd also have to leave behind the wounded who couldn't move. The medic said he'd stay with them, and three troopers volunteered to hold back and cover the withdrawal: Niland with his tommy gun, a PFC with a BAR, and a corporal loaded with grenades. Then Turnbull called Vandervoort on his SCR-300 and told him they couldn't hold out much longer. Vandervoort sent a reserve platoon led by Lieutenant Theodore "Pete" Peterson up along the west side of the N13 with specific orders not to engage with the enemy until they had contacted Turnbull. With any luck, their diversionary attack would allow him to withdraw safely.[28]

When Peterson arrived at Turnbull's position, he left his men behind a hedgerow, then crossed the road to find Turnbull. He found him "very calm, and he had the situation well in hand, for the rough position he was in," Peterson recalled later. As heavy large-caliber mortar fire exploded around them, Turnbull asked Peterson to concentrate his fire on a machine gun on the *manoir* to the left side, and to draw fire upon his position so Turnbull could withdraw. Peterson returned to his men and on his command had all his firepower—BARs, machine guns, M1s, a bazooka, and a mortar—open up on the *manoir.* Then they stopped. There was no more fire from the German machine gun, and when Peterson led two scouts to the farmhouse, they found no sign of the enemy. A few minutes later, another firefight erupted when a group of Germans ran into Peterson's left flank and was cut down. The few survivors took off in every direction as the rest of the platoon fired on Peterson and his men again.

Peterson had bought Turnbull some time. On the east side of the N13, Turnbull started his withdrawal with what was left of his platoon. The three volunteers laid down covering fire, and as Niland stepped over a low hedgerow to move across the road and set up there, the ripping sound of an MG42 split the air and he was knocked to the ground, lifeless. Turnbull had his men take off at full speed but at intervals. When they'd all run back far enough and gathered, they took off again, stopping regularly to turn and fire at the enemy. As soon as Turnbull's men were out of sight of the Germans, they slowed to a walk, and he sent a trooper to tell Peterson they were safe. He too withdrew his men at a run.

A quarter of an hour later, with the sun low in the west, Turnbull reached the outskirts of Sainte-Mère-Église with fifteen men. Peterson's platoon was right behind them; he hadn't lost a man. For most of the afternoon—four hours—Turnbull's platoon had managed to hold off the vanguard of two reinforced battalions of the 91st Luftlande on their way to destroy the village and assault the troops landing at Utah Beach, and kept the Germans from attacking Krause and Vandervoort's much smaller force from the north and south at the same time.[29]

TWELVE HUNDRED YARDS west of Sainte-Mère-Église, under the crude tarpaulin serving as his CP, Matt Ridgway was evaluating his division's situation. After the calamitous drops of two of his regiments and the disappointing early-morning glider supply operations, he had some kind of control over only a third of his command—some 2,100 men.[30] Four isolated groups of 82nd troopers on the west side of the Merderet were surrounded by the enemy: Timmes and more than a hundred mostly 508th men in an orchard a half mile north of Cauquigny; Lieutenant

Colonel Thomas Shanley and several hundred men on Hill 30, south of Cauquigny; 200 507th troopers north of Amfreville under the command of Captain Allen Taylor; and another 200 with Colonel George Millett, the 507th commander who had attacked Amfreville soon after landing but was beaten back by superior enemy numbers and retreated to a position several hundred yards west of the village. Just under a thousand 505th troopers—their ranks reinforced by misdropped men from the 507th, the 508th, and even the 101st Division—maintained a tenuous hold on Sainte-Mère-Église. They had fended off attacks from the north, east, and south, and there would be more.

But they had not achieved any other objective. Neither of the causeways over the Merderet had been taken—difficult missions made more so by the flooded Merderet marshlands, which had come as a surprise to everyone. The causeway and bridge at La Fière had been theirs, but shortsighted leadership, and just plain bad luck and timing, had allowed the Germans to retake Cauquigny. The 82nd had managed to hold the east side of the bridge and had secured—barely—both ends of the one at Chef-du-Pont, though, due to the artillery on Isle Marie, they didn't actually control movement over it. Two bridges over the Douve that were to be destroyed hadn't been, and areas and towns west of the Merderet that were to be taken, Amfreville and Étienville, were still under German control. And hundreds of injured men were being treated at the aid station in Sainte-Mère-Église and two more in farmhouses near Ridgway's CP and the La Fière bridge.

His men controlled a triangle of land with its points at Sainte-Mère-Église, the La Fière bridge, and Chef-du-Pont. German reinforcements were making their way to the area that night, and those would surely include tanks and self-propelled guns, which were difficult for lightly armed airborne troops to engage with. An armored task force led by Colonel Raff was supposed to drive inland from Utah that afternoon to bolster the 82nd. There was no sign of it. And there was no indication that the Utah landings had even occurred and, if they had, had been successful. The only radio Ridgway's CP had could send messages but not receive them, so he had no idea whether they were getting through to Corps HQ.

About 6:00 a.m., Ridgway drove in his jeep to the railroad overpass and found Gavin. They conferred for a while. They still hadn't made contact of any sort with the seaborne forces.

"Jim," Ridgway said, "how are things going?"

Gavin was typically low-key. "All right, I guess," he said. "We have had very heavy fighting and I have lost a couple of battalion commanders as well as quite a few troopers. We have not been able to get our first objective, but we are holding our own. Tanks at the bridge site are giving us a difficult time."

"Well," said Ridgway, "I have heard rumors that the amphibious landings did not come in on account of weather. We may have a hard time of it."

They talked about what they would do in that case. They decided to keep it from the troops and to make the best of things. If they had to, they'd pull all their forces into Sainte-Mère-Église and fight to the bitter end.[31]

After meeting with Ridgway, Gavin jeeped down to the bridge area to assess the situation. The 1st Battalion/505th had incurred heavy casualties—25 percent of Dolan's A Company was dead or injured—but the men were dug in and seemed to have the situation, at least on the east side of the bridge, under control. But the Germans 600 yards away near the Cauquigny church were formidable. There would be no crossing of the causeway that day.

The scene at Chef-du-Pont was no better, and Gavin wasn't happy about it. "If we had the 505th, we'd've had that bridge by now," he confided to Walton, the *Time* correspondent, that evening. It had originally been a 505th objective, but the La Fière bridge action had taken every 1st Battalion trooper available.[32]

Gavin returned to where the railroad ran under the D15. He decided to establish his command post close by, about a hundred yards east near a hedgerow in a field.[33] From there, he could stay in touch with the men two miles south in Chef-du-Pont and a half mile west at the Manoir la Fière, and with Ridgway's CP a mile closer to Sainte-Mère-Église. He'd finally established radio contact with the battalion of mostly 508th troopers trapped on Hill 30 across the river and a mile south of Cauquigny. Those men were under Lieutenant Colonel Thomas Shanley, the commander of the 2nd Battalion/508th. Shanley had been a superb combat commander in Sicily, and Gavin had faith in him.

One enemy attack on the La Fière bridge had been beaten back, but Gavin knew the Germans were massing for another one. There would be no retreat, he told his HQ staff gathered around him at his CP. "We'll be either killed or captured here," he told them.

In private, he was doubtful of their chances. A short while later, at dusk, he turned to Walton.

"You know, you don't have to stay here," he said.

"What do you mean?" said Walton.

"We can't hold, but we're not going to give up. They *might* save division headquarters."[34]

THAT EVENING, AT OKW headquarters just outside Berlin, the intelligence summary for the day reflected the success of Fortitude, the massive deception operation that had misled the Germans as to the location and timing of the invasion:

Sainte-Mère-Église, looking south down the N13 from the town square, on the left. The church is fifty yards beyond the trees.

The Sainte-Mère-Église church, seen from the south (town square) side

Pvt. Ken Russell, 505th

Lt. Harold Cadish, 505th
(courtesy of Marvin Catler)

Sgt. John Ray, 505th

Pvt. John Steele, 505th

Pvt. Ladislav Tlapa, 505th

Alexandre Renaud, mayor of Sainte-Mère-Église (second from left), with (from left) an American soldier, the town crier, and a *gendarme* officer

Pierre Maury, coordinator of Resistance activities around Sainte-Mère-Église, with two American soldiers in front of his shop

The D15, looking west, with the Manoir la Fière at bottom

The Manoir la Fière, shortly after June 9

The three Leroux children, Genevieve, Jeannine, and Louis, early in the war (courtesy of Jeannine Leroux)

An early twentieth-century photo of the La Fière bridge, looking east, with the *manoir* behind it on the right

The east (back) side of the Manoir la Fière

Lt. John Dolan, 505th
(courtesy of Heidi Dolan)

Lt. Louis Levy, 507th
(courtesy of DAV Louis Levy Chapter 11, Yuma, AZ)

Lt. Joseph Kormylo, 507th

Lt. John Marr, 507th

Along with some other 82nd Airborne men, Lenold Peterson (second from right) and Marcus Heim (far right) receive medals for their actions on June 6, 1944, at the La Fière bridge.

A German MG34 team in Normandy. Because the 34 and the MG42 were light, they could be carried easily by one man, and teams could move quickly, confusing the enemy.

Cpl. Ken "Hard Rock" Merritt, 508th

PFC Wilbur James, 508th

Pvt. Delbert "Pappy" Fairbanks, 508th (courtesy of Faye DiFrancia)

Aerial view of the Chef-du-Pont bridge (lower right) and the western edge of the village

Capt. Roy Creek, 507th

Lt. Turner Turnbull, 505th

Sgt. Billy Owens, 505th

Lt. Malcolm Brannen, 508th

Lt. Woodrow Millsaps, 508th

The Waco CG-4A glider held only about fourteen men, but its aluminum tube frame made it sturdier than the British Horsa.

325th soldiers disembark from a Horsa glider upon landing on June 7.

The Horsa was larger than the Waco and could carry twice the troops, but it was composed almost completely of wood, and more fragile. Few glidermen survived a collision with an obstacle. Eight of them died when this one landed just outside Sainte-Mère-Église.

Gliders transporting the 325th and their tow planes circle LZ "W," south of Sainte-Mère-Église, on June 7.

Sgt. Bud Olson, 325th GIR
(courtesy of Bud Olson)

Lt. Richard Johnson, 325th
(courtesy of Martin Morgan)

PFC Charlie DeGlopper, 325th GIR
(courtesy of Charles DeGlopper)

Lt. Waverly Wray, 505th

The StuG III destroyed by Pvt. John Atchley on June 6 on the outskirts of Sainte-Mère-Église (looking north)

The village of Sainte-Mère-Église after two days of heavy German shelling

An 82nd trooper dashes for the door of the church in Sainte-Mère-Église on June 8.

German prisoners captured by the 82nd Airborne on their way to Utah Beach on June 8 for evacuation

Lt. Paul Kinsey, 325th
(courtesy of Bill Kinsey)

Capt. John Sauls, 325th
(courtesy of John Sauls)

Capt. Robert Rae, 507th

Pvt. Melvin Johnson, 325th, with his wife, Ruby Ann, and their son, Kenneth, in 1943

Destroyed German tanks on the causeway just west of the La Fière bridge, soon after June 9

A soldier stands in front of the nearly destroyed Cauquigny chapel shortly after the June 9 battle.

The unimposing La Fière bridge, site of what Gen. Matthew Ridgway called "as hot a single battle as any U.S. troops had, at any time during the war."

> While the Anglo-Saxon enemy landing on the coast of Normandy represents a large-scale operation, the forces employed comprise only a relatively small portion of the total available. Of the approximately sixty divisions at present in the South of England, it is likely that at the most ten to twelve divisions are at present taking part, including airborne troops. The main objective of the landing must be regarded as the capture of the port of Cherbourg, and the simultaneous closing of the Cotentin Peninsula to the south.

The German impression of the Allied objective was partially correct. And the Germans continued to believe George Patton's 1st Army Group of twenty-five divisions, and a dozen other divisions located in Scotland or central England, had not been committed, which was also true—because those troops did not exist.

> The conclusion is, therefore, that the enemy command plans a further large-scale undertaking in the Channel area which may well be directed against a coastal sector in the central Channel area.[35]

That coastal sector, of course, was the Pas de Calais, the overwhelming choice of invasion site at the German High Command and of Hitler himself. The Allied ruse had worked better than anyone could have expected. The Führer would not be fooled into sending all his armored divisions to Normandy, and when the true invasion came somewhere near Calais, they would be waiting there. The invaders would be destroyed, and the war would be won.

"In the hedgerow areas, fighting against tough parachute opponents is difficult and time-consuming," read the evening report of the 91st

Luftlande.[36] But there were still plenty of German troops in the Cotentin fighting tooth and nail to destroy the Allied invaders—and more were on the way.

After receiving its orders earlier that morning, the 2nd Battalion/Fallschirmjäger 6 had moved steadily north through the fields and along the roads east of the N13. Corporal Eugen "Opa" Griesser and his comrades hadn't gone far when a massive barrage from the enemy warships off the coast found them and drove the men to the ground, where they lay, terrified, for an hour.[37] When it finally ended, the battered troops continued north, enduring mortar and artillery fire, strafing from occasional enemy fighter planes, and scattered firefights with small units of American paratroopers, until they reached a hamlet two miles east of Sainte-Mère-Église named Turqueville that was occupied by some *Osttruppen* of the 709th Infantry Division. By that point, everyone was covered with mud from constantly hitting the ground. There, the mortar fire was replaced by Allied naval artillery shelling on their position. They were stuck with no radio contact with flak units in the area, so the battalion commander, Captain Rolf Mager, summoned Griesser. He told Griesser to lead one of two recon squads into Sainte-Mère-Église to assess the enemy strength. Griesser made sure his dozen young *landsers* discarded every part of their equipment that could rattle or clank, and they headed out. They moved slowly and carefully toward the village, working around a few American outposts. He posted two men with MG42s to cover their withdrawal. They finally reached an alley and moved down it to a house near the church square, where they saw large groups of American paratroopers. It soon became clear that Sainte-Mère-Église was occupied by at least a battalion.

From a window six feet from them, a machine gun erupted, and from the other side of the square, others began firing—not at Griesser and his men but at the other recon squad to their right. He and another *landser* edged up and tossed grenades through the window and the machine-gun fire stopped. Griesser fired a few bursts from his Schmeisser into the window just to make sure, took a quick look inside, and then led his men back down the alley as fast as they could run as another machine gun opened up on them. When an American stepped out from behind a house, lifted his rifle, stood in their way, and yelled at them, they knocked him over and kept on running.

Both recon units made it back to report the presence of a battalion. By that time the sun was almost down. Von der Heydte ordered Mager by radio to pull his battalion back to Saint-Côme-du-Mont. They hadn't gone far when enemy gliders began landing in the open fields around them. The Fallschirmjäger 6 attacked, killing many of the enemies in the gliders and taking some prisoner. They also pillaged the gliders and found boxes of chocolate and cigarettes, cans of fruit juice and meat, and other treasures. Then they continued south to Saint-Côme-du-Mont.[38]

Colonel Edson Raff was no shrinking violet. He was about five foot six and known for his tough demeanor and training methods, so naturally his men nicknamed him "Little Caesar" after the 1931 film of the same name featuring diminutive tough guy Edward G. Robinson in the title role. The former commander of the 2nd Battalion/509th Parachute Infantry Regiment, the first paratroop unit to jump into combat in North Africa, he had written *We Jumped to Fight*, a book about the mission that had just been published in January 1944 and made him a celebrity—and done nothing to improve his reputation among many of his peers who thought him an abrasive publicity hound.[39] Since

North Africa, he'd been spending time as a D-Day airborne planner on General Omar Bradley's staff in London. But he hungered for another combat command, and Bradley had forced him on Ridgway.

Ridgway didn't like him—neither did Gavin—and the feeling was mutual. Instead of bestowing upon Raff the command of one of the 82nd's regiments, Ridgway gave him a lesser D-Day assignment, one normally assigned to a captain or major. He would lead an armored unit of seventeen Shermans, two armored cars, and ninety glider infantrymen of the 325th, who would ride on the tank hulls. Task Force Raff would land behind the first waves of the 4th Infantry Division and break through to the 82nd at Sainte-Mère-Église to provide it with much-needed firepower against German armor.

They came ashore with the other seaborne elements of the 82nd Airborne Division, which began landing on Utah at 2:00 p.m.—two battalions of artillery, engineer, quartermaster, and medical units, and more. After his force spent ninety minutes de-waterproofing the Shermans, Raff in an open jeep led it inland over one of the beach exits and over a narrow causeway through the flooded marshland to Sainte-Marie-du-Mont, which had been cleared of von der Heydte's Fallschirmjäger 6 earlier that day by the 101st Airborne. There, he headed west on a main road that intersected the N13 at a cluster of a half dozen houses called Les Forges. There was no opposition, no enemy fire—the result of the work of the 101st and advance elements of the 4th Infantry, which had preceded Raff—and the trip was a peaceful ride through the green French countryside until they reached the tiny crossroads hamlet and the N13. A left turn would take them to Carentan, seven miles south; Raff turned north toward Sainte-Mère-Église, two miles north.

A few minutes later, just before 7:00 p.m., they reached a point where the road dropped slightly into a small valley. In the distance they could see the village's church steeple. Off the road, some 4th Infantry cannon were firing north at a location designated Hill 20 on Raff's map. German artillery there began bombarding the column. He halted his forces and trained his binoculars north. Almost a thousand yards up the two-lane highway, on a wooded ridge on the west side that ran perpendicular to the highway, was a German artillery unit. Raff could see what looked like a pillbox.

He knew that the valley before him was LZ "W," the landing zone for a glider-reinforcement operation scheduled to arrive in two parts, at 9:00 p.m. and 11:00 p.m., on either side of the N13. If the Germans on Hill 20 weren't cleared off soon, the 177 gliders and their howitzers, jeeps, anti-tank guns, ordnance, food, medical supplies, and personnel would be sitting ducks.

He called to his lieutenant leading the reconnaissance platoon in an armored car.

"Take your scout car up the road and see what you can see," he said. Then he told the sergeant operating the nearest tank to go along and cover him. The glidermen dismounted.

The two vehicles got about 300 yards up the road before there were two explosions, and Raff saw the tank pile into the unmoving scout car. The lieutenant and a few other men made it back on foot. Raff regrouped and directed his Shermans to move off the road to the left side and move north. The two lead tanks made it through two of the fields before a barrage of shells knocked both out.

"That's eighty-eight fire," Raff's armor commander told him. "There are several, and I'm sure the fields ahead of us must be mined." Soldiers were quick to designate heavy artillery fire as 88mm cannon, but even if this was something smaller, it was wreaking heavy damage. As flames and smoke rose from the tanks, Raff called off the attack and pulled his force back. He tried several times to send a warning by radio, but he wasn't sure it would be routed to the planes on time.

A few minutes before 9:00 p.m., with the sun low in the west, the men heard a low rumble emanating from the east, and soon the armada of C-47s and their towed gliders—140 Horsas and 37 Waco CG-4As—came into view. As they approached the landing zone, Raff could hear rifles, machine guns, and artillery open up on them all at once. His remaining tanks fired at the German positions, but the effect was negligible. A few transport planes went down, but the rest turned around and headed back toward the Channel. The released gliders began circling and then landing. One newspaperman with Raff described it thus: "It was too small a landing field for so many gliders under any conditions. Only a few of them were able to make it. . . . They crashed into trees and hedgerows on each side of us. They pancaked down on the road. They skidded crazily and stopped." The Germans trained their 88s and machine guns on the crews as they scrambled out of their aircraft. One glider came to a stop next to the still-burning tanks, and the glidermen jumped out and ran before it too caught fire. Another one landed near the enemy emplacement atop Hill 20. Its crew pulled a jeep out of it, collected their equipment, bounced down to the road, and sped past Raff.[40] All but a few of the large wooden Horsas splintered upon landing, while few of the Wacos were destroyed.

As the survivors of the gliders were rounded up and the many wounded tended to by the few 4th Infantry medics behind Raff, he moved his remaining tanks and cars into a field well out of range of the German artillery, formed a circle with them, and had his men sleep within it. If the situation looked more hopeful in the morning, they would try again.[41]

THE FINAL AIR operation of the day arrived two hours after the first. An hour after sunset, a hundred C-47s began cutting loose their gliders—but not over LZ "W." After the disastrous first operation, Ridgway had engineered a plan to divert the LZ from "W" to the 505th's DZ "O" using a green-lit T, green smoke, and a Eureka signal. Fortunately, the lead towplanes picked up the Eureka signal and made for "O." But enemy fire was intense, and many men were killed or wounded before their gliders, most of them the larger Horsas, reached the ground. Few landed on the LZ; most of them crashed in fields and ditches or into trees, houses, and hedgerows, and disintegrated by the time they came to a stop.

In the dark, troopers moved out where they could to find the gliders and aid the wounded and salvage what guns, ammunition, and vehicles they could from the wrecked aircraft. They worked through the night, but the results were disappointing—not nearly enough of what they would need to stave off the Germans surrounding them.

Early that morning, Sergeant Rudi Escher, Corporal Rudolf May, and the thirteen other *landsers* of the two 1058th observation squads had bicycled a mile south down the N13 to Fauville, where their regimental HQ had taken over a château just off the road. They were sent to a sunken lane near it to wait for new orders. There was no food available. The men were hungry and exhausted after their long night in Sainte-Mère-Église, and several of them fell asleep. The others had to satisfy themselves with a piece of *Kommisbrot* (brown bread) or *Knäckebrot* (crispbread) they had with them. Escher had dropped down with his back to a tree stump and just dozed off when the sound of rifle shots woke him. One of them hit May in his upper left arm, and he stood and fired his MG42 from his hip in the direction the shots had come from. But there were no more shots, and though the *landsers* searched the area, they found no enemy soldiers.

They dug individual foxholes in the lane and settled in. Late in the afternoon, there was an artillery bombardment, so they hunkered down. A large piece of shrapnel zipped by Escher's head and smacked into the ground nearby, still smoking. Then, about an hour before sunset, more than a hundred planes roared into view from the east and began releasing gliders above the *landsers.*

From their foxholes just outside the hamlet of Fauville, Escher, May, and the others watched as a glider landed in the meadow in front of them. They ventured down to inspect the glider. Inside they found a jeep and an anti-tank gun, a dead pilot, an injured copilot, and two American soldiers petrified with fear. They removed the three survivors and tried to retrieve the jeep and cannon but gave up and set the glider on fire.

As midnight approached and the near-constant reports of German machine guns to the west faded away and then disappeared and were replaced by the sound of armored vehicle tracks in motion and then planes flying over them, Escher and his comrades began to suspect that they were surrounded by the enemy.[42]

EARLIER THAT DAY, two miles southwest of Fauville at the bridge outside Chef-du-Pont, where Lieutenant Colonel Ostberg's unmoving body lay with only his head above the surface, two troopers made their way down to him under heavy fire. They finally managed to reach him and pull his waterlogged body out of the Merderet. He was still alive, though badly injured. They carried him back to safety near the creamery. The next senior officer was Captain Roy Creek, CO of E Company/507th and a married man from New Mexico who'd grown up on a farm and earned his commission through ROTC in college.

Lieutenant Colonel Arthur Maloney, the 507th's XO, arrived soon afterward with seventy-five more men to add to Creek's one hundred. Two more attempts to storm the bridge failed. Maloney, a few days shy of his thirtieth birthday and a happily married father of two sons, led one of them. On the east side of the bridge, he jumped out of a foxhole behind the smoke cover of a white phosphorus grenade, and as he ran forward, a German threw a potato masher that landed at his feet. In a split second he decided he didn't have time to pick it up and throw it back; he turned to run as the grenade went off. Even though Maloney was six foot four and weighed 240 pounds, the explosion knocked him into the air. He got up unhurt and ran back to the foxhole to hear the men in their foxholes laughing at the sight of the "'old man' running in mid-air."[43]

The eastern approach was finally cleared when troopers crawled slowly down the causeway and, one by one, killed twenty-four Germans who were dug in about ten yards apart along the narrow shoulders of the causeway. Then the Americans rolled the Germans out of their foxholes and took their places. But constant rifle, machine-gun, and artillery fire from the right flank across the swamp made those positions untenable, and several men died as the afternoon wore on. Most of the troopers remained out of sight back at the creamery.

What appeared to be a stalemate took a turn for the worse when Maloney was called back to the La Fière area with most of the men present. He left Creek with thirty-four troopers—not a single one of them from his company, so not men he was familiar with. That number was soon reduced to twenty when a furious artillery barrage, including what Creek thought was probably an 88, bombarded the creamery area. Creek moved from foxhole to foxhole, figuring out who was dead and who was only wounded, organizing the men into squads, and putting in charge those he'd seen do good jobs since they'd organized. After Creek had established a CP in the courtyard, a trooper at a window up on the main building's third floor yelled down to him that what looked like a company of Germans was moving around their left rear about 300 yards away near the south edge of Chef-du-Pont.[44] Creek's small force was in danger of being surrounded.

That was when a lieutenant acting as a runner from General Gavin arrived with a summary of the situation at the La Fière bridge and a message: "Hold at all costs." *It's doubtful we can hold something we don't have,* thought Creek. He sent the runner back through the village and up the railroad tracks with a request for reinforcements.

Minutes later, a formation of C-47s appeared and began dropping bundles of weapons and ammunition. One parapack fell almost in the laps of Creek and his men. It contained 60mm ammo, which was convenient since they were out of rounds for their one 60mm mortar, which had a range of about a mile. They soon had the mortar firing on the Germans dug in on the far side, and the fire from that position lessened. Thirty minutes later, the officer who had delivered Gavin's order returned with a hundred men, some of them towing a 57mm anti-tank gun. Creek's men maneuvered it into position and began shooting down the causeway toward the island about a mile away, where the enemy fieldpiece was. Then Creek orchestrated another assault on the bridge. On a prearranged signal—a shot from the 57mm gun—the troopers fired on the western side of the bridge with the mortar and every machine gun they had. Then all fire stopped to let one officer and ten men dash across the arched bridge and deploy on the western side. Only five German grenadiers remained there, and as they vacated their foxholes and fled westward, they were gunned down. Though the long causeway beyond was still a no-man's-land, the Germans spotted on their left flank weren't seen again, and the bridge itself was finally in Allied hands. No German reinforcements crossed it to thrust northward to Sainte-Mère-Église or westward to the invasion beaches—and, Creek vowed, none would.

As darkness arrived about 11:00 p.m., the dead—eleven Americans and forty-three Germans—were collected and their bodies covered with parachutes, and the twenty-five newly wounded were tended to in the creamery courtyard. Then the men settled in, preparing for the worst—tanks were the biggest worry[45]—and everyone wondered: Where were the beach forces? They should already have made contact. Had the invasion failed or been called off?

At midnight, the troopers heard the sound of engines, and a minute later, reconnaissance elements of the 4th Infantry Division wheeled into the creamery yard with rations and supplies. The lieutenant in charge got out of his vehicle and found Creek. The landings had gone well, he said, "thanks to you fellows."[46]

SHORTLY AFTER SUNSET, Gavin asked Walton to take a message to Ridgway. When Walton got to Ridgway's CP, he found that the general had moved to a farmhouse. He learned that at 9:00 p.m., one of the general's radio operators had gotten through to the 4th Division near the beach. They'd had difficulties with minefields and then other things had slowed them down, but they were working their way inland. Some units would surely reach the 82nd's forces the next day. Finally, there was confirmation that the Utah landings and the others had indeed gone off as planned and that a beachhead had been established. It was bracing news for Ridgway and his troopers.

Walton gave Ridgway Gavin's message, then went into the barn, where all the wounded were—about 125 men. "It looked like something out of the Crimean War," he wrote in his notes. "They were shot through the face, lying on their back" . . . another trooper "sitting here, with his tongue half shot off, the lower part of his jaw missing . . . People were just hunks of flesh." There was a separate area just for all the men with legs broken on the drop.

Walton decided to get some shut-eye outside. There were some sleeping troopers lying outside wrapped in parachutes. He decided to join them and pulled over himself part of the parachute of the man on the end and rolled up next to him. A half hour later, a guard shook his shoulder and told him they were abandoning the area. Walton turned and shook the man next to him and found out he was dead. He trudged along the D15 back to Gavin's CP, crawled into a deep ditch under the exposed roots of a large overturned tree, and slept soundly through the night.[47]

After sundown, bone weary and shivering as the night cooled—the temperature would probably dip below fifty—Gavin too decided to get some sleep. He looked around for something to wrap himself in. He walked over to a dead paratrooper covered by his chute. A few wraps of the silk would keep Gavin warm. But he couldn't bring himself to take the dead man's shroud. He finally found a camouflage net, chose a place against the hedgerow that would provide some cover from the artillery fire that continued to fall, rolled himself in the net, and fell asleep.

He hadn't been asleep for long when someone shook him awake and told him that General Ridgway wanted to see him. Gavin thought that odd: Ridgway always moved forward to see his officers in combat rather than take them away from their commands. Gavin double-checked with the messenger. Yes, the general wanted to see him. Gavin found his aide, Hugo Olson, and decided it was safer to walk. Under a bright full moon, they trudged along the D15 east toward Sainte-Mère-Église. Both men were exhausted—especially Gavin, who had been up two nights and a day and on his feet for what seemed like forever—so the distance felt much longer. They found the division CP just off the road to the left. Someone there told them the general was asleep in a small ditch off to the side.

Ridgway had not slept for about forty-eight hours. Never in his life had he felt so tired. When Gavin woke him up, he wasn't happy about it. Ridgway told Gavin he had nothing for him and didn't need him, then rolled over and went back to sleep. Gavin and Olson walked the two miles back to their CP near the railroad crossing and did the same. But Ridgway, likely half asleep at the time, woke up with a different understanding of the incident and eventually allowed it to come between the two and permanently cool their relationship.[48]

A half mile east on the D15 in Sainte-Mère-Église, a third injury to Ed Krause—a bullet in his left thigh—had finally forced him to be jeeped up the N13 to the aid station, where a surgeon cut the bullet out and insisted that Krause spend the night. The 2nd Battalion commander was in a foul mood, certain that disaster awaited, but he reluctantly yielded command—at least for the night—to his executive officer, Major Bill Hagan.[49] There were 140 other men in the aid station, most of them from his 3rd Battalion, plus some injured Germans.[50] Colonel Ekman had shown up late in the afternoon to emphasize the importance of preventing the Germans from taking the village and continuing on to the beaches—not that anyone there needed reminding. A heavy artillery bombardment began falling on platoon positions about dusk. The shelling was so accurate that everyone was sure that one or more Germans were hidden somewhere close by and calling in coordinates to their artillery units south of town. The barrage eventually eased, but throughout the night, the occasional burst of nearby rifle fire from both American and enemy guns made it clear that some Germans had avoided the early-morning roundup. No one got much sleep.[51]

At the La Fière bridge, occasional mortar fire kept Dolan and Alexander's 1st Battalion hunkered down in their foxholes, some fortunate ones wrapped in parachutes they'd scavenged to ward off the cold air and the cold ground. Lowing cows in need of milking could be heard—there were cows everywhere either grazing on the thick green Normandy grass or lying dead upon it. Several dozen injured men were being administered to in the battalion CP behind the *manoir.* It was severely understaffed since only one staff officer was left.

Earlier that evening, the B Company troopers near them had been taken off the line at the bridge and sent to Sainte-Mère-Église to reinforce Vandervoort's 2nd Battalion against the Germans certain to attack from the north soon. The 507th men in reserve behind them had been sent to strengthen the weak position at Chef-du-Pont, though about forty under the command of Captain Robert Rae were still dug in on the high ground behind the *manoir* on part of a feudal mound. That left Dolan's depleted force—A and C Companies, which had both suffered heavy casualties—alone at the bridge, dug in along the edge of the marsh. From the far end of the causeway, they could hear German soldiers talking and tanks rumbling back and forth, preparing for another attack the next day.[52]

Sergeant William "Billy" Owens and his 1st Squad/1st Platoon/A Company were dug in close to the bridge. At thirty, Owens was a decade older than most of the young men in his squad, so they looked up to him like a father, which was made easier by his sense of humor and easygoing manner. He was still chuckling about something one of his buddies, Sergeant Joe "Andy" Anderson, had told him after the ferocious attack that afternoon. Owens had heard Anderson cussing and asked him what the trouble was. "Oh," Anderson said, "wait until I get my hands on that sergeant that enlisted me. He told me this was about the same as the Air Corps, and if I didn't like it, I could always transfer out."

Now, at 2:00 a.m., Owens listened to the rattle of the German tanks around Cauquigny. Then he heard one coming down the causeway toward the bridge. He checked on his men and waited. The tank reached one of the disabled tanks in the road and began pushing it off to the side. Owens knew if that burned-out wreck and the others were cleared from the roadway, it would be that much easier to barrel down the causeway in the morning. He took a couple of Gammon grenades and crawled to the edge of the flooded Merderet, then waded through the cold water until he was about forty yards from the tanks. He removed the protective cap from one Gammon and hurled it. He missed the working tank, but the grenade hit the disabled one and exploded. The tank commander put his Renault in reverse and began moving back down the causeway. Owens threw the other grenade and missed again, hitting the road, but the tank returned to Cauquigny. Except for desultory mortar shelling, the Germans didn't try anything else the rest of the night. But everyone knew sunrise would bring another attack.[53]

TWELVE

THE GLIDERMEN

We hit the Channel and sweated out the crossing in that fragile, vibrating kite.

JOHN MCNALLY, 325TH GIR[1]

June 7

2:30 a.m.

THE WHISTLE FROM the Ramsbury Airfield mess hall woke up the men of the 1st Battalion/325th Glider Infantry Division. They had gone to sleep on the ground, fully dressed, four hours earlier, their heads on their loaded knapsacks, their weapons by their sides. Everyone stretched, washed up, and walked to the mess hall for "our last hot meal for some time," remembered Lieutenant Wayne Pierce, XO of A Company, "and for a number of men, it would be their last meal on this earth."

Except for parachutes, the glidermen carried almost everything the paratroopers did. Pierce had little faith in the M1, so like a lot of noncoms and officers, he carried a Thompson machine gun because it "could throw a lot of lead." He had grown up on an Illinois farm, hunting squirrels and rabbits with a .22 rifle. But unlike most farm boys during the Depression, he'd finished high school, and after several low-paying jobs, he'd joined the army in June 1941. After Pearl Harbor, an army badly in need of officers had selected him for OCS, and three months later, he was a "90-day wonder" second lieutenant. He got married soon afterward and transferred to the 325th Infantry Regiment. He'd made a few glider landings, and they'd all been smooth.[2]

After breakfast, the men marched by platoons through a light mist to the airstrip and loaded into their assigned gliders—both the smaller American CG-4A, which carried eighteen troops and two pilots, and the larger British Horsa, capable of carrying thirty men and two pilots. Most of the companies climbed into Horsas and took seats along the aluminum benches on either side of the cabin, stuffed their packs below them, and buckled up. The strong aroma of spruce plywood permeated the air, which was made stuffy by thick cigarette smoke. At 4:40 a.m., barreling through rain and wind gusts, their C-47s labored down the runway with their Horsas—each one larger than its towplane—until the runway finally fell away and the rumble of the glider's three wheels gave way to the sound of air whooshing past the canvas surface.

The planes joined the formation in the sky above them and circled the area until the serial was complete; then they slowly turned south and flew toward the Channel as the rain stopped and the clouds cleared away. Soon they were over water, and the impending dawn brightened the horizon on the left side of the aircraft. The fighter plane escorts—mostly P-47s, P-38s, and British Spitfires—flew in a series of arcs above and back and forth among the slow-moving armada. Like with the glider operations of the previous evening, they would dispense with the roundabout subterfuge of a western approach and fly directly over Utah, whose large coastal guns had been silenced.

Due to aeronautics and weight, a glider normally rode higher than its towplane, but Pierce's had been overloaded with boxes of ammunition, mines, and cans of water tied to the floor in the center. The glidermen too carried extra mines, grenades, and ammunition that they hadn't had during training runs. Their towplane's engines began straining, then sputtering, and as the towplane slowed, the Horsa gradually lost altitude, to the increasing alarm of its occupants. It was clear to Pierce, standing behind the pilots and looking out the Plexiglas windshield at the C-47 one hundred yards away and much higher, that something would have to be done or they'd hit the water soon—it was only a few hundred feet below them, and they could see the waves below.

Pierce conferred with the pilots, then gave the order to open the canvas-and-plywood rear door and start throwing out supply boxes. Some men took emergency axes and stood ready to chop holes in the roof for crude escape hatches, since the wings were filled with thousands of Ping-Pong balls to keep the glider afloat. In the cockpit, the copilot had his hand on the release lever to cut the towrope loose, but the pilot said, "Just wait, just wait!" Finally, the C-47's engines smoothed out and it speeded up and the glider gradually gained altitude. The men put down the axes and secured the door, and everyone began to breathe easier.

Below them the sunlight gleamed on hundreds of ships of all sizes making their way toward France with men and matériel for the beachhead forces. An hour or so passed, and when the Normandy coast came into view ahead, Pierce gave the order to secure equipment and fasten seat belts, and he returned to his seat. As men put on their helmets and slung bandoliers over their shoulders and checked their weapons, they heard the *pom pom pom* of antiaircraft guns below and flak began to explode around them, buffeting the plane, and a few minutes later, as Pierce leaned over to pick up his knapsack, the glider lurched as the pilot reached overhead and pulled the release lever and the towrope skittered away. Then the pilot made a steep turn as they started gliding toward the earth. Pierce felt a wave of nausea and hugged his pack, hoping his men weren't watching.

Thirty seconds later the glider bounced onto the ground with a stomach-lurching thud, bounced again, and began rolling. Pierce stood up and unlatched the large side door across from him and kicked it open. When the glider stopped, he jumped out onto the ground, rolled over, and stood. The plane sat at one end of a small field near an apple orchard; in front of it was a tree-lined road, and Pierce ran toward it. The twenty-eight soldiers in his B Company platoon followed him out the door single file with the two pilots right behind them. As his men watched other gliders crash-landing around them, Pierce realized he had forgotten something and ran back to the plane, climbed inside, grabbed his rifle, and rejoined his column as the occasional mortar shell fell around them and two Messerschmitts zoomed overhead, strafing them. Somehow no one was hit.

It was 7:00 a.m. The sky was partly cloudy, and the air cool. Pierce pulled out his small map and, with the help of a nearby road sign, figured out where they were—about three miles southeast of their DZ. As more B Company men from other gliders joined them, Pierce led them toward the village of Sainte-Marie-du-Mont, from where they would move west toward their assembly point near Chef-du-Pont.[3]

Two hours later, in the lead glider of the next 325th armada, Sergeant Bud Olson crouched behind the two pilots and looked out through the windshield at the hundreds of ships 600 feet below off Utah Beach. It was a few minutes before 9:00 a.m. Behind Olson in the roomy British Horsa were twenty-eight other soldiers and two caged carrier pigeons to be released upon landing. They would return to England with confirmation of the lead plane's successful landing in case radio transmission failed.

Because of his extensive time spent at Eisenhower's HQ in London studying maps and aerial photos of the Normandy countryside behind Utah, Olson had been assigned to the lead glider of the 3rd Battalion/ 325th serial to help the pilots find the correct LZ. Behind Olson's glider were fifty-five more carrying the entire 3rd Battalion.

A few minutes after they made land, when their C-47 towplane came under heavy fire, the glider pilot released the towrope—long before they reached their LZ. He maneuvered the plane down to a field and the Horsa hit the ground at ninety miles per hour, rolled to the end of the pasture, and smashed into a hedgerow and trees. The nose cone fell off and Olson was thrown out of the plane.

He woke up to find himself pinned under one of the glider's tires, his legs and torso cut badly and his back injured. Some other soldiers helped extricate him as other gliders landed and crashed all around them. Olson could barely walk, but the first thing he did was find the pigeons and set them free. Dead soldiers were strewn throughout the wreckage. A medic patched Olson up, and he and the other members of the 325th's 2nd and 3rd Battalions moved out toward Chef-du-Pont several miles away.[4]

In another Horsa behind Olson's, Lieutenant Richard Johnson, a young Boston lawyer, sat right behind the pilot. As they flew across the Channel, he was bolstered by the lovely day and decided to encourage the men in his platoon with tales of British victories over much larger French armies at Crécy in 1346 and at Agincourt in 1415. He concluded with a few lines from Shakespeare's *Henry V*, when the young king addresses his followers before the latter battle:

We few, we happy few, we band of brothers;
For he today that sheds his blood with me
Shall be my brother. . . .
And gentlemen in England now abed

Shall think themselves accurs'd they were not here,
And hold their manhoods cheap whiles any speaks
That fought with us upon Saint Crispin's day.

When several of those who could hear him over the loud wind fell asleep, he tried to persuade himself it was the Dramamine pills they'd all taken before departure.

Johnson's Horsa landed in a swamp at ninety miles an hour. "The entire glider back to the wings disintegrated," recalled Johnson, "and the pilot and copilot sailed out through where the Plexiglass front had been, and my runner and I followed them." Their two seats had been fastened to a sturdy ramp that did not come apart but flew out, end over end, with them attached. "We landed face down in the water, which was only about four feet deep, with the ramp securely strapped to our backs by our safety belts. It was hard to find a footing in the swamp and I had just about decided that my part of the great invasion was going to end ignominiously by drowning." He finally found his footing and stood up, lifting both the ramp and his runner with him. When the two managed to disentangle themselves, they found they were unhurt—and, miraculously, so was every other man on the plane, even the two pilots.

They waded to dry land, where Johnson consulted his map. They were a few miles southeast of Sainte-Mère-Église and began moving with the rest of the battalion toward their assembly point at Chef-du-Pont.[5]

Like many other gliders that morning, all five of the Horsas carrying PFC Charles DeGlopper and his 140 C Company comrades landed several miles east of LZ "W" near Sainte-Marie-du-Mont. But there were only a few injuries, and the men assembled quickly and began moving west.[6]

The 200 planes carrying the 325th's three battalions suffered high casualties: thirty-two men dead, all but one of them in the all-wood, less maneuverable Horsas, and another 144 injured. That was about a 10 percent casualty rate, unfortunate but acceptable, and nowhere near the "futile losses" of 70 percent prophesied by Air Chief Marshal Trafford Leigh-Mallory. Included in the operation were twenty artillery pieces, more than seventy jeeps, trailers, and other vehicles, and more than fifty tons of ammo and supplies.[7]

As the 325th glidermen made their way to their battalion assembly points, the battle for Sainte-Mère-Église a few miles to the northwest had already renewed. Throughout the night, there had been several German attempts to break through the loose cordon around the village. But none involved large numbers, and each one was rebuffed.

On the north side, a large German *Kampfgruppe*—an ad hoc battle group consisting of two battalions of 1058th Grenadier Regiment reinforced by elements of the Sturm Battalion, ten self-propelled StuG III guns (a turretless, low-profile tracked vehicle with a long and potent 75mm gun), and parts of two other artillery units—had reached the northern outskirts of Sainte-Mère-Église by 5:30 a.m. On the east side of the N13, the 1st Battalion/1058th moved toward the village through the fields parallel to the highway. On the west side, the 2nd Battalion did the same. The Sturm Battalion and seven self-propelled guns came straight down the N13 and hit the northern roadblock at about 6:00 a.m.

Lieutenant Waverly Wray's D Company/505th was dug in on the east side of the highway. The village had been enduring steady artillery and mortar fire all night, and the result was a steady stream of casualties to the aid station near the Hôtel de Ville. When the Germans hit

Wray's company, all his men could do was fall back toward town. One German machine gun was doing major damage to D Company. But they gave ground slowly. Wray moved up and down the line, checking his men, making sure they had enough ammunition, and moving them around to fill in when a trooper was killed or evacuated.

Wray was a soft-spoken, devout churchgoer from rural Mississippi who neither drank nor smoked and who used no language stronger than "dad-burn" or "John Brown," a common Southern euphemism. He carried his Bible with him and read it in his foxhole on evenings when he had the chance. "He was armed with the conviction that he fought on the side of the Lord," remembered Vandervoort, his battalion commander. Wray wasn't particularly tall, just five foot ten, but he was as solid as an oak with legs like tree stumps—he'd been working on his family's farm since he was nine, but somehow completed high school. He hunted small game in the wooded hills around Batesville and became a crack shot with a rifle.

About 7:00 a.m., Wray went down to Vandervoort's CP to brief him on the situation. Vandervoort told him to return to his company and counterattack the German flank.

"Yes, suh," said Wray in his Mississippi drawl. He saluted, about-faced, and left to hurry back up the N13 to his company's position, where he collected as many grenades as he could carry, stuck a silver-plated .38 revolver in one of his boots, and, with his Colt .45 pistol and his M1, took to the fields on his own reconnaissance.

Through the dew-covered grass of small farm fields, orchards, and pastures and over and around the thick hedgerows and sunken lanes, he moved quietly toward the German units advancing south. This was terrain Wray knew, since his company had occupied it an hour earlier before falling back. He crept north 300 yards along the German left flank, then west 200 yards until he was only a couple of hedgerows from the N13. Steady rifle and machine-gun fire continued, though the hedgerows concealed the Germans' positions.

Wray followed a hedgerow south along a ditch until he heard German voices on the other side. He stepped up onto the embankment and looked over it. Seven German soldiers were gathered around a radio transmitter. He had apparently discovered the battalion command post. He pointed his M1 at them and yelled, *"Hände hoch!"* They turned toward him, and most of them raised their hands, but one quickly pulled his P38 pistol from its holster and fired, almost tearing Wray's cartridge belt off and barely missing his torso. Wray shot him as two other Germans in a slit trench forty yards to his left rear stood and opened up on him with Schmeisser machine pistols. Wray proceeded to shoot the six others below him as two Schmeisser rounds ripped through his right ear and another tore his helmet strap off. A B Company platoon leader, Tom McLean, saw the two Germans and directed his platoon to fire on them. Wray disappeared from view, then reappeared kicking two enemy prisoners in front of him and dripping blood from his ear onto his face, neck, and shoulder.

Wray had also found much of the battalion along a sunken dirt road between two hedgerows. He ran back to his lines and moved two platoons of D Company forward and placed them on the Germans' left flank. He deployed a 60mm and a .30-caliber machine gun to aim down the lane; then, after ordering the mortar to open fire, he observed the shell explosions and yelled adjustments that pinpointed the barrage on the German positions. As the machine gun fired down the lane on the enfiladed infantry, the grenadiers climbed over the hedgerows and into the open fields, where they met a furious fusillade from the platoon. Dozens of them fell under the relentless fire.

A few minutes later a German major carrying a white flag emerged from a hedgerow and walked through the field toward the platoon. A one-hour truce was negotiated to evacuate the wounded, but troopers on the right flank opened fire when they saw Germans withdrawing. That caused another exchange of small-arms and machine-gun fire until the last of the Germans moving north were out of range. That exposed the left flank of the Sturm Battalion on the N13, and those grenadiers began to withdraw.

Sometime after 10:00 a.m., Wray showed up at Vandervoort's CP to tell him that the B Company area was secure, with "his cartridge belt half-torn from his middle and with two large nicks in his right ear," remembered Vandervoort. "Dry blood was caked on his neck, shoulder and right breast of his jump jacket.

"I greeted him with, 'They've been getting kind of close to you, haven't they, Waverly?'"

Wray grinned and said, "Not as close as I've been getting to them, suh."[8]

Wray's actions and D Company's attack had repelled the German attack on the east side of the N13. But the Sturm Battalion, supported by several self-propelled StuG IIIs, pushed the troopers back along the hedgerows until they were only a few hundred yards north of the Hôtel de Ville and the crowded aid station just south of it.

There was only one 57mm anti-tank gun with the north-side defense, and the crew manning it zeroed in on a convoy of German troop trucks moving south on the N13. They hit the lead truck, stopping the convoy, and when an armored car began firing on them, they knocked that out. And when a StuG drove down the road, propelling smoke canisters before it for concealment, and emerged from the smoke screen just fifty yards from Vandervoort's CP, the gunners stopped its progress with two well-placed rounds. But its main gun continued to blast at the 57mm crew at close range. The gunners continued to exchange fire with the StuG until they dispatched its crew.

The gunners moved their two-wheeled gun up to and next to the StuG for a clear field of fire up the N13. They were loading the gun when a shell from another StuG farther up the highway hit them, wounding the crew and knocking the gun out of action. The StuG continued to move south into town behind a smoke screen. Several other StuGs followed it.

In a foxhole close by, Private John Atchley jumped up and ran to the anti-tank gun. A nineteen-year-old farm kid from Tennessee, he had never operated one before, but at almost point-blank range, he loaded a shell, crouched down behind the gun's metal shield, aimed, and fired up the street at the oncoming StuG. He missed but reloaded and took aim again. This round hit the StuG and knocked it out. Five other StuGs behind it retreated. Two more troopers, a lieutenant and a sergeant armed with Thompsons, jumped into the road and stood side by side, emptying magazine after magazine into the Sturm Battalion infantrymen coming down the highway until the Germans retreated several hundred yards north.[9]

A FEW HOURS earlier, just after first light, Dolan's 1st Battalion/505th men had been able to see the last of the 507th and 508th troopers trying to make it across the Merderet swamp. Some of them did and were helped onto dry land, wet and cold after a night partly submerged and hidden behind rushes. Others didn't make it, gunned down by Germans along the edge of the water on the other side of the causeway. The uninjured survivors were put in position among the 505th men.

About 7:00 a.m., the German mortar fire picked up, and at 10:00 a.m., the troopers could hear the sound of heavy armor moving down the causeway toward them from Cauquigny. Two French tanks led the way, followed by several trucks of infantry; grenadiers advanced among them. Two more tanks followed. The lead tank reached the bridge before shots from the 57mm gun up the hill found it and knocked it out of action.

Private Bob Murphy, the eighteen-year-old 505th pathfinder who had rejoined A Company, sat in a foxhole near the bridge and craned his neck at the tanks and grenadiers. One thought ran through his head: *Is today the day that I get it?* "Wet and shivering from the moist ocean and marsh air, we were dirty, thirsty, and hungry," he would remember. "We had no water, our throats were dry, and our K-rations were all expended." Even worse, there looked to be more Germans than their meager supply of ammunition could take care of.

Murphy scrunched down, then pushed his helmet back to get his right eye down close to the barrel of his M1 to sight on an enemy soldier. A piece of mortar shrapnel smacked into the back of his helmet and knocked his head forward into the dirt. He lifted his face, sighted, and began firing.[10]

Company A had only one remaining bazooka, manned by Peterson and Heim, but the tanks stayed back out of effective range. Dolan, near the front, realized he heard no 57mm fire and ran to the gun up the road. The crew had disappeared. He tried to fire the gun but found the firing mechanism had been removed. He'd just about given up on the 57mm when two members of the gun crew, both kids who should have been in high school, returned with the mechanism. They resumed firing and disabled the two tanks.

The noise was earsplitting. Owens, with his platoon on the front line at the bridge, knew what was coming next. Supported by machine guns and mortar behind them, the grenadiers charged along the causeway toward the bridge. The only communications Owens had, a private with a walkie-talkie, took a direct artillery hit that killed him and destroyed the walkie-talkie.

The first assault was beaten back. Then the Germans mounted another. Lieutenant William Oakley, who with Sergeant Oscar Queen had led the final attack on the *manoir* the day before, took a shrapnel hit to his lower back that produced a fist-sized hole. Owens crawled over to him and tried to bandage him, jabbed him with a morphine syrette, and told him he'd send a man back to find a medic, but Oakley said he could make it on his own. He told Owens to hold the bridge at all costs, then yelled at his platoon to obey Owens since he was now in command. He told him how proud he was of them, said he'd see them in England, and left. Up at the railroad crossing, he was placed in a jeep that took him to the aid station in Sainte-Mère-Église, where he went into shock and died.

After the second wave was driven back, Owens began crawling along the front line from foxhole to foxhole, collecting all the ammo and grenades he could from the dead and wounded. The few remaining men would need every round they could get. The machine guns in particular gobbled up ammunition. Fortunately, an A Company sergeant, Ed Wancio, ran tirelessly from the rear where the ammo had been collected to the machine-gun crews, lugging the heavy boxes through the barrage of mortar and artillery fire and keeping the crews supplied.

By now it was early afternoon. The Germans attacked again, this time with more firepower. "They must have received reinforcements," recalled Owens, "for the artillery shells and mortars were coming in like machine-gun fire. I don't know how it was possible to live through it."[11] He manned a machine gun whose crew had died or disappeared, and fired it until it was so hot that it wouldn't work anymore. He grabbed a BAR from an injured private and used it until he ran out of ammo. Then he ran to another machine gun whose two-man crew lay dead nearby. The gun lacked a tripod, so Owens rested it on a pile of dirt and blasted away. His platoon had only one other machine gun, manned by Queen, and a single mortar, but somehow Owens and his depleted platoon held. The Germans were just twenty yards away across the bridge when they pulled back behind the barricade of the disabled tank and overturned truck.

Owens counted his men—fifteen left. Some of them suggested they get out. He yelled over to Murphy, "Go ahead and find Lieutenant Dolan and tell him we're out of ammunition and we can't stand another tank or infantry attack and we need to move back."

Murphy climbed out of his hole and ran back up the hill and across the road to where Dolan was watching near the bend in the D15 where the aid station was. Murphy relayed Owens's message and asked if they could move back.

"No," said Dolan, and took a small piece of paper from a notepad and wrote something on it. "Here, give this to Owens."

Murphy ran back across the road—"ducking the incoming rounds," he recalled—and down to Owens. He handed him the note. When Owens finished reading it, Murphy asked him what it said.

"We stay—there's no better place to die." He looked at Murphy. "Okay, nobody moves—let's get ready when they come over the bridge."

They prepared for the next assault. Owens was sure they'd be overrun this time. He sent a corporal back to the railroad overpass to find Colonel Ekman and tell him to send some help. Then a Red Cross flag was held up and waved across the bridge, and the Germans stopped firing. Owens found a good view of the causeway and had a look. At least 200 dead or wounded German soldiers were scattered about among the burning tanks and other vehicles on the other side of the small bridge, with untold numbers in the water on either side. Owens stood up and yelled for his own men to stop. Then the thirty-year-old sergeant sat on the ground and cried. Later he realized he'd received a nasty shrapnel wound in one of his legs and hadn't noticed it.

A German came forward and asked for a thirty-minute pause to remove their wounded. Owens agreed, then set about preparing the surviving men of A Company to regroup and meet the next onslaught. But after the first aid groups made their way among the armored wrecks to collect and transport the injured back to Cauquigny—it actually took two hours—and a jeep came down the hill to load the 505th wounded and carry them back to the aid station, the remaining enemy troops began withdrawing.

Sporadic mortar fire continued to fall into A Company's forward positions on either side of the bridge, but there was no further attempt by the Germans to take the bridge. That evening, Lindquist's 507th men who had been sent to bolster the 505th forces north of Sainte-Mère-Église returned to relieve the 1st Battalion/505th at the bridge.

As A Company formed to move back to the railroad crossing, a sergeant looked at the line of exhausted troopers, now 66 fewer than the 145 who had assembled the day before. Twenty of them were wearing bandages or awaiting medical attention. "If people don't think that men get killed in war," he said, "they ought to take a look at this company." The 1st Battalion/505th moved to a reserve position west of Neuville-au-Plain, where they would get their first good night's sleep in three days.[12]

It was early afternoon when G Company troopers at the roadblock southwest of Sainte-Mère-Église heard the sound of tanks approaching from Chef-du-Pont. When the first one came into sight, every man there was relieved to see it was a Sherman. It was Colonel Raff's armored task force. The 8th Infantry had been strengthened overnight, and at 9:00 that morning, Colonel James Van Fleet, commander of the 8th Regiment of the 4th Infantry Division, had attacked Hill 20, his forces augmented by a battalion striking from the east; by 10:30 a.m., there was no more organized fire from the ridge. Most of the Wehrmacht forces there seemed to have slipped away during the night. By noon, save for a few snipers and unattached small groups, there was no German presence south of the village.

When the 8th Infantry began to move north, Raff had already left the area: After finally establishing radio contact with Ridgway, he had received an order from the general to bypass the German forces on Hill 20, so he'd headed west to Chef-du-Pont and then north.

Raff in his jeep led his tanks through the village and turned west on the D15 toward the La Fière bridge. A few minutes later, he pulled up near Ridgway's CP.[13] Ridgway was glad to see the armor, but Raff was not received warmly by his staff. Ridgway himself put personal feelings aside and made Raff, now without a job, his temporary chief of staff to replace the injured "Doc" Eaton. A few days later, in a letter to Eaton, he would write that he was "much pleased" with Raff's work. But the two would never reconcile. After the war, Raff would write that most of Ridgway's staff were sycophants, and say of the general, "I never saw General Ridgway do anything outstandingly brave in battle"—an opinion shared by no one else.[14]

Close behind Raff's tanks was Van Fleet in an armored car. His men were working their way up the N13 and would arrive in about an hour. And riding with Van Fleet was General J. Lawton Collins, the VII Corps commander known as "Lightning Joe" for his aggressive tactics. Lawton was a West Point classmate of Ridgway's and a friend.

Collins hadn't been too concerned about the 82nd. Shortly after noon on D-Day, when he'd made contact with the 101st, the fate of the 82nd was still unknown. When Omar Bradley asked him by radio if he'd had any word from Ridgway, Collins had told him, "Nope—but I'm not worried about Matt."[15]

Now Collins updated Ridgway on the invasion. Casualties at Utah had been light—197 and most of those had been caused by offshore mines. By the end of June 6, more than 20,000 troops and 1,700 motorized vehicles had been put ashore. And thanks to the two airborne divisions, which had seized the western exits and prevented any counterattacks on the seaborne forces, no German reinforcements had reached the beach. But the progress inland by the green 4th Infantry Division had been tentative and ragged, in most cases far short of the end-of-day objectives. At Omaha, several factors had contributed to a near defeat. Intelligence had somehow missed the fact that parts of a veteran German unit, the 352nd Infantry Division, had been moved in May from Saint-Lô to the Cotentin's east coast and had mounted fierce resistance; the naval and air shelling had been ineffective; and the terrain, which included higher bluffs than Utah, had featured machine-gun emplacements that rained death on the long beach below. Losses had been horrific, and the assault force there had gained just ten yards of beach in six bloody hours. (It would not be revealed until later that General Omar Bradley had come close to ordering the total evacuation of Omaha and diverting the surviving troops to Utah and the three British-Canadian beaches, which had also seen successful assaults.) But officers and noncoms had by degrees begun to rally their men and lead them through a hellish rain of machine-gun fire toward the seawall so far away. Finally, by early afternoon, American troops were advancing up the heights behind the beaches, where thousands of men lay dead and wounded—2,400 if the missing were included. The invasion appeared to have been a success—as was Operation Fortitude. In one day, the allegedly impregnable Atlantic Wall had been torn down, or at least permanently breached. Now it was a race to see if the beachhead could be held before the Germans' counterattacks could neutralize the Allied progress inland—and reinforce Cherbourg to keep it out of Allied hands.

Earlier that day, Ridgway had finally established radio contact with Collins, who had a problem. He had sent three green regiments toward Montebourg, six miles north of Sainte-Mère-Église, and they had run into the reinforced 1058th Regiment and come to a grinding halt. He needed help and suggested Ridgway send his seasoned 505th with Van Fleet's 8th Infantry north to bolster his forces.

That suited Ridgway fine. The 1058th and the Sturm Battalion, with several StuG IIIs, were still massing for another attempt to capture Sainte-Mère-Église. The mortar and artillery fire had let up some but never completely stopped, and much of the village was in ruins. Instead of waiting for the Wehrmacht's next counterattack, they would strike first. Ridgway, Collins, and Van Fleet formulated a joint operation that would kick off at 5:15 p.m. north toward Neuville-au-Plain. A battalion of Van Fleet's infantrymen would move north on the left flank of Vandervoort's battered and exhausted 2nd Battalion/505th. His men would head up the N13 and accompany the tanks Raff had brought. They moved into place just beyond the edge of town and waited.

By 5:00 p.m., Van Fleet's infantrymen had not arrived. A 2nd Battalion company was shifted to the west to take their place. As the assault was about to begin, a battalion of ten Shermans barreled into town from the east; they had been sent by Collins earlier that day to assist in the defense of Sainte-Mère-Église. Without stopping, the tanks rolled by the church square and turned right onto the N13 and continued north. Fifteen minutes later, they began to unload on the StuG IIIs, scoring hits on several and losing only one Sherman, and the 3rd Battalion troopers, supported by an efficient mortar barrage, attacked the German lines. The few StuGs left turned and made a run for Neuville-au-Plain, but several of the tankers swung northeast and then west along other roads to outflank them. The fast, nimble Shermans headed them off back at the N13 and drove them off the highway. The Shermans pursued the StuGs into the fields west of town and knocked them out in a free-for-all. Three more Shermans were lost.

The 3rd Battalion/505th attack quickly became a rout. Without any armor to support them against the Shermans and unable to protect themselves against the mortar barrage, the men of the German infantry could not defend their lines. A total of 414 Germans were killed, and hundreds more surrendered en masse. The 82nd paratroopers had shattered the 2nd Battalion/1058th Regiment and the Sturm Battalion. The village of Sainte-Mère-Église was no longer in danger.[16]

IN SAINTE-MÈRE-ÉGLISE, AS the American tanks rolled up the rubble-strewn N13 past the church square, townspeople emerged from where they had sheltered for two days in basements, in backyard dugouts covered in wood, and near hedgerows outside town. In front of the hair salon, two young girls watched as citizens wearing red rubber gloves loaded German corpses onto a cattle cart; to escape the stench, the children pulled back against the wall of a nearby building.[17]

The tanks were a welcome sight. Earlier that day, a paratrooper had told Mayor Renaud that if tanks didn't reach them in a few hours, they wouldn't be able to hold. *That means the end is near for us as well,* thought Renaud, since he knew without a doubt that the Germans would avenge themselves. His townspeople would be lined up against walls and shot, their houses would be burned, and there would be even more bombing by both sides as they tried to take his village.

Now, when the residents heard the metallic rattle of tanks, they ran out to cheer and greet them. "They meant victory, and for us, deliverance," recalled Renaud.

He walked to the square. The church was still intact, save for a hole in the wall and a buttress missing, and the ancient Roman milestone was untouched. There were shell holes all through the square. The church had stood for many centuries and would stand for several more. But for now there were injured to care for, dead to bury, and a village to rebuild.[18]

BY LATE AFTERNOON, from where he stood 1,200 yards north of Neuville-au-Plain, General von Schlieben had come to the conclusion that the 1058th Regiment, with or without what was left of the Sturm Battalion and elements of his 709th Infantry's artillery, was no longer able to recapture Sainte-Mère-Église—and, consequently, would not eradicate the enemy seaborne forces immediately to the east.

At noon, he had found Colonel Kurt Beigang, the 1058th's commander, at his command post and ordered him to attack immediately. "This very day," the general had told him, "take Sainte-Mère-Église! You know what is at stake!" But it had been no use. His anti-tank battalion of primarily StuG IIIs had taken heavy losses, and the ground troops had lost hundreds of men to death and injury; several hundred others had surrendered. The enemy tanks appearing at Neuville-au-Plain in midafternoon, combined with shelling from large-caliber naval guns off the coast, had been the deciding factor. Von Schlieben had barely succeeded in stopping the beginning of a panicked retreat coming north up the N13. Though he lacked any anti-tank defenses, adequate artillery support, or a panzer formation, he decided to assume the defensive and try to prevent the enemy from moving north to

Cherbourg—von Schlieben was sure the deep port there was the Allies' ultimate goal on the peninsula.

To make matters worse, the Allied air forces roamed the skies unopposed. The general had been promised before the invasion that a large panzer group would soon be shifted to his sector, supported by a thousand fighter planes. With that expectation in mind, he had established the defensive line almost a mile north of Neuville-au-Plain and summoned the remaining manpower from the coastal defenses and strongpoints to the northeast that had not been attacked, leaving only emergency garrisons. Their lack of mobility, and the enemy fighter planes that patrolled the roads and fired at the smallest German formations, would slow their arrival.

Morale among the troops was low, and the heavy losses to the officer corps—Beigang was now missing and probably dead—was making itself felt. And OKW had refused his suggestion of moving one of his better units, the 17th Machine Gun Battalion, south from near Cherbourg to bolster his defenses—they feared another airborne attack there. He would have to do what he could with his ragged forces.[19]

AFTER DARK, JUST northwest of Hill 20 in the sunken lane near the château functioning as a command post, Rudi Escher and his fourteen men, with their 1058th comrades—more than a hundred men, about a company's worth—began to move out. The Fallschirmjäger 6 reinforcements had never reached them, there was an enemy tank unit a half mile down the N13, and the gliders that morning had delivered hundreds more American soldiers into the area. The decision was made to withdraw to the west, the only direction open to them. The *landsers* left in a long—and noisy—single-file column. Escher was furious—men were talking loudly. They walked all night. At one point a group left to approach a farm and never returned. By dawn there were seventy men left. They tried to cross the railroad line above Chef-du-Pont but ran into the swamp on the west side and moved south along the tracks toward the village. When they were shot at, they took cover in ditches, then ran toward a large farmhouse. They had almost reached it when an American armored car burst into view at the entrance to the farmyard and opened fire on them. The rounds were above their heads, but Escher was sure it was a warning sign.

Landsers at the front began raising their arms. At the rear, Escher and his observation unit talked it over as the men in front of them were told to kneel down, which they did. Escher and his men could run, but facing tanks, artillery, and fighter planes with just Karabiners and a few Schmeissers seemed pointless. They threw their weapons on the ground and walked carefully into the farmyard, their hands held high above their heads.[20]

EVEN THOUGH HE didn't believe his own words, von Rundstedt reassured Hitler at the end of the day. "The troops engaged have fought bravely," he wrote in his daily report. "Where ground has been lost, this only occurred because of the enemy's material superiority. This will now change. Strong forces with panzers, artillery of all types and mortars are being brought up, and the Luftwaffe will considerably increase its operations. . . .

"Using its last man and last gun," he vowed, "Army Group B will attack and destroy the enemy forces which have landed. . . . Not only will our attack continue, but will end in the final re-capture of the main defensive line."[21]

But the Allies' complete mastery of the air prevented any coordinated large-scale counteroffensive, and any attacks had been, and would be, piecemeal and unsuccessful—though some had come close to success. The Allied lodgment was too large, as the five beachheads had merged.

In private, the old Prussian conceded that Rommel had been right—the panzer reserves should have been stationed closer to the coast, where they might have reached the beaches in time. His operations manager, General Bodo Zimmermann, summed up the situation succinctly: "We've thrown a whole day away."[22]

THE EVENING OF the next day, June 8, saw Ridgway reassessing the status of his command. The entire 505th, depleted as it was, had been attached to Collins's VII Corps along with the fresh 2nd Battalion/325th, and those men had moved out at 8:00 a.m. north toward Montebourg. That left him with fewer men than he'd had before the glider troops had arrived, and made the 82nd's mission even more difficult. His orders were to establish a lodgment west of the river to allow Collins's VII Corps to move smoothly through it and cut off the peninsula while his other forces moved north to take Cherbourg. That mission had not been accomplished; they still had not taken either of the two Merderet bridges. Sainte-Mère-Église was no longer threatened, but three large groups of troopers were still surrounded west of the Merderet—Taylor's 200 men had made radio contact with Millett and joined him that morning. They were all in desperate need of ammo, food, water, and medical supplies—especially plasma. Men were dying from blood loss.

Shanley's group on Hill 30 was in desperate need of blood plasma. For almost three full days, he and his 250 men had held out against a near-constant assault from a battalion of Germans reinforced with armor. At one point earlier that day, they had been attacked from three sides, when German infantrymen supported by captured French tanks and self-propelled StuG III guns hit the roadblock south of the hill near the end of the Chef-du-Pont causeway—Shanley had sent a force to establish the roadblock the previous day to prevent German troops from accessing the causeway and sending troops over it. After more than an hour of fierce fighting, he'd had to withdraw his men from the roadblock. By day's end, his wounded numbered in the dozens, and many of them were in bad shape. In response to his pleading by radio, three troopers in an isolated group about a mile south of Hill 30 had volunteered to try to get through the German lines and deliver twelve packages of the liquid. They never made it. One was killed, another went missing for a week after a hand grenade knocked him out, and the third returned barely alive after having been shot a half dozen times.[23]

But the night of June 8, Shanley had established contact with Colonel Lindquist, whose men had been holding down the Chef-du-Pont bridge on the other side of the Merderet since relieving Captain Roy Creek's meager and exhausted force the previous day. Lindquist wanted to send a relief convoy across the causeway, but the only way to do that was to reestablish the roadblock. Shanley gave the assignment to Major Shields Warren, who called on Lieutenant Woodrow Millsaps to do it.

Millsaps was thirty-one and had come up through the ranks since he'd enlisted ten years ago. His young wife, LaVerne, and their baby son were back in North Carolina, where Millsaps had been raised on a farm. He'd never finished high school—his mother died when he was eleven, and his widowed father had needed all the help he could get raising seven kids. But Millsaps was smart and resourceful, which was why Lindquist had specifically requested that he be assigned to his 508th PIR after Millsaps finished OCS—as a captain, Lindquist had been his company commander years before the war.

Earlier that day, Millsaps had helped out in the aid area and seen all the badly wounded, some of them with serious chest and stomach wounds, and the dying, men crying out for water they didn't have and pain relief they couldn't get. A few had died because there was no plasma. Millsaps hadn't slept in almost three days, but he was ready to do anything to relieve their suffering.

Warren told the 508th platoon leader to form a patrol and destroy the German roadblock, then cross the causeway to Lindquist at Chef-du-Pont. Millsaps wanted to use men he knew from his C Company—he'd already seen that strangers were harder to control—but he could find only a few of them; the remainder were troopers he didn't know, most of whom weren't happy about being volunteered for a dangerous assignment. Millsaps's second-in-command was Lieutenant Lloyd Polette, a big, powerful man and a dependable, well-respected squad leader known for his courage—and his temper.[24] But these troopers weren't his, either.

It was almost midnight when Millsaps led his group of twenty-three through fields and orchards down the gently sloping hill. They were able to slip through the enemy's outer defenses without raising an alarm, and get to a point 300 yards from the roadblock, which was at an intersection of two roads. A farmhouse and outbuildings lay just off the road. They waited for their artillery support—several guns at Chef-du-Pont were going to fire twenty-four rounds into the German position. Millsaps would move out toward the roadblock after the last round had landed.

At 2:30 a.m., the barrage began. But after only three rounds, which dropped around the roadblock, the artillery fire shifted south toward the Isle Marie, the German bastion almost a mile away on the other side of the causeway. Millsaps waited for the barrage on the roadblock to continue. When it didn't, he began to move his men down the dirt road toward the intersection. Polette led the group, with Millsaps near the rear. They had made only fifty yards when a German machine gun opened up on them with tracers, and flares illuminated the area in eerie light. A dozen of the troopers turned and ran back along the road.

Millsaps grabbed a sergeant running by and said, "What are you doing?"

"We're getting away from that fire," the sergeant said.

"Goddammit," Millsaps yelled, "you've got a job to do even if there is fire—go and collect those men!"

The sergeant left. Millsaps grabbed other men moving to the rear, yelling, "Everybody stop!" Some of them did. The sergeant returned a few minutes later with most of the stragglers.

The machine-gun fire continued—there were three of them now. Millsaps decided to shift his force to the right and hit the Germans on their flank. It took a half hour before he was satisfied with the group's position; then he led the men through an orchard. The tracers allowed Millsaps to pinpoint the guns, and he noticed that they were not mutually supporting—between two of them, there was an uncovered area. If he could get his men up and running quickly enough through the gap, which traversed an open field on the right, they could reach the enemy positions before the Germans could adjust.

As Millsaps and his troops neared the enemy positions along hedgerows just off the road, he passed the word along: "We will keep on moving until we close with them. You are to hold your fire until I give the word or until you hear my fire."

They left the orchard and approached a hedge. They were fifty yards from the farm buildings when they heard a challenge in German from twenty-five yards away. Millsaps fired his M1 at the German, who yelled and ran back toward the farm buildings, and behind Millsaps, his men hit the dirt and began firing—several of them had tommy guns, and the noise was tremendous—as Germans, some of them barefoot, poured out of the farmhouse.

Millsaps shouted at the men to get up. They didn't move. Schmeisser machine pistols started to fire on their flanks. If they didn't move, Millsaps knew, they'd be outflanked by what appeared to be a larger force. He ran forward twenty-five yards, yelling at the men to follow him. None did. He ran back and started pulling them up one by one.

"Goddammit," he said, "what's the matter with you? Are you afraid?"

Most of them said no, then offered one excuse or another—they were reloading, or bandaging a wound, or something else. Millsaps knew they were afraid; so was he. Then Polette came back. Instead of browbeating the men, he started talking to them softly. Was he speaking that way because he was younger and the other men responded to that? Millsaps wasn't sure. But with constant prodding by Millsaps, Polette, and the only other officer, another lieutenant, the troopers got to their feet and began to move forward. It took almost a half hour.

Then they were all moving forward out of the orchard through a gap in the hedgerow and toward the buildings. As Germans continued to emerge from the buildings, the troopers ran directly at them, tossing grenades ahead of themselves and firing and hitting enemy soldiers, horses, cows, and sheep—anything that moved. "We were all in the grip of mass hypnosis," remembered one PFC, "shooting anything that moved. . . . We were like robots, concussion and phosphorus grenades falling among us and being ignored in our distorted state of mind."[25] A German threw a grenade that hit a soldier's helmet and exploded, blowing his head off, and the explosions from other grenades knocked Millsaps and some others down, but they got up and kept on running forward and firing their weapons.

They didn't stop until all the Germans were dead, wounded, or gone from the area. Millsaps counted heads. Only eleven of his men still stood. The rest were dead or badly wounded. Many of the latter were laughing in a huge release of emotion at still being alive. Some were sobbing. Millsaps himself could hardly think clearly.

He turned to Polette. "You take over this position and hold it to the last man." Then he looked around. He needed someone to accompany him across the causeway to find Lindquist on the other side of the Merderet swamp. He told one of his B Company troopers, Sergeant Phillip Klinefelter, that he needed him.

"Okay, let's go," said Klinefelter, another farm boy but from Iowa.

They walked up to the road and followed it south to where it began to run over the swamp to the main causeway. Mortar fire and artillery fire were dropping around them. Ahead of them in the moonlight, they saw a German walking toward them. They dropped to the side of the road near the water, and when the German got near enough, Millsaps jumped up and bayonetted him. They walked on. Another German appeared. Millsaps bayonetted him also.

Klinefelter began falling behind. Millsaps stopped and waited for him to catch up.

"What's wrong with you?" he said. "Can't you keep up?"

"I think I'm shot," said Klinefelter.

Millsaps looked down at the other man's jacket. The left side of Klinefelter's chest was wet and black in the starlight. Millsaps stuck his hand into the jump jacket and pulled out a handful of clammy blood. "My God, man, you're shot!"

Klinefelter slumped to the ground, and Millsaps stripped off the sergeant's jacket and blouse. There were six bullet holes in his left arm and shoulder. By this time Klinefelter could hardly get to his feet. Millsaps helped him up and supported him as they made their way across the narrow causeway through the shelling from the German position on Isle Marie behind them on their right. As they reached the arched bridge and began crossing it, someone yelled, "Halt!"

They had reached Lindquist's troops. Millsaps left Klinefelter there and continued into town. He found Lindquist's CP and told the colonel that the roadblock had been retaken and the causeway was free from German troops.

But Lindquist decided that the artillery fire from the Isle Marie made it too dangerous to send the convoy. He told Shanley his decision by radio. Millsaps tried to persuade Lindquist to send the convoy but gave up. He hadn't slept in three days, and in the middle of briefing the colonel on the Hill 30 situation, he fell asleep.

It was nearing dawn. Shanley decided that Polette's small detachment couldn't hold against a German counterattack and told him to withdraw. Polette and his men who could walk, all seven of them, trudged up the hill to their lines. Later that day, when a patrol was sent down to the farmhouse to bring the wounded back, they counted forty-three dead German soldiers.[26]

JUST BEFORE SUNDOWN, Gavin jeeped east on the D15 to Ridgway's CP. That afternoon, Lieutenant John Marr, of Schwartzwalder's G Company/507th, had found a raised, brick-cobbled road just eighteen inches under the Merderet swamp; the road could be easily traversed by both men and vehicles—it was just wide enough for a jeep.[27] Colonel Timmes and his 120 men were still trapped in the orchard along the western edge of the swamp a half mile north of Cauquigny, and like the troopers on Hill 30, they were running out of ammunition and many other necessities. Timmes had sent Marr out with ten men the previous day to find an effective crossing. That patrol hadn't gotten far when it was turned back by machine-gun fire. In the morning,

Timmes had sent Marr out again. This time the lieutenant took only his runner, PFC Norman Carter.

They walked north until they ran into a Frenchman who directed them to the submerged road and told them it ran across the swamp to the Cherbourg-Paris railway. It was almost 1:00 p.m. when Marr and Carter found the road, which was several hundred yards east of Timmes's location. They waded through knee-high water to the railway, turned south, and eventually reached the bivouac of the 1st Battalion/325th, which had gotten to the area the previous evening. Its commander, Major Teddy Sanford, took them to Ridgway's CP in a jeep. But before they reached it, another jeep came toward them. Standing up in front next to the driver with his hands on the windshield was Ridgway, who stopped them. They all walked over to the side of the road, where Marr told the general about the ford. Ridgway pulled out a map and asked Marr to point out the location of the submerged road. Then they all drove back to the CP, and Ridgway summoned Gavin and 325th commander Colonel Harry Lewis. They came up with a plan that, if carried out successfully, would kill three birds with one stone: liberate Timmes's 120 men, link them up with Millett and his group of 400 trapped a half mile west of Amfreville, and take Cauquigny. The Germans had attacked Timmes's force again that morning with infantry supported by mortar and artillery fire, but they'd been repulsed. But Timmes's casualties were mounting, his ammo was running low, and he couldn't hold out much longer.

Cauquigny—and the bridge at La Fière and the causeway beyond it—had to be taken, and immediately. Earlier that day, General Bradley had been told that decoded German radio dispatches indicated that the Germans were moving three divisions from Brittany, which was to the southwest of the Americans. The divisions would go up the Cotentin Peninsula's west coast to Cherbourg to reinforce the 352nd and what remained of the 91st Luftlande. Bradley decided to order one of his reserve infantry divisions, the 90th, to race west through the 82nd's sector, block the German reinforcements, and cut off the peninsula at its base while Collins raced north to seize Cherbourg. The 90th, unloading at Utah, was ordered to cross the Merderet at the La Fière bridge on June 9, the next day.[28]

Ridgway had some decisions to make. His troopers had seized Cauquigny and the causeway, held them for a short time, and then, through a series of misunderstandings, lost them. The troopers had withstood several furious assaults by a superior German force, but the bridge itself was still no-man's-land—as was the Chef-du-Pont causeway. Bradley was now asking Ridgway to step aside and allow the green troops of the heavily equipped 90th Infantry Division to power across the causeway, rescue the three large 82nd groups on the west side of the Merderet, and finish the 82nd's job. Ridgway found the thought of this strategy humiliating, both for himself and for his division.

The 90th's success was not guaranteed; troops new to combat often wilted under heavy fire, and the enemy fire they would be charging into while crossing the bridge and the long causeway would be intense and focused. A collapse there might slow the advance west enough to allow the German reinforcements to reach Cherbourg and delay the American attack on the heavily defended port indefinitely. That result would endanger the entire invasion.[29]

The plan was simple but audacious and somewhat chancy—a lot depended on timing, and stealth, and these were troops whose only combat experience had been a couple of weeks in Italy. They would be moving in darkness through unfamiliar, confusing territory against an enemy of unknown size and location. Ridgway decided to throw the dice on Lewis's glidermen.

THIRTEEN

ATTACK AT MIDNIGHT

We were given a mission to cross that river. In fact, I was given three missions, which was a surprising thing. . . .

MAJOR TEDDY SANFORD[1]

TIMING, STEALTH, AND luck . . . those factors would play an outsized part in the operation.

Guided by the intrepid John Marr, Sanford would lead his 1st Battalion/325th—only about 350 men after the glider landing losses[2]—across the ford to Timmes's orchard and do it without raising alarms among the German units near Timmes. Together their two forces would attack and take Amfreville to the west, then move south toward Cauquigny and attack the German forces from the rear. Colonel Millett's isolated group northwest of Amfreville was also notified by radio of the plan, and he would join them. Though he had beaten back several attacks, he had done little to break through the German lines, and Gavin's low opinion of him seemed justified. Just after dawn that day, Millett's group of 200 men had been joined by 200 more.[3] Millett was radioed instructions to move onto the Amfreville road and link up with Timmes and Sanford.

Sanford, tall and lean, was a smart and courageous leader, but he'd seen no more combat than his men. He'd also been given another mission, one he was worried about: to take care of the Germans in a château 400 yards northwest of Timmes that had been dubbed the Gray Castle. No one was sure of the size of the château's garrison or how well armed it was, and Sanford thought he'd have his hands full without it—but he planned to send C Company there as soon as they linked up with Timmes.

That night around 11:00 p.m., Marr—after getting a few hours' sleep—led the battalion north along the railroad tracks and across the ford. Engineers guided by Carter had preceded the glidermen, marking the shoulders of the narrow road by pounding stakes marked with white tape into the ground on either side of it. The moon had not yet risen, and the sky was overcast, so there was little light to guide the long column of troopers sloshing through the cold knee-high water. Captain Dave Stokely's Company C led the way, followed by Company A and then B. Several jeeps—some towing 75mm howitzers, others carrying ammunition and medical supplies—crossed also. The column made plenty of noise, but no Germans saw them until everyone had crossed—only then did the column begin receiving small-arms fire from the Gray Castle. When they reached dry land, they turned south and quickly found Timmes, and the 120 men of C Company peeled off toward the Gray Castle—which, indeed, was a gray-stoned castle complete with corner turrets and a high wall surrounding most of it.

In the farmhouse Timmes was using as a CP, Sanford told him of the plan. Timmes thought it too complicated and one that would scatter Sanford's forces too much. He also thought the major was underestimating enemy strength. Sanford had been told that the German group defending the causeway consisted of one company reinforced with automatic weapons and two medium tanks, and Timmes knew that was wrong.[4] Then Sanford radioed to Colonel Lewis that he'd reached Timmes. Lewis told him to forget Amfreville and move toward Cauquigny with all haste—there was no sign of Millett's group, but they couldn't wait for him. Sanford quickly went over the mission with his two company commanders, then prepared to move out. Lieutenant Levy, who had traversed the area to and from Cauquigny more than once, guided B Company, and another lieutenant familiar with the area was attached to guide A Company. Marr stayed near Sanford at the orchard.

Stokely had been told to eliminate the threat from the Gray Castle, or at least to make a strong show to discourage the Germans from leaving it, then hurry south to assist Companies B and C in their attack on Cauquigny. Under small-arms fire, he led his 120 men through a few open fields toward the château. When they neared it, he ordered them to lay heavy fire on it. The Germans quickly responded with heavier fire. "The tracers were flying through the air, lighting up the area like daylight," remembered Lieutenant Wayne Pierce of Company A, which had just reached Timmes's orchard.[5]

Sanford, hearing the exchange of fire, feared C Company was getting into a major engagement, and they couldn't afford that. When they didn't return immediately, he sent Marr to get them. Marr found Stokely and guided his company south toward Cauquigny; Sanford joined them. But they had misjudged the effectiveness of their feint, for behind them, advancing from hedgerow to hedgerow, a force of Germans from the château was firing at them with rifles, machine guns, and Schmeissers.

Pierce's A Company moved through the orchard and onto the road to Amfreville. Company B swung left and south toward Cauquigny. Marr and the men of C Company, exhilarated at the fire they'd directed at the Gray Castle, caught up with A Company. A C Company platoon leader, a "Georgia cracker" named Lieutenant Buester Johnson, fell in next to Pierce in the dark. He slapped Pierce on the back and said, "They can't shoot worth shit." Then his company passed through Pierce's and took the lead, and Stokely put his men in skirmish formation, then moved through fields on the west side of the road while B Company did the same on the east side. It was almost 4:00 a.m., and the near-full moon had just risen in the east. It was right about then that the mission began falling apart.

Company B had just reached the edge of an apple orchard and moved into it when they were fired on by machine guns and rifles. In a matter of seconds, nineteen men fell dead,[6] and many others were wounded. The troopers established a perimeter defense.

Not far away, Marr was leading Company C behind the enemy lines at Cauquigny and across the main road to Amfreville. They were supposed to maintain contact with B Company, but visibility was only a few feet, and the soldier on the left flank who was responsible for keeping contact lost them when a hedgerow intervened. A few minutes later C Company reached the D15. They had gone too far south and were almost 300 yards from the Cauquigny chapel. Stokely ordered them to fix bayonets, and they continued through a field and then an orchard near a two-story farmhouse. When they reached the hedgerow on the far side and made their way around it to the sunken road bordering it, they could see, through the thin hedgerow on the other side, several German artillery pieces with their crews in the adjacent field. They were behind the German artillery park. Marr saw a howitzer and three larger guns he thought were 88s. They moved into the field, catching the Germans by surprise, and some of them called out *"Kamerad!"* and other things in German—it appeared they wanted to surrender.

Marr wasn't so sure. "This is a ruse," he told Stokely. "They don't want to surrender, they want to know where we are. I think we should just charge into them."

Stokely ignored him and ordered a sergeant who spoke German to negotiate. He started forward.

One platoon began to cross the road when machine guns on either side of them began firing down the road. Marr saw about a dozen men hit and fall to the ground, dead or wounded, and the rest of them dived into the ditch on the side of the road and remained there, unable to move. Another machine gun on the second floor of a farmhouse on their right side killed several more men. A moment later a German truck came barreling down the road toward them. Lieutenant Paul Kinsey, a tall, slender former motorcycle cop from Ohio,[7] had been hit in the leg and was limping, but he stood up in the road. When the truck came alongside him, a German in the passenger seat stuck his Schmeisser out the window and fired a burst at Kinsey. The lieutenant grabbed the gun barrel, pushed it to the side, and dropped a grenade into the cab. The explosion killed both Germans and knocked Kinsey to the ground. When he heard soldiers in the truck's bed yelling, he grabbed his M1903 Springfield rifle, which was capable of launching a rifle grenade, and shot one at the truck, which blew up.

The machine guns continued to blast into the troopers. One man was engulfed in flames when a round hit his cartridge belt. When the three Germans manning one machine gun got up and began moving, a trooper threw a phosphorus grenade that hit them and set all three on fire. Seven troopers from one of the other two platoons dashed across the road and through the thin hedge to charge the artillery crews. Only one man survived. Some of the men tried to cross the road to safety, but no one made it.

Private First Class Charlie DeGlopper, the six-foot-seven BAR man, stepped into the road. Holding his rifle at his hip, he began firing on full automatic at one of the machine guns as he walked toward it. He yelled to the men behind him, "Get out! Get out! Pull back!"

DeGlopper was not only tall but also wide; he weighed 240 pounds and made a large target. The Germans began to concentrate their fire on him, allowing most of his comrades to escape through the hedgerow. DeGlopper was hit, but he continued to fire his rifle, and when his twenty-round magazine was spent, he managed to pop in another one. A bullet hit him in the right arm, and he fell to the ground and shifted the BAR to his left shoulder and rose to his knees and fired until he was hit again and knocked flat. He lay on the ground and continued to fire until he was killed.[8]

Some of Stokely's men escaped across the fields—one crawled through a wheat field while bullets from a machine gun cut the stalks above his head and grain fell on the back of his neck. He made it back to safety alive, but Stokely decided to surrender. His troopers near him rid themselves of their guns and put their hands up. The Germans rounded them up and broke Stokely's arm with a rifle. A couple of men picked up Kinsey, who was bleeding from several gunshot wounds, and carried him to the German aid station.

Pierce was in a wheat field about twenty yards behind Sanford. Because of the intervening hedgerows, he couldn't tell what was going on, but from the furious fusillade, he knew it wasn't good. When the fire petered out and they could hear nothing but German voices, Sanford came back and said, "It looks like Company C is wiped out. We'd better move back." Then he started running north along a hedgerow with the rest of his CP staff.

Pierce watched their bobbing heads go over a rise in the wheat field. He thought Sanford's conclusion a bit hasty. There was still steady gunfire coming from B Company's position some distance to his left. He ran past an abandoned artillery piece to his right and then to the other side of the orchard. He looked through a hedge for signs of C Company but saw none, though he could hear someone in the lane next to it. It was close to 6:00 a.m., and the sun was about to rise. If he was going to be alive the next day, he needed to get moving. He rid himself of some unnecessary equipment and ran into the wheat field, bending over as much as he could. When he went over the small rise, he found a half dozen demoralized C Company men who told them their company had been destroyed. Together they moved north, heading back the way they'd come in the dark, but now in bright sunlight. They crossed roads and large open fields under machine-gun fire and picked up more C Company troopers. They reached Timmes's orchard without losing a man. Marr came in with two C Company men sometime later after calling in mortar fire from Timmes's group on a phone one of the C Company men had.[9]

As ordered, Millett had started out with his 400 troopers, then moved around enemy-held Amfreville. He neglected to establish a rear guard; fortunately, a captain took care of that. They were slowed by the ninety-six German prisoners they'd captured over the previous two days. Somehow in the darkness, his group became separated into two. Millett led one of them, a group of a hundred, straight into an enemy bivouac, and he was taken prisoner; most of his men were killed or captured. Most of the other group, led by the rear-guard captain, continued to move north and east. When dawn came, they could see the Merderet. They found a way to cross the swamp, reach the railroad tracks, and move down to the La Fière bridge area to rejoin the division with their prisoners.[10]

As THE REMNANTS of the 1st Battalion/325th came straggling back into Timmes's position, a heavy German artillery barrage fell on them, hitting the glidermen who hadn't had time to dig in. When the shelling finally died down, Timmes visited the farmhouse's attached shed, which was being used as an aid station. There were now ninety men in it. He didn't bother to count the dead.[11]

In the brutal ambush, Company C had lost half its effective strength. Every officer had been killed or wounded—Johnson, the Georgia cracker, was one of the dead. Sanford's other two companies fared little better; 220 men of the battalion, about half, were dead or wounded.[12] The operation had failed miserably, and the losses had been heavy.

But the La Fière bridge had to be taken. As soon as he heard the report, Ridgway told Gavin to use whatever means possible to take it and to do it immediately. The plan Gavin devised would be uncomplicated and direct—and, to some, suicidal.

PART IV

THE BRIDGE AND BEYOND

FOURTEEN

"COLONEL, IT'LL BE A SLAUGHTER"

It sounded like suicide.

LIEUTENANT LEE TRAVELSTEAD, 325TH GLIDER INFANTRY

THE SUN HAD just come up when Major Teddy Sanford, back in the farmhouse in Timmes's orchard, radioed Colonel Harry Lewis to tell him that the attack had failed—and that what was supposed to have been a reinforced company was a much larger body of Germans well prepared for a fight. Lewis in turn delivered the news to Ridgway at his command post near Sainte-Mère-Église. After talking to Lewis, Ridgway turned to Gavin and told him to get the Merderet crossing—and get it immediately.[1] There was no time to waste. The causeway, and Cauquigny, had to be seized. The 90th Infantry Division would reach the La Fière bridge later that day ready to move westward to seal the base of the Cotentin and to protect the American forces racing north toward Cherbourg from German reinforcements. The entire invasion depended on the success of that operation.[2]

"We could not lose a moment," Gavin wrote later, "in forcing our way across and rescuing troops on the other side, and the German strength was obviously building steadily."[3] The German divisions moving into the Cotentin from Brittany under Rommel's orders might peel off to Cauquigny to fortify the 1057th forces there. That could bottleneck the advance for days, or even longer—and stall the seizing of Cherbourg, and thus the vital buildup of men and materiél in Normandy, indefinitely.

In fact, the Germans across the Merderet swamp had already been reinforced. The 1st Battalion/1057th Infantry Regiment—about 600 strong on June 6—had been joined by troops from the 2nd Battalion on June 8. Its artillery battery now included two platoons of howitzers and at least nine small but effective PaK 40 anti-tank guns; each PaK 40 delivered a round that could pierce tank armor up to an effective range of 2,000 yards.[4] The intelligence that Sanford had received before his midnight raid—that there was only a reinforced company with automatic weapons and two medium tanks in Cauquigny—had severely underestimated the German force there, and his men had paid the butcher's bill for it. The previous day, regimental orders issued to all elements of the 1057th had made clear its mission: "Defense against an enemy attack from the east with main efforts on the river crossings of the Merderet, especially near La Fière, and annihilation of scattered enemy parachutists in the rear areas."

After three days, the German force in Cauquigny was well entrenched and prepared to withstand the inevitable attack with several layers of defense. Dozens of squads operating MG42, MG34, and captured French, Belgian, and Russian machine guns were dug in along the swamp's western shoreline, both north and south of the D15 road, with more machine-gun emplacements set back to cover roads and open fields. Hundreds of well-positioned riflemen in foxholes waited, hidden in and around the hamlet's chapel and its farmhouses and orchards, and a few hundred yards farther back, the howitzers, anti-tank guns, and mortars had been deployed in the fields bordering the road to Amfreville. Any attack across the narrow causeway would have to run through overlapping fields of machine-gun and rifle fire, plus constant mortar shelling.

Gavin knew some of this but not all. Still, he was not deterred, and he quickly drew up a plan. It was as simple and subtle as a rifle butt to the teeth: A battalion of men would charge across the La Fière bridge and 500 yards of unprotected causeway into the German front lines. The only fully organized and uncommitted battalion available was Lieutenant Colonel Charles Carrell's 3rd Battalion/325th; the "orphan" 401st battalion had recently been shifted from the 101st Airborne to the 82nd to beef up its glider regiment, and Carrell's troops were still mighty resentful. The 500 men were also relatively fresh, having experienced little or no combat since landing forty-eight hours ago. After "liberating" a few towns in the area that had been expected to have a German presence but had none, they had spent the previous two nights just north of Chef-du-Pont in relative peace as part of the division reserve.

Gavin radioed Lewis and told him that his 3rd Battalion would be leading a charge across the causeway. After the call, Lewis turned to a staff officer and told him that it was a suicide mission.[5] Then they drove to the division CP for confirmation. Gavin provided it with little sympathy. He told Lewis that the order was to be carried out. The attack would commence at 9:30 a.m. with a fifteen-minute artillery bombardment of the German positions, followed by the attack.[6]

Lewis told Carrell to hustle his men up the railroad tracks to the D15 near the 1st Battalion's bivouac—though there was little left of the 1st in the area that morning after the failed attack over the hidden ford.[7] Carrell, West Point class of '32 , was a short, mild-mannered officer with no combat experience, but he was always concerned with the welfare of his men and well liked by them for it. He quickly briefed his staff and his three company commanders.

Carrell was usually calm but not that morning. He was agitated and worried as he told them, in a halting manner, that he thought the mission "impossible"—a lack of confidence that no combat commander should betray to his men.[8] But he outlined the plan and designated Captain John Sauls's G Company to lead the attack, followed by E Company, then F Company, and finally the Headquarters Company. They would run down the causeway in two files, one on the left side of the road and one on the right, rifle platoons first, followed by weapons platoons with machine guns, bazookas, and mortars.

"It sounded like suicide," recalled one of his officers. "The entire span was exposed to concentrated small arms, artillery, and mortar fire. We thought we always got the dirty work, and it looked like this time we were to go through the meat grinder so the rest could follow more safely."[9] But there was no other fresh battalion available and no other option.

The 9:30 a.m. start time was pushed back an hour to ensure the arrival of a dozen 90th Infantry Division 155mm howitzers. When they arrived, they were placed in position on either side of the D15 where it rose twenty feet or so from the river plain among some low ridges 150 yards from the bridge—just close enough to provide a clear line of fire to the opposite shore and hidden enough, it was hoped, to discourage accurate anti-tank fire. Nearby were the 82nd's seven 75mm pack howitzers and eight larger 105mm howitzers. A dozen Sherman tanks, ten yards apart, had wheeled into position in front of and slightly lower than the artillery. Ridgway lay on the hill, on the north side of the road next to one of the tanks.

Every gun on the hill would fire nonstop for fifteen minutes in the hope that the barrage would bury the Germans and slow their recovery. At 10:45 a.m., smoke shells filled with phosphorus would be fired onto the causeway as a screen, at least for the first assault troops—or so they were told by Colonel Lewis.

Then Carrell's 3rd Battalion, the untried orphan unit, would charge across the bridge and around the wrecked vehicles and down the causeway through a wall of bullets into a well-entrenched enemy position with the strength of . . . well, no one on the American side knew for sure, though the latest estimates had increased. Carrell told Sauls that he would be attacking a reinforced regiment at least 2,000 strong. In their baptism under fire, the glidermen would have to run as fast as they could down a twenty-foot-wide corridor that offered almost no protection; after three days of near-constant fire, the scraggly bushes and small trees, mostly willows, on either side had been trimmed severely, providing only an illusion of cover. The chapel lay 610 yards away; dry land—where the marsh waters lapped up onto grass, and Germans with machine guns, Mausers, and Schmeissers were dug in along the edge—was about 100 yards closer. One officer present with the 90th Artillery was appalled when he was told of the plan. "Two well-defended machine guns could have denied that crossing to a regiment," he wrote later.[10]

While the artillery batteries a couple hundred yards behind the bridge and along both sides of the D15 were sighting in their guns, the glidermen started moving west toward the bridge from the area back around the bend near the railroad tracks. Sauls and Company G led, followed by E, F, and the Headquarters Company. His men had no knowledge of where the other two regiments of the 325th were, and they were only just beginning to know the full extent of their mission. But as word of it spread, so did the grousing—they'd been chosen for this suicide mission because they were new to the regiment. Some of them still wore their 101st patches on their left shoulders.[11]

Lieutenant Richard Johnson, the Boston lawyer, would lead E Company's 1st Platoon, right behind G Company. When his company commander, Captain Charles Murphy, had briefed his platoon and squad leaders and told Johnson that his platoon would lead off, Johnson said he'd go first. With tears rolling down his cheeks, Murphy said, "God bless you."

Gavin, meanwhile, couldn't understand Carrell's pessimism. The attack would be preceded by a sustained heavy artillery barrage and a smoke screen. Gavin's gamble was also bolstered by a belief he'd come to hold based on his own experiences in Sicily and Italy and on those of others: German troops, for all their vaunted reputation, did not care for close-quarters combat and would break or surrender if subjected to it.[12] And his men—even those of the 325th—had been drilled in close-quarter fighting constantly over the past year. A successful attack across the causeway, thought Gavin, required only the requisite degree of fortitude.

But Carrell's lack of enthusiasm seemed to have spread to his men. Because Gavin had never thought the glider infantrymen could measure up to his paratroopers, he decided on a backup plan.

About 9:30 a.m., Gavin called over two 507th officers: Lieutenant Colonel Arthur Maloney, now the battalion's commander after the badly wounded Ostberg was jeeped to Utah and then taken back to a hospital in England; and Captain Robert Rae, who was commanding a scratch 507th group Maloney had designated Rae Company. The company was made up of about ninety men Rae had picked up after dropping in the 101st Airborne area to the east, several miles away from the 507th DZ. They'd been dug in down at the east end of the bridge since they'd relieved Dolan's battered 505th men on the afternoon of June 7. Since then, the thirty-year-old Rae, six feet tall with wavy brown hair and an air of confidence, had shown his mettle as a combat leader.

His troopers were now in a foxhole line thirty yards back from the bridge and on both sides of the road.

The big, burly Maloney was a sight. His three-day red beard was streaked with dried blood, he had a bandage on his head, and his helmet had a hole in it. Earlier that morning, a mortar shell had exploded near him and a piece of shrapnel had gone right through his helmet, knocking him out. When other men reached him, he was bleeding profusely from a flesh wound that hadn't damaged his skull. After Maloney's eyelids started fluttering, they dragged him over to a tree and propped him up, and a medic applied a bandage to his head. Then he put his helmet on and stood up, ready to go.

Now Gavin told Maloney and Rae to gather a force of 507th troopers and stand by. "These glidermen are probably going to hesitate at some point when their losses are heavy and the shock hits them," he said. "At that instant, I'm going to wave to you. I want you to jump up with all your men yelling their heads off and go right through them and take them with you."[13]

Two more scratch 507th companies, each comprising the same number of troopers, would follow Rae across the causeway.

A few minutes later, when Maloney gathered his officers to discuss the plan, there was some complaining when they heard about the gauntlet they would be running.

"Colonel, it'll be a slaughter," said one officer. "They can fire on us from three sides for five hundred yards."

"I know," said Maloney, "but Timmes is over there and we must go to his help."

No one said a word. As one lieutenant put it later, "Timmes was on the other side being methodically cut to pieces by the Germans. No one could deny that we owed it to Timmes, no matter how thick the bullets on the causeway."[14]

Near the *manoir* about 10:00 a.m., Gavin found Carrell for a final discussion of the plan. The noise was so loud that they had to talk almost helmet to helmet, though the six-foot Gavin towered over the battalion commander. Carrell was still unenthusiastic.

"I don't think I can do it," he said.

"Why not?" Gavin asked.

"I'm sick."

It wasn't clear what he meant—was he suffering from an illness, an injury, or a bad case of nerves? But that was enough for Gavin. "Okay, you're through." He had never relieved a man in combat before, but "the whole battle was hanging by a thread," he said later.[15]

Gavin found Lewis and told him to put another man in charge. Instead of naming Carrell's XO, Major Charles Moore—a man known to, and respected by, the battalion—Lewis chose his staff operations officer, Major Arthur Gardner. No one in the former 401st battalion knew him except by name. Some confusion ensued—many of the men thought Moore was now in charge—and that dampened their spirits even more.

Gavin settled into a foxhole next to Maloney and about fifty yards back from the bridge, where he could see both Rae and Sauls.

The man who would be the first across the bridge, thirty-one-year-old Captain John Sauls, was from a small town in North Carolina; he had a wife and a little girl back home. He was one of the few junior officers in the 82nd with a college degree—his was in ceramic engineering.[16] Sauls was an outgoing, popular leader, but he was as new to combat as his men. When he began leading G Company west along the D15 from the railroad overpass and took the turn that became a straight shot down to the bridge past the *manoir* and first came into view of the small bridge, German machine-gun fire swept over them and the glidermen dived into the ditches on each side of the road for cover. About twenty dead 507th troopers lay scattered in the ditches and along the embankment, further discouraging anyone from rising and continuing down the D15. Below them, artillery and mortar shells were exploding all around the bridge and the road.

Sauls thought there had to be a better way to get to their jump-off place down near the bridge. He found a 507th officer nearby and asked him, but the man was no help.

"All I can tell you," he said, "is we've taken a hell of a beating here for two days and there's a million Germans over there."

Sauls left his men there and reconnoitered over to the south, following the curved ridge behind the *manoir*; he swung far enough around it to see a safer route leading down to a dirt lane into the courtyard and then along the shoulder-high stone wall running some thirty yards from a small building to the *manoir* entrance on the D15. Fifteen yards from the end of the wall was the road, which the wall approached at an acute angle—just enough, thought Sauls, to provide some protection. The only problem was a seven-yard gap the German artillery had opened up about ten yards from the end—an MG42 was trained on it and fired on anyone who attempted to move across it. Six dead 507th troopers lay along the lane. Sauls told one of Rae's sergeants to help him move them—he didn't want his men staring at the corpses while they were waiting and working up their nerve to charge. The two dragged the bodies out of sight, then Sauls retraced his steps and led his company a few at a time across the D15 and around the ridge and down past the ancient feudal mounds and through the courtyard.

When they arrived at the breach, most of the 2nd Platoon dashed across the opening to crouch shoulder to shoulder against the wall behind Sauls, until the forward area in the driveway was full. The next man to cross the gap would be Private Melvin Johnson, only twenty-two but married with a young wife, Ruby Ann, and a two-year-old son back in rural Wisconsin. He carried with him one photo; it was of the three of them and it had been taken in a studio while he was home on leave. Johnson would wait to cross when his buddies on the far side of the breach began moving out.

Sauls kneeled at the end of the wall, just fifteen yards from the road and twenty more from the bridge. Behind him were two reliable men: Sergeant Wilfred Ericsson, a sturdily built machinist from California, and Second Lieutenant Don Wason. Short but just as solid as Ericsson, Wason was a stock clerk from Greenwich, Connecticut, who'd been married for fifteen months. Sauls went over the company's assignment with them: to clear out the south sector, the left side, of the bridgehead—if they managed to reach the other side and establish one. Company E, behind them, had been assigned the right side, and Company F would mop up behind them.

At 10:30 a.m., the artillery barrage began, and the German cannon and small arms also increased their fire—the Germans knew artillery fire that intense presaged an attack and they hoped to disrupt units preparing to move out. The roar was deafening: men screaming and horses shrieking—most of the German artillery was horse-drawn—and mortar shells exploding, machine guns rattling, and shrapnel and bullets zipping through the dust- and smoke-filled air. A man could feel the concussion blasts from the explosions in his ears, his teeth, his bones, his lungs, his heart. The noise was thunderous and the chaos hellish and in no way encouraging to the men about to run through it. Sauls checked his M1A1 carbine and made sure he had a full fifteen-round magazine in it. The soldiers behind him did the same with their weapons—Garands, tommy guns, and BARs—and adjusted their helmets and made sure their extra ammo clips and magazines were at hand. Behind the first two platoons, the men of the weapons platoon nervously prepared to heft their mortars, machine guns, and ammo boxes and run down the long, open causeway.

Sauls had told his men that their best chance was to move as fast as they could and try to reach the other side in one long run. They could hear and feel mortar shells falling into the small strip of land between the wall and the water's edge, and hear machine-gun rounds hitting the wall and the stone garage on the other side of the driveway they crouched beside.

At 10:43 a.m., Sauls looked at his watch, held up two fingers, and yelled, "Two minutes to go!"

Some of the men asked when the smoke would start, because it hadn't yet. It never would—the smoke canisters Lewis had promised were still on ammunition trucks moving inland from Utah.[17] Then one soldier shouted, "Let's get to the other side. *Beaucoup mademoiselles* over there, none here." Those who could hear him laughed. Sauls looked back and winked, and those near him who caught his eye winked back. That made Sauls feel better. He thought the men seemed calm enough.

He glanced at his watch again and held up one finger. "One minute to go!"

At 10:45 a.m., the suppressive fire from the hill behind them eased, though some of the artillery continued to bombard German positions thirty yards or more beyond the far shore, which kept down the German fire except for the machine guns. Sauls waited thirty seconds, silently praying for the smoke shells. None appeared.

He grabbed his carbine with his left hand, stood and raised his right arm to wave his men forward, and yelled, "Let's go!"

FIFTEEN

THE CHARGE

The air was full of lead. . . .

LIEUTENANT RUFUS BROADAWAY[1]

As Sauls raised his right arm, a German round ripped through his hand, missing bone but tearing his palm apart. He ran to the bridge and across it on the south side. At the beginning of the long causeway, he went around the overturned truck and the first dead panzer and kept running. Behind him Wason peeled off to the north side, followed by Ericsson and his entire squad plus a BAR man from the next squad. Wason turned and yelled, "Get over left!" to balance the lines, and Ericsson and his men did as Wason ordered.[2]

Grenades and bandoliers jouncing, the men of Rae Company ran with their heads up and resisted the natural inclination to stoop over to avoid getting hit. Though the heavy barrage had indeed suppressed the small-arms fire somewhat, enemy mortar shells fell around them as they ran, and they passed Germans dug in along the sides of the causeway between the water and the pavement. They fired at the Germans as they neared and then passed them, but no one stopped. Sauls, who had been a boxer and swimmer in college, ran down the causeway past the two other burned-out tanks with little regard for the fusillade coming from several points on the far bank; he was followed by Ericsson, Wason, and others—all those long marches and runs they'd done in training were now paying off. Sauls reached the west side without another injury, though his right hand was bleeding badly. Friendly mortar fire was landing only twenty-five yards in front of him, but that was all right—it checked some of the machine gunners even farther ahead. Sauls stopped, breathing heavily after an uninterrupted 500-yard dash, and turned around for the first time. Right behind him was Ericsson, who jumped off the south side of the blacktop and started down a dirt lane that ran south along the water's edge. Through the smoke and haze, Sauls could see most of the 1st Platoon coming up toward him on either side of the causeway.

Sauls and about two dozen glidermen had penetrated the outer crust of the German defenses and achieved a tenuous bridgehead. The next few minutes would decide if they could hold it. But Sauls could see no one behind them. Something was wrong, and he couldn't see beyond the road's slight bend two-thirds of the way down the causeway to tell what it was.

The trouble was much farther back than that. At the *manoir* wall, after the 1st Platoon soldiers ahead of Private Johnson had run out to the road, he said, "Here I go," and rushed across the gap, but before he reached the other side, a machine-gun round smashed into his skull and he dropped to the ground dead. His death paralyzed the men behind him and none of them could summon the nerve to move across the bridge. Almost ten minutes went by before Lieutenant Frank Amino, a short former subway motorman from Pittsburgh, stood and yelled, "Let's go on and kill those sons of bitches!" He ran past the breach and onto the road. Most of the others started following him.

When Wason on the right side of the road reached Sauls, he continued past him straight ahead toward the first house thirty yards down the D15, where a German machine-gun crew was firing straight down the causeway. Several troopers followed him. He told them to stay back and ran toward the gun. As he got close, he pulled a grenade and threw it just as a round from the MG42 hit him and killed him. The grenade wiped out the Germans.

Sauls's runner, PFC Frank Thurston, had followed Wason and seen another machine gun farther up the road. He ran back to Sauls. "Sir," he said, "I know where there's a second machine gun beyond it. Can I go get it?"

Sauls told him to go ahead. Thurston crawled forward along a hedgerow to a position near the intersection of the D15 and the road that branched right and went over to the chapel. When he found a good vantage point behind a hedge, he settled down, trained his M1 on the crew, and quickly shot them one by one.

When he returned to Sauls, he was laughing. "I got the bastards," he said.

Ericsson on the south side of the D15 took one look at the line of German entrenchments along the water's edge and turned and yelled at the BAR man—a tall, blond coal miner from West Virginia named James Kittle—to come over to him. He positioned Kittle at the junction of the D15 and the dirt lane running south so that the BAR would cover a long, open field on the west side of the lane. Ericsson and his squad moved down the road, firing through the hedge and tossing grenades at the emplacements on their left. They flushed out Germans who began to retreat by crossing the road and running through the field, where Kittle fired at them with his BAR. Others still battered from the heavy barrage dropped their weapons and emerged with their hands held high. They were sent back down the causeway toward the east side of the river.

When Ericsson made it a hundred yards down the lane, he turned back to retrace his steps and get more men up and more ammunition. He had almost reached the main road when a bullet hit him in the back and knocked him to the ground. He was alive but found it difficult to move. He staggered to the blacktop and flopped down next to it.

Still standing near a hedgerow just off the D15, Sauls was trying to determine in the chaos how many men he had with him. Grenades began dropping all around. Every time one did, someone yelled, "Grenade!" and everyone else would hit the ground. But the German grenades didn't seem very powerful. One exploded five feet from Sauls while he stood there and only nicked him in the leg. His men started throwing their own grenades over the hedgerow, which produced more surrendering Germans.

As most of G Company followed Amino across the bridge and down the causeway, the German fire picked up and men began falling before the interlocking bands of machine-gun fire. "A lot of men were getting killed," remembered one 507th trooper who had been watching from the east side. The German small-arms fire "intensified to the degree that it was purely an unbroken whine. Sounded almost like a million mosquitoes in a very confined space."[3] Soon more than twenty of the men of G Company lay along the road and in the grass beside it, and the rest stumbled over and picked their way around the dead and wounded. Some of the glidermen sought cover in the shallow drainage ditches that ran along each side of the causeway. The weapons platoon came last, lugging ammo, bazookas, machine guns and tripods, and mortars and their base plates. Through the shelling and small-arms fire, most of those troopers ran twenty or thirty yards at most and flopped down, then got up and ran some more, gradually making their way down the causeway.

Then Lewis, desperate to provide his men assistance, waved one of the Shermans forward; it clanked onto the road and crossed the bridge to push the truck to the right side. Most of the mines laid down by Dolan's A Company on June 6 had just been picked up, but the tank hit one that hadn't, and stopped with a busted track. That increased the blockage there, so Ridgway ran down the hill and began helping the detail of 82nd engineers trying to get the tank moving again.

BEHIND G COMPANY was E Company's 1st Platoon, led by Lieutenant Richard Johnson. His company's mission was to clear the area on the north side of the D15, including the chapel. He led out from the *manoir* driveway behind the last men of G Company, and when he reached the road, he found they had stopped right in front of him. In the face of the withering German fire, their progress had come to a complete halt behind the truck and tanks. A 507th captain was there yelling, "Get these men moving," but few heard him over the roar of the artillery behind them. Johnson adjusted his glasses, took a deep breath, gripped his M1903 Springfield firmly, and walked onto the bridge. He saw a G Company soldier he knew, Andy Pavka, lying flat on his back. When the man began pushing and sliding himself backward, Johnson stopped.

"You're going the wrong way, Pavka," he said.

"I can't help it, sir," said Pavka. "I'm hit."

Bullets zipping past him and mortar shells exploding, Johnson continued over the bridge and down the causeway until he reached one of the French tanks on the right side of the road. He looked back to see only one man behind him, a private. He shouted to the private that he wanted E Company moving forward and sent him back. Then he pulled a cartridge out of an ammo belt hanging out of the tank and scrawled a large "E" on its side, hoping his men following him would see it. His runner, Private John Plicka, caught up to him and they ran along the right edge of the causeway until Johnson stepped in a hole and went sprawling into the swamp. Plicka pulled Johnson out using the butt of his rifle. A minute later, Plicka fell flat on his face with his M1 cradled in his arms.

Over the din Johnson yelled, "Don't stop here, Plicka."

"I can't help it, sir," said Plicka. "I'm hit."

Johnson noted that Plicka had used the same wording as Pavka and kept going. By that time most of E Company was strung out behind him. He had almost reached dry land when he saw a German machine gunner on the right raise his head and start firing in a steady, sweeping arc toward him, but before any bullets reached him, the gun hit the end of its traverse and stopped. The close call reinvigorated Johnson, and he ran off the causeway and tried to get behind the German, just twenty feet away. The German threw a potato masher at him. It landed in a pile of manure and Johnson jumped sideways back into the swamp. The grenade exploded and a piece of it slashed through his left arm.

Johnson grabbed a grenade, pulled the pin, and let go of the handle. He knew the grenade would go off in four and a half seconds. He counted *One a thousand, two a thousand* and lobbed it into the enemy foxhole. When the German picked it up to throw it back, it exploded in his right hand. Johnson waded out of the swamp to find himself facing the barrel of another MG42 right in front of him. But the Germans behind it were still head down in their foxhole, so Johnson poked them with his bayonet, said, *"Hände hoch!"* and gestured for them to start toward the other end of the causeway. They seemed willing to surrender, but not to venture out onto the causeway. He jabbed them lightly with his bayonet until they reluctantly headed in that direction.

He heard moaning and turned to see the first German, still conscious, with his left hand nearing the MG42's trigger. Johnson strode over, pulled him up, and tossed him away from the gun.

He turned to see how many of his men had made it to the west side. Only one, a sergeant, was in sight, and he ran up to Johnson. The air was filled with smoke, and a bullet from a machine gun on the east side, no doubt meant for Germans dimly seen through the smoke, went through both of Johnson's ankles. It didn't knock him down, but he fell to the ground anyway to avoid getting shot again. The sergeant was hit by a slug that went through his right arm, hit a rib, and came out in the middle of his back. He was alive but bleeding profusely in three places.

As Johnson tried to stanch the blood, some of his men arrived. He directed them to clear out the cluster of houses up ahead near the church, and they did, throwing grenades into the houses and shooting a sniper in an upper window of the chapel who had taken a shot at Johnson and barely missed. A medic appeared to patch up and stabilize the two men—and also to administer to a rabbit that had been wounded during the barrage.

The day was warm, but after the adrenaline wore off, Johnson found himself shivering uncontrollably.[4]

JOHNSON'S COMPANY COMMANDER, Captain Murphy, had been hit in the face with several shards of shrapnel before he'd made it over the bridge, but even with his face a bloody mess, he continued on, moving men forward until a third of E Company—all that would make it for now—was completely across the bridge. At the far shore, he kept on going and led a group down the road toward the chapel fifty yards on. The 507th's mortar fire was still landing around it; one shell injured seven glidermen, but it also helped persuade Germans to surrender. They rose out of their positions with their hands up and shouting, "*Kamerad!*" About thirty of them were herded onto the causeway and started east. Most of them would be killed or wounded before they reached the *manoir*, either by German or American fire.

A six-man patrol from E Company was sent to a few farm buildings beyond the church. They moved from building to building, shaking loose a few German prisoners from each one. At the last one, a barn, Sergeant John Selmer was just about to enter firing when a voice from inside said, "We have here only two wounded." Selmer relaxed, lowered his rifle, and stepped inside. A German against the wall behind him riddled him with a Schmeisser, and Selmer fell dead. A trooper who had been behind Selmer ran in and killed the German.[5]

Another group of E Company soldiers reached the western side of the bridge and continued moving down the main road. Two hundred yards from the causeway, they reached a hedge and looked over it. A German mortar crew was on the other side, the men firing as quickly as they could drop shells into the tube. The soldiers watched as five shells dropped onto the causeway. Then one of the men tossed a grenade over the hedge and killed all three Germans.[6]

When Amino and his platoon reached Sauls, he was directed by the officer to the lane on the south side that Ericsson's men had run down. After telling Amino to help clear the area, Sauls sent a sergeant to lead another group down the south side along a larger road that led to Pont l'Abbé.

With only two undermanned companies, the 325th was still managing to expand the bridgehead. As Gavin had hoped, the Germans had no stomach for the aggressive attacks. But there were hundreds more Germans than glidermen, and they appeared to have an endless supply of ammunition for their well-placed machine guns and mortars. Small, separated groups of 325th soldiers found themselves fighting pockets of determined grenadiers in close-quarter action that could have gone either way, and they were running out of ammunition and grenades.

All along the causeway junior officers were moving the men along, yelling at them and picking them up and pushing them down the road, and gradually the troopers were reaching the far side of the bridge, where, invigorated by their emergence from the gauntlet along the causeway, they followed the officers and noncoms and continued moving into the German positions.

Company E XO Lieutenant Bruce Booker, who had already fought in the Pacific as an enlisted man before attending OCS and joining the Airborne, had been assigned the task of prodding his men forward. But he got caught in the rush to the far side and reached it with some of the first men to make it, and when he realized that many more men were lagging behind, he ran back to the bridge and began to move them along. He had managed to herd most of them across when a mortar shell exploded near him and shrapnel sliced through both his calves and dozens of smaller fragments hit him. Unable to walk, he sat on the side of the asphalt to wait for a medic and waved at the last of the men strung out behind him, shouting, "Get on up there, goddammit! That's where the fight is!" Those who heard him got up and moved along. Before a medic found him, Booker saw a group of E Company soldiers coming back from the far side. Shouting and laughing, Booker pulled his .45 and fired several shots just above their heads. They turned back toward Cauquigny.

BACK AT THE *manoir* wall, Lieutenant Lee Travelstead—a slender, blond twenty-two-year-old commanding F Company's machine-gun platoon near the back of the line of 325th men—watched the chaos as he waited for his unit to move out across the bridge. Directly ahead of him was the mortar platoon with its heavy loads. Behind him, his men prepared to hoist their machine guns, tripods, or ammo boxes; Travelstead carried a tommy gun. Deep in one of his pockets was a box of chocolate-covered cherries he had been carrying since England, waiting for some special occasion. He pulled the box out and ate the entire contents before the order to jump off came. When it did, about 11:20 a.m., he began to run, making his way over and around the dead and wounded and terror-stricken soldiers on the ground and praying that he and his men wouldn't get hit by the heavy fire they could do nothing about.[7] He continued on down the causeway past the mortar and machine-gun men, many of them running with their heavy loads for twenty or thirty yards, diving down to the ground in search of cover, then getting up and doing it again.

It was about 11:30 a.m.—forty-five minutes had passed since Sauls had led the charge. Artillery, mortar, and small-arms fire were still coming from the west side. Gavin, in his foxhole fifty yards east of the bridge, trained his binoculars on the far side of the causeway, trying to get an idea of how the attack was going. But no information was coming back. Almost nothing could be seen of the far-side fighting save for the occasional puff of smoke or cloud of dust. The thick haze, scrub brush, and low trees along the causeway, combined with the slight bend to the right it took 200 yards beyond the bridge, obscured the view and made it impossible to know what was going on. There was no radio contact with the glidermen, and it looked like a good number of them were still hanging back near the tanks. Along the causeway, medics were running from man to man, trying to keep the wounded alive, applying compresses to gaping wounds gushing blood, tying off tourniquets, and jabbing arms, legs, and torsos with morphine syrettes. Gavin did not find the sight reassuring.

He discussed the situation with Maloney, at his side. He'd had his doubts about the glidermen back in England, and now he suspected that some of them might have been able to reach the other side, but certainly not enough, and he knew that Carrell's lack of confidence had spread through the ranks. He had to assume that the 325th's attack had failed—"the overwhelming fire power of the Germans was just too much," Gavin wrote later.[8]

He turned toward Rae, gave him the signal to move out, and yelled, "All right, go ahead! You've got to go and keep going!" Then he and Maloney headed to the bridge.

Rae jumped up and waved his men forward, and they came out of their foxholes shouting and ran across the bridge. Machine-gun fire from the far shore was still coming in, though it was nothing like what the first 325th companies had experienced. Just beyond the bridge, the last of the 325th men, most of them from F Company, were jammed so thick behind the disabled American tank and the panzer that Rae's troopers had to elbow their way through the scrum. An artillery shell exploded near Rae, and his runner, Private Richard Keeler, dived to the ground with several others.

"If you're going to get it," Rae told Keeler, "you're going to get it, and you might as well start walking down the road with me." He turned to those behind him. "Keep moving, keep moving, keep moving!"

Keeler got up and began working on the others who were still down. Soon most of Rae Company was following him, with the help of a few other lieutenants moving back and forth and encouraging them to move forward: "Come on, come on, keep firing as you go!" Corporal Earl Geoffrion, the man who had killed another trooper with one punch back in England, was also pulling 507th men up by their pants, getting them back on their feet, and pushing them down the causeway to dodge and step over and around the soldiers lying along the sides of the road.

Halfway across, Rae's men began to pass German prisoners of war coming their way, still holding their hands up. When he and about thirty-five troopers reached the far end, they were fired on by Germans—grenadiers Ericsson's patrol had missed who were along the edge of the swamp south of the road. Some of the troopers stopped in the road and stood there returning fire until the Germans withdrew. Rae heard small-arms fire coming from the right and led his men down the lane on that side to the chapel cemetery.

SERGEANT RUDI SKRIPEK and his squad were in a field near the D15, firing at the Americans as both sides threw grenades across the hedgerows. For three nights, his men and he had been dug in among the graves in the chapel's small cemetery, exchanging fire with the Americans on the other side of the causeway; the short stone wall around the graveyard had provided some protection, as they were made aware every time they heard a round bite into it. The mortar fire had been heavy, and many of his young grenadiers were already dead. Two days ago, he had held his best friend, Sergeant Peter Unsinn, in his arms while Unsinn died a painful death after a mortar shell exploded nearby and heavy shrapnel ripped apart his stomach.

Now someone ordered them to pull back to the chapel. Skripek and his men ran past a hedgerow to get to it, Americans firing at them and dropping some of his comrades. Moments later someone yelled at them to withdraw to Amfreville, almost a mile away. Small-arms fire from the Americans downed some of Skripek's comrades as they ran west, but most of them made it, Skripek included, though he was limping and in pain from a chunk of shrapnel in his left thigh and a few smaller pieces in his back.

He didn't think his injuries were that serious, and he didn't want to leave his men. That evening, when he visited an aid station, he told the captain there he just wanted a bandage on it. The officer took one look and decided otherwise, then decreed that Skripek would be sent to a hospital in Paris on a truck—or a train if the Germans could find a railroad line that hadn't been destroyed by Allied planes.[9]

GEOFFRION MADE IT across the bridge without getting hit and followed Rae toward the chapel. When he got near it, a bullet smashed into the stock of his Garand and broke it into pieces, knocking him into a foxhole with a dead German. His knee landed on a helmet, and he felt something tear in it. Someone yelled, "Get that goddamn gun." Geoffrion saw a sniper in an upper window of the chapel and others in the cemetery, and he grabbed the dead German's Schmeisser and began returning fire. Then another trooper threw him a Garand and he tossed the machine gun aside before someone behind him heard the Schmeisser's distinctive sound and shot at him. He trained his rifle on the cemetery, and when he saw movement, he pulled the trigger reflexively. A split second later he realized it was a German officer with his hands up. When the man fell back dead, Geoffrion felt a pang of remorse.[10]

After clearing the chapel area of Germans, Rae returned to the D15 and led his men west. Beyond the hamlet's small cluster of farmhouses, he ran into Captain James Harney, commander of F Company. Harney, preceding Rae, had made it across the causeway with his headquarters group in fifteen minutes. When he got there, he'd decided that he didn't have enough men to tackle his assigned mission of peeling off left and right to mop up after Companies G and E. Better, he thought, to push on down the road and establish his force along the slightly higher ground between them. His soldiers moved down the D15, spraying the hedgerows with fire and grenading German entrenchments at the edges of the field.

When Rae caught up to him, he asked Harney what he wanted him to do. Harney was surprised to see anyone but glidermen in the area, but he sent Rae on the left flank to make contact with Company G, then take up a defensive position on the high ground. Soon after Rae moved out, Harney ordered a group of E Company men to do the same on the right side. That established a firm center of the bridgehead and pushed the retreating Germans west.

ON THE EAST side of the bridge, the engineers had managed to get the Sherman moving, and now they were trying to use it to pull the truck and the panzer off the road. Ridgway ran over to it and helped secure a cable to the overturned truck, and Gavin, Maloney, and he were soon joined by Lewis, the 325th commander. All four were at the bottleneck, grabbing men, helping them to their feet, and pushing them in the right direction through the machine-gun fire. Mortar shells continued to fall around them—one exploded ten yards from Ridgway, killing one trooper and wounding eight others. The general ignored it. "The fire was so intense," Ridgway wrote later, "that the men were physically recoiling. The physical force of that firepower was such that they just stopped and started back—not from cowardice at all."[11]

"Son, you can do it," Gavin said to every soldier he picked up. The sight of two generals and two colonels standing where the action and the fire were the hottest inspired gliderman and paratrooper alike.

By noon the disabled tanks had been cleared to the sides of the causeway, and Gavin had walked back up the hill to exhort the Shermans to start moving across it. The last elements of F Company were finally moving along the causeway as another tank rattled onto the bridge. The battalion HQ company was next, with Sergeant Bud Olson among them. He was just passing the tank when its cannon fired, and the muzzle blast knocked him head over heels.

As he staggered to his feet, someone helped him. He looked up to see Ridgway. "If you're not wounded," the general said, "let's go."

Olson joined a cluster of men moving down the causeway. On the other side, he fired his M1903 into a machine-gun nest on the right side of the shore until some others and he knocked it out.[12]

WHEN TRAVELSTEAD REACHED the western end of the causeway, most of his men were still fairly close behind him. Harney sent him and his men straight ahead to the road that forked right toward the chapel. They had just turned onto the lane when a helmetless paratroop lieutenant leading a group of 507th men came running down the road toward Travelstead, yelling, "Show ourselves, and move 'em!" When he reached Travelstead, they both gathered their men and together led them to the chapel, where some of Rae's troopers were just clearing the cemetery of Germans. They all continued to push the Germans out of Cauquigny toward the crossroads hamlet of Les Helpiquets, a half mile west on the road to Amfreville. When they reached its main intersection, Travelstead directed two of his crews to set up there and fire at the retreating Germans still in sight.

As Travelstead stood in the center of the road behind his machine gunners, two of Rae's troopers—both much larger than Travelstead, who was five foot eight and only a hundred twenty pounds—had just walked up to him when a mortar round blew all three into the ditch on the left side of the road. Travelstead found himself underneath the two men. He waited for them to get up, but neither one moved. He pulled himself out from under them. They were both dead, having taken the brunt of the shrapnel. Travelstead was temporarily deaf from the concussion, and he was bleeding from shrapnel hits to an arm and a leg, but he was alive.[13]

The 1st Platoon of I Company/507th followed Rae Company across the causeway. When its leader, Lieutenant Donald O'Rourke, reached the chapel cemetery, he found fifteen glidermen standing in the road in front of it; they were around a foxhole on the side with a wooden cover. The grenadier in it "had apparently gone insane from shell shock," recalled O'Rourke, who lifted the lid and helped the man out by his arm, then directed him toward the causeway. Within minutes, eleven other Germans in the immediate vicinity emerged from their own foxholes and surrendered.[14]

Once the scrum around the tanks was cleared, most of the glidermen and paratroopers were moving steadily along the causeway. The other two scratch companies followed Rae, and by noon, almost all of the men of the 3rd Battalion/325th and the three 507th companies had made it across the bridge and driven most of the Germans out of Cauquigny save for a sniper here and there. On the west side of the hamlet, Rae had focused on the main road and pushed beyond the village. In doing so, he had strengthened the center of the bridgehead. That in turn had collapsed the German flanks, but only after Sauls's men south of the D15 had managed to knock out three machine-gun nests and beat back two anti-tank guns with the help of well-placed mortar rounds.

Unknown to Gavin at the time, the men of the 3rd Battalion/325th had indeed managed to establish a bridgehead—but without Rae Company's assistance, it's doubtful they could have maintained it against tough German opposition. Gavin's instincts had been correct, and he had made the right decision at the right time.

As more glider infantry and troopers arrived in the area and things quieted down, Rae decided to return to Cauquigny, since his men were low on ammunition. At the main crossroads, a 325th CP had been established in a stone farmhouse there. Rae's men collected in the orchard behind it, where they pulled out C rations and rested.

In midafternoon, Rae was summoned into the house. There he found Gavin, who told him to send a patrol north to find Timmes—indiscriminate American mortar shelling had prevented a 325th patrol sent with the same objective from making contact. Rae's patrol walked north to discover that the Germans holding Timmes's command under siege had disappeared. The patrol returned to Cauquigny, with Sanford's 1st Battalion/325th following them to link up with the 3rd Battalion. Timmes had about two hundred injured men, and he would wait until jeeps and trucks arrived to safely get them back to an aid station.

After things had cooled off in Cauquigny, Gavin walked down the lane running south from the D15. In a field a hundred yards beyond the water, he found a dozen mortars in large square holes in the ground, and plenty of artillery, half-tracks, and self-propelled guns—more than he'd expected. There were also many dead and wounded horses still in harness. He walked down the road along the south side of the swamp past dead Germans and the detritus of an army in retreat. Near an empty German CP, he saw a paratrooper still in his harness hanging from an apple tree. He had been shot. Then he returned to La Fière and later the division CP near Sainte-Mère-Église, where Ridgway and he gradually began to assess how the division as a whole was doing.

It wasn't till midafternoon that one of G Company's communications men, a sergeant, reached Wilfred Ericsson. He found the lieutenant badly wounded and on his stomach, unable to move, but with enough strength to motion to his tommy gun on the ground next to him.

"Take that with you," he told the sergeant. "You won't need your carbine over here."

About the same time, a medic finally looked at Sauls's hand and decided it was bad enough to get him shipped back to England—he had lost a lot of blood. After the causeway was secured, Sauls had taken on the task of guarding some prisoners while his men moved on, and he'd been forced to shoot and kill one German who wouldn't stop approaching him in a threatening manner and refused to respond to Sauls's warnings to stop. Sauls was a religious man, and he would rather have not done that.

Now he slung his carbine over his shoulder and began walking back across the causeway with dozens of other men injured but still able to walk, along with German soldiers on the way to Utah Beach and eventually a POW camp in England. Tanks and jeeps passed him, some loaded with ammunition boxes or towing artillery and others filled with badly injured American and German soldiers en route to aid stations. Dozens more wounded and dead men, most of them Germans but many glidermen and some paratroopers, lay in the ditches on either side of the road and in the swamp waters. Shermans had managed to move the disabled enemy tanks to the side of the road and were making their way westward. His hand bandaged and bloody, Sauls crossed the small bridge and walked past the half-destroyed *manoir*.

Sauls could feel justifiably proud of his men. In their baptism of fire, he had led his company—and his battalion—into what had seemed certain death. Some of the men had faltered, as some always did, but, given a second chance and a word of encouragement, they found the courage necessary to go on and joined their comrades on the far shore, where they fought well. The glidermen had done the job asked of them, and at the end of the day, few had been found wanting. That was evident in the casualty numbers the 3rd Battalion/325th had incurred: Of about 400 men involved, there were 40 dead and 180 wounded, a substantial 55 percent rate.[15] To cross the causeway, the glidermen had paid a steep toll in blood.

THE FOOTHOLD ON the west side of the Merderet seemed secure, and the other pockets of troopers had been rescued. Lindquist had just led a battalion of the 508th across the Merderet and down to Shanley on Hill 30—the Germans surrounding it had moved out. Jeeps and trucks would soon be carrying away the dozens of injured men there. The wounded at Timmes's position were also being moved to aid stations. Other troopers, single or in small groups, were steadily making their way into the lines after three days of playing a deadly game of hide-and-seek with the Germans.

At about 6:00 p.m., Ridgway and Gavin were still figuring out the state of the division when a call came through from the 325th CP at Cauquigny.

It was from the 325th's XO, Lieutenant Colonel Herbert Sitler. He reported that the bridgehead was in danger of collapsing under a German counterattack. Some of his men were retreating across the causeway, and reinforcements were needed immediately.

An infuriated Gavin jeeped there at once to find that Colonel Lewis had collapsed from sheer exhaustion, aided by a heavy sedative administered by his medical officer, and had been removed to an aid station. Sitler had taken command. He told Gavin he was spooked by the sound of the tanks that had been supporting him passing eastward and the sight of soldiers doing the same. It was impossible to hold the bridgehead, he said, and he intended to withdraw back across the causeway and re-form a defensive line on the east side of the Merderet.

Gavin got up near the front lines to see for himself. They did look thin, though the situation looked stable—and, to Gavin's eyes, ripe for offensive action. Better, he thought, to keep the Germans back on their heels; instead of waiting for the inevitable counterattack, the 82nd would counterattack. He returned to the CP and told Sitler that they were going to attack at once with everything, and everyone, at hand, including cooks, clerks, communications men—anyone with a weapon. "He blanched a bit, seemed rather startled, but accepted the order," Gavin wrote later. Sitler organized his HQ and service companies into a scratch force and sent it forward to plug the lines against the Germans. Then Gavin sent an armored car down to Shanley on Hill 30 to make sure he knew of the counterattack and to remain there to anchor the left flank. Sanford and his 1st Battalion/325th, a half mile north with Timmes, were told to do the same on the right flank. The objective: the German strongpoint Les Helpiquets, the hamlet 900 yards west on the road to Amfreville.[16]

Gavin sent his aide, Captain Hugo Olson, to instruct the tank commander to support the counterattack. Then he found Maloney and another officer and posted them at the head of the causeway. "We're going to attack," he told them. "I want you to stand on this bridge and don't let any man by. Turn them around." The hulking Maloney, his face and red beard still clotted with blood, was an imposing sight, especially after he picked up a heavy tree limb and wielded it, though he also carried a .45. Gavin knew no one would get by him.[17]

One man tried. Major Moore, the XO of the 3rd Battalion/325th, was running back from the front lines when he came up against Maloney, who ordered him back to the front. Moore began arguing. When he finished, Maloney said, "Your place is up front with your men at this time. You will go back up there or I will shoot you."[18]

Moore turned and went forward as ordered.[19]

After leaving the CP, Gavin shouldered his M1 and headed west toward the front lines again to find Rae. Whenever he ran into a trooper or gliderman coming back, he turned them around with "Where are you going, son? We're counterattacking and we need you up there." He ran into German fire and entered a wheat field and began walking across it when he noticed the stalks above his head being sliced "as though by a giant invisible scythe," he remembered.[20] He dropped to all fours and crawled the rest of the way.

The Germans had already counterattacked Harney's F Company, farther to the west near Les Helpiquets, and soon the glidermen were hit with mortar, artillery, and machine-gun fire. Harney had no choice but to pull back. Company F dug in behind some hedgerows and kept their heads down; the intense mortar barrage lasted about an hour. When it lifted, the glidermen looked through the hedgerows to see German soldiers moving toward them in the fields. They fired back until the grenadiers retreated.

Rae had been told to establish a defensive line on the west side of Cauquigny. He and his men moved again. They had just started digging in when the mortar barrage began and they could hear the sounds of a German counterattack approaching. About 9:00 p.m., with the sun low in the west, Rae was deepening his foxhole when he heard someone shouting his name. It was Gavin. The general told Rae that he'd decided a counterattack was needed to prevent the enemy from regaining Les Helpiquets. Rae was the man to lead it.

"Let's get these men moving," Gavin told him. "I want you to take your men and go forward."

"How far do you want me to go?" said Rae.

"Go to town!" Gavin said.

Rae assembled his men and led them back to Les Helpiquets. This time there was little opposition along the way as they moved up carefully, hedgerow by hedgerow, supported by Harney's platoon of 325th men on the right and three Shermans behind them. The remaining sixty exhausted troopers of Rae Company reached the hamlet's crossroads and dug in for the night. But when the Shermans began withdrawing and their crews resisted Rae's entreaties to stay, he walked back to the 325th CP to get them sent to Les Helpiquets again. That also proved unsuccessful, but he arranged for a jeep with food, ammunition, and medical supplies to be sent forward to his men. Mortar and machine-gun fire continued in the area until midnight, then eased off—the German counterattack had been beaten back before it could gain any steam, largely due to Gavin bolstering the front lines and aggressively pushing the units there forward.

SERGEANT BUD OLSON had survived the assault on Cauquigny without a scratch, though he was still sore from the injuries to his legs during the glider landing. After the German counterattack was pushed back, he spent the next few hours at the regimental CP. About 2:00 a.m., he was ordered to recross the causeway, locate the leading elements of the 90th Infantry, and guide them across. On the D15, he found the 2nd Battalion of the 357th Regiment of the 90th Infantry coming from Sainte-Mère-Église—the evidence of the fierce and bloody fighting they had seen on the way had unnerved them. Olson briefed the battalion's command on conditions and recommended they double-time on the causeway. At 4:00 a.m., he led the jittery infantrymen over the La Fière bridge and across the Merderet swamp. Mortar fire was still landing along its length, and some casualties were incurred. Olson was scared, but he was determined not to let these greenhorns know that.

Just after dawn, the vanguard of the 90th Infantry passed through Cauquigny and began relieving the 82nd troopers and glidermen on the front lines near Les Helpiquets. Rae and his men were held in the hamlet as a backstop just in case the 90th was attacked. They weren't relieved until late in the afternoon of June 10, when they returned across the causeway just behind Timmes's force and rejoined their regiment. It was only then that they finally got some real sleep.

Olson got only a few hours himself before he was woken up and told to report to Major Gardner. Since the 325th's Graves Registration officer was missing in action, Olson, one of whose assignments was Graves Registration assistant, was given the job. He was ordered to pick a three-man detail and move the bodies of dead 82nd men to a central area on the east side of the Merderet with a jeep and a trailer and a blanket with two poles for a stretcher. The day was warm and the work gruesome, since the dead bodies were in every sort of condition and often, in the case of those killed by mortar rounds, less than intact. After several trips, his enlisted men refused to finish. Olson called a break, and at a farmhouse whose inhabitants were gone, he found a cask of calvados in the cellar and shot into it. They filled their canteens, went upstairs, and began gulping the liquor down. "The detail got drunk as a skunk," remembered Olson, but eventually they resumed and finished their thankless task.

The final tally of dead soldiers was more than a hundred. Olson and the other men even picked some Germans up, but mostly dead Americans. That evening, when Olson reported back to Gardner at the CP, he told him flatly that he was not going to do that job again. Gardner allowed the threatened insubordination and told his sergeant he'd find someone else to handle Graves Registration. Then he ordered Olson to get some sleep.[21]

THE VICTORY AT Cauquigny allowed the 82nd Airborne to accomplish the last of its missions. Finally, the 82nd had established a firm bridgehead across the Merderet and cleared the area from Neuville-au-Plain in the north through Sainte-Mère-Église and Chef-du-Pont to the south. With its sister airborne division, the 101st, it had prevented German reinforcements from reaching Utah and attacking the seaborne forces, and it had virtually destroyed the German 91st Luftlande Division in the process. The paratroopers had also knocked out heavy artillery batteries that could have barraged the Utah beachhead, and kept the Germans in the Cotentin so confused that in the crucial first few hours of D-Day they waited too long to mount a counterattack. When the Germans finally did, they faltered against the smaller airborne units and their spirited, aggressive resistance.

The German defeat at Cauquigny marked the last chance for any Wehrmacht reinforcements to reach Utah. After June 9, the German High Command could only maneuver units to bolster the port of Cherbourg and try to prevent American troops from achieving their objective of cutting off the Cotentin Peninsula and then moving north and seizing the city. After two weeks of hard fighting, von Schlieben was captured on June 26; the port would finally fall to American and British troops three days later. By that time, the Allies had fourteen divisions in Normandy—twice as many as the Germans. Thanks to the resoundingly successful Operation Fortitude, Hitler and the German

High Command would persist in believing that the D-Day landings had constituted a diversion, and that the actual cross-Channel assault would occur somewhere near the Pas-de-Calais, where fifteen German divisions remained until late July. It was only then that the Germans understood the truth—that the D-Day landings *had been* the invasion. But by then it was too late. The myth of the impervious Atlantic Wall was only a memory. The full liberation of Europe was off to a good start and its final success inevitable—in no small part due to the men of the 82nd Airborne who had fought and died in those first few days in the hedgerows and fields of Normandy.

The dead were soon buried in a makeshift cemetery south of Sainte-Mère-Église, and the badly injured shipped back to England. The rest of the All Americans should have followed them in a few days to refit and prepare for the next operation requiring airborne troops. But circumstances, and the 82nd's new reputation as a fighting unit second to none, would prevent that from happening—and keep the tired and badly depleted division in almost constant combat for another month.

SIXTEEN

"YOU CROSSED THAT CAUSEWAY"

Courage was the common denominator. You just didn't notice it because everybody did it.

BILL WALTON[1]

OVER THE NEXT few days, the division continued to rest, resupply, and reorganize, as several hundred men misdropped throughout the peninsula finally reached their units, though hundreds of others, captured, wounded, or killed, did not. The ten 507th sticks that landed near Graignes, twenty miles southeast of their DZ, gathered there and fought off repeated German attacks until June 11, when 2,000 Waffen SS troops assaulted the village. Most of the 182 troopers were able to escape through the swamps, but half a dozen wounded men left behind were executed by the SS, along with thirty-two townspeople. The survivors made contact with American troops a week after D-Day.

THE 505TH AND the 2nd Battalion/325th, which had been fighting north of Neuville-au-Plain for almost a week, returned to the 82nd on June 13. The 508th assembled on and around Hill 30, which had not been reached until the late afternoon of June 9, when Colonel Lindquist led a force across the causeway at the La Fière bridge and down to Shanley's position; by then, the Germans besieging them and those manning the artillery at Isle Marie had already begun to withdraw to the west.

The 325th remained in reserve west of the Merderet, and the 505th and 507th returned to the east side of the river near the Manoir la Fière. Everyone expected to be returned to England soon since, according to SHAEF's "Employment of Airborne Forces" memorandum—written by Gavin himself—airborne troops were to be withdrawn as soon as they were relieved by ground troops immediately after they had accomplished their missions, ideally within forty-eight hours.

But the division had done such an outstanding job that they were now considered indispensable, and the success of the 82nd and the 101st was not lost on Eisenhower and other high-ranking brass. They had no more doubts about the effectiveness of airborne troops if they were provided with smart planning and well-trained air transport.

So when the green and ineptly led soldiers of the 90th Infantry Division faltered in their drive west to seal off the peninsula, General Joe Collins told Omar Bradley that he wanted the paratroopers back on line. When Bradley asked Ridgway, he agreed, and on D+7, June 13, the now veteran but badly understrength 82nd was thrown back to the front lines. The next day, troopers and glidermen attacked through the 90th Infantry and kept on going, enabling elements of the 90th to reach the west coast on June 18 and seal the peninsula from further German reinforcements. Then, after three more weeks of grueling combat in the fields, hedgerows, and sunken lanes of Normandy's bocage country, they made their final attack on July 3, driving south through Étienville and across the Douve River. There they turned southwest to capture the high ground around La Haye-du-Puits, a key crossroads town near the west coast, where they remained until relieved five days later.

Gavin, who had visited every battalion daily and spent much of his time on the front lines, protested the final attack order along with two of the parachute infantry regimental commanders, insisting that one more major operation might decimate the division; he felt the men should have been withdrawn long before. Even Edson Raff, now in command of the 507th and a glory hog himself, objected: "If we attack any more we won't have a cadre to make a regiment back in England," he told Gavin. "I think we ought to be withdrawn."[2] But Ridgway was unyielding. "I knew, though we were weak in numbers, their fighting spirit was still unimpaired," he wrote later.[3] The disagreement would increase the ill feeling between him and Gavin.[4] But the operation would proceed.

The last attack, on July 4—across an open field to a hill judged necessary to be taken—was especially costly. The previous day had seen brutal and constant combat involving the entire division to take Hill 131, the highest point in the area. Hill 95, less than a mile north of La Haye-du-Puits, was next. It was held by Germans with heavy artillery. Lieutenant Colonel Mark Alexander had taken Shanley's place as commander of the 2nd Battalion/508th after Shanley was badly injured, and his men would lead the attack, which was slated for dawn. But Alexander had scouted the terrain the evening before, and he thought the much wiser course would be to move the battalion onto a wooded ridge on the left that rose all the way to Hill 95. He had just returned to his CP and was on the phone telling the 508th commander, Colonel Roy Lindquist, his plan when a mortar round landed nearby and sent two shell fragments into his back. He suffered a collapsed lung and was jeeped back to a field hospital, where he would linger on the cusp of death for days and barely survive.

An inexperienced captain took his place, and Lindquist issued him his orders to cross the open valley and take Hill 95. When the captain asked Lindquist about Alexander's plan, he was told, "You have your orders." The battalion was down to 235 able-bodied men, including only eight officers.

The direct charge at 8:00 a.m. across the field without support and against a well-entrenched enemy backed by cannon appeared to be another ill-fated Charge of the Light Brigade. The Germans had twenty-eight machine guns and mortars zeroed in on the field.[5] The 82nd did gain control of the hill a few hours later, about noon, but only after horrendous casualties. The Germans counterattacked and took it back at 2:00 p.m. The troopers regrouped and finally took the crest again around midnight, this time for good. In doing so, they had killed more than 500 of the enemy and captured more than 700.[6] But the 82nd's losses had been severe. Lieutenant Louis Levy, who had held back the German armored advance on Cauquigny with eleven men, had died defending the hill, as had many others.

"We realized that we were through as a fighting unit at this time," recalled Tom Porcella, now a corporal. "There were not enough of us to continue." His regiment, the 508th, reported an effective strength after the battle for Hill 95 of fifty-eight officers and 780 enlisted men—roughly a third of its original 2,055 troopers.[7]

A few days later, on July 8, what remained of the division was put into reserve to return to England and its old camps in the Midlands. They had not received reinforcements or replacements since landing on June 6. After thirty-three days of continuous frontline fighting, 57 percent of the 82nd's combat personnel had been wounded or killed. Some units fared even worse. One company came out of the lines with only sixteen officers and enlisted men.[8] Teddy Sanford's 1st Battalion/325th boarded their LSTs at Utah Beach with just seven officers and 216 men; more than 500 had landed in France. His Company C, PFC Charlie DeGlopper's outfit, returned with six men and one officer.[9]

As testament to the division's courageous leadership, of its four regimental and sixteen battalion commanders—plus a few replacements who had come along and been plugged in where needed—fifteen had been killed, captured, or wounded, and more than two-thirds of all the lieutenants in combat companies were casualties.[10] In no other combat unit did officers do so much leading from the front, and they paid the price while inspiring their men. "We'd follow him anywhere," many troopers said of Gavin and, to a lesser extent, of Ridgway, but they also followed courageous battalion commanders and company officers into battle, and that kind of leadership often made the difference between success and failure, and life and death.

On the way back to the beach, the men of the 82nd spent a couple of days at a bivouac area where, after they were issued fresh fatigues and allowed to shower, they discarded the dirty, ragged jumpsuits they had worn more than a month straight without a bath. Then, on July 11, they loaded onto seventeen LSTs and were ferried back across the English Channel to Southampton, where they were greeted by the sounds of bands playing and crowds of civilians cheering. After they took a train ride to the English Midlands, trucks carried them to their camps.

The 505th arrived at Camp Quorn outside Leicester early in the morning. "We silently passed through the gates in columns of twos—not threes, as before," remembered PFC Bill Tucker. Only 44 men of his I Company were present; 144 had left Quorn at the end of May. At his company's "street," replacements and other troopers turned out to salute them. "We met the eyes of those who had stayed and of those [wounded] who had already returned," said Tucker. "Out of all those in the world, it was only those men of our company who could look at us and appreciate what was happening. They knew."[11]

THE GERMANS ALSO knew—at least, they knew what they'd been up against.

In a June 10 summary of events to the German High Command, the Seventh Army chief of staff reported that "the operation of the 'new weapon,' the airborne troops, behind the coastal fortifications, on one hand, and their massive attack on our own counterattacking troops, on the other hand, have contributed significantly to the initial success of the enemy."[12] In an official report two weeks after D-Day, von Rundstedt offered his own opinion. "The techniques and tactics of enemy airborne forces are highly developed," wrote the *feldmarschall*. "Particularly seasoned and prepared for battle, these soldiers proved to be powerful fighters, adapting quickly to the terrain."[13] And Gavin had been right about the Germans: Hard counterattacks and aggressive attack tactics had demoralized them, resulting in surrender or withdrawal. He had thoroughly trained his men to fight that way, and doing so had paid off in Normandy, where smaller American units had consistently outfought larger German forces, enabling them to achieve victory after victory.

"The Germans fear them now and give them lots of elbow room," Gavin wrote to his daughter on June 12. He was right.[14]

In England over the next few weeks, the men of the 82nd continued to rest and recuperate—and then resumed training. The end of their D-Day mission was only the beginning of the liberation of Europe, and they would be called upon again for tough missions requiring experienced, aggressive fighters who were superbly conditioned, trained, and led—their reputation had been made in the fields and hedgerows of Normandy.

AFTER THE WAR, some 82nd men remained in the military as a career. But most of them were happy to return to their civilian lives, content that they had done their part. They were unfailingly modest about their accomplishments. "We were not heroes. We had a job to do and we did it," Private M. S. "Mickey" Nichols, 508th, said.[15] "Nobody that's alive is a hero. The heroes are all those who were killed," said Sergeant Tim Dyas, 505th.[16] And many of them suffered emotionally and psychologically from the horrors they had witnessed or participated in. Captain John Sauls came home after the war and made a good life for his family as a ceramics engineer. But every so often, something would come over him and leave him trembling. One night in 1952, his young daughter heard crying from her parents' bedroom. She went in to find her mother comforting her father on the floor of the closet, where he sat shaking and sobbing.[17] Before he died in 1987, he was given a relatively new diagnosis, PTSD (post-traumatic stress disorder), previously labeled "shell shock" or "battle fatigue." That diagnosis would apply to a good number of 82nd men—as it did to many involved in combat—and its symptoms kept some of them from adjusting completely to everyday life. But few of them discussed PTSD as it applied to them, if they talked about the war at all—the men of the Greatest Generation hadn't been brought up that way. Only near the turn of the century, with the fiftieth anniversary of D-Day and an avalanche of books, movies, and TV shows about it, did many of them begin to open up about their experiences.

RIDGWAY AND GAVIN were both inordinately proud of their division's accomplishments. "The troopers had been splendid," wrote Gavin later.

"Resourceful and courageous in the attack, resolute in the defense, they fought superbly."[18] The feeling was reciprocal. The two generals' coolheaded leadership and courage under fire—particularly during the June 9 attack across the causeway—inspired respect, devotion, and even love in the men they led. The sight of the two in the thick of the fighting, on the bridge and elsewhere, inspired the men to follow them as no patriotic call to duty could. To a man, the paratroopers and glidermen of the 82nd would voice their pride in serving under the two and do so for the rest of their lives.

The achievements of the 82nd's two leaders were also recognized by their superiors. Eisenhower wrote George Marshall that Ridgway was "one of the finest soldiers this war has produced," and rewarded him with an immediate promotion.[19] He appointed Ridgway commander of a new airborne corps that would comprise the 82nd, 101st, and 17th Airborne Divisions.

Ridgway, in turn, recommended Gavin to replace him as the 82nd's commander and pushed hard for the promotion—despite the personal ill will that had developed between them. His recommendation was accepted, and Gavin, at only thirty-seven, became the youngest American two-star general since the Civil War. Over the next year, he would lead the 82nd to even more glory as the Allied armies slogged toward the heart of Germany and an end to the war.

THE PRIDE RIDGWAY and Gavin felt for their men extended to the 325th. Both commanders were surprised—astonished, even—that the 3rd Battalion/325th had fought as well as it had that morning. Its charge across the causeway, and its fighting over the next month in Normandy, changed Gavin's mind. "From then on," he wrote later, "the 325th became one of the great regiments of the war."[20]

That day on the Merderet was, Ridgway later wrote, "as hot a single battle as any U.S. troops had, at any time during the war."[21] And a month after D-Day, he succeeded in correcting the glider troops' pay inequity—he had been pushing for it for almost a year. They would henceforth receive the same hazard pay that their paratrooper brethren did: $50 extra for an enlisted man, $100 for an officer. They would also have the right to wear jump boots like the paratroopers, who, after watching the harrowing glider landings and fighting side by side with the glidermen, agreed. "After Normandy," remembered Lieutenant Lee Travelstead, "the paratroopers and glidermen had a sense of camaraderie that had never before existed, and I would hazard a guess that much of it had to do with that day on the Merderet."[22]

One day in the winter of 1976, Richard Johnson, by then a successful real estate attorney in Boston, asked Gavin to address the century-old Union Club. Gavin, after retiring as a three-star general in 1958, was now the president of the management consulting firm Arthur D. Little, based in Boston. He agreed to give a talk. As Johnson told the story:

> While I was helping him set up his slides and projector, he looked at me with a twinkle in his eye and asked, "Do you know why I'm doing this?" I replied I didn't, and he said, "You crossed that causeway, and I can't say no to any man who did."[23]

ACKNOWLEDGMENTS

Every book of this scope is reliant on many other people. Herewith:

Thanks especially to the 82nd Airborne World War Two veterans I interviewed: Walter Barrett, Leslie Cruise, Joe Gwaltney, Walter Hurd, Dick Klein, Kenneth "Hard Rock" Merritt, Bob Nobles, Bud Olson, Sam Sachs, Clifford Stump, and Fletcher Williams.

I'm also indebted to the following descendants and relatives of 82nd Airborne veterans of D-Day: Charles and Ray DeGlopper, Jim Nobles, Jason Geoffrion, Gary Olson, John B. Sauls Jr., Frankie Sauls Chapman, Bill Kinsey, Jason Lohner, Elyse Russell Rose, Christine Fleming, Courtney Taylor, Tim Campbell, James Loyd, Kevin Beaver, Nancy Richardson, Elyse Russell Rose, Christine Fleming, Anthony DeMayo, Frank DeMayo, Ann DeMayo, and Marie Winters (Tony DeMayo), Ben Masters, Fred and Edward Krause and Aurora Chichester, Melinda Bradley and Debi Cox (Daryle Whitfield family), Dianna Pflueger, Marvin Catler (Harold Cadish), Heidi Dolan, Bill Kinsey, Faye DiFrancia, John Kormylo, Gary Peterson, Teddy Sanford Jr., Tim Campbell, Ralph Skripek, Chris Skripek, and Steven Robert Zaley.

Individuals to whom I owe a special debt of gratitude are Ralph Alvarez, 82nd Airborne Museum; Greta Suiter and Erin Wilson, Ohio University Libraries; Bill Bonnamy, researcher; Marci Buchanan, Mineral Ridge Historical Society; Pierre Comtois, author of "Confusion and Triumph at La Fiere"; Dr. George Cressman at Camp Blanding Museum; Keri Belle at the Disabled American Veterans, Louis Levy, Chapter 11; Amy McDonald, Special Collections Research Center, Syracuse University Libraries; Patrick Elie,

6juin1944.com; Elizabeth Glasgow, Warren Trumbull County Public Library; Volker Griesser, author of *The Lions of Carentan*; Pete Henderson and Susan Geissler; Carole Howell, Lincoln City Historical Association; Kevin M. Hymel, author; Chelsea Johnson at Marshall District Library in Marshall, Michigan; Audrey John, Niles Historical Society; Laura Jowdy, archivist and historical collections manager, Congressional Medal of Honor Society; Gwen Kelley, Special Collections, Jefferson Parish Library, Gretna, Louisiana; Michelle Kopfer, Dwight D. Eisenhower Presidential Library; Josh DeJong at the Rigger Depot; Jessica Lyles at Casemate Publishing; Misty Mayberry in the Texas Room, Dallas Public Library; Edward Sanchez and Sylvia Aguillon, Dallas Public Library; Sharon McCullar, curator, Silent Wings Museum; Justine Melone, Tom Buffenbarger, Duane Miller, and Stephen Bye at the U.S. Army Heritage and Education Center; Andrew Rhodes, Special Collections, University of Southern Mississippi Libraries; Brian Siddall at Airborne in Normandy; Alea Stark at the Boston Public Library; Genoa Stanford at MCoE HQ Donovan Research Library; Jade Woodridge at Willard Library in Battle Creek, Michigan; Tatyona Bridges at the SMU Library; Colonel (Ret.) Keith Nightingale; Paul Woodadge; Martin Morgan; Mark Helm; and Claudia Rivers, Anne Allis, and Abbie Weiser at the University of Texas at El Paso Special Collections Library. At the National World War Two Museum in New Orleans, Joey Balfour, Assistant Director of Oral History, was helpful to a fault, finding dozens of oral and video interviews and accounts, many of them untranscribed and/or newly digitized, some barely audible, but all contributing to my knowledge of the subject. Thanks, Joey.

Special thanks to Marcia Cunningham, ace researcher; Mark Lee Gardner, who found many valuable old newspaper stories; Rachel Donovan, who keyboarded some chapters, and some translations; Joel Baret, French authority on the subject, who provided notes and answers to countless questions; Neils Henkemans, author of *Defending Normandy*, for his copious generosity and endless patience; Tom Kailbourn, Melissa Shultz, Jeff Guinn, John Oller, and Jacquelin Hipes, first readers, who read and provided invaluable commentary on selected chapters; and Baron Bustin, historian and tech editor extraordinaire, who knows more about this subject than I do, and provided the same. These people all made this book immeasurably better.

In Normandy, thanks to Yves Poisson for sharing his knowledge of the subject; Jean-Pierre and Marie Paviot, generous hosts at the Manoir la Fière and travel guides to the area, and their daughter Audrey Paviot, my excellent translator. Thanks also to Jeannine Leroux, who took the time one afternoon to patiently answer my questions, then walked me through the Manoir la Fière to vividly re-create her family's experiences on June 6, 1944; Marcel Cuquemelle, who generously shared his memories of the same day; and Henri-Jean Renaud, who did the same and provided valuable information about Sainte-Mère-Église, before, during, and after D-Day. Vivian and Rodolphe Rogers were also a great help, and provided valuable information about the *manoir* and the battle.

I can't imagine a literary agent better than B. J. Robbins, and I should know. She's my knight in shining armor, and a good friend. At Circle of Confusion, Michael Prevett is also a good friend and the best book-to-film facilitator there is in Hollywood.

At Dutton, thanks to John Parsley, whose excellent and sensitive editing made this book better, and his assistant, David Howe; my first editor, Brent Howard, whose idea this was, and who believed that I could do justice to the story; his assistant, Grace Layer, an excellent editor in her own right; publicity manager Sarah Thegeby; marketing director Stephanie Cooper; VP of subrights Sabila Khan; copy editor Frank Walgren; proofreaders Joy Simpkins and David Koral; IndexPros; designer Jason Booher for the excellent cover; Lorie Pagnozzi for the fine interior design; and managing editors Melissa Solis and Clare Shearer.

NOTES

Prologue

1. Nordyke, *Put Us Down in Hell*, 84–85; Robert Moss account at http://www.6juin1944.com/veterans/moss.php.

Introduction

1. David Eisenhower, *Eisenhower: At War 1943–1945*, 18–19.

One: A Last-Minute Change in Plans

1. "Overlord" was the code name assigned to the establishment of a large-scale lodgment on the European continent. The first phase, the amphibious invasion code-named "Neptune," included the airborne operations.
2. Wertenbaker, *Invasion!*, 36.
3. Bradley, *A Soldier's Story*, 232-233.
4. Balkoski, *Utah Beach*, 119.
5. Caddick-Adams, *Sand and Steel*, 482. This point may come as a surprise to readers more familiar with the fierce German resistance found at Omaha on D-Day. But after the war, Major General Thomas Handy, director of operations in the War Plans Division, said: "We all thought Utah was going to be more of a problem than Omaha—the damned terrain, swampy, with causeways on which a crew with one gun could stop tanks from coming through."

6. Dwight D. Eisenhower, *Crusade in Europe*, 240.
7. Wolfe, *Green Light!*, 79, 83; Gavin, *Airborne Warfare*, 41–44; Howarth, *Dawn of D-Day*, 80.
8. Bradley, *A Soldier's Story*, 232–34.
9. D'Este, *Decision in Normandy*, 85.
10. Ridgway, *Soldier*, 12.
11. Hastings, *Overlord*, 44–45.
12. Dwight D. Eisenhower, *The Eisenhower Diaries*, 112.
13. As quoted in Balkoski, *Utah Beach*, 48.
14. Hastings, 45.
15. Gavin, *On to Berlin*, 102.
16. Alexander and Sparry, *Jump Commander*, 163.
17. Balkoski, *Utah Beach*, 95.
18. David Eisenhower, 241.
19. Gavin, *On to Berlin*, 102.
20. Blair, *Ridgway's Paratroopers*, 208; David Eisenhower, 241.
21. Wertenbaker, 6–7.
22. Dwight D. Eisenhower, *Crusade in Europe*, 297.
23. David Eisenhower, 241–42.
24. Dwight D. Eisenhower, *Crusade in Europe*, 289.

Two: Jumpin' Jim and His All Americans

1. *Airborne Operations: A German Appraisal*, 28.
2. Zaley, *They Are Only Gone*, 106.
3. Booth and Spencer, *Paratrooper*, 156.
4. Creek, "The Operations of a Mixed Group," 4.
5. LoFaro, *The Sword of St. Michael*, 47–48; Letter 5, Series 2, Correspondence, Box 20, Matthew B. Ridgway Papers. Ridgway was also petitioning for jump pay for the glider troops, like the paratroopers received, as early as February 1944. Letters 9 and 44, Matthew B. Ridgway Papers.
6. Sanford, "Warrior and Commander"; Personal Diaries, Box 10, Diary 1944–45, February 23, 1944, James M. Gavin Papers; Nightingale, *The Human Face of D-Day*, 71.
7. Booth and Spencer, 157–58; Blair, *Ridgway's Paratroopers*, 193–94; Fielder, *A Matter of Pride*, 310–12.
8. Sorley, *Gavin at War*, 111.
9. Sorley, 170.
10. Sorley, 93; Lord, *History of the 508th Parachute Infantry*, 14; Blair, 203–4; Guild, *Action of the Tiger*, 38–40, 53; Sergeant Michael N. Ingrisano account at http://www.6juin1944.com/veterans/ingrisano.php.
11. Gavin, *War and Peace in the Space Age*, 28–29; Booth and Spencer, 19–31.

12. Gavin, *War and Peace in the Space Age*, 33.
13. As quoted in LoFaro, 34.
14. Astor, *June 6, 1944*, 62.
15. Graham, "My Memories of World War II," 4.
16. Megellas, *All the Way to Berlin*, 11. One 82nd officer stated of the weeding-out process at Camp Blanding in October and November 1942: "Of 6,000 enlisted men who were processed, only 1,800 were selected, and only 500 of 2,200 officers passed the rigid requirements successfully" (Graham, 3). See also Astor, *June 6, 1944*, 55, where a paratrooper referring to his jump class states that "less than fifty percent of the four hundred actually made it."
17. As quoted in Nordyke, *Four Stars of Valor*, 20.
18. As quoted in Astor, *June 6, 1944*, 51.
19. Diary April–December 1943, April 8, 1943, James M. Gavin Papers.
20. As quoted in Yockelson, *The Paratrooper Generals*, 9.
21. All Ridgway quotes from Ridgway, *Soldier*, 28–29.
22. As quoted in Blair, 196.
23. Blair, 196.
24. Blair, 111.
25. Mitchell, *Matthew B. Ridgway*, 10.
26. As quoted in Booth and Spencer, 86.
27. Booth and Spencer, 95.
28. Anderson and Eschle, "82nd Airborne Trooper."
29. Nordyke, *Four Stars of Valor*, 60.
30. LoFaro, 95–96; Blair, 97–98; Gavin, *On to Berlin*, 30; Ruggero, *Combat Jump*, 281. Ruggero implies that Gavin was told, but it seems hard to believe that Gavin would have considered sacking an officer who had followed orders from a superior officer.
31. Gavin, *On to Berlin*, 14.
32. LoFaro, 58; Fielder, 32; Ruggero, *Combat Jump*, 302.
33. Zaley, 196.
34. Breuer, *Drop Zone Sicily*, 130.
35. O'Donnell, *Beyond Valor*, 47–48.
36. O'Donnell, 48.
37. This account of the Sicily drop and the battle for Biazza Ridge is based on Gavin, *On to Berlin*, 30–36; Gavin, *Airborne Warfare*, 8–13; Booth and Spencer, 98–107; Devlin, *Paratrooper!*, 235–37; LoFaro, 94–101; Blair, 93–99; O'Donnell, 44–48; Breuer, *Drop Zone Sicily*; D'Este, *Decision in Normandy*, 293–95; Nordyke, *Four Stars of Valor*, 79–90; and Ruggero, *Combat Jump*, 280–319. Ruggero's Biazza Ridge account is the finest and most extensive; Breuer's is also excellent.
38. Blair, 99.
39. As quoted in Gavin, *Airborne Warfare*, 16.

40. Flanagan, *Airborne*, 88.
41. Sorley, 114.

Three: England in the Spring

1. Richardson, unpublished ms.; Nordyke, *All American, All the Way*, 184.
2. As quoted in LoFaro, *The Sword of St. Michael*, 200.
3. As quoted in Bastable, *Voices from D-Day*, 52. For an extended discussion of Axis Sally, see Guild, *Action of the Tiger*, 46–49.
4. Russell, "13 Hours: D-Day, June 6, 1944."
5. Earl Geoffrion interview, LOC History Project; Earl Geoffrion interview, Xavier Van Daele; "Earl J. Geoffrion—In Memoriam"; "World War II Veteran Earl Geoffrion in His Own Words"; personal communication.
6. Frank Haddy interview, Camp Blanding Museum.
7. Boroughs, *The 508th Connection*, 105; 505th briefing (505th PIR After-Action Reports, 14, Box 7, Folder 32, Cornelius Ryan Collection).
8. Cruise, "Normandy—June 1944"; Leslie Cruise, author phone interview, August 11, 2020; Leslie Cruise, author questionnaire.
9. Renaud, *Sainte Mère Église*, 137.
10. Balkoski, *Utah Beach*, 147; Astor, *June 6, 1944*, 18.
11. Ruggero, *Combat Jump*, 83–84.
12. Zaley, *They Are Only Gone*, 30–32. Zaley's book gives a fuller portrait of Krause than any other.
13. As quoted in Nordyke, *Four Stars of Valor*, 125; Devlin, *Paratrooper!*, 376.
14. "The Capture of Ste Mere Eglise," 8.
15. LoFaro, 221.
16. "One-Eyed Determination Took Nelson Bryant to Normandy," *Vineyard Gazette*, May 27, 2010.
17. Masters, *Glidermen of Neptune*, 9–13.
18. Nightingale, *The Human Face of D-Day*, 71.
19. Dank, *The Glider Gang*, 100; Letters 5, 9, and 44, Matthew B. Ridgway Papers.
20. Dank, 29–31.
21. Gavin, *Airborne Warfare*, 39; Nordyke, *All American, All the Way*, 184; Bryant, *Flying Coffins over Europe*, 17; Devlin, 374.
22. Charles DeGlopper, letter, May 26, 1944, courtesy of Ray DeGlopper.
23. Charles DeGlopper, letter, April 1, 1944, courtesy of Ray DeGlopper.
24. As quoted in Jakeway, *Paratroopers Do or Die!!*, 51.
25. Bud Olson, author interviews, June 22 and 25, 2020; Bud Olson, diary; Gary Olson, email questionnaire.
26. Zaley, 304.
27. Hubert Ross questionnaire, Box 7, Folder 37, Cornelius Ryan Collection.

28. LoFaro, 196.
29. Wolfe, *Green Light!*, 88.
30. McNally, *As Ever, John*, 42.
31. McNally, 42; the temperature is mentioned in Guild, 60.
32. Cruise, "Normandy—June 1944."
33. Zaley, 314.
34. airborne.com; Nightingale, 23.
35. Nordyke, *Put Us Down in Hell*, 40.
36. Frank Haddy interview, Camp Blanding Museum.
37. As quoted in Ambrose, *D-Day*, 190.
38. Tucker, *Parachute Soldier*, 28.
39. Bill Walton questionnaire, Box 9, Folder 4, Cornelius Ryan Collection.
40. As quoted in Langrehr, *Whatever It Took*, 77.
41. As quoted in von Keusgen, *Sainte-Mère-Église & Merderet*, 53; Bob Bearden questionnaire, Box 7, Folder 38, Cornelius Ryan Collection; Robert Mansel Hennon questionnaire, Box 8, Folder 9, Cornelius Ryan Collection.
42. McNally, 41–42.
43. Fauntleroy, *The General and His Daughter*, 105.
44. Fauntleroy, 107–8.
45. Blair, *Ridgway's Paratroopers*, 213.
46. Blair, 225.
47. Bob Dumke, radio interview, https://82airbornejs.c.com/robert-h-dumke
48. As quoted in Ambrose, *Band of Brothers*, 55.

Four: The Fortress, the Wall, and the Village

1. As quoted in Perrault, *The Secret of D-Day*, 4.
2. Ruge, *Rommel in Normandy*, 329.
3. As quoted in Belfield and Essame, *The Battle for Normandy*, 28.
4. Butler, *Field Marshal*, 131–53.
5. Young, *Rommel*, 12.
6. October 1943 report detailing weaknesses of the Western defenses.
7. Butler, 459; Caddick-Adams, *Sand and Steel*, 21.
8. As quoted in Mitcham, *Panzers in Normandy*, 34.
9. Pimlott, *Rommel*, 172–73.
10. Ruge, "Rommel's Measures to Counter the Invasion," 327.
11. Ruge, "Rommel's Measures to Counter the Invasion," 329.
12. Warlimont, *From Invasion to the Siegfried Line*, 11, 12.
13. D'Este, *Decision in Normandy*, 124–26.
14. Wilhelm Hümmerich interview, Box 26, Folder 23, Cornelius Ryan Collection.

15. As quoted in Hargreaves, *The Germans in Normandy*, 14.
16. Caddick-Adams, 487; Carell, *Invasion*, 18.
17. The Luftwaffe command planned to send thirty-six wings—approximately 1,200 planes—to the west when the invasion came (Ruge, "The Invasion of Normandy," 335).
18. Eckhertz, *D-Day Through German Eyes*, 254–55.
19. Pimlott, 175.
20. Ruge, "The Invasion of Normandy," 330.
21. The description and numbers of the tank battalion come from Reardon, *Defending Fortress Europe*, 309.
22. Christopher Skripek, author interview, May 10, 2022; email from Christopher Skripek, August 15, 2022; Rudolph Skripek obituary; Golz, *Paul Golz, the Pomeranian Grenadier*, 6–7; Floeter with Breen, *I'll See You Again*, 24–26.
23. Mitcham, *Rommel's Last Battle*, 61–63.
24. Villahermosa, *Hitler's Paratroopers in Normandy*, 25–26.
25. Anton Wüensch interview, File 27, Folder 45, Cornelius Ryan Collection.
26. Pöppel, *Heaven and Hell*, 172–74; Raibl, "The Operations of the 82nd Airborne Division," 4.
27. Von der Heydte, "A German Parachute Regiment in Normandy," 5.
28. Anonymous, *D Day at Utah-Beach*, 26.
29. Tucker, *Parachute Soldier*, 84.
30. Gavin, *On to Berlin*, 55–56, and many other places. Gavin thought very highly of the *Panzerfaust*: "As for the 82nd Airborne Division, it did not get adequate anti-tank weapons until it began to capture the first German panzerfausts. By the fall of '44, we had truckloads of them. . . . They were the best hand-carried anti-tank weapons of the war."
31. In a gas-operated firearm, high-pressure gas generated by the fired cartridge powers a mechanism that ejects the spent shell and inserts a new round into the chamber from the magazine. In other words, a soldier did not have to manually operate a bolt between rounds.
32. Gavin, *On to Berlin*, 56. Gavin carried a carbine into Sicily, and when it jammed, he picked up an M1 that he carried through the rest of the war. See also Kaufmann and Kaufmann, *The American GI in Europe in World War II: D-Day: Storming Ashore*, 193, where Lieutenant Jack Isaacs, 505th, mentions that the carbine had failed him twice in Sicily and Italy.
33. Milton, *D-Day*, 121.
34. Raibl, 8.
35. Turner, *Invasion '44*, 38.
36. Ryan, *The Longest Day*, 16; Ruge, *Rommel in Normandy*, 169; Liddell Hart, *The Rommel Papers*, 470.

37. Mitcham, *Rommel's Last Battle*, 44.
38. Liddell Hart, *The Rommel Papers*, 464.
39. Russell Miller, *Nothing Less Than Victory*, 207.
40. Perrault, 189; Breuer, *Hoodwinking Hitler*, 159–60.
41. Kenyon, *Bletchley Park and D-Day*, 159.
42. Breuer, *Hoodwinking Hitler*, 182.
43. Mitcham, *The Desert Fox in Normandy*, 65; Hargreaves, 34; Perrault, 196.
44. Box 27, Folder 3, Cornelius Ryan Collection; Carell, 6; von Schlieben, *The German 709th Infantry Division*, 24.
45. Isby, *Fighting the Invasion*, 189.
46. Von Keusgen, 42.
47. Pöppel, 174.
48. Murphy, *No Better Place to Die*, 205–6; von Keusgen, 37–38; Russell Miller, 263–64; Renaud, 27; von Keusgen, 27–28, 36–38, 57.
49. The population in 1936 was 1,136 (Wills, *Put on Your Boots and Parachutes*, 101). The U.S. Army estimated the population at a thousand (505th PIR After-Action Reports, Box 7, Folder 32, Cornelius Ryan Collection). With the arrest, conscription, or disappearance of many of the town's young men, it's likely the population by June 1944 was well below a thousand.
50. Coquart and Huet, *Le Jour le Plus Fou*, 92.
51. Alexandre Renaud interview, Box 25, Folder 53, Cornelius Ryan Collection.
52. Alexandre Renaud interview, Box 25, Folder 53, Cornelius Ryan Collection; Howarth, *Dawn of D-Day*, 92; Renaud, 20–21.
53. Wertenbaker, 68; Renaud, 20.
54. Russell Miller, 259; speech by Raymond Paris, "*Témoingage les 5–6 Juin 1944 a Sainte-Mère-Église*"; Coquart and Huet, 90, 101.
55. Von Keusgen, 41.
56. Léon, *Sainte-Mère-Église libérée*, 148–70.

Five: Jump into Darkness

1. As quoted in Hargreaves, *The Germans in Normandy*, 11.
2. Lelandais, *From Heaven to Hell*, 73; Joseph, "Operations of a Regimental Pathfinder Unit," 10.
3. As quoted in Keegan, *Six Armies in Normandy*, 87.
4. As one trooper described them: "The aerial photos were taken at high noon, so they didn't show the height of the hedgerows . . . those hedgerows looked like those little jumping hedges in England. We thought they were maybe two or three feet high, but no way man, they were eight and ten feet high!" (Covais, *Battery!*, 198).

5. Richardson; Francis Lamoureux interview, pts. 1 and 2, YouTube; Murphy, *No Better Place to Die*, 243–48; Michael Chester letter to James Gavin, March 30, 1959, James M. Gavin Papers; Pathfinders After Action Report, 82nd Airborne.
6. Balkoski, *Utah Beach*, 106.
7. Lord, *History of the 508th Parachute Infantry*, 21.
8. In many accounts, troopers asserted that their C-47 pilots took evasive action. Some surely did, but sometimes what troopers took to be evasive action was a pilot slowing down or speeding up or veering to avoid hitting another plane as it slowed to drop its men or changed direction or altitude for one of several reasons. Most of the troopers couldn't see anything happening outside the plane. See Hills, letter to Flanagan; Balkoski, *Utah Beach*, 113; Wolfe, *Green Light!*, 93–94, 115–23; and Rice, "Just for the Record."
9. "Preliminary Operations Around the La Fière Bridgehead," 8–9.
10. Rice, "Just for the Record."
11. James M. Gavin questionnaire, Box 8, Folder 21, *The Longest Day*, Cornelius Ryan Collection.
12. Gavin, *Airborne Warfare*, 58; Nightingale, *The Human Face of D-Day*, 164.
13. Gavin, *On to Berlin*, 56–57; Sorley, *Gavin at War*, 115; Nordyke, *Put Us Down in Hell*, 56–57; Nightingale, 164.
14. Graham, "My Memories of World War II," 3; Booth and Spencer, *Paratrooper*, 158. One of Gavin's few weaknesses was a penchant for judging others quickly and harshly, particularly in regard to their mettle in combat. See Roy Creek's National WWII Museum interview.
15. Astor, *June 6, 1944*, 55.
16. Some volunteers were deemed too lightweight for the Airborne; below-average height alone does not seem to have been a disqualifier. See Astor, *June 6, 1944*, 82, where a man who tried to join was judged "too light, too small."
17. Harold Kulju interview, Eisenhower Center; Astor, *June 6, 1944*, 12, 60, 152–54.
18. Kaufmann and Kaufmann, *The American GI in Europe in World War II: D-Day: Storming Ashore*, 187–88.
19. Hills, letter to Flanagan.
20. Bob Nobles, author interviews, March 10, 11, and 18, 2020; Hymel, "From Paratrooper to POW."

Six: The Swamp

1. Milkovics, *The Devils Have Landed!*, 14.
2. As quoted in Astor, *The Greatest War*, 478.
3. Ambrose, *D-Day*, 214.

4. Nordyke, *Put Us Down in Hell*, 82–84; Porcella, *Saut dans l'Obscurité*, 16–20; Tom Porcella oral history and written account, National WWII Museum; Christine Fleming (Tom Porcella's daughter), author interview, November 29, 2022.
5. Howarth, *Dawn of D-Day*, 90; Boroughs, *The 508th Connection*, 93; Breuer, *Geronimo!*, 227.
6. Howarth, 76–77.
7. George Miles interview, National WWII Museum. Miles watched as paratroopers wading through the flooded area were shot at by Germans. Several other trooper accounts mention this.
8. Neal Beaver questionnaire, Box 7, File, 39, Cornelius Ryan Collection; Nordyke, *Put Us Down in Hell*, 77; Boroughs, 112–13; accounts by Neal Beaver and members of his C-47's flight crew—Lieutenant Robert Nelsen, Sergeant Robert Lachmund, and Lieutenant Joseph Denson—at https://amcmuseum.org/history/troop-carrier-d-day-flights/.
9. Nordyke, *All American, All the Way*, 215–16.
10. Hutto, "World War II Memoirs."
11. Russell Miller, *Nothing Less Than Victory*, 234; Astor, *The Greatest War*, 475.
12. Morgan, *Down to Earth*, 149–50.
13. Morgan, 148.
14. Ambrose, *D-Day*, 200.
15. Hymel, "Dropping into Normandy."
16. Astor, *The Greatest War*, 481; Astor, *June 6, 1944*, 14, 33, 143–46.
17. Morgan, 152–53; Ed Jeziorski interview, National WWII Museum.
18. Geoffrion, "World War II Veteran Earl Geoffrion"; Geoffrion interview, LOC History Project; "Earl J. Geoffrion—In Memoriam"; Jason Lohner, author interview, December 6, 2022.
19. Kaufmann and Kaufmann, *The American GI in Europe in World War II: D-Day: Storming Ashore*, 190.
20. D. Zane Schlemmer oral history, National WWII Museum.
21. Jack Tallerday questionnaire, Box 8, Folder 46, Cornelius Ryan Collection.
22. Boroughs, 113–14.
23. Frank Haddy interview, Camp Blanding Museum.
24. Webster, *Parachute Infantry*, 30.

Seven: The Good Drop

1. Russell Miller, *Nothing Less Than Victory*, 453.
2. Michael Chester letter to James Gavin, March 30, 1959, James M. Gavin Papers.

3. Renaud, *Sainte Mère Église*, 75–76.
4. Anthony DeMayo questionnaire, Box 7, Folder 51, *The Longest Day*, Cornelius Ryan Collection; James Coyle interview, Box 7, Folder 50, *The Longest Day*, Cornelius Ryan Collection; Tony DeMayo letter to his parents, September 12, 1944, in Jacobus, *Echoes of the Warriors*, 229–30.
5. Ridgway wrote in his autobiography, *Soldier*, that he flew with the Second Battalion, but see Blair, *Ridgway's Paratroopers*, 547, notes 3, 4, 5, for persuasive evidence that he flew with the regimental HQ company.
6. Ridgway, *Soldier*, 3–8; Blair, 228–29; *The Island* (Hilton Head, SC) *Packet*, June 4, 1984.
7. Nordyke, *An Irresistible Force*, 88–98, 46; Sorley, 70.
8. Ridgway, 8.
9. "Debriefing Conference—Operation Neptune," USAMHI; "82nd Airborne Division, Action in Normandy," 8.
10. Cruise, "Normandy—June 1944"; Nordyke, *Four Stars of Valor*, 148; Blair, 227.
11. Griesser, *The Lions of Carentan*, 87–88.
12. Pöppel, *Heaven and Hell*, 172–75.
13. As quoted in LoFaro, *The Sword of St. Michael*, 204.
14. Von Schlieben, *The German 709th Infantry Division*, 30; Wills, 52.
15. Hargreaves, *The Germans in Normandy*, 39; Russell Miller, 265.
16. Von Schlieben, 27.
17. Isby, *Fighting the Invasion*, 181–82.
18. Von Keusgen, *Sainte-Mère-Église & Merderet*, 123.
19. Wilhelm Hümmerich interview, Box 26, Folder 23, Cornelius Ryan Collection.
20. Isby, *Fighting the Invasion*, 181; von der Heydte, "A German Parachute Regiment in Normandy," 8–11.
21. Reardon, *Defending Fortress Europe*, 37.
22. Russell Miller, 453.

Eight: Objective: Sainte-Mère-Église

1. Bré, *Chroniques du Jour J*, 22; Russell Miller, *Nothing Less Than Victory*, 260; Leon, 160; Henri-Jean Renaud, author email interview, April 1, 2023. Some sources mention that the curfew was 9:00 p.m. According to Henri-Jean Renaud, the mayor's son who was ten years old on D-Day: "The curfew time depended on several things. The garrison commander could change it under certain circumstances. . . . The time was therefore variable—I think in summer it was not the same as in winter. But in my opinion it was never after 10 p.m." (Henri-Jean Renaud, author email interview, March 30, 2023). Complicating this is the fact that some of the

French still set their clocks by solar time, an hour earlier than German (Berlin) time.

2. Renaud, *Sainte Mère Église*, 36–37; Carell, *Invasion*, 37; Coquart and Huet, *Le Jour le Plus Fou*, 89.
3. Marvin Catler (Cadish's nephew who was eleven years old when his uncle enlisted), author phone interview, May 28, 2023.
4. Ken Russell interview, Eisenhower Center; Zaley, 328; Kenneth Russell questionnaire, Box 8, Folder 38, *The Longest Day*, Cornelius Ryan Collection.
5. This account of the drops into the Sainte-Mère-Église town square employs the following sources: Renaud, 35–38; Alexandre Renaud interview, Box 25, Folder 53, *The Longest Day*, Cornelius Ryan Collection; Pipet, *Parachutés sur Sainte-Mère-Église*, 81–82; Bré, *Chroniques du Jour J*, 58–60; von Keusgen, *Sainte-Mère-Église & Merderet*, 71–75; Russell Miller, 260–62; and Langdon, *"Ready,"* 49–50.
6. This narrative of the F Company, 505th stick that fell into town is based on the following sources: Ken Russell interview, Eisenhower Center; Wills, *Put on Your Boots and Parachutes*, 70–71, 70–74; Guidry, *Treasures in My Heart*, 328; and Wurst and Wurst, *Descending from the Clouds*, 130. Ken Russell was nineteen years old at this time, not seventeen, as has been written in several books. Russell claimed in several interviews that the German soldier shot Ray in the stomach, but he was actually shot twice in the torso (hip and buttocks). See the Siddal Report at www.airborneinnormandy.com, where Brian Siddall has done impressive research work into many World War Two Airborne cases.
7. Ernest Blanchard interview, Box 7, Folder 41, Cornelius Ryan Collection.
8. Poyser and Brown, *Fighting Fox Company*, 92–96. These paratroopers, who dropped into and near the town square about forty-five minutes before the 505th did, belonged to two sticks of the 506th Fox Company.
9. Renaud, 35–38; "A Family Remembers Liberation: Sainte-Mère-Église, 1944," March 25, 2017, https://www.normandythenandnow.com/a-family-remembers-liberation-sainte-mere-eglise-1944/.
10. Wills, 70–71, 72–73; undated 1962 article in the Fort Bragg newspaper viewable at www.505rct.org; *Fayetteville* (NC) *Observer*, May 16, 1969; von Keusgen, 11, 73; Bré, *Chroniques du Jour J, 67*; Murphy, *No Better Place to Die*, 205–8; Wurst and Wurst, 130; Russell Miller, 264; Willard Young interview, Box 9, Folder 6, Cornelius Ryan Collection; Langrehr, *Whatever It Took*, 83. Some sources claim that Steele hung from the north side of the church, but the above sources make it clear that he hung above the main square on the south side: "The area I could see covered about one of our city blocks and I had a bird's-eye view of the action there," Steele said in the 1969 interview, and in the 1962 interview, he

said: "It was all lit up down there. Germans and GIs were running around shooting at each other. . . . I saw one of our boys land on the burning building. I heard him die." The German interviews also support this placement—above the square on the south side of the church—"the side of the bell tower that faced the churchyard," said Rudolf May in the account included in Robert Murphy's *No Better Place to Die*. And a resident of Sainte-Mère-Église, Jacques Muller, is quoted in Bré, *Chroniques du Jour J*, 67, as saying he witnessed this at about 0800 French solar time: "Near the church, at the level of the portal, there was a parachute on the ground; another was on the roof, towards the entrance to the side door, which faces the Roman boundary stone."

11. Von Keusgen, 72; Russell Miller, 263–65.
12. Russell Miller, 234; Edward Krause Army Service Experience Questionnaire, USAMHI.
13. Nordyke, *Put Us Down in Hell*, 131–32; Nordyke, *All American, All the Way*, 274-276; Brannen, "Four Days in Normandy"; Balkoski, *Utah Beach*, 118.
14. Devlin, *Silent Wings*, 186.
15. Tony DeMayo questionnaire, Box 7, Folder 51, *The Longest Day*, Cornelius Ryan Collection.
16. Lowden, *Silent Wings at War*, 71.
17. Dank, *The Glider Gang*, 125.
18. LoFaro, *The Sword of St. Michael*, 208–9; McManus, *The Americans at D-Day*, 182; Masters, *Glidermen of Neptune*, 64–66.
19. Dank, 126.
20. Esvelin, *Forgotten Wings*, 38–39.
21. Nordyke, *Four Stars of Valor*, 149.
22. Harrison, *Cross-Channel Attack*, 33.
23. Marshall, *Night Drop*, 23.
24. Jutras, *Sainte-Mère-Église*, 47.
25. As researcher Brian Siddall has proven beyond a shadow of a doubt, Ray died a week later from gangrene (www.airborneinnormandy.com).
26. Butcher, *My Three Years with Eisenhower*, 556–57.
27. As quoted in Russell Miller, 279.
28. Russell Miller, 460.
29. Reardon, *Defending Fortress Europe*, 40, 41. After repeated train delays and track cuts, these divisions—the 265th and the 276th—eventually resorted to proceeding on foot; they didn't reach the battle area near Carentan until three to five days later. See also Harrison, 378–79.
30. Blumentritt, *Von Rundstedt*, 222–24; Holland, *Normandy '44*, 128–30; Harrison, 332–33; Russell Miller, 279, 444–45.
31. Mitcham, *The Desert Fox in Normandy*, 79; Butler, *Field Marshal*, 480.

Nine: Le Manoir la Fière

1. Murphy, *No Better Place to Die*, 146.
2. This re-creation of life at the Manoir la Fière and the family's experiences on June 5–6, 1944, is based on the following sources: Audrey Paviot interview with Jeannine Leroux, February 28, 2023; Jeannine Leroux, author interview, October 27, 2021; Berthe Leroux account in Murphy, 201–4.
3. Email from Joël Baret, April 29, 2021.
4. Boroughs, *The 508th Connection*, 62.
5. In several accounts, Louis Leroux is cited as saying that he counted twenty-eight German soldiers when they arrived by truck. The earliest source of this is "Regimental Unit Study Number 3," published by the U.S. Army's Historical Section, European Theater of Operations, and written by S. L.A. Marshall, who says: "The witness is M. Louis Lerouex [*sic*], the resident at the MANOIR DE LA FIERE, the farm along the river; MME Leroux, who witnessed these events, corroborated his statements. . . . At that hour [2300 hours], 25-30 German infantry came to his home, got him out of bed and told him that they were setting up a defensive position around the farm." Aside from the unlikely events that Leroux managed to accurately count every one of the men in the dark as they got off the truck and that he was in a position to do so—and it's doubtful that all the soldiers walked into the courtyard to present themselves in full view of the farmhouse—accounts by 82nd troopers and officers describe far more than twenty-eight dead, injured, and captured around the Manoir la Fière that day: "Prisoners captured later, in addition to the German dead, amounted to the size of one of our platoons. There were no officers captured," wrote Lieutenant John Dolan, who arrived in the area of the *manoir* early in the morning and was there for the German surrender (Murphy, 148). Several other narratives that incorporate first-person accounts, such as Langdon's *"Ready,"* Murphy's *No Better Place to Die*, and especially Marshall's "Preliminary Operations Around the La Fière Bridgehead," cite several instances of Germans killed, wounded, and/or captured in and around the *manoir* that add up to far more than twenty-eight; Langdon writes that "20–25 Germans filed out of the house," and of several others who were killed, wounded, or captured in the fighting; and Thomas, in Lebarbenchon, *Américains et Normands dans la Bataille,* 43–44, says: "Nineteen Germans surrendered. They walked out the front door." Louis Leroux may have counted twenty-five to thirty Germans in his courtyard, but there were probably twice that amount in the area. Concerning the time of arrival, the later accounts of his wife, son, and two daughters make no mention of the troops' arrival at 2300, though plenty of other activities that evening are recounted. In three separate accounts, Madame Berthe Leroux related that the Germans arrived at daybreak:

"the Germans arrived at daybreak" (Murphy, 201); "The Germans, who had arrived at daybreak" (Lebarbenchon, 41); and "There were no Germans at that time at the farm of the Manor, and now, in the morning, the Germans arrived at the house and entered both the house and the stables" (Baret and Lapierre, *Cinq Jours sur la Ligne de Front*, 103–5). Daughter Geneviève claimed that the Germans came about five or six o'clock in the morning (Thiery Ferey, Leroux's grandson's letter, February 26, 2022). Finally, the account of Sergeant John Hardie, 508th PIR, relates how—at about 3:00 a.m., soon after dropping into the area—he and another soldier, John Strey, entered the *manoir* courtyard through the side gate, walked to the front gate, turned around, returned to the farmhouse, knocked on the front door, and then left. If there were any German soldiers there at the time, Hardie and Strey would have been killed instantly (Boroughs, 62). Leroux might have seen only twenty-eight German soldiers arriving outside his farmhouse door, but there were probably at least twice that many in the bridge-and-*manoir* area—at least two full platoons, since most infantry units were understrength at the time.

6. Balkoski, *Beyond the Beachhead*, 88. The author's explanation of a German rifle company's battle doctrine was also helpful.
7. Heidi Dolan, author phone interview, July 6, 2023; Nordyke, *All American, All the Way*, 247.
8. www.apps.westpointaog.org/memorials.
9. www.west-point.org.
10. Wills, *Put on Your Boots and Parachutes*, 103.
11. Murphy, 48–49.
12. Nordyke, *Four Stars of Valor*, 170; William Owens questionnaire, Box 8, Folder 27, Cornelius Ryan Collection.
13. Murphy, 50.
14. *Daily Missoulian*, June 15, 1945.
15. John Marr, oral interview, National WWII Museum.
16. "Preliminary Operations Around the La Fière Bridgehead"; Murphy, 46–52, 146–48; John J. Dolan letter to James Gavin, Box 7, Folder 52, Cornelius Ryan Collection; Fred B. Morgan interview, National WWII Museum; Marshall, *Night Drop*, 59–60. The timing of these rapid-fire events is uncertain, since few of the men involved were looking at their watches and noting the time.
17. "A few men, who had been able to get some automatic weapons from some of the bundles dropped . . .": Creek, "The Operations of a Mixed Group," 17.
18. *Time*, June 19, 1944.
19. Gavin, *On to Berlin*, 115–18; Wertenbaker, *Invasion!*, 46–48; *Time*, June 19, 1944; Marshall, *Night Drop*, 19–21; William Walton interview, Box 9, Folder 4, Cornelius Ryan Collection.

20. "Statement of Brigadier General James M. Gavin," in "82nd Airborne Action."
21. "Preliminary Operations Around the La Fière Bridgehead," 11; Nordyke, *Put Us Down in Hell*, 101–3; Nordyke, *Four Stars of Valor*, 170–76; Marshall, *Night Drop*, 16–18.
22. "82nd Airborne Action," 43.
23. Ridgway, *Soldier*, 10.
24. Anderson and Eschle, Clarence Ollom interview.
25. Boroughs, 62–71.
26. Jeannine Leroux, author interview, October 27, 2021; Baret and Lapierre, 102–6; Thomas, 41–43; Boroughs, 67; Bré, *Un Pont en Normandie*, 93–95; Murphy, 201–4. The number of surrendering Germans ranges in accounts from "ten to twelve" (Dolan, in Murphy, 149) to almost twenty (Thomas, 44).
27. Gavin, *On to Berlin*, 119.
28. Sources consulted for this narrative include: "82nd Airborne Action, Operations of 507th Following Drop"; Nordyke, *All American, All the Way*, 279–80; "Preliminary Operations Around the La Fière Bridgehead"; Murphy, 80–81; Balkoski, *Utah Beach*, 161–63; Morgan, *Down to Earth*, 185–86; Creek, 19–21; Ruggero, *The First Men In*, 164–69; Robert Vannatter account, airborneinnormandy.com; and aerial reconnaissance photo, May 9, 1944.
29. Nordyke, *All American, All the Way*, 254; "Movements on East Bank at Merderet Crossing" in "82nd Airborne Division, Action in Normandy"; "Preliminary Operations Around the La Fière Bridgehead"; Marshall, *Night Drop*, 64–70.

Ten: The Battle for the Bridge

1. Marcus Heim statement at http://www.505rct.org/album2/heim_m.asp.
2. "Levy's Group" in "82nd Airborne Division, Action in Normandy"; Marshall, "Preliminary Operations Around the La Fière Bridgehead"; Marshall, *Night Drop*, 69–72.
3. Nordyke, *Put Us Down in Hell*, 104–5, and *All American, All the Way*, 260; "508 Regiment After the Drop" in "82nd Airborne Division, Action in Normandy"; Adolph "Bud" Warnecke correspondence to Gerald Astor, Gerald Astor Papers; William A. (Bill) Dean letter, Camp Blanding Museum.
4. Email from Colonel (Ret.) Keith Nightingale, June 19, 2024. Years later, Nightingale was told by several participants, including Marcus Heim and John Norris, of the overturned truck.
5. Nordyke, *Four Stars of Valor*, 173.

6. Ruggero, *The First Men In*, 204.
7. Nordyke, *All American, All the Way*, 261. Sergeant Elmo Bell's account, which Nordyke includes, is the only one that mentions this detail.
8. Several accounts describe all three of the tanks involved in this action as French Renaults. But Dolan, in his account of the June 6 battle, wrote: "They attacked with three tanks, which I was unable to identify for sure; but they appeared to be similar to the German Mark IV-type, or maybe a little lighter" (Murphy, *No Better Place to Die*, 149). A photo taken several days after the June 6–9 battles at the bridge shows three French tanks (including one involved in the June 7 attack), but one tank is missing from the photos—likely the lead tank of the June 6 battle, which was pushed out of the road by the second one after it was knocked out. In the foreground of the same photo, a loose track and part of an axle belonging to a Panzer Mark III can be seen. And on page 47 of "Preliminary Operations Around the La Fière Bridgehead," written by S. L. A. Marshall from interviews conducted in August 1945 (and collected in "82nd Airborne Division, Action in Normandy"), the author writes: "At that moment, a medium German tank moved up to the road fork, trailed by a large group of infantry." This is based on a statement from Lieutenant Joseph Kormylo, in "Levy's Group" in "82nd Airborne Division, Action in Normandy": "Just at that time a big German tank moved up to the road fork with a number of infantry coming along with it." This was the next tank to show up after Private Orlin Stewart and two other men knocked out two other tanks, and it was likely the lead tank down the causeway to the bridge that afternoon. See also Henkemans, "Notes on Panzer Ersatz und Ausbildungsbteilung 100."
9. "Buffalo Horatio Holds the Bridge; Another Gets Aid," *Buffalo Evening News*, August 5, 1944.
10. John J. Dolan letter to James Gavin, Box 7, Folder 52, Cornelius Ryan Collection.
11. Nordyke, *Put Us Down in Hell*, 98, 144, 161, 190.
12. Tom Porcella oral history and written account, National WWII Museum.
13. Boroughs, *The 508th Connection*, 82–83.
14. Faye Fairbanks DiFrancia, author phone interview, June 14, 2024.
15. Ken Merritt, author interviews, May 5 and 11, 2020; June 6, 2020; and August 26, 2020; Ken Merritt interview at www.westpoint.edu; Ken Merritt oral history, National WWII Museum; Nordyke, *All American, All the Way*, 278; Milkovics, *The Devils Have Landed!*, 58. Merritt told this story many times over the years in interviews and accounts. There are differences in almost all of them.
16. Von Schlieben, *The German 709th Infantry Division*, 24–30, 158–61; Isby, *Fighting the Invasion*, 181–82.

17. Wilhelm Hümmerich interview, Box 26, Folder 23, Cornelius Ryan Collection.

Eleven: Counterattack

1. Russell Miller, *Nothing Less Than Victory*, 506.
2. Ambrose, *D-Day*, 278.
3. NBC Broadcast Day for June 6, 1944, at https://www.otrcat.com/nbc-broadcast-day-for-june-6-1944-d-day.
4. Renaud, *Sainte Mère Église*, 42–43.
5. Russell Miller, 426.
6. James Coyle account, National WWII Museum.
7. Alexandre Renaud account, Box 25, Folder 53, Cornelius Ryan Collection.
8. Coquart and Huet, *Le Jour le Plus Fou*, 86–87; Renaud, 50–51; Henri-Jean Renaud, author questionnaire, April 30, 2023; Tucker, *Parachute Soldier*, 38. Both Alexandre Renaud and his son, Henri-Jean, saw the dead German in the square; Tucker saw the dead German by the church.
9. Russell Miller, 427.
10. Bré, *Chroniques du Jour J*, 78, 142.
11. Renaud, 61–62, 66–67.
12. As quoted in Nordyke, *An Irresistible Force*, 60.
13. Benjamin H. Vandervoort letter, March 11, 1959, Box 9, Folder 1, Cornelius Ryan Collection. According to Vandervoort, all but two platoons of his regiment—about 160 troopers plus a few dozen other misdropped men—assembled; a total of "39 officers and 564 men who had boarded the troop carriers."
14. Nightingale, *The Human Face of D-Day*, 167.
15. Charles Miller account, National WWII Museum.
16. Marshall, *Night Drop*, 26.
17. Alexander and Sparry, *Jump Commander*, 168. Lieutenant Colonel Mark Alexander, who knew both men well, discussed how petty Kraus could be and how stubborn Vandervoort could be.
18. Charles E. Sammon letter, March 21, 1959, Box 8, Folder 38, Cornelius Ryan Collection; Benjamin H. Vandervoort letter, March 11, 1959, Box 9, Folder 1, Cornelius Ryan Collection. In Vandervoort's account, F Company CO, Lieutenant Hubert Bass, supplied this description of some of the twelve prisoners his men had taken.
19. Cruise, "Normandy—June 1944"; Leslie Cruise interview, Michigan NPR, August 8, 2019; Leslie Cruise, author phone interview, August 13, 2020; Leslie Cruise, author questionnaire; Leslie Cruise interview, LOC History Project.
20. Nordyke, *An Irresistible Force*, 60–63.

21. Distinguished Service Cross citation, PFC Dominick DiTullio, https://www.findagrave.com/memorial/9300082/dominick-ditullio.
22. Pipet, *Parachutés sur Sainte-Mère-Église*, 81: Pierre Maury is quoted as saying of the early-morning celebration of the village's residents at the church square: "Colonel Krause left, dragging his leg because he had an ankle injury."
23. Nordyke, *Four Stars of Valor*, 160–62; Tucker, 39–41; "The Capture of Ste Mere Eglise"; Charles Matash hospital admission card file, Fold3.
24. Nordyke, *All American, All the Way*, 239–41; Balkoski, *Utah Beach*, 270–74.
25. *Buffalo Evening News*, July 8, 1944. The story of the four Niland brothers—three of whom died during the invasion of France—was the basis of the film *Saving Private Ryan*.
26. Nordyke, *All American, All the Way*, 234.
27. Benjamin H. Vandervoort letter, March 11, 1959, Box 9, Folder 1, Cornelius Ryan Collection.
28. "Neuville-au-Plain" in "82nd Airborne Division Action in Normandy"; Theodore Peterson letter, March 22, 1959, Box 8, Folder 29, Cornelius Ryan Collection; Wills, *Put on Your Boots and Parachutes*, 79–80; Nightingale, 167–71.
29. This account of the action at Neuville-au-Plain is based on "Neuville-au-Plain" in "82nd Airborne Division Action in Normandy"; Theodore Peterson letter, March 22, 1959, Box 8, Folder 29, Cornelius Ryan Collection; Benjamin H. Vandervoort letter, Box 8, Folder 29, Cornelius Ryan Collection; Wills, 79–80; Nordyke, *All American, All the Way*, 234, 241–44; Nordyke, *An Irresistible Force*, 60–61, 67–71; Nordyke, *Four Stars of Valor*, 163–67; and Marshall, *Night Drop*, 30–39.
30. Huston, *Out of the Blue*, 183.
31. Ridgway, *Soldier*, 27.
32. Bill Walton interview, Box 7, Folder 4, Cornelius Ryan Collection.
33. Lebenson, *Surrounded by Heroes*, x.
34. Bill Walton interview, Box 9, Folder 52, Cornelius Ryan Collection.
35. As quoted in Delmer, *The Counterfeit Spy*, 170–71, and Hesketh, *Fortitude*, 199. There are slight differences in the two texts due to translation.
36. Nauroth and Steinberg, *Die Geschichte der 91.Luftlande-Division*, 46.
37. Anonymous, *D Day at Utah-Beach*, 56.
38. Griesser, *The Lions of Carentan* 100–2; Volker Griesser, email Q and A, April 19, 2024; von der Heydte, "A German Parachute Regiment in Normandy," 13; von Keusgen, *Sainte-Mère-Église & Merderet*, 116; Carell, *Invasion*, 73–74; Harrison, *Cross-Channel Attack*, 298. The exact movements of the 2nd Battalion/Fallschirmjäger 6 may never be known, as reports during and after were spotty and maddeningly incomplete. Some accounts, including von der Heydte's written after the war, claim that the

battalion reached only the outskirts of Sainte-Mére-Église. Others, including Carell and von Keusgen, claim that at least part of the battalion veered northeast off the N13 to Turqueville. Griesser based his assertion on the account of his grandfather, Eugen Griesser.

39. Clay Blair letter to Matthew Ridgway, August 14, 1984, Clay Blair Papers.
40. As quoted in Marshall, *Night Drop*, 95.
41. This account of the June 6 actions of Task Force Raff are based on the following sources: Blair, *Ridgway's Paratroopers*, 253–56; Nordyke, *All American, All the Way*, 281–83; Marshall, *Night Drop*, 92–98; Edson Duncan Raff questionnaire, Box 8, Folder 32, Cornelius Ryan Collection; Balkoski, *Utah Beach*, 278–84; Chaisson, "Task Force Raff's Race Against Time."
42. Von Keusgen, 114, 121, 129.
43. Arthur Maloney questionnaire, Box 8, Folder 19, Cornelius Ryan Collection.
44. Ruggero, *The First Men In*, 225.
45. Milkovics, *The Devils Have Landed!*, 187.
46. Roy Creek oral history, National WWII Museum; Creek, 23.
47. Wertenbaker, *Invasion!*, 49; Bill Walton interview, Box 7, Folder 52, Cornelius Ryan Collection.
48. Blair, 257–58; Gavin, *On to Berlin*, 120–22.
49. Blair, 244–45; Marshall, *Night Drop*, 102.
50. Langdon, *"Ready,"* 55.
51. Tucker, 41–42.
52. Murphy, *No Better Place to Die*, 94.
53. William Owens questionnaire, Box 8, Folder 27, Cornelius Ryan Collection.

Twelve: The Glidermen

1. McNally, *As Ever, John*, 42.
2. Baret, *"Nobody Lives Forever,"* 12.
3. Pierce, *Let's Go!*, 112–14; O'Donnell, *Beyond Valor*, 153–54; Wayne Pierce interview, National WWII Museum.
4. Bud Olson interview, National WWII Museum.
5. Johnson, "RBJ's Adventures in Normandy."
6. After-Action Reports, 82nd Airborne, 8.
7. Nordyke, *All American, All the Way*, 296, 302; Masters, 76,79.
8. Sources for this account of Wray's story include Nordyke, *An Irresistible Force*, 75–79; Benjamin H. Vandervoort letter, March 11, 1959, Box 9, Folder 1, Cornelius Ryan Collection; and Nordyke, *Four Stars of Valor*, 183–86.

9. LoFaro, *The Sword of St. Michael*, 218–19; Nordyke, *Four Stars of Valor*, 182–83; Nordyke, *An Irresistible Force*, 74–75.
10. Murphy, *No Better Place to Die*, 94–95.
11. As quoted in Gavin, *On to Berlin*, 125.
12. "Preliminary Operations Around the La Fière Bridgehead"; Langdon, *"Ready,"* 72.
13. Gavin, *On to Berlin*, 124–26; Nordyke, *Four Stars of Valor*, 178–80; LoFaro, 229–30; Marshall, *Night Drop*, 119.
14. Blair, *Ridgway's Paratroopers*, 264.
15. Bradley, *A Soldier's Story*, 276.
16. Nordyke, *All American, All the Way*, 311–21.
17. Nordyke, *All American, All the Way*, 161.
18. Renaud, *Sainte Mère Église*, 79–81.
19. Von Schlieben, *The German 709th Infantry Division.*
20. Von Keusgen, *Sainte-Mère-Église & Merderet*, 157, 162.
21. As quoted in Hargreaves, *The Germans in Normandy*, 72.
22. Hargreaves, 74.
23. Nordyke, *All American, All the Way*, 328.
24. George Miles interview, National WWII Museum; William Biagoni interview, National WWII Museum.
25. Bill Dean interview, Camp Blanding Museum.
26. Sources for this account include Millsaps, "This Is My Story"; Bill Dean interview, Camp Blanding Museum; Boroughs, *The 508th Connection,* 84; "Lt. Millsaps Patrol" in "82nd Airborne Division, Action in Normandy"; and Marshall, *Night Drop*, 138–49.
27. The hidden road is described as a "brick roadway" in Nordyke, *All American, All the Way*, 330; Marr describes it as a "cobblestone road" in his National WWII Museum interview.
28. Bradley and Clay, *A General's Life*, 259.
29. Blair, 269–70.

Thirteen: Attack at Midnight

1. "Conversations Between Major," 85.
2. In "Conversations Between Major," 83, Sanford said: "In my battalion we lost something like five or six officers and about a hundred men landing."
3. Nordyke, *All American, All the Way*, 326.
4. Pierce, "Normandy! Let's Go!," 8; "Conversations Between Major," 85.
5. Wayne Pierce interview, National WWII Museum; *Let's Go!*, 131–35.
6. Nordyke, *All American, All the Way*, 359.
7. Paul Kinsey, author phone interview, February 28, 2023.
8. Dave Stokely's description is in the *Knoxville News-Sentinel*, March 18, 1946; Teddy Sanford's description is in "Conversations Between Major," 89–90.

9. Wayne Pierce interview, National WWII Museum; Pierce, 135; John Marr interview, National WWII Museum.
10. Nordyke, *All American, All the Way*, 330–31.
11. Nordyke, *All American, All the Way*, 330–42.
12. LoFaro, *The Sword of St. Michael*, 241.

Fourteen: "Colonel, It'll Be a Slaughter"

1. "Statement of Brigadier General James M. Gavin" in "82nd Airborne Action."
2. Unless otherwise specified, sources for this account of the June 9 attack across the causeway include: "Statement of Brigadier General James M. Gavin," "Composite Force Under Captain Rae at Merderet Crossing," "The Crossing of Merderet by 325-3," "Continuation of Merderet Crossing," and "Crossing of the Merderet—Notes" in "82nd Airborne Action"; "The Forcing of the Merderet Causeway"; Nordyke, *All American, All the Way*, 343–68; Gavin, *On to Berlin*, 127–31; Marshall, *Night Drop*, 151–93; LoFaro, *The Sword of St. Michael*, 277–97; Morgan, *Down to Earth*, 214–31. As with any large-scale operation involving disparate units often in different places, there are sometimes discrepancies in details large and small in different accounts. Marshall's *Night Drop*, published sixteen years after the events it recounts, is based on the narratives he wrote that are collected in "82nd Airborne Division, Action in Normandy," which are in turn based on group interviews conducted in England in August 1944. In most cases where there is a difference of fact, I have chosen to use the information in the latter narratives, the earliest ones, which are available at USAHEC.
3. Gavin, *On to Berlin*, 127.
4. Henkemans, *Defending Normandy*, 176-77, 184: "According to several prisoners, the two battalions functioned as a single battlegroup under Hptm. Reiter—an arrangement that apparently started around 8 June." Additionally, records of German POWs taken on June 9 include several from the 3rd Battalion; Regimental Order for the Defense of the Merderet Sector, June 8, 1944, in author's possession.
5. Nordyke, *All American, All the Way*, 343.
6. The original time of 9:30 a.m. for the attack was noted by Lieutenant Colonel Frank Norris, who was at Ridgway's CP on the morning of June 9; he gave his account in Colby, *War from the Ground Up*, 21.
7. In Richlak, *Glide to Glory*, 213, Medic Chester Walker confirms the 3rd Battalion's location on June 8–9: "After doing some patrolling, we finally bivouacked near Chef-du-Pont in late afternoon of June 8th. After daylight on June 9th was when we learned we were going to attack the causeway." See also Marshall, "The Forcing of the Merderet Causeway."

8. LoFaro, 235; Lee Travelstead, letter to Edward G. Miller, April 17, 1992, courtesy of Edward G. Miller.
9. As quoted in Nordyke, *All American, All the Way*, 344.
10. As quoted in Blair, *Ridgway's Paratroopers*, 271.
11. Pierce, *Let's Go!*, 142.
12. See Booth and Spencer, *Paratrooper*, 54, for an excellent discussion of this subject.
13. As quoted in Blair, 273; Gavin, *On to Berlin*, 128.
14. As quoted in Nordyke, *All American, All the Way*, 347.
15. Blair, 273; LoFaro, 236. Sergeant Bud Olson, in a National WWII Museum interview and in a letter to his wife (in the author's possession), said that Carrell had been injured when his glider landed but didn't state what the injury was. Creek in Pierce's *Let's Go!*, 142, also stated that Carrell had been injured in the glider landing. See also Matthew B. Ridgway statement, Box 6, Folder 7, Operation Overlord, James M. Gavin Papers, in which he states: "Col. Lewis reported to me at a point about 25 yards from the East end of the bridge at about 1015 hr stating that he had relieved Col. Carrol [*sic*] of command of the battalion because he had told him that he did not think he could take it physically, he had been shaken up on the glider landing."
16. Frankie Sauls Chapman, author phone interview, June 1, 2021; John Sauls Jr., author phone interview, May 17, 2021.
17. In "The Crossing of Merderet by 325-3" in "82nd Airborne Action," Marshall mentions that some smoke canisters might have been fired, but Lieutenant Colonel Frank Norris, commanding the 345th Battalion howitzers, stated that there were no smoke canisters on hand, as most of his munitions were still on trucks en route from Utah Beach; Nightingale, *The Human Face of D-Day*, 180.

Fifteen: The Charge

1. Richlak, *Glide to Glory*, 230.
2. This account of the June 9 charge across the causeway is based primarily on the following sources: various sections of "82nd Airborne Division Action," USAHEC; Marshall, "The Forcing of the Merderet Causeway"; Nordyke, *All American, All the Way*, 343–58; Morgan, *Down to Earth*, 222–30; Marshall, *Night Drop*, 151–93; Pierce, *Let's Go!*, 141–65; and many other sources individually cited.
3. O'Donnell, *Beyond Valor*, 156.
4. Johnson, "RBJ's Adventures in Normandy, June, 1944"; Woodadge, "Richard B. Johnson."
5. Marshall, *Night Drop*, 165.
6. Marshall, *Night Drop*, 165–66.

7. Nordyke, *All American, All the Way*, 353.
8. Gavin, *On to Berlin*, 129. Gavin never completely understood or accepted that the 325th had established a bridgehead in Cauquigny and was in the process of flushing out the Germans there. More than three decades later, in his 1978 autobiography, *On to Berlin*, he wrote of Rae's actions after crossing the causeway: "From then on the battle was decided. Rae took command of the forces on the far side and continued for several miles before finally digging in." And in a 1981 letter, he wrote that Rae "took part of a battalion of glidermen, who were about to retreat, into an attack into the German positions." Even Rae in a later account admitted that he had placed himself under the direction of Captain Harney (Morgan, 225–29). After interviewing dozens of men involved in the action, S. L. A. Marshall, in both his "The Forcing of the Merderet Causeway" and his book *Night Drop*, correctly concluded that Rae's men made the difference in the victory, but that Rae did not exercise any outsized leadership over the glidermen.
9. Joël Baret interview with Rudi Skripek; Chris Skripek, author email interview, August 15, 2022.
10. Geoffrion interview, LOC History Project; Jason Lohner, author phone interview, September 18, 2022.
11. As quoted in McManus, *The Americans at Normandy*, 90.
12. Bud Olson interview, National WWII Museum; Bud Olson, author interview, June 22, 2020.
13. Nordyke, *All American, All the Way*, 356; Travelstead, letter to Miller.
14. O'Rourke, "The Operations of the 1st Platoon."
15. "Notes on the 325th Narrative," "82nd Airborne Action."
16. In "The Forcing of the Merderet Causeway," S. L. A. Marshall incorrectly labeled Les Helpiquets as "Le Motey," the name given to a cluster of a few farmhouses 300 yards northwest of Les Helpiquets that had no crossroad and only a dirt road through it and that was not on the main road to Amfreville. Other writers have followed suit.
17. Blair, *Ridgway's Paratroopers*, 276.
18. Booth and Spencer, *Paratrooper*, 198.
19. Major Willard Harrison statement, July 27, 1944, in Box 6, Folder 6, Operation Overlord, James M. Gavin Papers.
20. Gavin, *On to Berlin*, 131.
21. Bud Olson, author interviews, June 22, 23, 2020; Olson, "My Memories of WWII."

Sixteen: "You Crossed That Causeway"

1. Bill Walton interview, Box 9, Folder 4, Cornelius Ryan Collection.
2. As quoted in Blair, *Ridgway's Paratroopers*, 292.

3. Blair, 292.
4. For a fuller description of this controversy, see Ridgway, *Soldier*, 15; and Blair, 292.
5. Nordyke, *Put Us Down in Hell*, 241.
6. Alexander and Sparry, *Jump Commander*, 223–33.
7. Alexander and Sparry, 241, 245.
8. Anzuoni, *"I'm the 82nd Airborne Division!,"* 134.
9. "Conversations Between Major," 105, 107–8.
10. Nordyke, *All American, All the Way*, 407.
11. Tucker, *Parachute Soldier*, 69.
12. As quoted in Gavin, *On to Berlin*, 133.
13. Generalfeldmarschall Von Rundstedt, After Action Reports, Battle of Normandy.
14. Fauntleroy, *The General and His Daughter*, 111.
15. Jutras, *Sainte-Mère-Église*, 96.
16. Tim Dyas interview at https://www.tankbooks.com/interviews/dyas1.htm.
17. Frankie Sauls Chapman, author phone interview, June 1, 2022.
18. Gavin, *On to Berlin*, 132.
19. As quoted in Blair, 297.
20. As quoted in LoFaro, *The Sword of St. Michael*, 241.
21. As quoted in LoFaro, 241.
22. As quoted in Murphy, *No Better Place to Die*, 184.
23. Johnson, "RBJ's Adventures in Normandy, June, 1944."

BIBLIOGRAPHY

Books

Alexander, Mark J., and John Sparry. *Jump Commander: In Combat with the 505th and 508th Parachute Infantry Regiments, 82nd Airborne Division in World War II*. Casemate, 2010.

Ambrose, Stephen E. *Band of Brothers*. Simon & Schuster, 1992.

Ambrose, Stephen. *D-Day: June 6, 1944—The Climactic Battle of World War II*. Simon & Schuster, 1994.

(Anonymous). *D Day at Utah-Beach*. OCEP, 1976.

(Anonymous). *Handbook on German Military Forces*. LSU Press, 1990.

Anzuoni, Robert P. *"I'm the 82nd Airborne Division!"* Schiffer Military History, 2005.

Astor, Gerald. *The Greatest War: Americans in Combat, 1941–1945*. Presidio Press, 1999.

Astor, Gerald. *June 6, 1944: The Voices of D-Day*. St. Martin's Press, 1994.

Atkinson, Rick. *The Guns at First Light: The War in Western Europe, 1944–1945*. Henry Holt, 2013.

Badsey, Stephen. *Utah Beach*. (Battle Zone Normandy Series.) Sutton Publishing, 2004.

Balkoski, Joseph. *Beyond the Beachhead: The 29th Infantry Division in Normandy*. Stackpole, 1989.

Balkoski, Joseph. *Utah Beach: The Amphibious Landing and Airborne Operations on D-Day*. Stackpole, 2005.

Baret, Joël. *I Wouldn't Want to Do It Again . . .* Helion & Company, 2011.

Baret, Joël. *"Nobody Lives Forever": Forcing the Causeway la Fière-Cauquigny by the 325th Glider Infantry Regiment*. Self-published, 2011.

Baret, Joël. *Une Tombe en Normandie*. Self-published, 2014.

Baret, Joël, and Émile Lapierre. *Cinq Jours sur la Ligne de Front*. L'Association U.S. Normandie, 2012.

Bastable, Jonathan. *Voices from D-Day*. Greenhill, 2018.

Bearden, Bob. *To D-Day and Back: Adventures with the 507th Parachute Infantry Regiment and Life as a World War II POW*. Zenith Press, 2007.

Beevor, Antony. *D-Day: The Battle for Normandy*. Penguin, 2009.

Belfield, Eversley, and H. Essame. *The Battle of Normandy*. B. T. Batsford, 1965.
Bennett, G. H. *Destination Normandy: Three American Regiments on D-Day*. Praeger, 2007.
Bernage, Georges, Philippe Lejuée, Laurent Mari, and Henri-Jean Renaud. *Objectif Sainte-Mère-Église: Jour J, Les Paras U.S.* Éditions Heimdal, 1993.
Blair, Clay. *Ridgway's Paratroopers: The American Airborne in World War II*. Dial Press, 1985.
Blandford, Edmund. *Two Sides of the Beach: The Invasion and Defence of Europe in 1944*. Airlife Publishing, 1999.
Blumentritt, Gunther. *Von Rundstedt: The Soldier and the Man*. Odhams Press, 1952.
Booth, T. Michael, and Duncan Spencer. *Paratrooper: The Life of Gen. James M. Gavin*. Simon & Schuster, 1994.
Boroughs, Zig. *The 508th Connection*. Self-published, 2013.
Bowman, Martin. *Remembering D-Day: Personal Histories of Everyday Heroes*. HarperCollins, 2004.
Bradham, Randolph. *"To the Last Man": The Battle for Normandy's Cotentin Peninsula and Brittany*. Praeger, 2008.
Bradley, Omar N. *A Soldier's Story*. Henry Holt, 1951.
Bradley, Omar N., and Clay Blair. *A General's Life*. Simon & Schuster, 1983.
Bré, Gilles. *Chroniques du Jour J*. Éditions Christian, 2006.
Bré, Gilles. *Un Pont en Normandie: Les combats à l'Ouest de Sainte-Mère-Église du 6 juin 1944*. Self-published, 2003.
Breuer, William B. *Drop Zone Sicily: Allied Airborne Strike July 1943*. Presidio Press, 1983.
Breuer, William B. *Geronimo! American Paratroopers in World War II*. St. Martin's Press, 1989.
Breuer, William B. *Hoodwinking Hitler: The Normandy Deception*. Praeger, 1993.
Bryant, James E. *Flying Coffins over Europe: The Odyssey of a Glider Infantryman with the 82nd Airborne Division During World War II*. Self-published, 2003.
Burns, Dwayne T., with Leland Burns. *Jump into the Valley of the Shadow*. Casemate, 2006.
Burriss, T. Moffatt. *Strike and Hold: A Memoir of the 82nd Airborne in World War II*. Brassey's, 2000.
Butcher, Harry C. *My Three Years with Eisenhower*. Simon & Schuster, 1946.
Butler, Daniel Allen. *Field Marshal: The Life and Death of Erwin Rommel*. Casemate, 2015.
Caddick-Adams, Peter. *Sand and Steel: The D-Day Invasion and the Liberation of France*. Oxford University Press, 2019.
Campbell, David. *U.S. Airborne Soldier Versus German Soldier*. Osprey, 2018.
Carell, Paul. *Invasion: They're Coming!* Translated by E. Osers. Bantam, 1964.
Carruthers, Bob, ed. *The German Army in Normandy*. Pen and Sword Military, 2013.
Carruthers, Bob, and Simon Trew. *The Normandy Battles*. Cassell & Company, 2000.
Carter, Ross S. *Those Devils in Baggy Pants*. Appleton-Century-Crofts, 1951.
Cobb, Matthew. *The Resistance: The French Fight Against the Nazis*. Simon & Schuster UK, 2009.
Colby, John. *War from the Ground Up: The 90th Division in WWII*. Nortex Press, 1991.
Coquart, Élizabeth, and Philippe Huet. *Le Jour le Plus Fou*. Albin Michel, 1994.
Covais, Joseph S. *Battery! C. Lenton Sartain and the Airborne G.I.'s of the 319th Glider Field Artillery*. Andy Red Enterprises, 2010.
Crookenden, Napier. *Dropzone Normandy*. Charles Scribner's Sons, 1976.

Dank, Milton. *The Glider Gang: An Eyewitness History of World War II Glider Combat.* J. B. Lippincott, 1977.
Delmer, Sefton. *The Counterfeit Spy.* Harper and Row, 1971.
Desquesnes, Rémy. *Normandy 1944: The Invasion and the Battle of Normandy.* Translated by John Lee. Éditions Ouest-France, 2009.
D'Este, Carlo. *Bitter Victory: The Battle for Sicily, 1943.* E. P. Dutton, 1988.
D'Este, Carlo. *Decision in Normandy.* Konecky & Konecky, 1993.
De Trez, Michel. *The Way We Were: Colonel Ben Vandervoort.* D-Day Publishing, 2004.
Devlin, Gerard M. *Paratrooper! The Saga of U.S. Army and Marine Parachute and Glider Combat Troops During World War II.* St. Martin's Press, 1979.
Devlin, Gerard M. *Silent Wings.* St. Martin's Press, 1985.
Doubler, Michael D. *Closing with the Enemy.* University Press of Kansas, 1994.
Drez, Ronald J. *Twenty-Five Yards of War.* Hyperion, 2001.
Drez, Ronald J., ed. *Voices of D-Day: The Story of the Allied Invasion Told by Those Who Were There.* LSU Press, 1994.
Duboscq, Geneviève. *My Longest Night: A Twelve-Year-Old Heroine's Stirring Account of D-Day and After.* Arcade, 2012.
Dunn, Bill Newton. *Big Wing: The Biography of Air Chief Marshal Sir Trafford Leigh-Mallory.* Airlife Publishing, 1992.
Eckhertz, Holger. *D-Day Through German Eyes.* (New paperback edition containing Book One and Book Two.) DTZ History Publications, 2016.
Editors of Time-Life Books. *Fortress Europe.* (The Third Reich Series.) Time-Life Books, 1992.
Editors of Time-Life Books. *Time Capsule/1944: A History of the Year Condensed from the Pages of Time.* Time-Life Books, 1967.
Eisenhower, David. *Eisenhower: At War 1943–1945.* Random House, 1986.
Eisenhower, Dwight D. *Crusade in Europe.* Doubleday, 1948.
Eisenhower, Dwight D. *The Eisenhower Diaries.* Edited by Robert H. Ferrell. W. W. Norton, 1981.
Eisenhower, Dwight D. *The Papers of Dwight David Eisenhower, Vol. III: The War Years.* Edited by Alfred D. Chandler Jr. Johns Hopkins Press, 1970.
Esvelin, Philippe. *Forgotten Wings: Gliders in Normandy and Southern France.* Éditions Heimdal, 2006.
Fauntleroy, Barbara Gavin. *The General and His Daughter.* Fordham University Press, 2007.
Fielder, Bob. *A Matter of Pride.* Self-published, 2007.
Flanagan, E. M., Jr. *Airborne: A Combat History of American Airborne Forces.* Presidio Press, 2002.
Floeter, Ernst W., with Lynne Breen. *I'll See You Again, Lady Liberty.* WingSpan Press, 2014.
François, Dominique. *The 507th Parachute Infantry Regiment.* Éditions Heimdal, 2000.
François, Dominique. *The 508th Parachute Infantry Division.* Éditions Heimdal, 2001.
François, Dominique. *Normandy: Breaching the Atlantic Wall.* Translated by Gayle Wurst. Zenith Press, 2008.
Fraser, David. *Knight's Cross: A Life of Field Marshal Erwin Rommel.* HarperCollins, 1994.
Gavin, General James M. *Airborne Warfare.* Infantry Journal Press, 1947.
Gavin, General James M. *On to Berlin.* Viking Press, 1978.
Gavin, General James M. *War and Peace in the Space Age.* Harper, 1958.

Golz, Paul. *Paul Golz, the Pomeranian Grenadier, and the Invasion of Normandy.* Self-published, (2014?).

Griesser, Volker. *The Lions of Carentan: Fallschirmjäger Regiment 6, 1943–45.* Translated by Mara Taylor. Casemate, 2014.

Guidry, Paula F. *Treasures in My Heart.* Self-published, 2004.

Guild, Frank, Jr. *Action of the Tiger: The Saga of the 437th Troop Carrier Group.* Battery Press, 1978.

Hargreaves, Richard. *The Germans in Normandy.* Pen and Sword Military, 2006.

Harrison, Gordon A. *Cross-Channel Attack.* (The United States Army in World War II, The European Theater of Operations.) Office of the Chief of Military History, 1951.

Hart, Russell A. *Clash of Arms: How the Allies Won in Normandy.* Lynne Rienner Publishers, 2001.

Hart, Stephen. *German Weapons of World War II.* Amber Books, 2018.

Hasley, Lucien, and Joël Baret. *Colline 30: Une Vie de Souvenirs.* L'Association U.S. Normandie, 2014.

Hastings, Max. *Overlord: D-Day, June 6, 1944.* Simon & Schuster, 1984.

Henkemans, Niels. *Defending Normandy* (vol. 1A). Panzerwrecks Ltd., 2024.

Hesketh, Roger. *Fortitude: The D-Day Deception Campaign.* Abrams, 2000.

Howarth, David. *Dawn of D-Day: These Men Were There, 6 June 1944.* Collins, 1959.

Huston, James A. *Out of the Blue: U.S. Army Airborne Operations in World War II.* Purdue University Press, 1972.

Ingersoll, Ralph. *Top Secret.* Harcourt, Brace & Co., 1946.

Isby, David C., ed. *Fighting in Normandy: The German Army from D-Day to Villers-Borcage.* Greenhill Books, 2001.

Isby, David C., ed. *Fighting the Invasion: The German Army at D-Day.* Greenhill Books, 2000.

Jacobus, George. *Echoes of the Warriors.* Self-published, 1992.

Jakeway, Don. *Paratroopers Do or Die!!* Self-published, (1999?).

Johnston, Lew, ed. *The Troop Carrier D-Day Flights: A Fully Documented Review* (third edition). Self-published, 2003.

Jutras, Philippe. *Sainte-Mère-Église: Les Paras du 6 Juin.* Éditions Heimdal, 1991.

Kaufmann, J. E., and H. W. Kaufmann. *The American GI in Europe in World War II: The Battle for France.* Stackpole, 2010.

Kaufmann, J. E., and H. W. Kaufmann. *The American GI in Europe in World War II: D-Day: Storming Ashore.* Stackpole, 2009.

Keegan, John. *Rundstedt.* Ballantine, 1974.

Keegan, John. *Six Armies in Normandy.* Viking Press, 1982.

Kenyon, David. *Bletchley Park and D-Day.* Yale University Press, 2019.

Knickerbocker, W. D. *Those Damned Glider Pilots.* Static Line Books, 1993.

Langdon, Allen. *"Ready": The History of the 505th Parachute Infantry Regiment, 82nd Airborne Division, World War II.* 82nd Airborne Division Association, 1986.

Langrehr, Henry. *Whatever It Took.* William Morrow, 2020.

Lebarbenchon, Roger-Jean. *Américains et Normands dans la Bataille.* Azeville, 1993.

Lebenson, Len. *Surrounded by Heroes: Six Campaigns with Divisional Headquarters, 82nd Airborne Division, 1942–1945.* Casemate, 2007.

Lelandais, Benoît. *From Heaven to Hell: Men like No Others.* OREP Éditions, 2005.

Lemonnier, Amiral. *6 Juin 1944: Les Cent Jours de Normandie.* Éditions France-Empire, 1961.

Léon, Monique Maury. *Sainte-Mère-Église libérée.* Éditions du Gref, 2007.

Liddell Hart, B. H. *The German Generals Talk.* William Morrow, 1971.

Liddell Hart, B. H., ed. *The Rommel Papers.* Harcourt, Brace & Co., 1953.

LoFaro, Guy. *The Sword of St. Michael: The 82nd Airborne Division in World War II.* Da Capo Press, 2011.

Lord, William G. II. *History of the 508th Parachute Infantry.* Infantry Journal Press, 1948.

Lowden, John L. *Silent Wings at War: Combat Gliders in World War II.* Smithsonian Institution Press, 1992.

Marshall, S. L. A. *Night Drop: The American Airborne Invasion of Normandy.* Little, Brown, 1962.

Masters, Charles J. *Glidermen of Neptune: The American D-Day Glider Attack.* Southern Illinois University Press, 1995.

McKenzie, John D. *On Time, On Target.* Presidio Press, 2000.

McManus, John C. *The Americans at D-Day: The American Experience at the Normandy Invasion.* Forge, 2004.

McManus, John C. *The Americans at Normandy: The Summer of 1944—The American War from the Normandy Beaches to Falaise.* Forge, 2004.

McNab, Chris, ed. *The D-Day Training Pocket Manual 1944.* Casemate, 2019.

McNally, John. *As Ever, John: The Letters of John V. McNally to His Sister, Margaret McNally Bierbaum, 1941–1946.* Roberts Press, 1985.

Megellas, James. *All the Way to Berlin.* Ballantine, 2003.

Milano, Vince, and Bruce Conner. *Normandiefront: D-Day to Saint-Lô Through German Eyes.* History Press, 2011.

Milkovics, Lew. *The Devils Have Landed!* Creative Printing and Publishing, 1993.

Miller, Edward G. *Nothing Less Than Full Victory.* Naval Institute Press, 2007.

Miller, Russell. *Nothing Less Than Victory: The Oral History of D-Day.* William Morrow, 1993.

Milton, Giles. *D-Day: The Soldiers' Story.* John Murray, 2018.

Mitcham, Samuel W., Jr. *The Desert Fox in Normandy: Rommel's Defense of Fortress Europe.* Praeger, 1997.

Mitcham, Samuel W., Jr. *Panzers in Normandy.* Stackpole, 1999.

Mitcham, Samuel W., Jr. *Rommel's Last Battle: The Desert Fox and the Normandy Campaign.* Stein and Day, 1983.

Mitchell, George C. *Matthew B. Ridgway: Soldier, Statesman, Scholar, Citizen.* Stackpole, 2002.

Morgan, Martin K. A. *Down to Earth: The 507th Parachute Infantry Regiment in Normandy.* Schiffer, 2004.

Mrazek, James E. *The Glider War.* St. Martin's Press, 1975.

Murphy, Robert M. *No Better Place to Die.* Casemate, 2009.

Nauroth, Helge Sven, and Boris Steinberg. *Die Geschichte der 91.Luftlande-Division.* Tredition Gmbh, 2017.

Neillands, Robin, and Roderick de Normann. *D-Day, 1944: Voices from Normandy.* Weidenfeld and Nicholson, 1993.

Nightingale, Colonel (Ret.) Keith M. *The Human Face of D-Day.* Casemate, 2023.

Nordyke, Phil. *All American, All the Way: A Combat History of the 82nd Airborne Division in World War II (From Sicily to Normandy).* Historic Ventures, 2009.

Nordyke, Phil. *The All Americans in World War II.* Zenith Press, 2006.

Nordyke, Phil. *Four Stars of Valor: The Combat History of the 505th Parachute Infantry Regiment in World War II.* Zenith Press, 2006.

Nordyke, Phil. *An Irresistible Force: Lieutenant Colonel Ben Vandervoort and the 2nd Battalion, 505th Parachute Infantry in World War II.* Historic Ventures, 2011.

Nordyke, Phil. *Put Us Down in Hell: The Combat History of the 508th Parachute Infantry Regiment in World War II.* Historic Ventures, 2012.

O'Donnell, Patrick. *Beyond Valor: World War II's Rangers and Airborne Veterans Reveal the Heart of Combat.* Free Press, 2001.

Ospital, John. *We Wore Jump Boots and Baggy Pants.* Willow House, 1977.

Penrose, Jane, ed. *The D-Day Companion.* Osprey, 2004.

Perrault, Gilles. *The Secret of D-Day* (Reprint). Bantam, 1967.

Pierce, Wayne. *Let's Go! The Story of the Men Who Served in the 325th Glider Infantry Regiment.* Professional Press, 1997.

Pimlott, Dr. John, ed. *Rommel: In His Own Words.* Greenhill Books, 1994.

Pipet, Albert. *Parachutés sur Sainte-Mère-Église.* Presses de la Cité, 1984.

Pöppel, Martin. *Heaven and Hell: The War Diary of a German Paratrooper.* Spellmount, 1996.

Porcella, Tom. *Saut dans l'Obscurité.* Imprimerie Houchet, 1986.

Poyser, Terry, and Bill Brown. *Fighting Fox Company.* Casemate, 2013.

Preisler, Jerome. *First to Jump: How the Band of Brothers Was Aided by the Brave Paratroopers of Pathfinders Company.* Berkley Caliber, 2014.

Reardon, Mark J., ed. *Defending Fortress Europe.* Aberjona Press, 2012.

Renaud, Alexandre. *Sainte Mère Église: First American Bridgehead in France—June 6, 1944.* Famille Renaud, 2004.

Reynolds, Michael. *Steel Inferno: I SS Panzer Corps in Normandy.* Sarpedon, 1997.

Richlak, Jerry Lee, Sr. *Glide to Glory: 325 Glider Infantry Regiment, 82nd Airborne Division.* Cedar House, 2002.

Ridgway, General Matthew B., with Harold H. Martin. *Soldier: The Memoirs of Matthew B. Ridgway.* Harper & Brothers, 1956.

Roberts, Mary Louise. *D-Day Through French Eyes: Normandy 1944.* University of Chicago Press, 2014.

Ruge, Friedrich. "The Invasion of Normandy." In *Decisive Battles of World War II: The German View,* edited by H. A. Jacobsen and J. Rohwer. Translated by Edward Fitzgerald. G. P. Putnam's Sons, 1965.

Ruge, Friedrich. *Rommel in Normandy.* Presidio Press, 1979.

Ruggero, Ed. *Combat Jump: The Young Men Who Led the Assault into Fortress Europe, July 1943.* HarperCollins, 2003.

Ruggero, Ed. *The First Men In: U.S. Paratroopers and the Fight to Save D-Day.* HarperCollins, 2006.

Ruppenthal, Major Roland G. *Utah Beach to Cherbourg (6 June—27 June 1944)* (American Forces in Action Series). U.S. War Department, Historical Division, 1947.

Ryan, Cornelius. *The Longest Day: June 6, 1944.* Simon & Schuster, 1959.

Shenkle, George A., with Adam G. R. Berry. *My Clear Conscience.* Overlord Publishing, 2015.

Smith, Carl, and Mike Chappell. *U.S. Paratrooper 1941–45* (Warrior Series No. 26). Osprey, 2000.

Sorley, Lewis, ed. *Gavin at War: The World War II Diary of Lieutenant General James M. Gavin.* Casemate, 2022.

Speidel, Lieutenant-General Hans. *We Defended Normandy.* Herbert Jenkins, 1951.

Stafford, David. *Ten Days to D-Day: Citizens and Soldiers on the Eve of the Invasion.* Little, Brown, 2003.

Thompson, Leroy. *The All Americans: The 82nd Airborne*. Donald & Charles, 1988.
Thompson, R. W. *D-Day: Spearhead of Invasion*. Ballantine, 1968.
Thornton, Nancy C. *Tales from Choteau Montana*. Canal Heritage Enterprises, 2020.
Tucker, William H. *Parachute Soldier* (second edition). International Airborne Books, 1944.
Turnbull, Peter. *"I Maintain the Right": The 307th Airborne Engineer Battalion in WW II*. AuthorHouse, 2005.
Turner, John Frayn. *Invasion '44: The Story of D-Day in Normandy*. G. P. Putnam's Sons, 1959.
Villahermosa, Gilberto. *Hitler's Paratroopers in Normandy*. Frontline Books, 2019.
Vlahos, Colonel Mark C. *"Men Will Come": A History of the 314th Troop Carrier Group 1942–1945*. Merriam Press, 2019.
von Keusgen, Helmut Konrad. *Sainte-Mère-Église & Merderet*. Éditions Heimdal, 2010.
Webster, David Kenyon. *Parachute Infantry: An American Paratrooper's Memoir of D-Day and the Fall of the Third Reich*. LSU Press, 1994.
Wertenbaker, Charles Christian. *Invasion!* D. Appleton-Century, 1944.
Wertz, Jay. *D-Day: The Campaign Across France*. Weider History Publications, 2011.
Whitlock, Flint. *"If Chaos Reigns": The Near-Disaster and Ultimate Triumph of the Allied Airborne Forces on D-Day, June 6, 1944*. Casemate, 2013.
Wills, Deryk. *Put on Your Boots and Parachutes*. Self-published, 1992.
Wilt, Alan F. *The Atlantic Wall: Hitler's Defenses for D-Day*. Enigma Books, 2004.
Wolfe, Martin. *Green Light! Men of the 81st Troop Carrier Squadron Tell Their Story*. University of Pennsylvania Press, 1989.
Wood, James A., ed. *Army of the West: The Weekly Reports of German Army Group B from Normandy to the West Wall*. Stackpole, 2007.
Wurst, Spencer F., and Gayle Wurst. *Descending from the Clouds: A Memoir of Combat in the 505 Parachute Infantry Regiment, 82nd Airborne Division*. Casemate, 2004.
Yockelson, Mitchell. *The Paratrooper Generals*. Stackpole, 2020.
Young, Desmond. *Rommel: The Desert Fox* (Reprint). Berkley, 1950.
Zaley, Steven Robert. *They Are Only Gone If They Are Forgotten*. Tense Moment, 2014.
Zaloga, Steven J., with illustrations by Howard Gerrard. *D-Day 1944 (2): Utah Beach & the US Airborne Landings*. Osprey, 2004.
Zetterling, Niklas. *Normandy 1944*. Casemate, 2019.

Articles

Anderson, Steve, and Louis Eschle. "82nd Airborne Trooper: From Sicily to the Siegfried Line." *Military History*, June 2003.
Anonymous. "St. Mère Église." *After the Battle*, 1973.
Booth, T. Michael, and Duncan Spencer. "The Airborne's Watery Triumph." *MHQ*, Spring 1994.
Comtois, Pierre. "Confusion and Triumph at La Fière Causeway." *World War II*, May 1998.
Haulman, Daniel L. "Before the D-Day Dawn." *Air Power History* 61, no. 2 (2014): 6–13.
Marshall, Colonel S. L. A. "Affair at Hill 30." *Marine Corps Gazette*, February–March 1948.
McCaul, Ed. "82nd Airborne Paratrooper at Normandy." *Military History*, June 1997.
Sanford, Lieutenant Colonel (Ret.) Teddy Hollis, Jr. "Warrior and Commander." John Endicott Family Association Newsletter, March 2022.

Online Articles

Chaisson, Patrick J. "Task Force Raff's Race Against Time." *Warfare History Network*, August 2021, accessed February 14, 2024, https://warfarehistorynetwork.com/article/task-force-raffs-race-against-time.

Chambers, Richard. "The Fallschirmjäger in Normandy." *Flames of War*, accessed January 17, 2023, https://www.flamesofwar.com/Default.aspx?tabid=112&art_id=816.

"Earl J. Geoffrion—In Memoriam." *US Airborne*, https://usairborne.be/Biographie/bio_us_geoffrion.htm.

Hymel, Kevin. "From Paratrooper to POW: Bob Nobles of the 82nd Airborne." Warfare History Network, Summer 2015.

Hymel, Kevin. "The WW2 Paratrooper: First-Hand Accounts of the D-Day Invasion." Warfare History Network, Winter 2015.

Kelvington, Mike. "Battle of the Bridge: A Company, 1-505th at La Fière Bridge." *Havok Journal*, June 7, 2019, https://havokjournal.com/culture/military/battle-of-the-bridge-a-company-1-505th-at-la-fiere-bridge/.

Morgan, Martin K. A. "Walk Where They Fought: La Fière, 82d Airborne, D-Day 1944." *Armchair General*, May 10, 2006, http://armchairgeneral.com/walk-where-they-fought-la-fiere-82d-airborne-division-d-day-1944.htm.

Nightingale, Keith. "The Taking of La Fière Bridge." *Small Wars Journal*, May 28, 2012, https://smallwarsjournal.com/jrnl/art/the-taking-of-la-fiere-bridge.

Rice, Julian A. "Just for the Record: A Pilot's Story." *6 Juin 1944*, http://www.6juin1944.com/veterans/rice.php.

Whitlock, Flint. "Airborne at La Fière: Slugfest in Normandy." *Warfare History Network*, December 15, 2016, https://warfarehistorynetwork.com/article/airborne-at-la-fiere-slugfest-in-normandy/.

Others: U.S. Military Documents, Publications, After-Action Reports, Studies, Monographs

Abraham, Captain Robert. "The Operations of the 508th Parachute Infantry (82nd Airborne Division), Normandy, France, 5–10 June 1944 (Normandy Campaign)." Academic Department, The Infantry School, Fort Benning, GA,1947.

Airborne Operations: A German Appraisal. MS20-232. Department of the Army, Washington, DC, 1951.

Albright, Captain Barry E. "Operations of the 2nd Battalion, 508th Infantry Regiment, 82nd Airborne Division, in the Invasion of Normandy, 5–13 June 1944" (Normandy Campaign)." Academic Department, The Infantry School, Fort Benning, GA, 1949.

"The Capture of Ste Mere Eglise: An Action by 505th Infantry Regiment of the 82nd Airborne Division." (Regimental Unit Study Number 6.) Academic Department, The Infantry School, Fort Benning, GA.

"Conversations Between Major General Teddy H. Sanford and Captain Teddy H. Sanford, Jr." (Senior Officers Debriefing Program.) U.S. Army Military History Institute, Carlisle Barracks, PA, 1974.

Creek, Major Roy E. "The Operations of a Mixed Group from Units of the 507th Parachute Infantry (82nd Airborne Division) in the Invasion of France, 5–7 June 1944 (Normandy Campaign)." Academic Department, The Infantry School, Fort Benning, GA, 1948.

Donovan, Lieutenant Colonel Michael J., USMC. "Strategic Deception: Operation Fortitude" (USAWC Strategy Research Project). U.S. Army War College, Carlisle Barracks, PA, 2002.

"82nd Airborne Division, Action in Normandy, France, June–July 1944." U.S. Army Unit Records, Box 6, 82nd Airborne Division in Normandy, France—Operation Neptune," National Archives, Washington, DC.

Joseph, Captain John T. "The Operations of a Regimental Pathfinder Unit, 507th Parachute Infantry Regiment (82nd Airborne Division) in Normandy, France, 6 June 1944 (Normandy Campaign)." Academic Department, The Infantry School, Fort Benning, GA, 1947.

Keil, Lieutenant-Colonel Guenther. "Grenadier Regt. 919, Kampfgruppe Keil." MS C-018. Historical Division, European Command, Foreign Military Studies, USAHEC, Carlisle, PA, 1944.

Keil, Lieutenant-Colonel Guenther. "Report Covering the Questions of the Historical Division About the Operations of Inf. Reg. 1058 and Combat Team Keil." MS B-844. Historical Division, European Command, Foreign Military Studies, USAHEC, Carlisle, PA, 1946.

Marshall, S. L. A. "The Forcing of the Merderet Causeway at La Fière, France: An Action by the Third Battalion, 325th Glider Infantry" (Regimental Unit Study Number 4). Academic Department, The Infantry School, Fort Benning, GA.

Marshall, S. L. A. "Preliminary Operations Around the La Fière Bridgehead, Merderet River, Normandy: An Action by Various Elements of the 82nd Airborne Division" (Regimental Unit Study Number 5). Academic Department, The Infantry School, Fort Benning, GA.

O'Rourke, Lieutenant Donald C. "The Operations of the 1st Platoon, Company I, 507th Parachute Infantry (82nd Airborne Division), at the Forcing of the Merderet River Causeway at LaFiere, France, 9 June 1944." Academic Department, The Infantry School, Fort Benning, GA, 1947.

Raibl, Captain Tony J. "The Operations of the 82nd Airborne Division Artillery (82nd Airborne Division) in the Airborne Landings Near St. Mere Eglise, France, 6–8 June 1944 (Normandy Campaign)." Academic Department, The Infantry School, Fort Benning, GA, 1948.

Ruge, Vice Admiral Friedrich. "Rommel's Measures to Counter the Invasion." MS A-982. Historical Division, European Command, Foreign Military Studies, USAHEC, Carlisle, PA, 1946.

Triepel, General Major Gerhard. "Sector Cotentin, from 6 June until 18 June 1944." MS B-260. Foreign Military Studies, USAHEC, Carlisle, PA, 1946.

von der Heydte, Friedrich Freiherr. "A German Parachute Regiment in Normandy" (U.S. Army Foreign Military Studies No. B-839). U.S. Army Historical Division, Washington, DC, 1954.

von Schlieben, *Generalleutnant* Karl Wilhelm. *The German 709th Infantry Division During the Fighting in Normandy.* MS B-845. Historical Division, United States Army, Europe, USAHEC, Carlisle, PA, 1948.

Warlimont, General Walter. *From Invasion to the Siegfried Line.* U.S. Army Historical Division, Washington, DC, 1945.

Warren, Dr. John C. "Airborne Operations in World War II, European Theater" (USAF Historical Studies No. 97). USAF Historical Division, Maxwell Air Force Base, AL, 1956.

Unpublished Accounts, After-Action Reports, Morning Reports, Combat Interviews

Baret, Joël. Notes from interview with Rudolf Skripek, 2007.
Brannen, Malcolm. "Four Days in Normandy."
Creek, Roy. Written account.
Cruise, Leslie Palmer. "Normandy—June 1944."
Daglish, Ian. "Extract from a Short History of the 82nd Airborne in Normandy." Unpublished manuscript.
Geoffrion, Jason. "World War II Veteran Earl Geoffrion in His Own Words." Unpublished.
Graham, Chester E. "My Memories of World War II." Unpublished.
Henkemans, Niels. "Notes on Panzer Ersatz und Ausbildungsabteilung 100."
Hills, Randy. Letter to Lieutenant General (Ret.) E. M. Flanagan, January 17, 2003, www.warchronicle.com.
Hutto, James C. "World War II Memoirs." Courtesy of Sharon Hutto Marks.
Johnson, Richard B. "RBJ's Adventures in Normandy, June 1944."
Millsaps, Woodrow W. "This Is My Story."
Pierce, Wayne. "Normandy! Let's Go! My First 60 Hours!"
Richardson, Fayette. Unpublished manuscript.
Russell, Kenneth E. "13 Hours: D-Day, June 6, 1944."
Travelstead, Lee. "LCT's Adventures in Normandy, June 1944."
Vandervoort, Benjamin H. "Waverly Wray."
Woodadge, Paul. "Richard B. Johnson—The Forgotten Hero of the Causeway Charge," 2008.

Collections

Camp Blanding Museum interviews.
Cornelius Ryan Collection, Mahn Center, Ohio University.
Gerald Astor Papers, USAHEC.
James M. Gavin Papers, USAHEC.
Library of Congress History Project.
Matthew B. Ridgway Papers, USAHEC.
National WWII Museum interviews. S. L. A. Marshall Collection, University of Texas at El Paso.

Films

D-Day Down to Earth—Return of the 507th (PBS).
Seize & Secure: The Battle for La Fière (National WWII Museum and Louisiana Public Broadcasting).

82nd Airborne Author Interviews

Horace Barrett, Leslie Cruise, Joe Gwaltney, Walter Hurd, Dick Klein, Kenneth "Hard Rock" Merritt, Bob Nobles, Bud Olson, Sam Sachs, Clifford Stump, Fletcher Williams.

Online Sites

www.fold3.com
www.thedropzone.org
www.6juin1944.com
www.database-memoire.eu
www.airborneinnormandy.com
www.dday-overlord.com
www.ww2-airborne.us
www.tracesofwar.com
www.americanairmuseum.com
www.tabletopdeutschland.com

INDEX

ABOUT THE AUTHOR

James Donovan is the author of *Shoot for the Moon*, *A Terrible Glory*, *The Blood of Heroes*, and several other books. He has been a literary agent since 1993 and lives in Dallas.